Borderlands of Slavery

AMERICA IN THE NINETEENTH CENTURY

Series editors
Brian DeLay, Steven Hahn, Amy Dru Stanley

America in the Nineteenth Century proposes a rigorous
rethinking of this most formative period in U.S. history.
Books in the series will be wide-ranging and eclectic, with
an interest in politics at all levels, culture and capitalism,
race and slavery, law, gender, and the environment, and
regional and transnational history. The series aims to expand
the scope of nineteenth-century historiography by bringing
classic questions into dialogue with innovative perspectives,
approaches, and methodologies.

BORDERLANDS

of

SLAVERY

THE STRUGGLE OVER
CAPTIVITY AND PEONAGE
IN THE AMERICAN SOUTHWEST

WILLIAM S. KISER

PENN

UNIVERSITY OF PENNSYLVANIA PRESS

PHILADELPHIA

Published by
University of Pennsylvania Press
Philadelphia, Pennsylvania 19104-4112
www.upenn.edu/pennpress

Printed in the United States of America
on acid-free paper
1 3 5 7 9 10 8 6 4 2

A Cataloging-in-Publication record is available from the Library of Congress
ISBN 978-0-8122-4903-3

For Nicole, the love of my life

Contents

Prologue

In a January 1864 communication with Indian Commissioner William P. Dole, New Mexico Superintendent of Indian Affairs Michael Steck provided a concise description of Indian slavery that alluded to every fundamental aspect of the practice as it existed in the Southwest. Upon being taken into captivity, he explained, indigenous slaves "are usually adopted into the family, baptized, and brought up in the Catholic faith, and given the name of the owner's family, generally become faithful and trustworthy servants, and sometimes are married to the native New Mexicans."[1] In a single breath the superintendent summarized—albeit somewhat superficially—Indian slavery as it existed not only in American times but in earlier Spanish and Mexican periods as well. Steck's previous decade of experience with New Mexico Indian affairs rendered him eminently qualified to comment upon the nature of captivity. His letter to Dole asserted the widespread cultural hybridity and concomitant transformation of human identity that emanated from captivity and dependency, practices that predated Steck's arrival in New Mexico by three centuries.

Human captivity was a critical component of indigenous warfare, labor, and social interaction in the Southwest long before the influx of European explorers and colonists that began in the sixteenth century. Complex trade networks linked nomadic peoples of the Plains with sedentary Puebloan inhabitants of the upper Rio Grande region through intricate commercial mechanisms, primarily involving commodities obtained through hunting, gathering, and cultivation. The exchange of human subjects, however, also formed an element of this culturally entrenched kin-based system, with adoption, dependency, and assimilation being important components. Intertribal warfare in the Southwest perpetuated a continuing captive trade, one based more on honor, community, gender roles, and kinship demands rather than on economic necessity.[2] When Francisco Vasquez de Coronado reached northern New Mexico in 1540–41, he found a thoroughly enmeshed system of slavery emanating from warfare and raiding between sedentary Puebloan peoples and nomadic tribes occupying neighboring regions. Coronado himself enlisted a former Indian slave—a Pawnee held in servitude at the Tiguex Pueblo—as a guide for his expedition from the upper Rio Grande Valley to the South Plains.[3]

With the arrival of the first Spanish imperialists—many of whom subverted Native inhabitants to servitude using the *encomienda* and *repartimiento* systems—multiethnic slavery institutions took on new importance in the Southwest and quickly burgeoned into a permanent fixture of community interaction. Political, military, and ecclesiastical support buttressed Euro-American influence over Indians in the Rio Grande Valley of north-central New Mexico during the early decades of colonization. Although European systems of coerced labor proliferated to a larger degree in Spain's South American and Central American outposts, where labor-intensive sugar plantations and silver mines required large numbers of workers, colonists representing the cross and crown carried the impetus for involuntary servitude into the more northerly provinces as well.[4] When Spaniards colonized New Mexico, they established a predominantly agricultural and pastoral economy, one that required a liberal supply of manual labor to ensure optimum production.[5] With demand for labor exceeding the number of available working-age men and women, colonists began forcing Indians into servitude, a phenomenon first manifested in the *encomienda* and later in captive enslavement. Whatever their sobriquets, such systems introduced a more profit-centered form of slavery into the Southwest.[6]

The practice of forcibly removing indigenous women and children (who collectively were some two-thirds of all captives) from their tribes and subverting them to servitude entailed a widespread assimilation of Indians into Spanish culture—and vice versa—and often resulted in a transformation of identity on the part of the victim.[7] In New Mexico, the *encomienda* system, which the Spanish crown formally inaugurated in 1503, legitimized the subjugation of Pueblo Indians. Through this legal apparatus, Spaniards manipulated power relations and allowed for Indians to be claimed by settlers and soldiers who, as masters, exposed them to Christianity and protected them from enemies. In return, indigenous subjects performed menial chores and acted as either domestic servants or shepherds in the field, depending on age and gender; they also paid tributary taxes in the form of corn and other foodstuffs that they cultivated throughout the year. Perceiving this to be a noble undertaking, colonists taught Puebloan subjects to speak the Castilian language while ecclesiastics forcefully instructed them in the tenets of

Catholicism, believing that this so-called salvation warranted servitude as a means of remuneration.[8]

Spanish officials not only condoned but even encouraged miscegenation between Indians and New World colonists, recognizing the social and religious benefits entailed in demographic incorporation and believing that the absorption of Native blood into Catholic lineages through the ideology of *limpieza de sangre* (purity of blood) would more readily foment spiritual conversion and civility.[9] Although it continued to sanction the *encomienda* and remained supportive of settlers who held others in bondage, the crown insisted that such a system not be identified as "slavery" and banned settlers from holding Indians in that capacity. In 1542, the Spanish monarchy outlawed Indian slavery with the New Laws, and leaders reiterated that decree in the 1681 *Recopilación de Leyes* (a nine-volume set of laws governing all aspects of colonial affairs), which prohibited the ransoming of captives but simultaneously and incongruously encouraged that noncompliant Indians be attacked and subverted.[10] Even so, the redemption and exchange of captives occurred frequently throughout Spain's colonies and effectively counteracted any prohibitory edicts issued from across the Atlantic. Like English colonists in seventeenth-century Virginia, whose statutes-at-large mandated that "all Indians taken in warr [*sic*] be held and accounted slaves," New Mexicans easily circumvented antislavery royal *cedulas* by invoking the "just-war doctrine," enabling them to take captives during hostile encounters without fear of being reprimanded.[11]

In 1638, Fray Juan de Prada criticized the *encomienda* as a system of persecution and ominously predicted that Indians, "oppressed with new impositions and annoyances," would lash back at the ecclesiastics who collected their tribute.[12] Time would ultimately prove him correct. At the onset of the 1680 Pueblo Revolt, an estimated one-half of the approximately two hundred Spanish households in New Mexico held Indians in varying forms of servility. The rebellion occurred because of not only cultural tensions between Natives and newcomers, but also the widespread use of Puebloan peoples as unwilling and uncompensated laborers. The successful Native insurgence ousted colonists from New Mexico for more than a decade and invoked a profound sense of fear among Euro-Americans, with the ripple effect being felt as far away as Seville.[13]

Following Don Diego de Vargas's 1692 *reconquista* and subsequent reestablishment of Spanish rule in New Mexico, settlers came to better appreciate the limits to which the Pueblos could be subverted. Like the 1676

Bacon's Rebellion in colonial Virginia—which prompted a tactical shift in coerced labor from the predominantly white method of indentured servitude to a race-based chattel system of African slavery—the Pueblo Revolt altered slaving practices in the Southwest. By the early 1700s, enslavement of indigenous peoples began to shift toward nomadic and seminomadic Apaches, Comanches, Navajos, and Utes. Catholic missionaries actively contested the enslavement of Pueblo Indians, hoping instead to convert them to Christianity through conciliatory strategies. Long-standing rivalries between secular and clerical elements stemming from the Inquisition fanned the flames on these already firmly established hegemonic quarrels. Ecclesiastics emerged largely successful in their protestations, although Spanish captive raiding and violence toward slaves perpetuated a process of hostile reciprocation that did not dissipate until the mid-nineteenth century.[14]

Predicated upon imperial interlopers exerting symbolic psychological power and physical control over Native peoples and the spaces they inhabited, the proliferation of Indian slavery in the Southwest during the seventeenth and eighteenth centuries coincided with the development of similar slave systems in the eastern part of the continent. On North America's Atlantic and Gulf coasts, and throughout its hinterlands, English and French settlers also subjected Indians to comparable forms of denigrating and exploitative bondage. Spaniards acted unintentionally in concert with rival European imperialists in promulgating new systems of involuntary servitude across much of the continent, and in so doing all three of those foreign nations influenced the indigenous forms of labor and exchange that Indian tribes practiced.[15]

Indigenous captivity continued unhindered in part because of the material and symbolic wealth that slaves represented within frontier societies. Ideally, colonies existed for the benefit of the mother country, with settlers expected to produce tangible goods to augment the monarchy's riches. Whereas silver and gold could be shipped back to Spain, slaves represented a wholly different type of commodity. New Mexico's landholders found captives to be a convenient means of retaining a publicly visible form of wealth, a type of symbolic capital.[16] Indian slaves served a purpose even greater than precious metals or specie to many New Mexicans in that they not only provided labor, but also could be exchanged as a sort of organic currency in a region where, until the late 1700s, hard coinage remained scarce.[17] Spain attempted to impose strictures on colonial slave markets despite its ongoing inability to regulate commerce in human captives, enabling the colonies to retain capital and resources that the crown believed should belong solely to the mother country.

By the late 1700s, lower-class New Mexicans utilized the captive trade to repay their own debts and avoid falling into servitude themselves as peons. Slaves became a medium of exchange, with some people using Indian captives to purchase and barter for merchandise or other inanimate items, creating an economic dynamic that swapped living for nonliving commodities and that dehumanized those held in bondage. Oftentimes, individuals participated in raids on Indian camps and villages for the sole purpose of taking captives and selling them after returning to the Rio Grande settlements. With indigenous women and children in high demand, marauders could accrue handsome profits by providing captives to land-owners, some of whom owned dozens of servants.[18]

Catholic Church records indicate the extent to which Indian slavery flourished in the Southwest during the eighteenth and early nineteenth centuries. Spanish priests frequently baptized Indian children, at which point they became accepted members of the adoptive families who initially served as their captors. New Mexico's clergymen were only too happy to oblige any such request, recognizing anointment in the holy faith as a symbolic means of achieving religious conversion and thereby stripping Indians of their spirituality, tribal identity, and previous kinship associations while simultaneously instilling and broadcasting the mystic power of the Church. Theological conversion served as a secondary form of enslavement, one that priests hoped would bind a person spiritually in addition to their precon-ceived physical bondage and geographic isolation from their tribe of origin, thus augmenting a psychological state of subjectivity.[19]

Catholic priests recorded 3,237 Indian baptisms in New Mexico between 1700 and 1849, a calculation that doubtless fell short of the actual figure. Navajos had the most baptisms after Mexican independence, repre-senting 37.5 percent of the total. Apaches comprised 24 percent, Utes repre-sented 16 percent, and Comanches just 5 percent. In a brief period from 1750 to 1754, the Church anointed more than three hundred abductees, indicating a drastic increase in captive taking during that period. A consid-erable percentage of all baptisms (1,171 of them, or roughly one-third) occurred in the Spanish settlements north of Santa Fe, with a relatively even distribution across other provincial regions as far south as Paso del Norte (modern Ciudad Juárez) on the Rio Grande.[20]

Church registries from the Spanish colonial era are replete with individual examples of indigenous baptism, each entry giving voice to a human subject that would otherwise remain invisible in the historical record. Priests noted an approximate age—almost invariably under ten years—and assigned a new name to each Indian child, a common practice in slave cultures worldwide that served as a symbolic ascription of hybridized identity.[21] Six Comanche children baptized at Santa Clara Pueblo in 1743 became, by virtue of receiving the sacrament, María la Luz, Polonia, Antonia, Josepha, Lorenza, and Cristobal.[22] Through the simple and superficial act of Catholic conversion, these Indian youths immediately became less of an "other" within the adoptive society, as baptism and renaming marked the beginning of the cultural assimilation process.[23] Typically, several captives would be baptized in one day, an indication that they had been taken from their tribe during a single slave raid. Although most ceremonies involved only a small number of children, mass baptisms did occasionally occur. Fray Manuel Sopeña baptized twenty-two Apache children at Santa Clara in 1743; Fray Otero did the same with nineteen Apaches at Laguna Pueblo that year; and Fray Manuel Zambrano anointed an additional eleven Indian children in one ceremony on August 27, 1759, at Santa Fe.[24]

More than three thousand Indian baptisms in New Mexico resulted in a corresponding 3,302 mixed-ethnicity childbirths. The number of slave baptisms and illicit conceptions through unsanctified exogamous unions remained relatively constant over a period of 150 years and had not begun to wane even after the 1846 American conquest. The frequency of childbearing among captive Indian women, not only in New Mexico but throughout the colonial New World, indicated the extent to which the Spanish—and later the Mexicans—practiced miscegenation as a method for assimilating indigenous peoples. Such intimate relations directly contradicted the teachings of Catholicism regarding sexuality but nonetheless occurred with noticeable regularity.[25] The progeny that resulted from such unions bound women to their captors through their shared offspring and, in some instances, also raised the societal status of the mother. Most mixed-blood children spent their entire lives in the Spanish settlements, giving rise to the racial castes that emanated from interethnic relationships between European masters and Indian slaves.[26]

Very few baptized Indians appeared in church records as slaves, because many ecclesiastics avoided placing that title upon them in an attempt to veil the prevalence of involuntary servitude from the Spanish crown. In mission baptism books, priests recorded ancestry in one of three quasi-euphemistic ways that described the biological origin of the child being baptized and identified blood purity, reiterating the importance that Spaniards placed on genealogical origin. Most eighteenth-century baptisms involved an *hijo(a) legítima*, meaning a male or female of, literally, legitimate Spanish pedigree. Another notation that friars used was *hijo(a) de padre(s) no conocido*, indicating that either one or both of the child's parents remained unknown. This category typically appeared in registries when one of the parents claimed Indian ancestry, in which case the Church only recognized the Spanish parent and disregarded the Native father or mother by recording them as "unknown." The third and final notation, used primarily for Puebloans and nomadic Indian captives, simply denoted *indio/a*.[27]

New Mexicans also went to great lengths to cloak intermarriage and cohabitation with Indian captives. Of 6,613 extant Spanish and Mexican marriage records between 1694 and 1846, a mere twenty-one involved actual slaves, with the more anonymous method of concubinage being substituted in place of formal wedlock.[28] Many clergymen convinced themselves that baptism and marriage ceremonies involving Indian captives constituted a form of spiritual salvation, and they therefore believed that they were fulfilling a noble religious project.[29] Once baptized, in fact, a captive would no longer be considered a slave in the literal sense. As generations passed and visible genetic distinctions such as skin pigmentation began to coalesce in a single Hispanic ethnicity, ecclesiastics became increasingly lax in notating ancestry in their record books. By the time Mexico achieved independence in 1821, racial differences had indeed become less salient, and census records containing discrepancies in regards to ethnic origins indicated that those in power concealed the true nature of gender and race relations in the province.[30]

Over the course of two centuries, a multilateral captive network had developed in the Southwest that involved not only Spanish colonists but also numerous peripheral Indian tribes, giving rise to hegemonic rivalries across the region. Through relentless raiding of colonial outposts in New Mexico, Texas, and northern Mexico, the Comanches especially—and to a lesser extent the Apaches, Navajos, and Utes—contributed to the redefinition and repurposing of enslavement and also the redistribution of social power and spatial control, carrying Euro-Americans into captivity and inciting sustained fear and anxiety throughout New Spain's isolated imperial outposts.[31] All of this occurred within a plurality of sovereignty contingent upon a borderlands backdrop, wherein multiple indigenous and Euro-American power brokers coexisted in oscillating conditions of peace and warfare that revolved in large part around processes of enslavement and repatriation.[32] The considerable value of slaves in the New Mexican marketplace, as well as the utilitarian uses for captives as both servants and fictive kin among indigenous tribes, also pitted Indian polities against one another, dividing tribal resources and fighting men in multiple directions and thus limiting the capability of individual Native communities to resist colonial violence and predation. Just as Euro-Americans raided Indian camps for captives and Indians in turn confronted colonial settlements, Comanches also marauded Apaches, Apaches pillaged Comanches, Utes plundered Paiutes and Navajos, Navajos attacked Utes and Paiutes, and the processes of intertribal warfare went on ad infinitum.[33]

As time wore on, slave raiding emerged as a ruthless profession among both New Mexicans and the more powerful equestrian tribes surrounding the province, all of whom preyed upon and exploited weaker groups for their own benefit. While Spanish and Indian intermediaries often assisted in transporting captives to New Mexican masters, the system originated with and was perpetuated by European colonists themselves, whose economic interests and social hierarchies demanded the continuation of involuntary labor systems and concomitant senses of dependency. Weaker groups of people served as a convenient means of obtaining this labor, giving rise to intertribal slave raiding once the more powerful Apaches, Comanches, Navajos, and Utes realized that they could exploit the colonists' insatiable desire for servants. By attacking weaker tribes for captives and slaves to trade in Spanish markets, some Native groups recast themselves as core societies that dominated socially and economically, while disempowering and denigrating neighboring peoples to the status of weaker and poorer peripheral components of that larger borderlands social system.[34]

As slave trafficking increased, seasonal trade fairs became common events at Santa Fe, Taos, and Pecos, with hundreds, sometimes thousands, of Indian attendees bringing captives with them to redeem for various goods of Euro-American manufacture.[35] These trade fairs marked the emergence of a system of intercultural commercial exchange involving multiparty negotiations in which one of the principal products—human captives—had no input in their ultimate disposition, a characteristic that

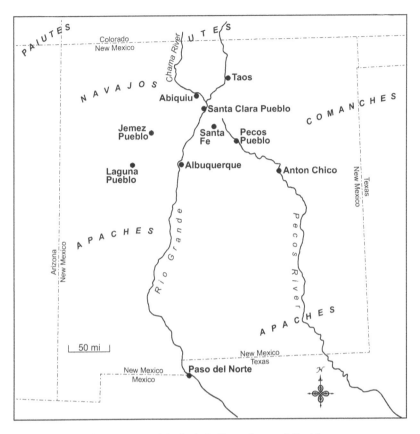

Figure 1. New Mexico's Indian tribes and Pueblos,
prior to the U.S. conquest.

New Mexico shared with the American South. Pueblo Indians acted as intermediaries in this network, becoming quasi-capitalists as they realized substantial profits in captives and horses, two of the most valuable commodities on the northern New Spain frontier. Fray Andrés Varo observed in 1749 that "these Infidel Indians are accustomed to come in peace to the Pueblos, and bring buffalo and elk skins, and some young Indians from those that they have imprisoned in the wars that they have among themselves." They traded those captives to Spanish colonists and Pueblo Indians for horses and mules, knives, clothing, beads, and other items of foreign manufacture not otherwise available to them. Colonial settlers hoarded trade items prior to these fairs because, according to Varo, Indian slaves constituted the "gold and silver and the richest treasure of the governors."[36] Fray Miguel de Menchero noticed that the powerful Comanches were especially prone to selling Plains Indian captives to Spanish colonists.[37] All of this occurred despite the issuance of orders to the contrary, including a proclamation by Governor Gervasio Cruzat y Gongora forbidding the sale of captives, a toothless order that went unheeded and unenforced.[38]

An armistice brokered in 1786 between Comanche chief Ecuerecapa and New Mexico governor Juan Bautista de Anza solidified preexisting but porous trade relationships, encouraging greater numbers of Comanches to mingle at the Santa Fe and Taos fairs.[39] Following the accord, Anza's superior authorized him to ransom all captives under the age of fourteen that the Comanches held.[40] As many as three thousand captives were redeemed in northern New Mexico between 1700 and 1850, entering society as *indios de rescate* and *genízaros* (detribalized captives) through a process that historian James Brooks calls "a thinly disguised slave market."[41] In New Mexico, *genízaros* originated with and evolved almost exclusively through the Indian slave trade.[42] Spanish officials exploited *genízaros* for two important purposes. Colonel Don Fernando de la Concha, a onetime governor of New Mexico, explained the first role when writing in 1794 that *genízaros* served as interpreters during diplomatic meetings between Spaniards and independent Indians.[43] The second role involved the protection of New Mexico's interior settlements. By segregating *genízaros* on the periphery of Spanish villages, colonial officials established a buffer zone to shield settlers from the raids of nomadic tribes living to the north, west, and east of the province. In 1776, three distinct *genízaro* communities lived at Santa Fe, Abiquiú, and Los Jarales south of Albuquerque, numbering 137 families.[44] Governor Pedro Fermín de Mendinueta believed that these people had a duty to patrol and monitor the frontier because, if left unprotected, New Mexico's more secluded villages would be "exposed to total ruin." Independent Indians attempting to raid colonial outposts would first encounter tangential *genízaro* settlements, which would offer preliminary resistance—"a defensive shield," in the words of Fray Juan Agustín de Morfí—to thwart hostile invaders.[45]

As a result of their detribalization, many captives and *genízaros* acculturated to Spanish (and later Mexican) society and refused opportunities for repatriation later in life. Colonists preferred to obtain Indian children under a certain age to ensure such an outcome. Writing of Apaches in

1789, Commandant General of Interior Provinces Jacobo Ugarte y Loyola observed that many captives who had been taken as youths did not "retain any memory of their Country or [have the] evil intention to return as adults to search for their relatives." He stressed the importance of acquiring only children under seven years of age, because those would be more likely to develop a sense of dependency and remain with their captors. "Little by little," Ugarte y Loyola wrote in an explanation of the Spanish assimilation process, these captives would "become instructed in our customs, acquire Christian instruction, and breathe purer air."[46] Over the course of many years, such acculturation tactics proved highly successful, as many abductees attached themselves closely to their new adoptive families.[47]

The Indian slave trade continued to expand geographically even as Spain's grasp on the New World loosened during the Age of Revolutions.[48] The Enlightenment-era models for these upheavals were the American and French revolutions, the republican ideologies of which not only helped to precipitate the independence of many Latin American countries, but also laid the theoretical groundwork for the eventual emancipation of chattel slaves in the U.S. South—as well as peons and captives in the Southwest—during the mid-1800s.[49] Growing Euro-American populations in New Mexico and Alta California during the early nineteenth century increased the demand for servants in both regions.[50] In California, *hacendados* and *rancheros* subverted mission Indians through a system of debtor servitude in which elites and religious missionaries lent merchandise and then required that it be repaid through labor. Despite California having outlawed the exchange of indigenous servants in 1824, one observer noted as late as 1846 that, with Indians as the primary labor force in the region, "the business of the country could hardly be carried on" without their servitude.[51] In contrast to the systems of involuntary labor that prevailed in colonial California, however, slaving mechanisms in New Mexico required greater armed force and coercion to sustain them.

In the late 1700s, the emergence of debt peonage alongside Indian captivity signified the fragmentation of involuntary labor into two systems, both of which revolved around economic dependency. The various semblances that slavery assumed by the early nineteenth century indicate its bifurcation into distinctive forms and demonstrate the strategic maneuvering of authoritarian masters seeking to perpetuate such institutions under misleading guises. Peonage became a transitional phase of dependency— one that lay at the interstices of slavery and wage labor—that characterized

Latin America's agrarian and pastoral areas, most often targeting Indians, mulattos, and mestizos. By the dawn of the nineteenth century, Hispanos had adopted credit extension and debtor servitude as a method of securing cheap labor on estates, or *latifundios*, throughout Mexico as well as New Mexico.[52]

Indian slavery and debt peonage were in fact quite similar in operation and remained inextricably linked through kinship bonds and interethnic bloodlines. Not only did captivity and peonage form institutions of involuntary human bondage that would later, in American times, be compared to chattel slavery in the South, but they also bore a cause-and-effect relationship upon one another. Many peons could trace their ancestry back over many generations to Indian slaves who cohabited with and bore offspring to Spanish colonists. Brigadier General James H. Carleton, commanding New Mexico's military department during the Civil War, wrote that "[Indian] servants . . . bear children from illicit intercourse [and] the offspring of this intercourse are considered as *peons*." Carleton was describing the ethnic interconnectedness of captivity and peonage: Indian slaves gave birth to mixed-blood children who often grew up to become a part of New Mexico's lower class and incurred debts for subsistence, thus becoming peons after reaching adulthood.[53]

Conniving members of the upper class and clergy devised methods that guaranteed interminable subjectivity on the part of many New Mexicans. Catholic priests charged exorbitant amounts for marriages, baptisms, and funerals, to the extent that most individuals had to secure a third-party loan to pay for such services. Under those circumstances, a person necessarily went into debtor servitude in order to baptize a child, get married, or bury a deceased family member.[54] Price-gouging creditors charged four to five times the wholesale cost of goods, a tactic that worked in tandem with continuously compounding interest to ensure that debts grew larger with time. "The initial debt is truly the tie that binds him to servitude from which he finds it impossible to escape for the rest of his life," Fray Juan Agustín de Morfi wrote in reference to New Mexican peons. "In this way, a man who yesterday lacked a square of cloth to cover himself, today is forced by necessity to enter domestic service much to his shame," he concluded.[55]

The fact that Spain never enacted laws either establishing or regulating this type of coercive labor makes it impossible to determine its precise date of origin. A widespread system of debtor servitude involving sedentary

Indians and indigent citizens developed in South and Central America during the seventeenth century, largely as a result of Spain's abolition of the *repartimiento* system and the subsequent need to devise new methods of labor acquisition.[56] The practice did not spread into New Mexico until much later, due primarily to its localized subsistence economy (as opposed to labor-intensive extractive economies in more southerly portions of the empire), and the availability of captive Indian slaves therefore fulfilled the need for workers in the upper Rio Grande Valley. While there is no discernible moment in time when debt peonage appeared in New Mexican villages, there are hints of its existence as early as 1778, and strictures on the relationship between masters and servants in Mexico's 1824 constitution indicate that it had become fully developed by that period.[57]

Peonage provided the perfect complement to the preexisting regime of Indian slavery, and it bolstered the labor force in a province experiencing gradual economic and demographic expansion. In a predominantly pastoral and agrarian economy, a plentiful supply of uncompensated tribute-paying workers ensured modest but sustainable profits, and *patrones* exploited the productive capacity of captive Indians and indebted citizens at every opportunity. Debtor servitude among landless sheepherders emerged as one of the primary forms of peon labor in colonial New Mexico beginning in the late 1700s and endured for nearly a century through *partido* contracts.[58]

The establishment of the Santa Fe Trail in 1821 and subsequent commercial intensification between New Mexico and Missouri recalibrated the economic dynamics of peonage and captive servitude and widened the gap between rich and poor in the Southwest.[59] During the Industrial Revolution of the early nineteenth century, these processes coincided with similar economic and demographic expansions in the Deep South, where the rapid emergence of a so-called Cotton Kingdom forever altered the nature and importance of chattel slavery. In both instances, varying levels of capitalist market integration precipitated changes in slaving practices and increasingly reoriented servitude toward economic imperatives, in addition to preconceived kinship obligations and social relationships.[60]

By 1824—just three years after the first American merchants arrived in Santa Fe—caravans consisting of up to one hundred men and "almost every kind of dry goods" imaginable were setting out for the Southwest on an annual basis.[61] Profits surged higher each year, beginning at a mere $15,000 worth of merchandise in 1822 and reaching the six-figure range before the end of that decade.[62] Just as exported raw materials that Southern slaves harvested proved a boon to the industrializing Northern economy throughout the antebellum era, so too did the labor of New Mexico's involuntary servants, who produced "sheep, copper, tobacco, buffalo robes, and dressed skins," directly benefit the Missouri—and, by extension, the U.S.—economy.[63] This diverted the produce of northern New Mexico to external markets and enveloped the region in continental commercial forces driven by the capitalistic nature of the Santa Fe trade and its Missouri merchants.[64] By 1825, one observer estimated that New Mexico's northern communities took in profits exceeding $300,000 annually, a phenomenal sum in a province previously unaccustomed to the circulation of specie and material wealth.[65] Accordingly, peonage and captivity took on greater economic importance after 1821. With added incentive for profits and a new market for their goods, New Mexicans no longer used servants solely for subsistence purposes and to demonstrate social standing, but instead sought to accumulate wealth through the coerced productivity of captives and peons.

By the early nineteenth century, the Southwest's involuntary labor regimes had expanded in two separate yet not dissimilar directions in order to subject a greater number of persons to a lifetime of dependent bondage. Debt peonage and Indian slavery were firmly entrenched in local society and culture, becoming nearly as common in some New Mexico communities as chattel slavery in the South's Cotton Kingdom. The arrival of Americans in New Mexico, however, would forever alter these preexisting regional systems of coerced labor, with sectional struggles catapulting the issue of slavery in the West to the forefront of public and political discourse. Ensuing congressional discussions about New Mexico's two forms of involuntary servitude would not only impact the nature of those systems as practiced locally, but also begin to modify American understanding of slavery and free labor during the age of emancipation.

Introduction

Two months after the Civil War ended, President Andrew Johnson issued an executive order that some Americans might have found strange and unimportant, considering the monumental and urgent task of reunifying a deeply divided nation. Johnson's mandate required that government officials take concrete action to end the practice of Indian enslavement in New Mexico.[1] A year and a half later, on March 2, 1867, the president affixed his signature to another seemingly obscure piece of legislation, entitled "An Act to abolish and forever prohibit the System of Peonage in the Territory of New Mexico and other Parts of the United States."[2] In the Southwest, however, few if any inhabitants would have deemed either of these actions peculiar. By the Reconstruction era, Hispanic peons and Indian captives throughout territorial New Mexico had long hoped that American democracy might free them from bondage. Their anxious masters feared they could be right and fought shrewdly to fend off systemic change.

It is today taken as a simple fact that the Civil War and the Thirteenth Amendment to the Constitution ended slavery in the United States. This book argues otherwise. Debt peonage and even captive slavery outlived the Civil War, often to the shock and consternation of the nation's champions of freedom. More than that, the fight over peonage and captivity in New Mexico demonstrated the importance of those systems in America's nineteenth-century transition to free labor and the concomitant evolution of United States jurisprudence in the post–Civil War era. The constitutional amendment banning slavery in 1865 failed to encompass all forms of coercive labor in the United States and its territorial appendages. The presence of peonage and captivity in the Southwest caused many Americans to realize that slavery and involuntary servitude were not limited to blacks in the South, but also subsumed many Hispanics and Indians in New Mexico who suffered the similarly stigmatizing effects of human bondage, or "the other slavery," as historian Andrés Reséndez has called it.[3] After coming to this understanding in the immediate post–Civil War years, American reformers embarked upon a renewed quest to eliminate compulsory labor in the United States. In so doing, they effectively expanded the scope of the Thirteenth Amendment and, in the parlance of the times, set out to make "freedom national" in the reunified republic.[4]

In the Southwest, as in the South, slavery was both a labor regime and a social system, and the number of enslaved people in late eighteenth-century New Mexico roughly mirrored that in the United States. An estimated 12 percent of New Mexico's population in 1790 lived in a servile status, a statistic that closely coincided with the early American republic, where 15 percent of the national population in 1780 was enslaved.[5] Until recently, however, scholars have tended to overlook the Southwest's multiethnic institutions of human bondage, especially during the period following the 1846 American conquest. This owes in large part to the long-standing propensity of U.S. historians to focus on racialized chattel slavery in the antebellum South, casting alternative forms of involuntary labor into the shadows of academic and public awareness. As historian Joseph C. Miller points out, however, the institutionalization of slavery in the early American republic "was the least representative instance of the processes of slaving in the global perspective" and has therefore become a "politicized paradigm of slavery" in the modern imagination.[6] Perhaps nowhere on the nineteenth-century North American continent did this hold truer than in the West, where alternative forms of coerced labor and dependency in the Mexican Cession lands stripped thousands of people of their freedom and mobility.[7]

Academic debates continue as to whether or not debt bondage should be classified as a form of outright slavery.[8] Although peonage and captivity differed in certain particulars, both relied on coercion and subjected weaker groups to involuntary, wageless servitude for extended periods of time. But contrary to hereditary chattel slavery, peonage involved a contractual verbal agreement between creditor and debtor, making it a negotiated relationship of servility and dependency at the outset. Yet this shared power dynamic immediately and permanently shifted in favor of the master once a labor deal was finalized. While it might be true that nobody held a gun to a person's head and forced them to become indebted to a landlord (*patrón*), and indeed prospective peons understood the consequences of their failure to repay a creditor, the system nonetheless operated upon manipulated conditions of dependency that typically ensured perpetual bondage. Both parties knew that the ultimate outcome would likely be a lifetime of servitude, and unfortunate peons necessarily subjected themselves to that condition anyway because no plausible alternative existed. As contemporary observers described it, debt peonage constituted a hybridized form of slavery, servitude, and serfdom, drawing characteristics from each while bearing certain traits inimitable unto itself.[9]

The most straightforward description of peonage in New Mexico comes from a descendant of a Spanish colonial family that was part of the land-holding element of society. "In feudal times," according to Fabiola Cabeza de Baca, "there were many poor people who became indebted to the *ricos*, and the rich were never at a loss to find men to be sent with flocks of sheep." In colonial and territorial New Mexico, she explained, herding was among the few methods of employment outside the household. As a consequence, "if a man became indebted to a *rico*, he was in bond slavery to repay," and few peons ever questioned the legitimacy of the system that perpetuated their servitude. Because of such machinations, "entire families often served a *patrón* for generations to meet their obligations." Cabeza de Baca described several crucial elements of peonage, including its comparability to slavery, types of work performed, the sense of dependency that developed between master and servant, and the hereditary nature of the institution. She implicitly revealed one reason why large outbreaks of violent resistance never occurred—because of family obligation and a sense of honor—and her use of the terms "*ricos*" and "poor people" acknowledged the socioeconomic hierarchy that undergirded the entire system.[10]

While debt peonage remains comparatively obscure in the historiographies of American labor, slavery, and the western frontier in general, the subject of indigenous captivity has received considerable attention and scholars generally agree that it was a form of slavery. Building on the pathbreaking work of James Brooks, recent authors have increasingly recognized the historical roles of various southwestern tribes and continue to elevate Native Americans—especially Apaches, Comanches, Navajos, and Utes—to a higher level of importance as actors in the gradual evolution of regional societies.[11] Others have focused on the participation of indigenous peoples, and women especially, in southwestern slave raiding and the resulting contention for social and cultural hegemony in that porous borderlands region, a conflict that often saw Indians emerging as a dominant force during multilateral interactions.[12] The existence of racial castes and social hierarchies meant that most New Mexican communities exhibited some level of segregation, with marginalized Indian captives and indigent peons occupying positions at the periphery of communal interaction.[13] The work in these fields of study has been remarkable over recent years, but two blind spots in the new historiography have ensured that the history of labor coercion in the Southwest continues to be seen as a regional rather than a national story. First, while these respective works have analyzed Indian slavery in great depth, they largely ignore debt peonage. Second, although some of these writers acknowledge the ways in which the nation impinged on the region, many of them have overlooked the ways in which the region impinged on the nation. Thus, my arguments expand on the existing literature by contextualizing captivity and peonage within the broader themes of antebellum sectionalism, wartime emancipation, and postwar Reconstruction.

Slaves can be seen in several different ways: as commodities, as workers, or, in some instances, as both. As commodities, slaves are directly convertible to cash, while as workers, they are similarly subjected to servitude and varying levels of dependency but seldom have significant marketplace value. In the Southwest, captives and peons toiled as unfree laborers in fields and households and therefore did have economic value as producers of goods and providers of services. But rarely were they commodifiable to the same degree as Southern slaves, who could be sold at auction for princely cash sums. Herein lies a significant difference between peonage and captivity in the Southwest and chattel slavery in the South. The Southern dilemma—which scarcely existed in New Mexico—was that plantation owners had become reliant on slaves, both as a labor source and as a monetary asset, to such an extent that slaves were crucial to individual affluence as well as sectional economic prosperity.[14] By 1860, for instance, almost half of all Southern assets were tied up in chattel slaves: The states below the Mason-Dixon Line had a collective wealth of $6.33 billion on the eve of the Civil War, of which the cash value of slaves constituted $3.05 billion.[15]

Southerners' reliance on slaves as chattels and producers became especially acute as the nineteenth century wore on, with emerging capitalist markets prompting commercial expansion and intensification in both the North and the South. The increasing commercialization of slavery after 1800, attendant with the contemporaneous communication and transportation revolutions, made slavery an increasingly imperative institution for Southerners' economic success, particularly those in the burgeoning Cotton Belt.[16] While Hispanos enjoyed the fruits of their servants' labor in fields and households, they also relied to a remarkable degree upon peons and captives as a reflection of elevated social status. Like seventeenth-century Virginia plantation owners, New Mexico's landholders lived in a society where, up until the Civil War era, specie remained scarce and a barter economy prevailed. In each place, the demonstrable socioeconomic status of patriarchs depended primarily on their dependent laborers rather than bank accounts. In nineteenth-century New Mexico, as in early colonial Virginia, proprietors exercised direct control over labor and the means of production within a social system contingent upon patriarchy, enslavement, and the overt disempowerment of entire classes and racial groups.[17]

When New Mexico came under the jurisdiction of the United States in 1846, debt peonage and captive slavery were thrust into sectionalist debates in the U.S. Congress. Preexisting Mexican laws regulating human bondage were continuously called into question during discussions over slavery in the newly acquired territories. Legislators temporarily mitigated these incendiary issues with the Compromise of 1850, allowing popular sovereignty for New Mexico and Utah territories and free-soil statehood for California.[18] By that time, however, dependent servility had become a mainstay in southwestern culture and economy, and federal attempts to uproot it met with staunch resistance at the local level. Although on several occasions they did take up the issue of African American rights and chattel slavery, New Mexico's territorial legislators typically avoided mentioning peonage and captivity during official proceedings. Most Hispanic policymakers belonged to an elite echelon of society that traced its lineages to the earliest Spanish colonists and they themselves often held Indian captives and indigent debtors as servants. For this reason, local lawmakers nonchalantly perpetuated peonage through their silence on the issue, while simultaneously expressing a deep aversion to a chattel slavery in which they held no vested economic or social interests. In the mid-1850s, however, the ascension of proslavery Democrats during the presidential administrations of Franklin Pierce and James Buchanan, as well as the Supreme Court's decision in the Dred Scott case, prompted a shift in policy objectives on the part of New Mexicans. The territorial legislature first adopted a measure regulating the mobility of blacks in 1857, then passed an infamous "slave code" in 1859 that mirrored those of many eastern states. In the eyes of most Americans, this placed New Mexico firmly in the camp of proslavery interests.[19]

Events during the Civil War ultimately induced the repeal of New Mexico's slave code, and not long afterward the federal government, influenced by Radical Republican ideology and Reconstruction policy, ventured a step further and outlawed peonage as well. By 1867, the peculiar institutions of Indian captivity and debt bondage, as they had existed and evolved over three hundred years and three political sovereignties, were finally nearing their demise. The systems remained so entrenched, however, that it would take several more years and numerous judicial proceedings to finally liberate captives and peons. Not until the 1870s did most servants attain freedom—more than three centuries after Spaniards introduced the system, almost three decades after American debates on slavery in the southwestern territories began, and several years after the final shots of the Civil War had been fired.

Captive slavery had a profound impact on the social, economic, and political development of the Southwest, both prior to and following its geopolitical absorption into the United States. Kinship components of human bondage proliferated to a larger degree in the Southwest—where racial prejudice was less pervasive among indigenous and Hispanic inhabitants—than in the South, where the spread of chattel slavery in place of indentured servitude had propagated increasing racism toward blacks since the early 1700s. This led to many misconceptions among easterners not familiar with the region.[20] The multifaceted institution of Indian slavery and the ethnically amalgamated society that resulted from it undermined New Mexico's political advancement once it became a part of the United States, as evidenced in debates over issues of mixed-blood identity and involuntary servitude in both the territorial legislature and the U.S. Congress during the antebellum years.

The existence of captives and peons in New Mexico communities following the American conquest also trivialized the territory in the minds of many Protestant white easterners. While anti-Hispanic ethnocentrism and anti-Catholic nativism contributed to New Mexico's stifled political aspirations during the years following the U.S. conquest, Indian slavery and debtor servitude—within the context of antebellum sectionalism—became another reason for the territory's struggle to achieve statehood prior to the Civil War. New Mexico languished in territorial status for more than sixty years, in part because the continuing presence of involuntary servitude discouraged favorable action toward statehood on the part of Northern free-soilers and Radical Republicans.[21] When social change did occur in the Southwest vis-à-vis the eradication of peonage and captive slavery during the Civil War era, it came not as a movement from within, but was instead driven by external political and ideological forces and backed by legislative and judicial doctrine that originated in evolving American ideas of republicanism and democracy.

The presence of two distinct systems of servitude, coupled with the enactment of discriminatory slave codes in the territorial legislature, sent a confusing message to Southerners and helped to encourage a Confederate invasion of New Mexico at the onset of the Civil War. After that war, with the manumission of African American slaves, Northern politicians expected to see a similar liberation of bound laborers in all parts of the country. In the remote Southwest, citizens ignored emancipation laws and retained many of their servants, contending that captives had nowhere to go if freed and that peons, who went into debt voluntarily, did not fall into the category of slaves. In so doing, Hispanos further exacerbated Anglo-Americans' pessimistic opinions of the culturally and socially "backward" territory.

Most important, the existence of debt peonage and Indian captivity in New Mexico culture and society played a prominent role in the political debates that brought about America's midcentury transition from slavery to free labor. With the implementation of popular sovereignty, peonage and captivity became critical factors in congressional deliberations over the future of slavery because of their entrenchment in the newly acquired Mexican Cession lands. Although most federal leaders soon realized that these institutions existed in the Southwest, Northerners and Southerners disagreed over whether or not debt peons and Indian captives were slaves.

Antebellum political discourse surrounding these unfamiliar systems of bondage ultimately informed federal policy during the Reconstruction era, helping to expand abolitionist legal doctrine to include peonage in addition to the "involuntary servitude" mentioned in the Thirteenth Amendment. During the fifteen years preceding the Civil War, the existence of debt bondage and captive servitude in New Mexico forced Americans to think more broadly about slavery and brought awareness to the fact that involuntary labor was not limited to the chattel system in the South. This recognition informed profound political debates during the 1850s regarding the future role of unfree labor in the country. In the immediate postwar years, federal leaders realized that the constitutional ban on slavery failed to encompass all systems of servitude, due to varying definitions of voluntary and involuntary labor. Postwar investigations, along with President Johnson's 1865 executive order banning Indian captivity and the 1867 congressional moratorium on peonage, broadened federal policy on coercive dependent labor. The subsequent implementation of debtor servitude and sharecropping in the rural South indicates that those efforts, while eventually effective in New Mexico, lacked nationwide resonance. Despite this shortcoming, federal deliberations over peonage and captive slavery prior to and during the Civil War had a significant impact on the future legal perception of compulsory labor in the United States. Indeed, early twentieth-century court proceedings in the Deep South cited New Mexico peonage cases as guiding precedent when formulating legal decisions about the status of African Americans bound to similar forms of unfree labor.[22] The legal and political implications of debt peonage and Indian captivity in territorial New Mexico thus resonated for decades after the Thirteenth Amendment purportedly ended the practice of enslavement in the United States of America.

Chapter 1

Debating Southwestern Slavery
in the Halls of Congress

An embattled James K. Polk stood in front of a vehemently divided Congress on December 5, 1848, poised to deliver his first State of the Union address since the culmination of the Mexican-American War earlier that year. The United States had just absorbed a tremendous amount of land through the Mexican Cession, and the president understood that the ensuing admittance of that region as either free or slave territory would be extremely contentious and might ultimately drive the nation to internal conflict. Realizing the high stakes, he implored his colleagues to enter the process of political incorporation with open minds and conciliatory hearts. Polk declared that Congress ought to establish "regularly organized territorial governments" for California and New Mexico, stressing that legislators would do well to set aside "the agitation of a domestic question which is coeval with the existence of our government itself." Allowing the slavery issue to disrupt the admittance of these newly acquired regions would, in Polk's estimation, undermine national prosperity, embarrass the country internationally, and jeopardize the federal Union itself. The president's well-founded exhortations, as it turned out, would be in vain. The congressional leaders sitting in the audience that day had no intention of incorporating the Southwest into the Union without unprecedented levels of sectional fanfare and debate over slavery.[1]

Debt peonage and Indian captivity first ascended to the forefront of national discourse following the culmination of the Mexican-American War in 1848. By the terms of the Treaty of Guadalupe Hidalgo, the United States came into possession of almost half of Mexico's previously claimed territory. Conspiracy theorists believed that Southerners participated in and promoted the war in an attempt to gain land for the expansion of their peculiar institution. Horace Mann, a staunch Massachusetts abolitionist, wrote an accusatory letter in 1850 declaring that "the south waged war with Mexico from one, and only one, motive; for one, and only one, object,—the extension of slavery." Mann supposed that slavery in the western territories would doom the United States to an "unobstructed career of conquest, of despotism, and of infamy," postulating that the introduction of chattel bondage into either California or New Mexico would be "a vastly greater crime than was the African slave trade itself."[2]

Mann was clearly referring to President Polk, a Southern slaveholder from Tennessee, who helped to incite the war and had insisted on Mexico's cession of territory as a prerequisite to peace. Polk vehemently denied allegations that his administration waged the war in view of advancing slavery westward. "I did not desire to extend slavery," he confided to his diary, noting that neither California nor New Mexico would have been likely to support slavery anyway and that the mere acquisition of those provinces for future American settlement satisfied him.[3] Even in his inaugural address, in which he stressed the importance of American imperialism, Polk insisted that "the bonds of our Union, so far from being weakened, will become stronger" with westward expansion, insinuating that he fought the war with no fractious intentions in mind.[4]

Polk could not have been more mistaken in his assumption that acquiring the Mexican Cession lands would foster national unity. Contrarily, this newly seized domain, comprising what would eventually become the State of California and the territories of New Mexico and Utah, sparked intense sectional debates in Congress that lasted for more than two years. Politicians argued incessantly over the existence of slavery in the West, exemplifying the overall ignorance of many Americans regarding peonage and Indian captivity. Polk himself unwittingly acknowledged the widespread presence of captive slaves in the Southwest when his administration assured Mexican dignitaries that the U.S. government would quell Indian raiding around the new international border "and compel them to release these captives, and restore them to their families and friends."[5] The president recognized that the borderlands region hosted a large population of enslaved captives and debt peons and pledged that the federal government would work to liberate them, in effect making an antislavery pronouncement that went unnoticed because it involved Indians and Mexicans rather than African Americans.

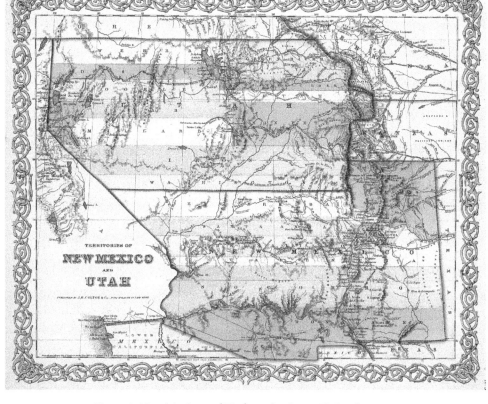

Figure 2. New Mexico and Utah territories, c. 1850s. Courtesy
David Rumsey Map Collection, www.davidrumsey.com.

Once the Southwest became a U.S. possession, regional forms of
coerced servitude underwent a rapid politicization at the federal level. The
issue of slavery in western territories had already plagued Congress for decades and would have a profound influence on sectional debates in the years
leading up to the Civil War.[6] The precedent for congressional regulation of
slavery in newly acquired lands stemmed from the Northwest Ordinance of
1787, which specifically prohibited "slavery and involuntary servitude" in
any new territories north and west of the Ohio River.[7] Questions regarding
the geographic extension of slavery arose repeatedly as America continued
to expand westward. The idea of territorial self-government, or "popular
sovereignty"—which effectively sectionalized the slavery issue—arose with

the creation of the Southwest Territory in 1790 and was tested multiple times over the ensuing decades, first with the Louisiana Purchase in 1803; again with the 1820 Missouri Compromise; and finally with the vast domain that Mexico relinquished to the United States in 1848.[8]

The path to territorial status for New Mexico, which took almost three years, proved to be an object of great controversy and placed it at the forefront of a heated national discourse on slavery. The admission of New Mexico and Utah into the Union as either free or slave territories prompted numerous debates in Congress and exacerbated sectional turmoil between Northern and Southern lawmakers.[9] Political leaders in both houses argued over whether or not slavery should be sanctioned in the Southwest, discussing the aptitude of the arid climate and mountainous topography for supporting involuntary servitude, the sentiments of the civilian inhabitants toward such an institution, and the validity of preexisting Mexican laws banning human bondage. In most of these exchanges, legislators failed to distinguish between slavery in the South, and captivity and peonage in the Southwest. One of the great peculiarities about debates on slavery in the Mexican Cession lands was that the topic of discussion—plantation-style chattel slavery—mattered very little to most of the recently naturalized Mexican Americans living there. Only a handful of U.S. politicians ever recognized this discrepancy and, when attempting to explain the true nature of regional systems of servitude to their peers, they often received laughter and jeers in response.[10]

Congressional debates on the regulation of slavery in New Mexico began even before the signing of the Treaty of Guadalupe Hidalgo.[11] But when Mexico ceded California and New Mexico to the United States in 1848, the question of admitting those two provinces into the Union took on increased urgency. A year later it became evident that California would seek entry as a free-soil state, meaning that New Mexico must be admitted as either a slave state or territory in order to maintain sectional balance, a stipulation that traced its precedent to the Missouri Compromise.[12] In a speech delivered on June 27, 1848, South Carolina senator John C. Calhoun outlined one critical consideration involving whether or not the Northern states, through their congressional representatives, should have the power to block Southern migrants from relocating to the new territories with their slave property.[13] While the Compromise of 1850 offered a temporary solution to the problem, the 1857 Supreme Court case *Dred Scott v. John F. A. Sandford* provided a more conclusive (and controversial) verdict on the future of slavery in the territories.[14] The arguments undergirding the 1857 decision help to explain the eccentricities of the political debates over slavery in New Mexico that occurred between 1848 and 1850, and they provide a broader contextual framework in which to view and interpret southwestern slave systems.

One of the primary dilemmas addressed in the Dred Scott case involved the transport of slaves into U.S. territories. Senator John M. Berrien of Georgia, a former attorney general in Andrew Jackson's administration, posed that question to Congress as early as 1850. "If the Constitution of the country recognizes my title to the slave within my State, beyond my State, and within a sovereign State that inhibits slavery, does it forbid, does it deny that title within a territory that is the common property of the United States?" he asked rhetorically.[15] The senator was referring to an American legal principle known as the "right of transit," wherein the constitutionally protected property rights of slaveholders enabled them to bring bondsmen into states that had abolished slavery, although by the 1850s most Northern states had stopped recognizing this purported right.[16] Berrien's inquiry and others regarding slavery in the territories would be answered in the Supreme Court's 1857 ruling.

Some scholars have criticized the Dred Scott case—a landmark victory for proslavery ideologues and a stunning defeat for the free-soil movement—as a failure of American jurisprudence and one of the earliest examples of overt judicial activism on the part of the U.S. Supreme Court.[17] In a vote that transcended sectional lines, six of nine Supreme Court judges sided with Chief Justice Roger B. Taney in the opinion that Congress had no power to regulate slavery in the territories, nor did it have the ability to prohibit citizens from transporting their slave property into such regions.[18] The constitutional interpretations and legal theories sustaining the Supreme Court decision could be traced back to the Northwest Ordinance.[19] The Dred Scott case cemented lingering ambiguities on territorial jurisdiction to the benefit of proslavery interests, although its failure to address involuntary servitude more broadly left plenty of latitude for New Mexicans to interpret the ruling loosely in regards to captivity and peonage.

Through Dred Scott, the Supreme Court answered many of the questions that had arisen in Congress surrounding the admission of new states and territories in the Mexican Cession lands. Following the Mexican-American War, political leaders spent more than two years sparring over the regulation of slavery in the Southwest and debating whether or not territorial legislatures could legally sanction systems of involuntary servitude. If Congress admitted New Mexico and Utah without a clause protecting the peculiar institution, Southerners feared that, however economically and agriculturally impractical the implementation of plantation slavery in those regions might be, slaveholders who relocated there might be forced to surrender their human property upon arrival.

Most congressmen acknowledged the vast differences between state and territorial governments and, by extension, their capacity as federal lawmakers to legislate over them. Long before the Dred Scott case, Representative David Wilmot described states as independent and highly organized political entities while explaining that territories, on the other hand, "are unorganized, dependent communities, destitute of sovereignty, looking to us for political existence."[20] As quasi-colonial bodies, territories existed at the behest of the federal government; most high-ranking officials received their appointments from Washington bureaucrats, including governors, whom the president appointed directly. This placed territories in a subordinate political position, denigrating their inhabitants as veritable wards of the government and allowing for a higher degree of federal oversight.

Because each territory had only a single congressional representative who could do little more than give speeches when allowed the opportunity, the addition of a new territory did not disrupt sectional political balance to the same degree as did the admission of new states with multiple congressmen and full voting powers. With California receiving free-soil statehood status in 1850, Southerners were perturbed that two popular sovereignty territories (New Mexico and Utah) did not adequately compensate for the disruption of political representation in Congress. Senator Calhoun despaired the outcome of debates on California's admission as a free-soil state and spoke vehemently against it, recognizing that no solution was likely to preserve national unity forever. From the moment the Northwest Ordinance became law in 1787, he lamented, the South had been "deprived of its due share of the territories," the result being the destruction of "the equilibrium which existed when the government commenced." Calhoun interpreted sectional inequity in terms of political power and population—both of which influenced the allotment of congressional seats and had been the basis of earlier compromises—to assert the importance of balanced representation between the North and South. The growing population imbalance between the two sections, which the 1840 census placed at a difference of 2.4 million people, meant that power in the House had shifted significantly in favor of the North.

Calhoun pointed out that Northern states had forty-eight more seats in the House than did Southern states, a gap that would only widen with time. The admission of new slave territories would do nothing to mitigate this discrepancy because their representatives did not have voting powers and, even if they did, the population of western territories remained negligible compared to that of states in the East.[21]

Calhoun's points about political representation in Congress and the limited power of territorial governments precipitated widespread anxiety over new territories. Those tensions arose in part from the unforeseen ramifications that sometimes attended the admission of these geographically immense regions, where populations often became divided over the slavery issue. When the Northwest Territory was broken up into multiple smaller states, for example, the settlers in southern Illinois and Indiana related more to neighboring slave regions like Kentucky and Missouri, than they did with northerly Wisconsin and Michigan residents. This meant that territories might become internally divided and seek admission as multiple states with either pro- or antislavery constitutions. The same held true for New Mexico, a vast region that, prior to the creation of Arizona Territory in 1863, stretched from Texas to California and covered some 250,000 square miles. Because it encompassed such a large area and included diverse groups of people, New Mexico was susceptible to ideological divergences on the slavery issue among its widely dispersed and ethnically diverse population. This prevailing uncertainty frightened political leaders in the North and South alike and militated against the admission of new territories without extensive debate and compromise.[22]

Both Northern and Southern interests claimed that their perceived constitutional rights—including private property ownership—must be affirmed and protected within the boundaries of any and all new territories. By attempting to prohibit slavery in territorial appendages, Senator Calhoun thundered, the North made "the most strenuous effort to appropriate the whole [Mexican Cession] to herself, by excluding the South from every foot of it."[23] He pointed out that thousands of men from both sections and from all ideological persuasions fought in the Mexican-American War and shed blood in that struggle for the collective American cause. In a similar vein, other legislators noted that the *federal* government, representing *all* of the states, purchased the Mexican Cession using assets from the "common fund" of the U.S. Treasury, which entitled citizens to equal rights within those new territories. "They are as much the territories of one state as another . . . of the Southern as the Northern States," Calhoun reasoned. "They are the territories of all, because they are the territories of each." The South Carolina statesman believed that congressional oversight in territorial governance must not privilege one section's interests over the other.[24]

As the Dred Scott decision later affirmed, constitutional property rights included the ownership of slaves. This notion did not sit well with Northern free-soilers, and even representatives from some border states expressed dissatisfaction with that idea. After his retirement, former Missouri senator Thomas Hart Benton explained that Southerners felt aggrieved by their inability to take slave property with them when immigrating to the western territories. "In reality," an unsympathetic Benton countered, "it was that he was not allowed to carry the State law along with him to protect his slave."[25] Truman Smith of Connecticut concurred when informing fellow senators that slaveholders could move westward into New Mexico or Utah "on an exact footing of equality with the non-slaveholders," inasmuch as any American citizen, regardless of sectional origin, "can take their families, and, on arrival, can go to work and earn their bread by the sweat of their brows." Migrating slaveowners could transport all personal property with them should they so choose, "if they will only convert [their slaves] into money" before entering the territories. Any prohibition against the movement of slaves into the new territories, Smith maintained, had nothing to do with constitutional doctrine but could instead be attributed to slave property being "against common right."[26]

Stephen A. Douglas, a Democratic senator from Illinois, similarly maintained that the prohibition of human trafficking had nothing to do with sectionalism or slavery, pointing out that it applied to other articles of trade as well. Alcohol, much like slaves, could not be taken into certain territories because of prohibitory local laws that were "directed against no section, and impair the rights of no State of the Union," Douglas explained. Such codes pertained to the sale and use of specific types of goods and property, "whether brought from the North or the South," and therefore had no bearing on sectional or antislavery ideology.[27] Although the landmark Supreme Court opinion in the Dred Scott case had yet to be rendered at the time these political deliberations took place between 1848 and 1850, preexisting notions of constitutionality lent credence to a belief among Southerners that they held the rational advantage in congressional debates. The basic republican principle of equal rights for all individuals, established during the revolutionary generation, spawned a variety of arguments over slavery and servitude that, by the antebellum era, had come to be fueled by sectional interests.

These political viewpoints and the Supreme Court's 1857 decision invigorated the ongoing debate over slavery that culminated in civil war. Senator Benton believed that the issue of slavery in the territories, as it arose in 1848, and as later manifested in the Dred Scott case, represented one of the instigating factors in the sectional conflict. "And there commenced the great slavery agitation," he wrote, "founded upon the dogma of 'no power in Congress to legislate upon slavery in the territories,' which has led to the abrogation of the Missouri compromise line—which has filled the Union with distraction—and which is threatening to bring all federal legislation, and all federal elections, to a mere sectional struggle, in which one-half of the States is to be arrayed against the other."[28] New Mexico was strewn directly into these political and ideological struggles following the Mexican-American War, largely as a result of slavery, peonage, and captivity.[29]

In regard to the southwestern territories, abolitionists and free-soilers immediately invoked the argument that chattel slavery could not exist there with any practicality, owing primarily to the climate and geography of the region. The most well-known proponent of this line of reasoning was the Whig senator Daniel Webster. In 1850, he delivered an impassioned speech based on a notion of providential design, declaring that chattel slavery could never survive as an institution in California or New Mexico for reasons of "physical geography," and both regions would therefore remain "free by the arrangement of things by the Power above us."[30] His frequent allusions to the will of God and laws of nature as the leading factors precluding slavery from the western territories drew harsh rebukes from less-pious congressmen, particularly Senator Douglas, who understood the importance of ideological underpinnings in the slave debates. With poignant sarcasm, Douglas responded that he was "exceedingly gratified" by Webster's conclusions about the impossibility of slavery in the West, but pointed out how useless such theological reasoning would be in determining pro-or antislavery sentiment and the ideological nature of political representation in the new territories.[31]

In a sense, Webster and Douglas were both right. While Douglas asserted that laws of nature and providential design would not direct the flow of ideology, Webster's observations about western geography being antithetical to profitable plantation-style slavery also had merit. Any person who traveled to the Mexican Cession could attest to the fact that the land-scape varied significantly from that of the American South, and the atten-dant differences in agricultural practices and economic exchange precluded the sensibility of introducing chattel slavery into the region on a mass scale. Known for its basin-and-range topography, the Southwest consists of arid and sparsely inhabited deserts bisected from north to south by lofty, rugged mountain ranges at intervals of fifty to one hundred miles. The vast major-ity of the region lacks the necessary rainfall and humidity to grow year-round market crops for export, with only the occasional river valley provid-ing the appropriate ecosystem for agricultural production.

In New Mexico, only three such rivers—the Chama, the Pecos, and the Rio Grande—provided enough water to support farming on any significant scale, and even then irrigation was necessary in most places and for most crops.[32] Taken collectively, the farmlands in those three valleys composed an infinitesimal fraction of the total land area, and that tiny percentage was in turn subdivided into hundreds of long-lots of twenty to forty acres each, based on family inheritance of property, a distributive tradition that traced its origins back to colonial land grants. Most of northern New Mexico was therefore relegated to a pastoral economy based largely on sheep-raising and wool harvesting. This combination of pastoralism on the grassy hill-sides and at higher elevations, along with agriculture in the more arable valleys and lowlands, necessitated involuntary labor in the form of Indian captives and Hispanic peons. The number of man-hours needed to sustain the Southwest's seasonal subsistence economy, however, never remotely approached what was required for export-driven cotton and tobacco plan-tations in the South.

New Mexico also operated in large part on what historian Dan Usner has called a "frontier exchange economy," with Hispanos obtaining many of their goods through barter-driven trading networks that involved peripheral Indian tribes.[33] Exemplified by the trade fairs at Pecos and Taos, this component of the southwestern economy involved the exchange of animals, food, and items of Native manufacture for staples of Euro-American origin and captives. In this sense, mid-1800s New Mexico lacked the telltale features of western capitalism—industrialization, the capacity for mass production, and extractive market resources—that many Ameri-can newcomers hoped to encounter there. What they discovered instead was a variegated economic system that included hunting and gathering, pastoralism, subsistence agriculture, involuntary servitude, and even the extension of credit in the form of merchandise, but rarely the circulation of hard currency or bank notes.[34] Despite the advent of the Santa Fe Trade in 1821 and the concomitant commercial network established with Missouri merchants, New Mexico remained a quasi-feudalist society with a hierarchical social order—a primitive civilization, in the eyes of most American newcomers—that hardly beckoned for the implementation of chattel slavery and market agriculture on a grand scale. Southern efforts to extend slavery westward were in large part a political ploy to secure additional proslavery representation in Congress and to prevent any significant dissolution of the peculiar institution in places where it already existed.

Southerners valued the Southwest primarily for its geographic and political importance, not because they hoped to establish profitable plantations and transport large numbers of black slaves there, although this was the very ideological objective to which they turned during debates on the topic. Since New Mexico linked slaveholding Texas with Southern California, the region would complete an uninterrupted coast-to-coast empire should the South succeed in conquering New Mexico and California at the onset of a civil war. During his tenure as secretary of war in the 1850s, the future Confederate president Jefferson Davis commissioned the Pacific Railway Surveys and endorsed the Gadsden Purchase in advancement of a futuristic Southern strategy that saw New Mexico as the location of a transcontinental railroad linking the Gulf of Mexico to the Pacific Coast.[35] Thus, Southern attempts to establish and uphold the right of slaveownership in New Mexico were predominantly ideological, a strategic machination seeking sectional geographic expansion not for the purpose of implanting chattel slavery and plantation agriculture, but rather for establishing a continental empire that would enable Southern cotton to be more easily exported worldwide.

Some politicians readily acceded to the fact that the southwestern environment did not appear conducive to chattel slavery or plantation agriculture. Speaking to Congress in 1848, George P. Marsh, a Vermont representative, stated that the Mexican Cession lands "lie without the natural limits of slavery, and the institution cannot exist in those provinces, because it is excluded by physical conditions, and the economical law of profit and loss which they dictate." In their arguments against slavery, some abolitionists and free-soilers contended that the Southwest, with its subsistence agriculture and pastoral economy, must "be inhabited and tilled only by freemen" because the absence of labor-intensive export crops like rice, cotton, sugar, and tobacco precluded any extensive demand for manual slave labor.[36] That observation, while partially true, also assumed that slavery existed in only certain environments where particular crops grew, a fallacious notion that neglected to account for the thousands of unfree peons and captives toiling in southwestern fields, pastures, and households. Expounding upon Marsh's claims, Senator Truman Smith pledged that New Mexico "will and must be [a] free state, proviso or no proviso," referencing the provocative but moribund proposal of Representative David Wilmot in 1846.[37] As supporting evidence, Smith introduced published travelogues and reports from the Army Corps of Topographical Engineers to describe the southwestern climate. All of these firsthand accounts sustained the contention that chattel slavery could not profitably exist in the arid deserts and high altitudes of New Mexico and Utah.[38] Describing the Santa Fe region, Lieutenant William H. Emory reported quite bluntly that it "presents nothing but barren hills, utterly incapable, both from soil and climate, of producing anything useful."[39] Even Southerner Henry Clay, in attempting to lead a highly factionalized Congress to a compromise measure in 1850, pointed out that New Mexico, with its dry climate, had nature itself on her side, which he equated to "a thousand Wilmot Provisos."[40]

Senator John Bell from Tennessee joined antislavery congressmen in alluding to the dryness of the Southwest, proclaiming that "African slavery can never find a foothold in New Mexico."[41] Even if territorial residents favored slavery in practice, in principle, or both, Southerners would be unlikely to transport chattels there because, according to one Pennsylvania senator, "Masters will hardly carry their slaves into a territory in which they will be likely to be free as soon as their feet touch its soil."[42] In making such claims these politicians reasserted the statements of a New Mexico congressional delegate, Hugh N. Smith, who in April 1850 acknowledged the region to be "entirely unsuited for slave labor." Smith then paradoxically admitted that debt peonage, existing "in a quantity quite sufficient for carrying on all the agriculture of the territory," effectively fulfilled regional demand for labor.[43]

During discussions over a proposed compromise measure, Bell's antislavery colleague, Senator Daniel Webster, remarked that "no man would venture a farthing today for a great inheritance to be bestowed on him when slavery should be established in New Mexico."[44] Longtime New York politician Washington Hunt sarcastically offered a reward of $1,000 "for the discovery of a slaveholder who even wished to take his slaves thither."[45]

Others refused even to lend credence to the issue, believing the impracticality of slavery in the Southwest to be so obvious that it scarcely warranted their time and attention. By invoking the climate as an argumentative point, such claims reverberated around the more familiar plantation slavery and maintained that, so long as irrigation was needed to grow crops, slavery could not logically or profitably exist. This Northern Whig stance offered a practical nature-based alternative to the ideological abolition movement, which many saw as overly incendiary and antithetical to preserving the Union.[46]

Webster commended fellow Northerner Truman Smith for having adequately proven, "beyond the power of any conscientious man's denial," that slavery could never exist in New Mexico and for demonstrating to Northerners "that that which they desire to prohibit will never need any prohibition there."[47] He then insisted that the debate should proceed no further because "there is not, & there cannot be slavery" in California, New Mexico, or Utah.[48] Webster remained convinced that New Mexicans, "to a man, are opposed to slavery" and believed all territorial inhabitants to be "as warmly and decidedly" averse to it as the people of Maine were. The statesman assured his listeners that "slavery of the African race does not exist in New Mexico" and explained that the social and economic atmosphere of the region had no need for such a system because "the use of cheaper labor [peonage] rejects it." Invoking a final hyperbolic analogy, Webster swore that chattel slavery was about as likely to gain a foothold in New Mexico as it was to "be established on Mars' Hill."[49]

The forceful congressional interchange over compromise proposals resulted in a number of Northern newspaper editorials that specifically cited New Mexico's statutory retention of peonage, drawing comparisons between debt bondage and chattel slavery and attracting publicity to an already politically charged issue.[50] Despite Webster's impassioned speeches in the halls of Congress, Horace Greeley, a New York newspaperman and renowned abolitionist, lambasted the senator for not taking more forceful action to prevent slavery from being established in the western territories. Greeley criticized the congressman for what he perceived to be a lukewarm resistance to slavery. According to Greeley, Webster's opposition to the peculiar institution in New Mexico stemmed from slavery's moral reprehensibility, but he had done little to effect the passage of laws to definitively prevent it in practice. "Ten years have since passed," he wrote, "and Slavery is already there—there both in the abstract and the concrete—in the form

Figure 3. Daniel Webster, antislavery Massachusetts senator. Courtesy
National Archives and Records Administration, Washington, D.C.

Figure 4. Truman Smith, antislavery Connecticut senator. Courtesy
National Archives and Records Administration, Washington, D.C.

of a slave law and in that of slaves." Greeley grasped the realities of south-western slavery with much greater acuity than most Americans, recognizing peonage as an "abstract" form of slavery. His perceptive allusion to the "concrete" referenced New Mexico's Slave Code and the fact that the territorial legislature continued to sanction involuntary labor in the form of "master-servant relationships."[51]

While Webster's belief that all New Mexicans, "to a man," opposed slavery was an obvious fallacy for its universal inclusivity, the majority of the territory's native Hispano inhabitants did seem either opposed to or ambivalent toward the institution, in part owing to Mexico's earlier prohibition of slavery. Richard Weightman, a New Mexico congressional delegate, wrote that his constituents mostly opposed the introduction of chattel slavery and, he believed, would one day seek statehood on a platform of free labor. Having already suffered undue hardship in recent years "as a political battlefield over which to settle the slavery question," most Nuevomexicanos had no desire to choose sides on an issue "which in no way practically concerns them."[52] Responding to Weightman's claims, the antislavery National Era newspaper accused him of "bending his knee to the ruling power" in order to retain his position as a congressional delegate. "What can be expected of a Territory," an editorialist quipped, "the first act of whose first Delegate is one of abject submission to the slave power?"[53]

Most Anglo-Americans residing in New Mexico also acknowledged the irrationality of black slavery in the territory. Joab Houghton, a Santa Fe resident with a background in politics and law, informed Senator John M. Clayton that "any owner of slaves who should bring slaves to New Mexico would be ruined," because plenty of peons and captives already satisfied the demand for labor there. The introduction of African American slaves into the territory, he believed, would "produce the most deleterious effects upon the morals and the industrial interest of the country."[54] Two politically connected New Mexicans, Henry Connelly and James L. Collins, buttressed Houghton's argument when writing that most inhabitants, including Hispanos and Pueblo Indians as well as recent Anglo-American arrivals, were unequivocally averse to slavery.[55] Even New Mexico's territorial governor on the eve of the Civil War, Abraham Rencher—a man whose public statements pandered to Northerners but whose personal sympathies espoused Southern interests—admitted that "no efforts on the part of designing men can ever disturb the public peace by agitating the question of slavery."[56]

Yet another obstacle to the introduction of chattel slavery in the Mexican Cession lands stemmed from geopolitical concerns. The Southwest shared an extensive international border with Mexico, a nation that abolished slavery years earlier and that therefore became a place where escaped slaves sometimes sought refuge. Many people believed that slaves taken to New Mexico would have ample means of escape and, like runaways from East Texas, would enjoy the protection of Mexican citizens once they crossed either the Rio Grande or the newly drawn east-west boundary from El Paso to the Pacific Coast.[57] Because mountain ranges with dense vegetation afforded cover and nearby Mexico already prohibited slavery, opportunities to escape abounded to such a degree as "to render such property valueless," declared one Connecticut senator, who merely repeated the prior testimonials of many New Mexico residents.[58] Several of the territory's leading citizens explained that, unlike the deep waters and powerful currents of the Mississippi, Missouri, and Ohio rivers, the Rio Grande was nothing more than a shallow stream at most points and would do nothing to inhibit escapees. Once they crossed the river and reached Mexico, such slaves "would be as free as in the land of his forefathers" because Mexican citizens, opposed to slavery and still reeling from the loss of half their national domain in the recent war with the United States, would protect them from recapture and prevent their extradition.[59] The continued existence of debtor servitude and Indian captivity throughout the Southwest and in Mexico, however, suggests that Hispanics were not as averse to slavery as some Americans imagined.

To be sure, New Mexico's original constitution—written in 1850 by a group of delegates in anticipation of statehood—expressed a distaste for slavery, although the document was conceived with the assistance of Anglo-American newcomers who had their own political and sectional agendas and therefore did not necessarily reflect local sentiment. The framers resolved that slavery "is naturally impracticable" and could never tangibly exist in the region, noting that it only affected them with politically "evil tendencies" and must therefore be unambiguously rejected.[60] Only a few months later, New Mexico would be admitted into the Union as a territory rather than a state, and the constitution never went into effect. Territorial judge Joab Houghton, a transplant from New York, wrote many of the document's antislavery provisions, and the free-soil overtones reflected his own views more than those of regional occupants.[61] Regardless of what New Mexico's constitution dictated relative to slavery, its ideological implications were widely ignored in congressional circles.

In May 1850, Collins and Connelly met with Senator Truman Smith to discuss slavery in New Mexico. The Connecticut politician based his subsequent congressional speeches on both that meeting and his prior written correspondence with those two individuals. At that time, Collins and Connelly remained sympathetic to the slavery cause; the former edited a proslavery newspaper, the *Santa Fe Weekly Gazette*, and the latter held dozens of Hispanic peons, although he freed them several years later. At Smith's insistence, Collins and Connelly produced a detailed description of the slavery issue as it pertained to New Mexico. "Experience has shown," they wrote, "how infinitely more dangerous—*more savage*—is an escaped negro, than the worst of an Indian tribe." The two men called specific attention to the numerous Native groups inhabiting the territory, pointing out that, like Mexican citizens below the border, they too would likely assist and protect fleeing black slaves. "The known sympathy of the Indian for a fugitive slave would secure him every protection at their hands which he could desire," they predicted.[62]

In addition to the nomadic tribes inhabiting outlying regions, thousands of Pueblo Indians occupied permanent settlements in the more central portions of New Mexico and they too might protect black slaves. As with the lower and middle classes of the Hispano population, many Pueblos sympathized with the enslaved and entertained "none of the prejudices against the color of the negro," meaning that they would likely abet their escape whenever possible.[63] Any compassionate disposition toward slaves on the part of New Mexico's people emanated at least in part from the ongoing captive trade. Having been so frequently exposed to the horrors of human bondage, it stood to reason that many Indians and lower-class Hispanics would be sensitive to the plight of escaped black slaves. In their general ambivalence to race, New Mexicans represented the polar opposite of most easterners, whose prejudices drove them to abhor not just African Americans, but also the Indians and mixed-blood mestizos of the Southwest.

Setting aside the geographical and racial arguments against human bondage, Representative Marsh invoked the popular abolitionist claim of morality, positing that only the human conscience could truly check the spread of slavery. "Slavery is everywhere profitable, under the management of a prudent master," Marsh proclaimed, and mere geographic or climatic concerns could therefore never prevent its spread entirely. Commending the abolition of slavery in some New England states, he delivered a pious diatribe to his Southern opponents, claiming that slavery in the North "was abolished, not because it was contrary to the economical law of profit and loss, but because our fathers held it . . . to be contrary to the law of conscience and of God."[64] Horace Mann, a Massachusetts representative, shared this theological tenet of abolitionism; insisting that the existence of slavery was strictly a matter of conscience, he provocatively declared that "wherever the wicked passions of the human heart can go, there slavery can go."[65] Building upon this rationale, Senator Smith pronounced that the only real obstacle to chattel slavery in New Mexico "results from principles and jurisprudence acknowledged by the whole civilized world."[66] Thus, from the ideological standpoint of staunch abolitionists, the issue of slavery in newly acquired territories should be viewed as a matter of ethics and humanity rather than economics or legality.

Abolitionists and free-soilers echoed a wide range of Northerners in their general assertion that chattel slavery could not exist in New Mexico or any other southwestern territories. As one army lieutenant noted in 1846, peonage predominated throughout New Mexico, and the negligible profits to be gained from yet another form of involuntary servitude did not justify "the existence of negro slavery."[67] Senator Smith reiterated this supply-and-demand concept when telling his colleagues that slavery could never "be advantageously used in competition with the cheap peon labor of New Mexico," and any Southerner venturing into New Mexico would therefore find it most economical to simply sell his plantation slaves and "employ the native labor of that country."[68] Thus some easterners—albeit a minority—rightly connected the debate on slavery in the territories to the preexistence of peonage in those regions and the comparatively minimal demand for manual labor in a localized subsistence economy.

Despite their moral aversion to slavery in New Mexico, antebellum abolitionists rarely demanded that peonage or Indian captivity be banned there. This anomalous oversight suggests that, while some Americans recognized these two systems at face value as forms of human bondage, most did not view them with the same abhorrence as they did black slavery. Many easterners had personally witnessed Southern slavery, been exposed to both pro- and antislavery rhetoric and propaganda, and had read the heartrending slave narratives that began to appear in the 1830s, but they had never been offered a firsthand glimpse of peonage and captivity in the western territories, nor did any published accounts from Indian slaves or Hispanic peons exist.[69] Observers reported what they saw for publication in newspapers, pamphlets, and books, although in so doing they merely condemned without acting. That is, most travelers were passive witnesses who criticized the evils of slavery not so much to elicit direct action against the system, but rather to assert their own morality in appeasement of conscience.[70] This was precisely the disingenuous position that Horace Greeley accused Daniel Webster of taking during the debates over slavery in the territories.

The prevailing ignorance of southwestern slave systems among easterners also emanated from strong Anglo-American prejudices against Hispanics and Indians, whose racial, linguistic, religious, and cultural backgrounds made them seem different and strange to newcomers. A piece appearing in the *Santa Fe Weekly Gazette* took a sardonic tone intended to capture the attention of seemingly oblivious Northern free-soilers and antislavery Whigs. "There is in this country a state of things existing which is much more worthy of the efforts of your philanthropists, your Abolitionists, and your nigger-loving whites, than the question of slavery," the article read, "and that is the fact that there are thousands . . . of Indian women and children who have been stolen from their families and sold into slavery, worse than *Southern Slavery*."[71] The author of the letter clearly intended to ruffle some feathers by pointing out the hypocrisy of certain antislavery groups.

Further evidence of such prejudices surfaced in military reports as well. A medical officer named J. F. Hammond believed that New Mexico's servile population lacked any "spark of culture," evincing instead a "painful combination of astuteness with impotency."[72] His observations reflected a common idealistic mentality during an era when many Americans perceived Indians and Hispanos on the western frontier as socially and culturally flawed, essentially nothing more than an impediment to the nation's providential imperialistic expansion and a scourge upon more pure Euro-American bloodlines. Even Northern abolitionists who abhorred chattel slavery and disseminated a rhetoric of morality retained strong racial prejudices toward the very same peoples whose plight for freedom they espoused, as evidenced by the fact that many antislavery activists supported the African colonization movement. Hammond's viewpoint coincided with that of many others—Northern and Southern alike—who believed Hispanics and Indians to be intellectually inferior and culturally incompatible with the divine scheme of Manifest Destiny.[73] For these reasons, some easterners completely overlooked the existence of peonage and Indian slavery in New Mexico and often failed to even view them as forms of coercive labor.

The widely acknowledged impracticality of chattel slavery in the western territories did little to deter Southerners in their insistence that the institution be extended there in ideology if not in practice. Plantation-style agriculture never gained a foothold in the Southwest, but the practice of holding humans in servile bondage continued to enjoy the wholehearted ideological support of Southerners from the moment the territory fell under the dominion of the United States. More than anything else, black slavery was a nonstarter in New Mexico because *hacendados* and political elites already possessed sufficient means for oppressing indigent citizens and captive Indians into a condition of permanent servitude and simply did not need an additional labor force.[74] Seemingly undeterred by Northern onslaughts, proslavery interests fought to preserve New Mexico's peculiar institution in any form possible, endeavoring to make it a slave territory under the guises of peonage and captivity if nothing else.

Systems of involuntary servitude existed in the Southwest long before the installation of western capitalism and constitutional principles. Throughout the colonial period, New Mexico's social structure resembled that of the American South in that a small, land-rich contingent of the inhabitants were a veritable provincial aristocracy. At the outbreak of the Civil War in 1861, a Union soldier noticed that only a few hundred "rich Mexicans" lived in the territory.[75] Although they represented a small percentage of the total population, these *ricos* reigned supreme over territorial affairs and controlled vast tracts of land, oftentimes traceable to Spanish and Mexican land grants. To develop and maintain the arable portions of these lands and to raise livestock on the grassy hillsides, *patrones* employed the traditional methods of debt peonage and Indian slavery.[76] Small villages frequently appeared within the boundaries of these large landholdings, with laboring peons as the principal occupants. On vast pastoral ranges, lower-class peon laborers "made little villages around the ground of the lord of these estates," a practice that often segregated the lower classes of peons from the families of the landed gentry.[77]

James Josiah Webb, a merchant and trader on the Santa Fe Trail, noted in his memoirs that by the time he arrived in the province in the early 1840s peonage "was a fixed institution."[78] When General Kearny occupied New Mexico during the Mexican-American War, the temporary legal code that he implemented implicitly acknowledged the existence of slavery by mandating that only "free male citizens" would be able to vote in the new territory.[79] Touring New Mexico a decade later, United States Attorney

William Davis observed that debtor servitude remained the predominant form of labor, having originated during the Spanish colonial era and being recently codified in a territorial statute.[80] When debating the slavery issue as it pertained to the land acquired from Mexico, many congressional leaders cited this preexistence of involuntary servitude as ample precedent for its retention and legal sanction. One politician explicitly understood peonage as a form of slavery when outlining its legal history in the Southwest, noting that it existed under former Mexican statutes and was merely perpetuated in recent master-servant codes.[81] These legal precedents became a focal point for congressional deliberations prior to New Mexico's admission into the Union as a territory on September 9, 1850. Another senator sardonically summarized the crux of the entire debate when he insisted that any assertion of previous Mexican laws remaining valid "is to say, in other terms, that we are subject ourselves to the laws of a foreign nation."[82]

Hugh N. Smith corroborated the shaky ground upon which this viewpoint rested. Regarding the statutory preexistence of slavery in New Mexico, he informed Daniel Webster that it "had been altogether abolished by the laws of Mexico," although such abolitionist doctrine effected only racial slavery and did nothing to suppress or limit peonage and captivity.[83] Mexico did indeed approve several measures outlawing slavery and regulating relationships between masters and servants between the years 1821, when it gained its independence from Spain, and 1846, when the Mexican-American War commenced. Southerners contended that preexisting anti-slavery laws became extraneous the moment Mexico ceded the territory to the United States, at which time the mandates of the U.S. Constitution immediately applied to those lands. Contrarily, Northerners insisted that Mexican slavery statutes continued in full force until territorial officials abrogated them, an understanding with roots in the American conquest of New Mexico. When the Army of the West took possession of Santa Fe in August 1846, Kearny immediately issued a proclamation declaring that "the laws hitherto in existence will be continued until changed or modified by competent authority," thereby acknowledging congressional authority to legislate more definitively on the issue at some future date.[84]

The first such controversial decree appeared in Mexico's 1824 constitution and primarily involved the transatlantic slave trade. The law forbade trafficking or commerce in slaves and granted instantaneous freedom to any bondsmen brought into the country. It required the immediate seizure of sea-bound slave-trading vessels and called for the imprisonment—for a period of up to ten years—of any persons found to be complicit in such activities. The edict reinforced earlier Spanish regulations banning the slave trade and prohibited any person from taking slaves into Mexico, whether for the purpose of selling them or for retaining them as personal servants.[85]

Another regulatory measure of April 15, 1829, marked the second time that Mexico abolished slavery and reiterated that all persons formerly held in a condition of servitude were henceforth free. The primary difference between this law and Mexico's 1824 constitutional provision arose from the fact that it allowed slaveowners to be compensated for their freed slaves "when the condition of the Treasury admits it."[86] The stipulation that masters be remunerated for their liberated slaves sought to ease the transition to a nonslaveholding society and stifle any public outcry that might emanate from such a decree. Unfortunately for Mexican slaveholders, a chronically overspent national treasury never facilitated the issuance of such reimbursements. The Mexican president at that time, Vicente Guerrero, could scarcely have imagined that his government's slave code would become an object of debate in the United States Congress twenty years later. One U.S. senator, while denying the validity of the law as it pertained to New Mexico after the 1846 conquest, referred to Guerrero's decree as "waste paper," an assertion to which Northern abolitionists vehemently objected.[87] Senator James Cooper of Pennsylvania, for one, not only believed these Mexican antislavery laws to be commendable but also insisted that they remained valid and effective in the southwestern territories, a suggestion that many in the room found audacious and even laughable.[88]

A third and final Mexican statute of April 4, 1837, repeated the stipulations of the preceding two laws, once again banning slavery and reaffirming the right to compensation for any master despoiled of his human property upon entering Mexico.[89] The passage of three nearly identical mandates betrayed the Mexican government's failure to effectively enforce the first two. The country's vast territorial domain made it hard for the government to uphold such regulations in its sparsely populated frontier provinces, especially New Mexico, a difficulty that American lawmakers came to appreciate in later years. Continuous reverberations in governmental leadership, an omnipresent threat of political coups, and financial insolvency made it tough for the Mexican national government to exert any meaningful effort toward the enforcement of antislavery provisions.

Congressional dialogue on the validity of Mexican laws during the 1848–1850 sessions reflected the rampant sectionalism that fueled such debates, with all rationality sometimes being thrown to the wind during the course of rhetorical exchanges. Because Mexico's statutes prohibited slavery, Northerners voiced strong support for their continuance and sought to incorporate them into a new set of regulations for New Mexico. Conversely, Southerners denied that the laws remained applicable. John Berrien summarized his section's position when stating that earlier laws, "with whatever authority they may have been enacted while California and New Mexico were a part of the Mexican republic, ceased instantly upon their transfer to the United States."[90] Had Mexico's laws upheld the institution of slavery, Northern and Southern positions on the matter would no doubt have been reversed.

Northerners cited legal precedent in support of retaining the preexisting laws of conquered territories, alluding to instances in which the U.S. Supreme Court ruled that civil and municipal codes relating to property ownership in ceded foreign land remained in force until government officials annulled or replaced them. Senator Cooper mentioned seven different court cases that established this legal standard.[91] The primary basis for his argument emanated from an 1828 Supreme Court case in which Chief Justice John Marshall addressed the issue as it pertained specifically to territorial acquisitions. Upon reverting to American sovereignty, a ceded territory dissolved all formal relations with its former country and came under the jurisdiction of the United States. Marshall explained that the transfer of land from one nation to another involved a complementary and obligatory shift in allegiance on the part of those residing there but acknowledged that any law regulating "the intercourse and general conduct of individuals," including property rights and, by extension, slavery, would remain in effect until modified "by the newly created power of the state."[92]

In other words, upon the acquisition of foreign territory, the existing law of the land continued in full effect until the conquering nation abrogated or amended it. Northern abolitionists used this ruling to argue for the continuation of Mexican antislavery laws, pointing out that no new edicts had yet been enacted to replace the old ones. According to Southern logic, however, this argument did not apply to the present situation because the Supreme Court ruling pertained to civil laws involving "the intercourse between citizen and citizen" and therefore had no impact on political mandates involving slavery.[93] Senator Calhoun conceded that foreign municipal laws proven to be consistent with the American political system might remain unchanged, but he insisted that this should have no impact on slavery in New Mexico. Based on his interpretation of preexisting Mexican municipal law, Calhoun concluded that "the peonage system would continue, but not to the exclusion of such of our citizens as may choose to emigrate with their slaves or other property."[94] In Calhoun's eyes, the Northern argument contradicted itself inasmuch as Mexican statutes prohibited chattel slavery but upheld peonage, which in principle and practice was merely a modified form of involuntary servitude. Because slaves were not considered citizens, Northerners countered that Mexico's civil and municipal laws could not, under the U.S. Constitution, continue to regulate slavery in New Mexico. The entire debate hinged upon one question: Did a law regulating slavery constitute a "civil or municipal law" or a "public or political law"? If the former, then Mexican legislation could not remain in effect beyond the moment of American conquest.

Speaking to the House of Representatives on July 29, 1848, Richard Donnell of North Carolina announced once again that Mexican law abolished enslavement and proclaimed in no uncertain terms that "African slavery, as it exists in the Southern States, was forbidden in that territory at the time it became, by cession, a part of our country."[95] Senator Benton, who claimed to have been averse to slavery in principle since early adulthood, concurred in the view that Mexico's antislavery provisions had not been automatically repealed when the southwestern domain shifted to American jurisdiction. In New Mexico and California, he pointed out, slavery had already been abolished at the time of the American conquest and could be reintroduced there only if Congress passed a new law to that effect.[96]

Addressing political colleagues on July 8, 1850, Senator Truman Smith offered a detailed description of slavery laws in New Mexico, beginning his diatribe with the straightforward comment that slavery had been prohibited there prior to the region being ceded to the United States. "If the ordinances and laws of Mexico abrogating slavery do not continue, yet it may be assumed that *there is no law authorizing it*," he reasoned, "and this is just as serious an obstacle to the introduction [of slavery] as a positive law forbidding it."[97] Because Mexican statute applied to the region at the time of the American conquest, Smith contended that those laws remained valid and enforceable, and by simply recanting such edicts Congress could not "reintroduce slavery" without passing an entirely new law to that effect.[98]

Still other Northerners feared that previous Spanish and Mexican mandates outlawing slavery would prove insufficient in preventing its eventual extension into the Southwest, demanding that Congress enact additional measures to ensure that black men and women could never be taken to those territories as slaves. Representative Marsh again questioned the validity of Mexico's laws, warning fellow Northerners about the veracity of such abolitionist doctrine and suggesting that U.S. courts would be unlikely to recognize another nation's legal codes. Skeptical of what judges might rule in the event of litigation, he cited this ambiguity as sufficient justification for the enactment of additional measures outlawing slavery in the Southwest.[99]

Marsh focused on Mexico's 1824 federal constitution, which he claimed had regulated slavery but not abolished it entirely, because the document banned involuntary servitude only in that republic's states. New Mexico and Alta California had been provinces—similar to territories in the U.S. body politic—and it remained a matter of interpretation as to whether the Mexican constitution had indeed outlawed slavery there along the same lines as the more southerly states. Subsequent laws passed in 1829 and 1837 were also questionable in their ultimate effect, in part due to civil and social unrest in that country. The general instability of Mexico's government made it difficult for American lawmakers to determine whether or not that country's congressional bodies even had the power to pass acts that superseded the 1824 constitution.[100]

These legal loopholes jeopardized the Northern movement to ban slavery in the Southwest. "Though slavery may have been abolished by Mexico," Marsh concluded, "yet American slaveholders may now revive it, by removing to the Territories and carrying their slaves with them," a possibility that, however unlikely, nonetheless necessitated congressional action.[101] Broadcasting the Southern viewpoint, Senator Calhoun sprang to his feet and condemned all antislavery interpretations of New Mexico's legal situation. At the moment Congress ratified the Treaty of Guadalupe Hidalgo in 1848, he insisted, Mexican sovereignty "became extinct" in the ceded territory and the U.S. Constitution took effect.[102] As one of the most vocal and preeminent proslavery representatives of his time, Calhoun voiced the sentiments of many Southerners when he asserted the irrelevance of all Mexican laws. Their Northern counterparts had, they believed, strayed woefully awry in embracing the notion that another country's statutes prohibited the extension or regulation of slavery within the American national domain.

Jefferson Davis, at the time a U.S. senator from Mississippi, likewise deflected the Northern argument with his own forceful invective. "Did we

Figure 5. John C. Calhoun, proslavery South Carolina senator. Courtesy
National Archives and Records Administration, Washington, D.C.

admit territory from Mexico subject to the constitution and laws of Mexico? Did we pay fifteen millions of dollars for jurisdiction over California and New Mexico, that it might be held subordinate to the law of Mexico?" the senator asked rhetorically during a February 1850 speech.[103] Davis recalled the negotiation process antecedent to the signing of the Treaty of Guadalupe Hidalgo, during which time a United States minister plenipotentiary, Nicholas Trist, discussed the slavery issue with Mexican commissioners. Trist purposely sidestepped the topic of slavery in the actual treaty to avoid setting a controversial precedent, informing his ambassadorial counterparts that "the bare *mention* of [slavery] in any treaty . . . was an absolute impossibility." He understood that any provision either including or excluding slavery in the ceded territory could not be considered without inciting political turmoil in the halls of Congress. Trist only slightly exaggerated the gravity of the situation when he told Mexican diplomats that "if it were in their power to offer me the whole territory described in our project, increased tenfold in value [and] covered a foot thick over with pure gold, upon the single condition that slavery be excluded therefrom, I could not entertain the offer for a moment, nor think even of communicating it to Washington."[104]

Davis alluded to this intentional omission of Mexico's slave laws as evidence that such mandates could not remain in effect after the treaty had been signed. He quoted the constitutional recognition of slave property as validation for the Southern cause, noting that the founding document ensured all American citizens the same legal protections regardless of sectional affiliation. Mexico's abolition of slavery during the 1820s, he insisted, became irrelevant the moment that it ceded New Mexico and California to the United States, whereupon that entire region came under "a sovereignty to be measured by our Constitution, not by the policy of Mexico."[105]

The most comprehensive analysis of preexisting Mexican laws and their impact on the extension of slavery into New Mexico came from Judge Kirby Benedict. Explaining his ruling in an 1857 peonage case, Benedict expounded upon previous Spanish and Mexican slavery statutes, analyzing the intended effects of those laws and addressing many of the same unresolved issues that congressmen had raised several years earlier. Benedict began by acknowledging the longtime existence of debt peonage in New Mexico. Comparisons first had to be drawn between the common perceptions (and misperceptions) of peonage versus slavery as institutions of involuntary servitude. Identifying them as essentially one and the same system in principle, Benedict opined that slavery "ceased to exist" during the Spanish colonial era, citing an act of Spain on August 6, 1811, as the official moratorium. Spanish law thereafter prohibited any person from selling another's liberty or engaging in any other act that might be perceived as human trafficking. In Benedict's estimation, all forms of involuntary servitude had been banned in New Mexico by decree of its mother country in 1811.[106]

After gaining independence in 1821, Mexico's lawmakers passed their own edicts defining and regulating slavery, all of which reinforced previous Spanish law and included additional sanctions for violations. According to Benedict, such legislation demonstrated "the Mexican spirit" on the topic of slavery and would be the guiding principle for his pending legal interpretation.[107] Mexico's 1829 decree defined master-servant relationships, acknowledged the existence of servitude, and placed numerous restrictions upon masters. Nobody in Mexico would ever again be born into slavery, and six months after the law's inception "the introduction of slaves" would be forever prohibited.[108] The law also forbade whipping and other forms of corporal punishment, with a provision allowing servants and slaves to sue an abusive master for "excessive chastisement."[109] This and other Mexican statutes applied equally to New Mexico and had effectively banned racial slavery—while specifically allowing peonage—many years prior to the 1846 U.S. conquest.

Having thus established the parameters of preexisting Spanish and Mexican laws relative to slavery in New Mexico, Benedict examined the territory's midcentury transition in sovereignty. He cited the inception of the Kearny Code in September 1846 as the first instance of American law being implemented, noting that the document failed to address servitude and therefore left the institution intact by virtue of salutary neglect. Because the code lacked specific wording relative to masters and servants, Benedict reasoned that a *patrón* could only "recover his debt from his servant or peon, as in the ordinary way from another debtor."[110] Although this opinion highlighted the system of peonage more so than that of chattel slavery, it nonetheless defined both institutions as involuntary servitude. Benedict's comments relative to Mexico's peon regulations applied to all forms of coerced labor, and he reaffirmed that slavery had been outlawed multiple times through the mandates of both Spain and Mexico. Of all the commentary on Mexico's slavery laws, however, a German-born doctor, Adolph

Wislizenus, provided the most concise explanation. Describing the system of debt peonage that he encountered almost everywhere he went, Wislizenus wrote that "this actual slavery exists throughout Mexico, in spite of its liberal constitution; and, as long as this contradiction is not abolished, the declarations of the Mexican press against slavery in the United States must appear as hypocritical cant."[111]

While remaining mostly ambivalent toward chattel slavery—viewing it through the tunnel vision of political expediency rather than economic practicality or moral standing—many inhabitants of New Mexico vehemently defended their right to retain captives and peons. Superintendent of Indian Affairs James S. Calhoun noticed in 1850 that the recent transformation in political sovereignty and nationality had little effect on New Mexicans when it came to their outlook on Indian slavery and debt bondage. "They yet think that the right to buy and sell captives is perfect, and that no human power can disturb that right," he wrote, explaining that "trading in captives has been so long tolerated in this territory, that it has ceased to be regarded as wrong."[112] Although Calhoun referred to Indian servants, his allusion to exchanging human property extended to peons as well. Widespread confusion about the differences between Southern slavery and New Mexico's traditional forms of bondage continued among federal lawmakers. As late as January 1861, with the first shots of the Civil War just weeks away, those in the East remained perplexed as to New Mexico's stance on slavery. Congressional leaders could not discern the true sentiments of the people, having been bombarded with innumerable "contradictory and self-stultifying reports" from territorial residents.[113]

Even leading territorial officials did not quite understand the actual prevailing sentiment on slavery in the Southwest. Daniel Webster asked Hugh Smith to explain "what the fact is, at the present time, respecting the existence of slavery in New Mexico."[114] The response contradicted Governor Calhoun's earlier claim that local residents retained slave labor. Smith assured Webster that New Mexico "is a free territory" and that he knew of no persons there "who are treated as slaves," with the exception of a few black men accompanying military officers and other temporary residents. "The strongest feeling against slavery universally prevails throughout the whole territory," he concluded in a rather simplistic analysis, carefully avoiding any mention of the peons and captives that his Hispano constituents held and, with political acumen, deflecting attention toward chattel slavery.[115]

Still others believed that Hispanics would reject the implementation of chattel slavery on racial pretenses. While serving as Polk's secretary of state during the Mexican-American War, James Buchanan—who proclaimed in 1826 that slavery constituted "a great political and a great moral evil" from which the nation might never recover—foresaw the impending crisis that would follow annexation of Mexican territory. In 1847, he stated that it would be unlikely for Hispanos to "reestablish slavery" after banning the institution years earlier vis-à-vis the three Mexican statutes. Buchanan's reasoning, however, revolved around a personal prejudicial belief that Nue-vomexicanos were themselves "a colored population," and he betrayed his own ethnocentrism when writing that "among them the negro does not socially belong to a degraded race."[116] In other words, Buchanan saw both Hispanics and African Americans as racially and socially inferior and did not believe that two such groups could interact on a civilized level without the paternalistic oversight of white men.[117]

According to a New York editorialist, New Mexico's Hispanic popula-tion deserved little if any blame for either pro- or antislavery movements in the territory, and regional agitation over the issue could be attributed to the implanted federal officials who propagated such political maneuver-ings.[118] In an attempt to counter local proclamations in favor of slavery and to encourage citizens to oppose human bondage, the American and Foreign Anti-Slavery Society published a lengthy statement and distributed it among territorial residents. Provocatively entitled *Address to the Inhabitants of New Mexico and California . . . on the Social and Political Evils of Slavery*, the pamphlet implored Hispanos to reject the introduction of a "detestable institution" into their territory. Heedless of the fact that their audience had just recently been naturalized as American citizens and that many of them continued to identify with their former nation, the abolitionist authors declared that "Patriotism and Christian benevolence" must be the guiding lights for them in their resistance to slavery. The booklet urged that they "tolerate no servile caste kept in ignorance and degradation" and claimed that the society's members would rather see New Mexico and California "forever lost" to another country than allow them to "be converted by the American people into a region of ignorance, vice, misery, and degradation by the establishment of human bondage."[119] Ironically, involuntary servi-tude had existed for generations in the area and had indeed propagated a discernible "servile caste" but, due to the swarthy efforts of New Mexicans, those institutions remained mysterious to many Americans. The failure of the proclamation to condemn peonage and captivity suggests that the organization was halfhearted in its pursuit of abolition and indicates that a political and sectional intent may have superseded any pietistic one. Had the society's members sought unequivocal universal emancipation on moral pretenses, they might have included peons and captives in their crusade for slave liberation.

United States military authorities in Santa Fe attempted to suppress the Anti-Slavery Society's potentially incendiary edict by preventing dissemination of the organization's propaganda. Such maneuvering, however, failed in its intended effect because the editor of Santa Fe's newspaper, William G. Kephart, served as an agent for the organization and had been dispatched to New Mexico with orders to "show the inhabitants the advantages of free over slave labor."[120] He used the newspaper as a platform to broadcast an abolitionist agenda and conspired to enlist Catholic priests to his cause, noting that with ecclesiastical aide "and God's approbation of the work," his success would be ensured.[121] The Protestant missionary lodged malicious verbal assaults "of the rankest character" against any Anglo-American who brought slaves into the territory. Judge Spruce M. Baird, a native Texan, avowed Southerner, and victim of Kephart's antislavery rhetoric, complained that his adversary repeatedly used the newspaper as an outlet for "his abolition doctrines."[122]

Kephart's abolitionism in New Mexico caught the attention of many congressional lawmakers, some of whom feared that he might provoke violence in the same manner that agitation over slavery brought turmoil to Kansas in 1854. Richard H. Weightman, the territory's delegate to Congress and a personal rival of Kephart, publicly attacked his foe and accused him of using the "garb of a missionary" to conceal his machinations under a disingenuous veil of morality.[123] Deeply concerned about the situation, Weightman belittled antislavery activists as conspirators who hoped to incite "*treason and rebellion*" against the federal government and assured Congress that Kephart's efforts to bring New Mexico's people to their knees over slavery had been in vain. The society's pamphlet was circulated throughout New Mexico, with copies printed in both English and Spanish, in order to urge the people "to set up an independent government unless exempted from the curse of slavery." Ultimately, the abolitionist undertaking failed to sway public sentiment, in part because Kephart did not speak Spanish himself and showed disdain toward the Hispanic culture. Despite the society's control of the only territorial newspaper and its distribution of abolitionist ideas, "no excitement took place in New Mexico," Weight-man wrote with undisguised relief.[124]

Kephart's stay in Santa Fe lasted less than three years; with his newspaper nearing bankruptcy and personal expenditures mounting, he had little choice but to abandon the antislavery mission and return to the Eastern states in January 1853.[125] "The controlling influences here are pro-slavery," he griped, "and almost the whole of the American population is from the slave states."[126] Kephart's experience epitomized the ongoing confusion among American outsiders relative to New Mexicans' perspectives on the slavery issue. Whereas Hugh Smith and Richard Weightman—both of whom represented the territory in Congress—swore that Hispanos disavowed the peculiar institution in both practice and principle, Kephart believed the entire population to be wedded to the Southern proslavery cause.

Congressional deliberations over slavery in the territories lasted for the better part of two years, commencing with the Treaty of Guadalupe Hidalgo in February 1848 and culminating on September 9, 1850, with the passage of the congressional compromise accord. The brainchild of an aging but determined Henry Clay, the conciliatory legislation temporarily assuaged both pro- and antislavery factions but also laid the groundwork for the impending political conflagration of the 1850s.[127] It allowed for the admittance of California as a free-soil state and for Utah and New Mexico to be appended as territories under the premise of popular sovereignty, granting residents the ability to decide for themselves on the slavery issue. Clay's efforts brought temporary closure to some of the most heated sectional debates the nation had yet seen, averting Southern secession for another decade.

These discussions at the national level almost exclusively addressed chattel slavery, which scarcely existed in New Mexico and, many argued, could never be profitably implemented there. Debt peonage and Indian slavery, long entrenched in southwestern culture, had become a mainstay of everyday life just as black slavery was an omnipresent characteristic of the South. Congressional leaders neglected to account for the disparities in these systems of servitude when formulating policy objectives. On one telling occasion, during a Senate debate over the 1850 compromise measure, an amendment sought to include a provision "that peon slavery [be] forever abolished and prohibited" in the territories. Many legislators scoffed at the proposal, with one senator standing and proclaiming sarcastically, "I move to amend that amendment by striking out the word 'peon,'" a quip that instigated laughter throughout the chamber. Senator Benton retorted by pronouncing the amendment to be worthy of consideration. In place of the word "slavery," he suggested that the more all-encompassing term "servitude" be substituted.[128] Another senator thought that "this peonage . . . was servitude existing by virtue of the contract of the individuals . . . [and] by the recognized law of that country," meaning that Congress had no right to interfere.[129] The entire debate on peonage versus slavery ultimately failed to provide any meaningful solutions, with many senators believing that Congress lacked the power to legislate on slavery in the territories. In this, one gets a sense of the general ambivalence toward Hispanic peons and Indian captives. Many officials either neglected or refused to recognize such persons as involuntary servants and thus avoided legislating on what they perceived to be a nonissue.

In the years immediately following the Mexican-American War, congressional discourse on slavery in the Southwest had little direct impact on preexisting systems of bondage. Nor, for that matter, did the Compromise of 1850 satisfactorily resolve the issues that arose concerning the extension of chattel slavery into New Mexico. The debates did lay the rhetorical groundwork for future Reconstruction policymakers seeking to expand the Thirteenth Amendment to encompass peonage and captivity, because antebellum political arguments developed precedents that helped to define and even expand the free labor ideology of postwar legislators and reformers. Within the context of prewar sectionalism, however, more than two years of deliberation on slavery within the Mexican Cession lands revealed the indecisiveness of federal lawmakers on such issues, and their indeterminacy culminated in the Civil War a decade later. The debate carried on and, ultimately, the territorial legislature passed laws throughout the 1850s that would have more immediate consequences for the nature of debt peonage and Indian slavery, while simultaneously placing New Mexico firmly within the camp of the Southern cause. In the meantime, as more and more Americans traveled to and settled in New Mexico after 1850, the nation would gradually become more familiar with the nature of debt peonage and Indian captivity.

Chapter 2

Indian Slavery Meets American Sovereignty

In 1867, under the direction of Republican James R. Doolittle of Wisconsin, a Senate special committee released a voluminous 532-page report outlining the "condition of the Indian tribes" occupying America's western domain.[1] Impelled by widespread accusations alleging mistreatment of indigenous peoples all across the continent, the published testimonial initiated a period of restructuring in approaches to Indian affairs. With moral reformers demanding modified federal Indian policies and the "Doolittle report" (as it has come to be known) substantiating previous allegations of abusive conduct, officials felt pressured to pursue corrective action. Under the political leadership of Republicans and the moral guidance of religious activists, this far-reaching movement promulgated the liberation of many debt peons and Indian captives in the Southwest Borderlands, a vast area that included New Mexico, Arizona, southern Utah and Colorado, and the trans-Pecos part of Texas. It also prompted federal investigations to ensure compliance on the part of regional servantholders.[2]

The 1867 report, which included the sworn testimony of several prominent New Mexico citizens and bureaucrats, revealed a grim portrait of circumstances in that region, one where systems of human bondage persevered and prospered even after the Civil War's culmination brought about the manumission of African American slaves. The informants—including Brigadier General James H. Carleton, Judge Kirby Benedict, ex-governor Henry Connelly, former Superintendent of Indian Affairs James L. Collins, and famed frontiersman Kit Carson—concurred in one thing if nothing else: Forms of coercive labor remained firmly implanted in the Southwest at that time.

Carleton's testimony set the tone for what lay ahead. "The number of Indians, men, women, and children, who have been captured or bought from the Utes, and who live in the families in the Territory," he told investigators, "may be safely set down as at least three thousand." Implicitly describing the cultural and filial dependency that this fostered, he noted that many of these captives learned to speak Spanish and "become attached to the families they live in." Carleton also acknowledged that New Mexicans frequently rode into Navajo country, where they "capture some of the women and children and make slaves of them." He spoke of only two tribes—the Utes and Navajos—while neglecting to mention the roles of Apaches, Comanches, or other groups who acted with similar complicity in the captive slave network.[3]

Judge Benedict took the stand next. Nearly a decade earlier, in a case that had legal implications into the early twentieth century, this official from Illinois had established himself as the face of antislavery judicial activism in New Mexico by ruling in favor of a peon in an 1857 lawsuit. "There are in the Territory a large number of Indians, principally females (women and children), who have been taken by force, or stealth, or purchased," Benedict explained. "It is notorious that natives [Hispanos] of this country have sometimes made captives of Navajo women and children when opportunities presented themselves; the custom has long existed here of buying Indian persons, especially women and children; the tribes themselves have carried on this kind of traffic." Lest his intended audience misunderstand any of his testimony, he concluded by bluntly telling them that "the Indian persons obtained in any one of the modes mentioned are treated by those who claim to own them as their servants and slaves." Once again, however, the informant alluded only to a solitary tribe—this time the Navajos.[4]

Connelly, following the lead of Carleton and Benedict, seemed merely to reiterate what his colleagues had already made quite clear. Describing relations between Navajos and New Mexicans, he noted that "they mutually also captured and held as slaves the women and children of each other," explaining that reciprocal slave raiding "had existed since time immemorial."[5] James L. Collins, who developed a deep knowledge of slaving practices during his tenure as an Indian agent, similarly testified that at least two thousand Indians "are held and treated as slaves, but become amalgamated with the Mexicans and lose their identity."[6] A fifth informant, Kit Carson, revealed that "even before the acquisition of New Mexico there had always existed a hereditary warfare between the Navajoes and Mexicans; forays were made into each other's country, and stock, women, and children stolen."[7]

When these five men testified in the summer of 1865—with the nation still reeling from the deadliest conflict it has ever experienced—they doubt-less realized the political, legislative, and juridical implications of the coer-cive labor systems that they described. Even so, all of them understated the extent of captivity in New Mexico. The decades following Mexican inde-pendence saw a noticeable increase in captive slaving throughout upper Rio Grande villages, as New Mexico's absorption into capitalist commercial networks via the Santa Fe Trail increased the demand for uncompensated labor and contributed to the proliferation of slave trafficking.[8] Triumphant military campaigns during the Mexican national period enabled soldiers and civilian auxiliaries to capture large numbers of women and children servants.[9] In 1825, Juan de Abrego returned from a Navajo campaign in which his men took twenty-two "slaves of both sexes."[10] In a particularly destructive expedition during 1838, New Mexicans killed seventy-eight Navajo warriors near their Canyon de Chelly homelands and took another fifty-six captives back to the Rio Grande settlements, a devastating tragedy for the tribe.[11]

While New Mexicans continued to carry Indians into captivity through-out the 1820s and 1830s, peripheral tribes reciprocated and exacted a simi-larly heavy toll on Hispanic villages. When a civic leader, Donaciano Vigil, addressed the New Mexico Assembly in June 1846—just two months prior to the American invasion—he lamented the large number of captives living within Indian camps. Expressing particular concern about "young Mexican women who serve the bestial pleasures of the barbaric Indians," he insisted that the national government provide a liberal supply of arms and ammuni-tion so that Nuevomexicanos could protect themselves from Indian attacks.[12] On some occasions, abductees managed to flee from their captors and found refuge at agencies or military posts. In 1855, New Mexico Indian agent Michael Steck received no less than six liberated captives at his Fort Thorn agency, including two boys aged fourteen and sixteen who arrived "nearly naked" after escaping from the Mescalero Apaches.[13] That same year, James H. Carleton of the First Dragoons received four captive Mexican boys who absconded from the Comanches and sought refuge in his camp at Hatch's Ranch near the Pecos River. Carleton sent the escapees—named Louis Martinez, Felix Bonciargo, Theodoro Garcia, and Ivan Salgado—to headquarters in Santa Fe, where the department com-mander arranged to have them reunited with family members.[14] Like the thousands of so-called contraband slaves during the Civil War, who ran to Union troops for protection from recapture, these captives sought out the military in hopes that soldiers might assist them in their plight for freedom.

By the 1850s, sanctioned trade fairs rarely, if ever, occurred and captive exchanges took place predominantly through individual transactions. Hispanos made annual voyages to trade with Navajos and Utes and, during the course of those commercial expeditions, traders frequently bartered for Indian slaves among the tribes they encountered. "All children bought on the return trip would be taken back to New Mexico and then sold, boys fetching on an average $100, girls $150 to $200," the western explorer Daniel Jones explained. Private James Bennett of the First Dragoons was surprised to learn that Indian captives brought to Santa Fe were "sold as slaves," with prices ranging from $100 to $400 worth of trade goods each. According to Jones, exploitative Mexican slave traders "were fully established and systematic in this trade as ever were the slavers on the seas." They especially targeted southern Utah's starving Paiutes, who sometimes swapped a child for a horse and then killed the animal for food.[15]

Many masters placed a monetary value on their Indian servants, whom they sold and traded with greater frequency than the indebted peons being similarly held in bondage. The "domestication" of indigenous captives increased their market value, providing an incentive for assimilation through baptism and further exacerbating the frequency with which masters initiated intimate interethnic relationships and fostered filial connections. Writing about Paiute slaves in 1852, one Indian agent explained that their adoption into New Mexican families effectively bound them to that society and precluded most attempts at running away.[16] The practice of selling and trading assimilated captives continued well beyond the initial American occupation of New Mexico in 1846. "There is no law of the Territory," Steck confessed in 1864, "that legalizes the sale of Indians, yet it is done almost daily, without an effort to stop it."[17]

New Mexico's captive exchange favored females as the more valued commodity, owing not only to their usefulness as domestic servants, but also because of their appeal as potential wives and childbearers. Governor Calhoun attested to the value of women as both servants and concubines, noting that men purchased them based on their physical appearance. "The value of captives depends upon age, sex, beauty, and usefulness," he explained. "Good looking females, not having passed the 'sear and yellow leaf,' are valued from fifty to one hundred and fifty dollars each," while boys typically brought only half that amount, a testament to the value that masters placed on a servant's sex appeal.[18] Thomas Farnham, a traveler during that time, reiterated that "the price of these slaves in the markets of New Mexico varies with the age and other qualities of the person," alluding to sexual availability when noting that younger captives fetched higher prices. Once abducted, the Englishman wrote, captives "are fattened, taken to Santa Fe and sold as slaves . . . a 'likely girl' in her teens brings often £ sixty or £ eighty."[19] As Judge Benedict noted in 1865 when asked to testify about the nature of slavery in New Mexico, "a likely girl of not more than eight years old, healthy and intelligent," would be valued around $400, because "when they grow to womanhood" they could be forced to serve in sexual capacities.[20]

The phrase "likely girl" implied a direct correlation between Indian slavery in the West and chattel slavery in the Southern states. In nineteenth-century parlance, professional slave traders and auctioneers used terms like "fancy girl" and "likely girl" to indicate sexual availability when advertising upcoming slave auctions in local newspapers. Whenever a potential buyer read an advertisement describing a slave woman as "likely" or "fancy," he could be fairly certain that she was young, physically attractive, and vulnerable to being raped. Once purchased, such women took on a twofold purpose in that they not only labored as slaves, but also provided sexual services and, in many cases, bore children and future servants for their master.[21] By using this terminology in reference to New Mexico's Indian captives, Farnham and Benedict implicitly acknowledged two critical similarities between nineteenth-century America's regional systems of slavery. First, that indigenous captives could be bought and sold like chattel slaves in the South, and second, that Hispano masters had sexual exploitation in mind when purchasing Indian girls.

Years of slave trafficking and ransoming had a noticeable cultural and demographic impact on the Southwest. Like many enslaved families in the antebellum Upper South, where a mass redistribution of chattels to the more southerly Cotton Belt propagated forced migrations that broke filial bonds through spatial disassociation, countless Indian families, whose kinfolk were forcibly redistributed among households across a large geographic area, underwent an indelible psychological imprint from this form of captivity.[22] One U.S. special agent, writing to the commissioner of Indian affairs in 1867, lamented that he would not be able to locate and redeem many of the captives recently taken from the Navajo tribe. The abductees,

he explained, were scattered throughout the northern New Mexico settlements of Tierra Amarilla, Ojo Caliente, El Rito, Arroyo Seco, and Taos, as
well as Los Conejos in the Colorado Territory.[23]

As New Mexicans variously hoped and feared, the system of captive slavery that developed over the course of three centuries began to wane following
the arrival of American troops in 1846. After New Mexico's conquest in
August of that year and the subsequent implementation of the Kearny Code
(a set of civil regulations that his officers devised), the territory became subject to the laws of the United States.[24] At that time, national slavery debates
proliferated and required the undivided attention of federal officials. Ultimately, the appointment of Anglo-Americans to fill many of New Mexico's
political offices would have a pronounced impact on indigenous slavery and
the regional societies of dependency that it propagated. As territorial governor David Meriwether stated in his 1853 inaugural address, "The elevated
and the lowly, the rich and the poor, the native-born and the immigrant, are
all alike entitled to the protection of the laws."[25] Sectional developments,
coupled with the increasing vigor with which the United States military
implemented and enforced Indian policy in the West, altered the fundamental
characteristics and severity of local slaving practices.

Whereas civilian militias typically avenged—or at least tried to avenge—
Indians' captive raids during the period of Mexican sovereignty, the task of
punishment fell to federal troops after the midcentury American conquest.
In 1853, territorial governor William Carr Lane revealed the lofty goals of
civil and military officials when informing Steck that the southwestern
tribes "shall eschew violence and bloodshed, and the law of retaliation shall
be forever annulled."[26] With permanent army outposts at Abiquiú, Albuquerque, Cebolleta, Doña Ana, Las Vegas, Los Lunas, Rayado, Santa Fe,
Socorro, and Taos, the Indians' propensity to take captives decreased during the 1850s as the Apaches and Navajos concentrated instead on stealing
livestock for subsistence purposes. In 1851, when Colonel Edwin V. Sumner
oversaw a complete reorganization of the military department, troops were
redistributed to newly established forts constructed in the heart of Indian
homelands. Fort Defiance monitored the Navajos, Fort Union watched over
the Southern Plains tribes, Fort Massachusetts policed Ute country, and
Forts Fillmore and Webster supervised southern New Mexico's Apachería.[27]
As the commanding officer at Fort Defiance pointed out in 1853, the place-
ment of troops closer to Indian villages and encampments had a "controlling influence" and discouraged captive taking during depredations.[28]

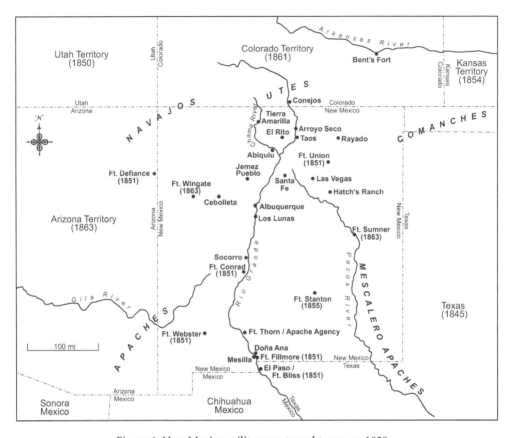

Figure 6. New Mexico military posts and towns, c. 1850.

Contrarily, captive raiding did not immediately begin to wane among New Mexicans, as civilians continued to exact a heavy toll on Native groups and in so doing perpetuated the tradition of enslavement and blood feuding. In 1861, Miguel A. Otero, a New Mexico congressional representative, referred to Indians as nothing more than "sullen and reluctant" slaves, and the territorial secretary noted that "the people obtain possession of their children by purchase or otherwise, whom they rear in their families as servants, and who perform a lifetime servitude to hard task masters and mistresses."[29] The 1850s and 1860s would be a tumultuous time for relations between New Mexicans and Indians, with increasing violence and frequent military campaigns inflicting tremendous demographic hardships on both sides.

Because multilateral warfare carried on even after the American occupation, southwesterners continually memorialized Congress on the subject, claiming that "hostile Indians penetrate the country in every direction and rob, and kill, and carry into captivity" New Mexico's women and children.[30] Civilians' independent pleas to federal politicians echoed the many resolutions that local legislators approved relative to the issue. During the 1849 constitutional convention at Santa Fe, representatives adopted numerous instructions for New Mexico's delegate to present in Congress, one of which bewailed that "many of our citizens of all ages and sexes are at this moment suffering all the horrors of barbarian bondage, and it is utterly out of our power to obtain their release from a condition to which death would be preferable."[31] Another declaration in 1852 said, "This territory has been a continual scene of outrage, robbery, and violence carried on by the savage nations by which it is surrounded . . . our citizens . . . are daily massacred before our eyes . . . our wives and daughters violated, and our children carried into captivity."[32] Similar petitions would arrive in Washington, D.C. almost annually for the next fifteen years. Although Indian depredations happened less regularly than the exaggerated petitions indicated, raids nonetheless occurred with enough prevalence to substantiate the alacrity with which Nuevomexicanos approached the issue. Between 1846 and 1860, Navajos alone attacked territorial settlements no less than fifty-eight times, killing and capturing hundreds of people. New Mexican militias took the field on twenty-six different occasions during that same time period, killing ninety-eight Navajos and capturing 283 more.[33]

In response to civilian entreaties, Texas senator Thomas Rusk implored his fellow lawmakers to take immediate action to thwart raiding and captive taking. The statesman's concern owed in part to the fact that his constituents had long suffered similar hardships at the hands of some of the same tribes. Speaking before Congress in June 1850—just three months before New Mexico and Utah officially became U.S. territories—he described the hazardous circumstances under which residents of that region lived. Captive raiding, he noted, "is not only continued from day to day, but is increasing from day to day, by the culpable neglect of this Government to protect its citizens there." Rusk asked his colleagues to take whatever action necessary in order to protect women and children "from being carried off and made slaves to savage Indians."[34] The senator, however, overlooked the reality that New Mexicans, as newly christened American citizens, were equally guilty of his allegations and had abducted many Indian captives

themselves. The federal government ultimately did take action to counter-
act the slaving practices that plagued the region, sending large numbers of
troops to garrison several of the larger villages and implement new Indian
policies. But these initiatives, while partially effective, proved insufficient in
preventing slave raids altogether.

Whereas previous Spanish and Mexican governments maintained only
a nominal military force in New Mexico (the presidial garrison at Santa Fe
rarely had more than one hundred troops), the U.S. military dispatched
thousands of soldiers to the West, hindering Indians' ability to raid settlements for plunder and captives.[35] A combination of political policy and
military force acted to limit—and eventually eliminate—slave raiding in
the Southwest, albeit very gradually, as attested to by the fact that New
Mexicans continued to memorialize Congress well into the 1860s in hopes
of securing additional military protection.

During the earliest years of American occupation, the predatory warfare
between Hispano civilians and independent tribes hamstrung the U.S.
Army's ability to enforce Indian policy. After 1846, American troops permanently occupied New Mexico in order to guard the civilian inhabitants
from Indian raiding and depredations, protection from which General
Kearny had promised to them during his conquest. "From the Mexican
government, you have never received protection," he had declared from
atop a roof in the village of Las Vegas. "The Apaches and Navajos come
down from the mountains and carry off your sheep, and even your women,
whenever they please. My government will correct all this."[36] Kearny's specific mention of women being carried away as captives during the course
of raids acknowledged the commonality of the practice. His pledge to coun-
teract such behavior, however, indicated that he underestimated the severity of raiding at the midpoint of the nineteenth century. His colleagues, in
fact, employed Indians for their own use while at Santa Fe, with one officer
admitting that a Ute slave made his bed each night, while another lieutenant enjoyed the service of "a few female serfs" when dining.[37] Even the man
Kearny appointed to serve as New Mexico's first civil governor, Charles
Bent, had an Indian servant named María Guadalupe in his household, and
he also owned a black slave known as Dick, who was severely wounded on
January 29, 1847, at the Battle of Embudo, south of Taos.[38] So common
were Indian slaves in New Mexico in the mid-1800s that even the army
officers charged with suppressing captive raiding benefited from the services of such abductees while at their posts.

In a testament to the importance that residents of the Southwest placed on quelling Indian raids, Mexican diplomats insisted that a clause (Article 11) be included in the 1848 Treaty of Guadalupe Hidalgo relative to the repatriation of captives held among tribes.[39] The stipulation traced its precedent to an 1832 treaty of commerce between the United States and Mexico, which contained an article mandating that both nations endeavor to repatriate captives taken during Indian raids.[40] American diplomats grossly underestimated the extent to which reciprocal slave raiding occurred in the region, and officials in both the civil and military branches of government found themselves burdened with the task of locating and redeeming captive women and children. As U.S. bureaucrats soon learned, many captives had been assimilated into tribes as servants and fictive kin and had little if any desire to return to their original homes. Nor did administrators fully appreciate the scope of captivity; only after they began attempting to enforce Article 11 did Americans realize that a considerable number of tribes, whose homelands covered a broad geographic area, habitually took captives during raids in northern Mexico. Upon transporting those captives across the newly formed international boundary, Indians often traded them to other Native groups, and thus many abductees vanished in the commerce and kinship networks of the Southwest.[41]

Attempting to secure the return of captives on the Southern Plains in 1849, Indian agent Thomas Fitzpatrick and Major Benjamin Beall of the First Dragoons gained firsthand familiarity with slave trading among regional tribes. Having parleyed with chiefs representing the Apaches, Arapahoes, Cheyennes, Comanches, and Kiowas at Bent's Fort in March of that year, the two officers discovered that members of all five tribes regularly commingled in camps along the Arkansas River and that their captives openly participated in tribal ceremonies and raids, in addition to serving as laborers and fictive kin. Beall informed his superiors in Santa Fe that it would be impossible "to obtain the Mexican captives by peaceable means," and Fitzpatrick was equally certain that the Indians would never turn over any captives without ransom being paid in return. Liberating the slaves by armed force, he conceded, "will not only cause the death of some of the prisoners but will drive them once more into an inveterate state of hostility."[42]

Beall and Fitzpatrick held their council at Bent's Fort on the eve of James S. Calhoun's arrival in New Mexico to serve as the territory's first Indian superintendent, and their letters to Santa Fe served as a harbinger of impending frustrations for federal officials. As the new head of Indian affairs, Calhoun bore responsibility for overseeing the repatriation of Mexican captives in compliance with Article 11. Although only periodically successful in his endeavors, he was not entirely at fault for the government's failure to fulfill its treaty obligation, inasmuch as negligible funding and lukewarm bureaucratic support continually hamstrung his exertions toward that end.[43]

The efforts of Calhoun and others to recapture women and children held in captivity frequently sparked hostilities between Americans and Indians, exacerbating an already precarious relationship between the two groups. In December 1849, Major Enoch Steen of the First Dragoons, commanding the military post at Doña Ana in southern New Mexico, met with a delegation of Mescalero Apaches who sought to negotiate a peace treaty. The major immediately seized two of the chiefs, Santos and Buffalo, and assured the others through his interpreters that he would hang the prisoners unless the tribe returned three Mexican boys taken captive earlier that year. The Indians eventually complied with his demands and the two chiefs were set free, but not before Steen muddied the waters on what had promised to be a peaceful diplomatic interchange.[44] Just a few months later the veteran army officer met with a group of Gila Apaches and nearly duplicated his blunder when he demanded that they surrender two captive Mexican children, Teofilo and Mateo Jaramillo, who had been taken from their family at Doña Ana several months earlier.[45]

Similarly aggravating situations—all traceable to Article 11—arose throughout southern New Mexico during the early 1850s. John Russell Bartlett, serving as the international boundary commissioner at Santa Rita del Cobre in 1851, unabashedly snatched two Mexican boys, José Trinfan and Saverro Heradia, from their Chiricahua Apache captors during the tribe's visit to his camp. His offer to compensate the Indians with a few gifts offended their leaders and fanned the flames of an already shaky relationship between the two parties.[46] A year later, an officer at nearby Fort Webster proclaimed that he had ceased offering presents in return for captives and instead had begun simply confiscating them from the Apaches by force.[47] While officials understood it as their lawful duty to return abducted women and children to Mexico, they did not fully appreciate the kinship ties and feelings of dependency that had been forged through years of bondage and thus, in all likelihood, did not realize the cultural ramifications of their actions. Such misunderstandings widened the rift between two already disparate polities and often jeopardized peace negotiations between the groups. In April 1855, during a conference with Mescalero Apaches at Dog Canyon in the Sacramento Mountains of southeastern New Mexico, Colonel Dixon S. Miles observed that one chief had a captive Mexican from the village of Manzano "tied up" in plain view of the troops. Miles asked Chief Palanquito to effect the boy's release but, unlike Steen and Bartlett before him, opted not to reclaim the child forcefully, recognizing that such action would have "disturbed the whole affair of peace."[48]

Another example of illicit trade in captives involved the officers at Fort Webster and the surrounding Gila Apaches in southwestern New Mexico. When James Gadsden began meeting with Mexican dignitaries in 1853 to negotiate the treaty that bore his name, he was under pressure to ensure that his countrymen cease paying ransoms for captives. He wrote to General John Garland, commander of the Military Department of New Mexico, expressing deep concern about officers at Fort Webster who purportedly allowed illegal commerce with nearby Apaches and repeatedly purchased Mexican prisoners from them.[49] Garland and his civil government colleagues worked quickly to stem the tide of what promised to be a controversial issue in Gadsden's upcoming treaty negotiations. Governor David Meriwether informed the Apache agent at the fort, James Smith, that the purchase of captives "can never be tolerated," pointing out that such action would only encourage the Indians to take more prisoners and instructing him to "reclaim and if necessary take by force any captives belonging to Mexico." Under no circumstances, however, was Smith to issue or authorize any type of indemnities for the Indians, as it would "stimulate the Indians to make other captives with a view to their sale."[50] Major Israel B. Richardson insisted that only four Mexicans had been ransomed at Fort Webster, two of whom were forcibly taken from the Apaches in conformity with the department's preferred method, although such confrontational tactics remained uncodified as official policy. As for the other two, a boy and a girl, Richardson blamed another embattled Indian agent, Edward H. Wingfield, for authorizing their ransom.[51] Michael Steck, who replaced Wingfield as the agent at Fort Webster, reported that the four captives "are all comfortably situated and not costing the government anything except a trifle for clothing." The Chihuahua governor, Angel Trías, promised Steck that he would send agents to take custody of the captives and return them to their families in Mexico.[52] The entire debacle cast light on the controversy surrounding captive taking among both Indians and Mexicans and on the inability of civil and military officials to curb the practice, despite the recent shift in sovereignty to the United States.

Nor did it seem to dawn on many American officials that Mexicans below the border held hundreds—perhaps thousands—of Indian captives themselves. Less than a year before Bartlett met with the Chiricahuas at Santa Rita del Cobre, four hundred Sonoran soldiers under Colonel José María Carrasco ambushed a large band of Apaches near the town of Janos in Chihuahua. In the melee that followed, they took sixty-two captives and promptly redistributed them "among the haciendas and ranchos as servants, too far off ever to reach their homes again."[53] Among the Apaches slain or captured in the Janos attack were several of Geronimo's family members. Only about thirty years old at the time and yet to achieve notoriety outside of his own tribal community, Geronimo organized a vengeance raid that claimed the lives of many Sonorans and perpetuated a vicious cycle of violence.[54] Despite these ongoing trends, Article 11 contained no mandate requiring that Mexican officials reciprocate by repatriating abducted Indians, an incongruous oversight that understandably perturbed the Apaches when confronted about their own captives.

Just as Indians resisted the attempts of officials to reclaim their captives, so too did residents in northern New Mexico defy such efforts. As Governor Calhoun noted in 1850, "Unless the Mexicans are paid for such captives . . . very few of them will be released."[55] Much to the delight of U.S. officials, the dilemma arising from the Treaty of Guadalupe Hidalgo would prove to be short-lived. Mexico's leaders came to realize the counterproductive nature of Article 11, as American efforts to repatriate captives often meant paying ransoms in order to secure their release. The issuance of such presents actually encouraged abductions; once Indians discovered the lucrative nature of the business, they capitalized by taking even more captives to exchange for various goods at U.S. military posts.[56]

Once Article 11 was abrogated with the ratification of Gadsden's treaty in 1854, civil and military administrators placed less importance on reclaiming captives. This held especially true in the more southerly reaches of the territory, where Mescalero and Chiricahua Apaches took women and children from the northern Mexican states of Chihuahua and Sonora and, accordingly, the United States no longer had an obligation to protect such persons because of their foreign citizenship.[57] Contrarily, captives from the Rio Grande communities of northern New Mexico, despite being ethnically Hispanic, were legitimate American citizens and, as such, held certain rights that demanded action on the part of the federal government. In any event, localized efforts to free captives did continue to occur, primarily because a small handful of civil and military officials saw the diplomatic and humanitarian benefits of such action. When Pablo Melendres, a former *alcalde* (mayor) and prominent citizen of the Mesilla Valley, purchased a Sonoran boy from a band of Apaches in 1858, Captain Richard S. Ewell of the First Dragoons wrote the department commander and asked that he "lay the matter before the governor, as it is understood that Melendrez [*sic*] bought the captive for a peon and [his] restoration would have an excellent effect upon the Mexicans" from whom he had been taken.[58]

Throughout the 1850s and into the 1860s, New Mexico's bureaucrats grappled with the task of captive redemption but experienced little success in such pursuits. This owed in part to the effectiveness of Indians' assimilation methods. When Chief Huero delivered two Hispanic captives to the commanding officer at Fort Defiance in January 1858 in compliance with recent treaty stipulations, both abductees "elected to remain with the Navajos" and vehemently opposed repatriation to their Mexican families. The post commander, Major Electus Backus of the Third Infantry, honored their request and allowed them to remain with their adoptive Navajo clans. One of the captives had been with the tribe so long that he could not remember his original birth name.[59] After the Civil War, a Navajo Indian agent observed that most captives did not wish to be liberated and compared the situation to "guarding a jail to keep criminals from breaking in."[60]

Long-standing enmity between Hispanics and Indians also contributed to the military department's failure to curtail slave raiding. "This system of warfare will interfere very much with my [military] measures," Colonel Sumner grumbled in 1851, asking that his counterpart Calhoun "abstain from sending any war parties of Mexicans" or civilian militiamen into the Indian homelands.[61] Sumner's protest was not without merit; when taking office as the territory's first civil governor, Calhoun suggested that militias be dispatched into Indian country as a means of augmenting the inadequate number of U.S. troops garrisoning the military posts. By condoning such action, however, the governor perpetuated the captive-taking tradition. Intercultural animosity proliferated as civilian-led expeditions focused not merely on chastising nearby Indians but also on attacking peaceful subgroups, often for the sole purpose of securing captives to sell as slaves in the New Mexico marketplace.[62] Civilian warfare with the Indians would continue to pose challenges in upcoming years for military officers attempting to discourage

depredations, oftentimes counteracting federal treaty negotiations with territorial tribes and unwittingly contributing to endemic slave raiding. Not until
1864 would New Mexico's governor issue a proclamation positively forbidding civilian militias from taking independent retributive action against
Indians.[63]

The difficulties that American troops experienced in their efforts to
restrain Indian raiding and captive taking during the first decade of occupation in New Mexico stemmed in large part from the inability of civil and
military officials to reach an agreement over appropriate Indian policies,
and the pressure to enforce Article 11 only intensified that interdepartmen-
tal contentiousness. With the civil government (Bureau of Indian Affairs)
devising Indian policy and the military (War Department) responsible for
enforcing those measures, inherent ideological differences between the two
disparate bureaucracies undercut attempts to conceive a mutually agreeable
course of action.[64] The unintended consequence was that, throughout much
of the Southwest, captive enslavement continued with minimal abatement
for many years following the American conquest, despite several U.S. officials not only proclaiming an aversion to the practice, but also pledging to
halt it through a mixture of reform-minded policy initiatives, judicial coercion, military action, and multilateral diplomacy.

Many early territorial officials coming from the South remained partial
to the slaveholding cause and refused to interfere, essentially sanctioning
the practice through their ambivalence and silence. Because he was from
the slave state of Georgia, Governor Calhoun became the target of numerous accusations that he ignored the existence of Indian slavery and even
promoted it through his policies. Much of his personal correspondence,
however, refutes such allegations. Calhoun frequently complained of the
ongoing exchange of captives, especially among the Comanches and Navajos, and admitted that he had yet to devise a means of suppressing the
trade.[65] He professed an overall disenchantment with New Mexican slavery
and likened it to the peculiar institution existing in his home state. "All will
agree that this revolting trade should be stopped," he told Commissioner
of Indian Affairs Orlando Brown, admitting with some frustration that the
proposed methods of doing so differed widely. The new governor felt a duty
to reclaim captives whenever possible, and he expected the government to
reimburse him for any ransoms paid to liberate such persons.[66] Despite his
abhorrence to captivity, though, Calhoun rarely purchased the freedom of
any servants during his time as governor, usually doing so only through the

recompense of intermediaries who brokered such transactions in his stead. On one rare occasion in October 1849, Calhoun procured five former Mexican slaves from the Navajos, of whom all but one readily consented to return to their natal families. On that occasion he did not offer any form of ransom to the tribe, and the headmen surrendered the captives merely as a gesture of good faith and to avoid being the targets of future military action.[67]

When negotiating treaties with New Mexico's tribes, Calhoun followed the lead of his many predecessors who, since well before Mexican independence in 1821, had repeatedly included clauses mandating the return of captives. This held especially true with the Navajos, who brokered numerous peace accords with Mexican officials prior to the 1846 American occupation. In 1805, following a massacre at Canyon de Chelly in which soldiers killed 115 Navajos and captured thirty-three others, tribal leaders met with Governor Joaquín Real Alencaster to arrange an accord that would allow for the mutual exchange of captives and prisoners.[68] Seventeen years later, during the first year of Mexican rule, Governor Facundo Melgares arranged a treaty mandating that all captives held among the tribe be delivered to the governor in Santa Fe. Should the Navajos wish to recover their own kinfolk held in the New Mexican villages, however, they would be required to "make a claim on the government" and hope that sympathetic officials carried out the request.[69]

Whereas Navajos faithfully returned prisoners following each treaty, the tribe frequently complained that officials in Santa Fe failed to reciprocate. After two five-hundred-man campaigns—composed of civilian militia and peon auxiliaries—marched into Navajo country in 1840 and killed twenty-three warriors and captured fourteen slaves, tribal leaders agreed to meet with officials once again to discuss terms for peace.[70] During a negotiation at Jemez Pueblo in 1841, Navajos refused to make any agreements until their counterparts honored previous treaties and returned all women and children taken during the previous expedition. "They have handed over all of our people held captive by [their] Nation, this being the basis upon which true peace can be guaranteed," wrote one fair-minded observer. "On delivering these to us, they have become convinced that your Excellency [the governor] does not want to turn over to them their captives. . . . [T]hey state that on more than ten occasions they have handed over our captives and to them none have been returned."[71] In a process that had become woefully redundant, Mexican leaders again sought to meet with Navajo

Figure 7. James S. Calhoun, New Mexico's first territorial governor,
c. 1851. Courtesy Museum of New Mexico, negative #050460.

headmen three years later and somewhat audaciously proposed that the chiefs, "as proof of good faith," return all captives detained among the tribe.[72]

Contrarily, New Mexicans held themselves to no such obligation. Instead, Navajo families would be required to ransom captives on their own, and if the tribe wished to reclaim their kinfolk they would have to negotiate terms with each captiveholder on an individual basis and without the assistance of government officials. Mexican bureaucrats also avoided any agreement that would mandate the repatriation of captives seeking religious conversion. If any Navajos desired "the beneficial waters of baptism," they concluded that it would be improper for good Catholics to deny such wishes and therefore encouraged clergymen to administer the sacrament at their own discretion.[73] Between 1812, when Spain abolished slavery outright, and 1847, after the United States had procured sovereignty over the territory, at least 330 Navajo captives underwent baptismal rights in New Mexico parishes.[74] As one American observed in 1851, "This slave trade gave rise to cruel wars between the native tribes of this country." Four years later, when a group of Nuevomexicanos from Abiquiú and Ojo Caliente raided an Indian camp, killing two and taking a pair of captives, an Indian agent named Lorenzo Labadi noted sardonically that "this is not the first time they have done this."[75]

By the time Americans arrived in the late 1840s, decades of bad faith and broken treaties between Navajos and New Mexicans precluded the ability of government officials to negotiate any meaningful peace agreements. Lieutenant James W. Abert visited several New Mexico villages in 1846, where inhabitants repeatedly complained of hostilities with the Navajos. At José Chavez's hacienda north of Socorro, the "señor" informed the young officer that Navajos had recently captured his son, along with most of his peons' wives and children.[76] An 1849 treaty between Navajos and U.S. officials typified the captive repatriation clause that appeared in almost every compact ever negotiated with that tribe. One article stipulated that the Indians must surrender all captives, regardless of ethnic or national origin, to military authorities at Jemez within one month and required that any slaves being held in New Mexico's villages likewise be turned over to the same officials for repatriation. A decade later, Colonel Benjamin Bonneville and Superintendent of Indian Affairs James L. Collins repeated this clause almost verbatim in yet another wishful peace pact.[77]

Under such circumstances, Governor Calhoun would have been hard-pressed to offer ransoms even if he wanted to; when assuming office as superintendent of Indian affairs in 1849, the department advanced him a sum of $3,800 to be expended in New Mexico, of which a trifling $300 was earmarked to effect the release of captives.[78] Commissioner of Indian Affairs William Medill admitted this amount to be negligible and instructed his agents to avoid paying ransoms altogether if possible, noting that "to make compensation would encourage a continuance of the practice of making captives."[79] Even so, agents in the field periodically compensated tribes with horses or supplies for the return of captives, a practice that drained government coffers and burdened the department with expenses that superintendents saw as unnecessary. When Indian agent John W. Whitfield, pursuant to the governor's request, doled out $25 apiece for two captives held by the Southern Cheyennes, he readily admitted the impropriety of doing so. The official afterward stressed (somewhat hypocritically) that "we cannot establish the precedent of buying Mexican prisoners" and predicted that a policy of purchasing captives would "bankrupt [the] treasury."[80] As an agent to the Utes in the 1850s, Kit Carson likewise offered ransoms but claimed to do so only in the name of humanity. When two Muache Utes brought a captive Navajo woman to the Taos agency, Carson "thought it better for the squaw to be with me than with the Mexicans or Utahs." With that in mind, he gave two horses for her exchange and wrote to James L. Collins requesting remuneration.[81] A month later, Carson again redeemed a captive, this time an Apache girl held in bondage with a local Hispanic family; having been severely maltreated by her captors, she informed the agent that "it would be impossible for her to live with her mistress." Whether he actually received compensation from the department for ransoming these captives remains unknown, but certainly Carson's superiors frowned upon the associated costs and headaches.[82]

New Mexico's civic leaders became the center of controversy in 1851–52 when rumors circulated that Governor Calhoun had issued slaving licenses to territorial residents. Calhoun gave dozens of trading permits to Hispanics and Pueblo Indians, but none of the vaguely worded documents specifically sanctioned trade in human flesh.[83] His accusers maintained, however, that the passes allowed slave traders to enter Utah Territory in search of Indian captives. The *Deseret News Weekly*, a Mormon publication founded in 1850 as Utah's first newspaper, informed its readers that Calhoun authorized rogue traders "to purchase Indian children as slaves, for the benefit of persons in New Mexico," and slandered the governor as being "no better than an infamous kidnapper."[84] News of Calhoun's supposed complicity in the Indian slave trade reached a broad audience when the *National Era*, an abolitionist weekly published in Washington, D.C., reprinted the article under a suggestive headline: "Scoundrelism in Our Territories: Kidnapping Under a Governor's License."[85]

These newspapers referred to licenses that Calhoun issued on July 30 and August 14, 1851, to Pedro León and several companions, who traveled to Salt Lake County to trade with Ute Indians in that region.[86] León had established himself throughout northern New Mexico as a well-known slave dealer, having been involved in the business since the 1830s and being a frequent leader of militia campaigns into both Ute and Navajo country.[87] Because the permits did not specify the meaning of the word "trading," León's group bartered in various goods, including slaves. Whether Calhoun deliberately omitted any reference to captives remained unknown, but the ambiguity of the passes in that regard made it difficult for critics to prove his complicity. By sanctioning trading voyages into Utah, the governor actually did nothing new, inasmuch as New Mexicans had been venturing into the Great Basin for over a century to trade and take Paiute captives back to the markets in Santa Fe and Taos.[88] When Mormon colonizers arrived in the Salt Lake and Utah valleys in 1847, they blamed New Mexicans for the hostilities that arose with neighboring tribes. One Latter-Day Saint, Thomas Bullock, wrote of the Great Basin Indians that "all they r fit for is Slaves . . . they r wild as Beasts—they r outrageous against White People, because the Spaniards killed many, & stole their children."[89]

Paiutes held a predetermined disadvantage in that they constituted, according to one contemporary witness, "the most destitute and degraded of all the Indian tribes" in the West.[90] Mounted groups like the Navajos and Utes easily preyed upon less mobile Paiute villages and rode away with captives, leaving parents and spouses helpless to reclaim their displaced kinfolk. Passing through Utah in the 1850s, Dr. Garland Hurt found the Paiutes' plight to be deplorable and described the people as "so abject and degraded" that they thought little of trading their children to the Utes for "a few trinkets or bits of clothing." The Utes would then transport these commodified juveniles to northern New Mexico, "where they find a profitable market for them among the Navajoes."[91] George W. Armstrong, an Indian agent at Provo, informed his superiors in 1856 that the semi-sedentary Great Basin tribes had suffered noticeable demographic decline as a result of Ute raiders, who had become adept at "stealing their squaws and children and selling them as slaves to other tribes, as well as to the Mexican people."[92] When federal officials approached the Southern Paiutes in 1865 to negotiate a treaty, the Paiutes refused to relocate onto a shared reservation with Utes because of their long-standing animosity toward that tribe.[93]

According to John Greiner, a New Mexico Indian agent, the Paiutes themselves encouraged (albeit inadvertently) the slave trade by swapping their children for articles of subsistence. The blunt agent noted that "the Mexicans in time past carried on quite an extensive trade with these Indians for their children who make excellent house servants."[94] Paiutes found themselves increasingly susceptible to enslavement in New Mexican villages as the first half of the nineteenth century wore on. Not until New Mexico became a part of the United States at midcentury did the practice begin to taper off, although it continued to linger at the time Armstrong wrote in 1856. Many Anglo-Americans venturing into the Great Basin region after 1850 found themselves appalled by the violent exchanges that characterized the relationship between the Utes and their less powerful Paiute and Shoshone neighbors.[95]

The slaving mission that Pedro León and his party undertook in 1851 signaled the culmination of nearly a century of Paiute victimization for slaving purposes. Mormon authorities confronted León and his companions after they arrived in Utah and took them to meet with Governor Brigham Young, who declined to renew their permits. He also refused to allow León's company to deal with Indians, citing the invalidity of Calhoun's passes outside of New Mexico and lecturing them on the moral reprehensibility of trading for children. Young did, however, authorize them to barter briefly with Mormon merchants for supplies before returning to New Mexico.[96] Once discharged, León promised that he and his men would go straight home without dabbling any further in the slave trade.[97]

After trading in Utah's Sanpete Valley settlements for eight days, León returned to his camp, whereupon he discovered that Paiutes had driven off eighteen of the party's animals during his absence. He immediately pursued and confronted the culprits, who refused to return the animals but instead offered four girls and five boys as recompense. Thus, according to Agent Greiner, Pedro León and his party had not gone to Utah for the specific purpose of taking captives, but instead they had been coaxed into it by circumstances beyond their control. In defense of the slave traders, Greiner stated that the men accepted the captives only because they saw no other option, and he insisted that León planned to deliver the children directly into the governor's custody upon their return to New Mexico.[98]

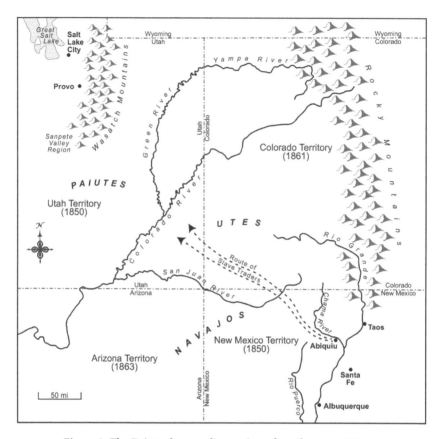

Figure 8. The Paiute slave-trading region of northwestern New
Mexico, southwestern Colorado, and southeastern Utah, c. 1860. New
Mexican slave traders like Pedro León embarked from the Chama
River to search for potential slaves in these more northerly regions.

Once they learned that León had Paiute slaves in his possession, Utah
authorities arrested and imprisoned his entire party for violation of the
Indian Trade and Intercourse Act of 1834.[99] All of the traders' equipment,
animals, and merchandise—along with the nine captives—were confiscated
and, according to Greiner, the Indian slaves "were sold to the Mormons as
servants, by the Mormon authorities."[100] Within weeks of their capture,
León and his party appeared before Mormon judge Zerubbabel Snow in a
Salt Lake City courtroom. A jury convicted the men for trading without a
valid license, the penalty being forfeiture of all personal property, including

the Paiute captives. After the verdict, attorneys argued that the confiscated Indians should be sold to remunerate legal fees and court costs accrued during the proceedings. Judge Snow, however, refuted this notion based on various American legal precedents, and he allowed Mormon families to adopt the children instead.[101]

Utah's territorial legislature used the ruling in this case as precedent to devise a resolution entitled "An Act for the Relief of Indian Slaves and Prisoners," outlawing Indian slavery while simultaneously sanctioning the purchase of indigenous children for adoption into Mormon households.[102] Utah officials perceived León's arrest and conviction as a fortuitous opportunity to seek legal justification for a new law that condoned the purchase and indenture of Indian children while concurrently banning the interterritorial Indian slave trade and shutting Utah off to any future New Mexican expeditions.[103] The circumstances surrounding the León incident prompted Young to issue a proclamation in 1853 berating Hispanics generally and raising a thirty-man detachment of Mormon troops to patrol the countryside. "There is in this territory, a horde of Mexicans, outlandish men," the governor announced, noting that they had furnished the Indians with guns and ammunition in addition to their illicit trade in human flesh. Showcasing more ethnocentrism than pragmatism, the governor ordered fellow Mormons to "arrest and keep in close custody, every strolling Mexican party."[104]

With all of their animals confiscated, León and his fellow traders left Utah as pedestrians on February 6, 1852, but did not return to the New Mexican settlements until April because of deep mountain snows that slowed their progress. By the time León arrived in New Mexico, the *Deseret News Weekly* had already broken the story. In issuing the trading passes, Agent Greiner argued, Governor Calhoun had complied with all government regulations pertaining to Indian trade.[105] Richard Weightman, New Mexico's congressional delegate, also supported Calhoun. Speaking in the House of Representatives on March 15, 1852, he accused the media of publishing unsubstantiated propaganda and chided them for being "reckless and unscrupulous" in their reporting.[106] Weightman claimed that both he and Calhoun had been victims of conniving political enemies who sought to undermine their influence, specifically naming the *Santa Fe Weekly Gazette* and its staunch abolitionist editor, William Kephart, as the culprits. Through the efforts of Kephart and others, rumors that Calhoun and Weightman advocated the slave trade reached national media outlets as far away as New York City.[107] Whatever the immediate repercussions, however, Calhoun never had to vouch for his actions. In May 1852, with his health rapidly failing, he left Santa Fe for Missouri and died en route, bringing a quiet end to the controversy.[108]

The Pedro León case exemplified the drastic cultural, ethnic, and legal changes that affected the western domain after it came under American jurisdiction, and it highlighted the impact of political and ideological transformations on preexisting institutions of servitude. Since the mid-1700s, Hispanos had traveled into the Great Basin to trade for slaves, and Indians from that section ventured into northern New Mexico settlements for the same purpose. Prior to 1850, no geopolitical boundary yet separated New Mexico from what ultimately became Utah. Slave traders were understandably baffled when told that newly arrived Mormon settlers prohibited such activity in what to them still constituted a portion of New Mexico. The extension of American laws regulating slavery in the territories confounded longtime residents of the Southwest, who either resisted or altogether ignored these sudden legal constraints upon their customary lifestyles.

Despite their antislavery rhetoric, Brigham Young's followers did sometimes keep Indian captives under the auspices of community laws, although the extent to which Mormons actually enslaved the people they bought or detained remains debatable.[109] Latter-Day Saints tolerated chattel slavery because, according to scripture, black persons had descended from Cain and were damned to a lifetime of servitude. Contrarily, they saw Indians not as slaves or servants but as gentiles whose heathenism necessitated their salvation through purchase and incorporation into Mormon society.[110] According to the *Book of Mormon*, North American Indians emanated from an Israelite family in Jerusalem sometime around 600 B.C. and were directly related to the Mormon colonizers of Utah.[111] The responsibility thus fell to these nineteenth-century pioneers to "save" their Lamanite Indian neighbors, a salvation that they sought to effect through direct purchase, domestic captivity, and religious conversion. With this "humanitarian" mind-set, Utah officials allowed citizens to buy or trade for captives among the Great Basin tribes in order to salvage their souls through education and theological submersion, a view not altogether different from the Spanish Catholics in New Mexico who converted captives through baptism. When a young Paiute man showed up at Fort Defiance in 1859, for example, he informed the post commander that "the Mormons had baptized him into their church, and gave him a paper, certifying he was a Latter-Day Saint, and a good man."[112] As with many other colonizing groups, the possession of indigenous children within Mormon households was viewed as a means of uplift through assimilation and acculturation.[113]

In a somewhat disingenuous perversion of the compensated emancipation scheme that some Northerners advocated for the eradication of slavery in the South, Brigham Young himself declared in 1852 that Mormons had begun a grand experiment, "a new feature in the traffic of human beings" that essentially amounted to "purchasing them into freedom instead of slavery."[114] Utah theocracy met California democracy when it came to the enslavement of indigenous peoples, as the latter state had already adopted a law in 1850 that condoned the purchase of Indian children as apprentices and wards in white households as a means of "civilizing" them at an early age.[115] Just one year after Utah's passage of an act condoning the practice, Solomon Nunes Carvalho, traveling with John C. Frémont's 1853 western expedition, witnessed this newly sanctioned purchasing of Indian children firsthand. Following a treaty between Young and renowned Chief Walkara, Carvalho observed that the governor bought two young Snake Indian captives from the Utes. The children had been reduced to a state of hopeless starvation and "were almost living skeletons." As Carvalho saw it, Young was merely engaging in an act of humanity and had saved the captive infants from certain death, although what became of them once they reached Mormon households remains unknown.[116]

In a similar vein, and with an uncloaked expression of approval, Indian agent Armstrong described a situation he witnessed in Utah's Santa Clara River Valley in 1857. A settler there, Jacob Hamblin, had "four apprenticed Pied [sic] children" herding sheep, spinning wool, and "attending to other household duties." The children, all between ten and twelve years of age, had been in Hamblin's possession for four years after being purchased from the tribe, although Armstrong downplayed the reality of their enslavement through his use of the less suggestive term "apprentice" when describing their status. While official reports from Utah's Indian agents sometimes alluded to Indian children serving in Mormon households, they avoided mentioning that those servants had been purchased, instead referring to them as laborers who were being transformed into "very useful members of society."[117] The circumstances surrounding Mormons, Paiutes, and Nuevomexicano slave traders represented one of the most visible public controversies involving Indian captivity during the 1850s and, in the minds of those who read about it in newspapers, helped to situate the matter within the broader context of American slavery.

Indian captivity rose once again to the forefront of public attention just prior to the Civil War, when New Mexico's territorial legislature attempted to amend previous slave codes to apply to "male or female Indians that should be acquired by barbarous nations." Governor Abraham Rencher refused to sign the amendment into law and explained his reasoning in a speech to the legislature on December 6, 1860. His twisted logic reflected the proslavery sentiment that pervaded New Mexico politics during the antebellum era. Rencher explained that the proposed amendment "seemed to be based upon the supposition that male or female Indians, acquired from barbarous Nations, are slaves, which is not the case." He also stated that New Mexican lawmakers had no legal power to enslave, informing his audience that "the Legislature can neither create, nor abolish slavery, they can only regulate it where it already exists," a viewpoint that conformed with federal legal precedent relative to the political powers of territories. "The normal or native condition of all our Indian tribes is that of freedom," Rencher proclaimed, "and they cannot, under our laws, be made slaves either by conquest or purchase." Then, in a stark twist, the governor concluded with an anomalous statement: "We may hold them as Captives, or peons, but not as slaves."[118]

In a single statement, Rencher unwittingly summarized the entire basis of the misinformed rhetoric on New Mexican slavery. The idea that Indians could be captives or peons—but *not* slaves—would drive the misguided congressional and territorial debates on the institution for years to come. Americans held preconceived notions of what constituted slavery based on what they observed in the Southern states, and after arriving in New Mexico some newcomers failed to perceive involuntary servants in the form of Hispanic peons and Indian captives as falling within their own cultural and legal definitions of slavery. The fundamental purposes and motivations that sustained coercive labor systems in the Southwest differed little from the peculiar institution that existed in the American South, but ethnocentric ideologies and cultural prejudices against Indians and Hispanics rendered many American newcomers oblivious to the level and extent of involuntary servitude existing in local communities. In New Mexico, antebellum political biases favoring the Southern cause permeated territorial politics during the presidential administrations of Democrats Franklin Pierce (1853–57)

and James Buchanan (1857–61), and many lawmakers turned a blind eye
to the plight of indigenous slaves until Radical Reconstruction directed
increased abolitionist attention toward New Mexico.

After the Civil War, the U.S. government conducted an investigation of
Indian affairs throughout the West, reporting there to be approximately
two thousand Navajos and Utes held "as domestic servants in a state of
bondage or slavery."[119] A number of other witnesses supported this finding,
variously estimating New Mexico's Indian slave population at between
1,500 and 4,000 persons.[120] Appearing before a federal grand jury in a case
concerning illegal ownership of Indian slaves, Juan Jose Santistevan of Taos
County testified that captives continued to be the most convenient source
of labor in northern New Mexico. A former slaveholder himself, Santistevan explained that "before the American conquest [Indians] used to sell
and trade their children to the citizens of New Mexico as slaves," acknowledging that the descendants of these captives lived as servants among Hispano families throughout local settlements.[121]

Reiterating the harsh realities of Indian enslavement, citizens of the territory reminded Massachusetts senator Charles Sumner in 1867 that the
reciprocal captive trade had been the root of animosity in the Southwest
for generations. "It was no unusual thing," they informed the abolitionist
politician, for the territorial newspaper to announce the loss of citizens
"carried into captivity," especially by the Navajos. They also admitted that
New Mexicans retaliated by forming unsanctioned civilian militias that
swept through Navajo country on equally violent raids, "taking all the
women and children they could prisoners and bringing them to the settlements and selling them as slaves, or using them as such in their own household."[122] After spending three years in the Southwest, James O. Pattie
described the reciprocity that characterized a culture of hatred between
Hispanos and Natives, writing that "the amount of robbery is about equal
between the lower classes of New Mexicans and the Indians."[123] So too did
Colonel Sumner recognize the mutual acrimony that defined these intercultural relationships. "This predatory warfare has been carried on for over
200 years, between the Mexicans and the Indians," he observed, "quite
enough time to prove that unless some change is made the war will be
interminable. They steal women and children . . . and in fact carry on the
war in all respects like two Indian nations."[124] Even army officers charged
with chastising depredating Indians readily admitted that citizens acted

wantonly in their interactions with tribes. After Mescalero Apaches stole a herd of stock and rode away with two captive Mexican boys from the vicinity of El Paso, Colonel Dixon S. Miles acknowledged that he had difficulty sympathizing with the victims on either side. "The hatred and animosity which is nurtured between the Mescaleros and the Mexicans," he wrote, meant that "they are constantly stealing and depredating on each other."[125]

By the Civil War era, Navajos had become the most victimized tribe in the captive wars. When John Greiner met with several tribal headmen at Jemez Pueblo, their spokesperson informed the Indian agent that "three of our chiefs now sitting before you mourn for their children who have been taken from their homes by the Mexicans." Claiming that over two hundred Navajos had been abducted and enslaved in recent years, one emotional chief declared that "my people are yet crying for the children they have lost."[126] Greiner mailed a letter to the commissioner of Indian affairs in Washington, D.C., stressing the importance of securing a moratorium on such practices, but his efforts seem to have been in vain. His protestations contradicted the views of military department personnel, many of whom remained at ideological odds with civil officials. At the same time that Greiner sought to curtail captive raids, Major Henry Lane Kendrick, in command at Fort Defiance, wrote that the most efficient means of forcing the Navajos into submission would be to take advantage of their fear that the federal government might begin assisting Mexican slave raiders and sanctioning their deeds. Kendrick thought that granting such authorization to civilians would be "wise and philanthropic" and, he believed, might occasion a more abrupt end to hostilities.[127] New Mexico's Superintendent of Indian Affairs Michael Steck suggested during the Civil War that the best way to facilitate peaceful relations between Natives and civilians would be to establish reservations for each tribe, allowing the military to monitor activity and prevent raiding. In reference to the Navajos, Steck thought that such a policy would protect the tribe from slave raids and thus eliminate their retributive measures against the settlements.[128] When the government did pursue this initiative with the establishment of the Bosque Redondo Reservation in 1863, the ensuing hardship that Navajos endured proved Steck's suggestion to have been overly optimistic.

Kit Carson's 1863 campaign of total warfare against the Navajos exacted a heavy toll on the tribe and exacerbated an already dire set of circumstances. When New Mexican volunteers, allied with Ute warriors (traditional Navajo enemies), swept through the Diné homelands, they aimed not only to crush the tribe into submission and displace them onto a faraway reservation, but also to acquire slaves.[129] As Carson himself admitted, his Ute auxiliaries joined the expedition primarily to take captives, a pursuit in which they enjoyed considerable success. Because he so desperately needed their assistance as guides, Carson recommended that the Utes be allowed to keep all Navajo prisoners.[130] A census taken at the Ute agency near Conejos, Colorado, in the summer of 1865 enumerated 148 captives spread throughout local communities, of which 76 percent claimed Navajo ancestry.[131] The fact that so many Navajo captives turned up in the vicinity of the agency just two years after Carson's scorched-earth campaign revealed that many Ute warriors had been successful during those expeditions and, upon returning home, had traded or sold their captives to local residents.

Militiamen who participated in Carson's campaign, along with other civilian noncombatants, likewise seized the opportunity to take captives. Small parties preyed upon the Navajos during their "Long Walk," striking the Indians as they trekked toward the woebegone reservation set aside for them on the plains of southeastern New Mexico. In one telling incident, the commanding officer at Fort Wingate reported that a Navajo girl staggered into the post after citizens attacked the group with whom she traveled, killing all the men and capturing the women and children to be "sold into peonage." The girl had been held captive in a village north of Jemez Pueblo before escaping and making her way to the fort, where an officer cared for her while awaiting further instructions from headquarters "with regard to her future disposal." The fate of her family members, like that of so many captives, remained a mystery.[132]

General William Tecumseh Sherman arrived at the Navajos' Bosque Redondo Reservation in May 1868, five years after the removal campaigns commenced, to discuss a treaty with tribal leaders that would relieve them and their followers of the suffering associated with their internment. Many Navajos perished from starvation, famine, and a variety of illnesses that swept through the area. In a single rather typical month during the winter of 1865, at least forty-three detainees died from sickness at Fort Sumner, while a measles epidemic that same year packed the post hospital—built to accommodate just twenty people—with more than four hundred Indians seeking treatment.[133] Having already spent nearly half a decade in miserable confinement at the reservation, officials assumed that the tribe would happily accept any terms the government offered allowing them to return to their homelands.

Because of these calamitous circumstances, federal agents who spoke with the Navajo headmen at Fort Sumner must have been surprised when the subject of captives took center stage during the negotiations. Barboncito, one of the most influential Navajo chiefs, wasted little time in addressing the topic. During the second day of deliberations, the elder headman minced no words when informing General Sherman, "I want to drop this conversation now and talk about Navajo children held as prisoners by Mexicans." The veteran army officer might have been taken aback by Barboncito's straightforwardness, but he addressed the concern with commendable resolve. Through a translator, Sherman informed him of the United States' recent war to end slavery and assured the chief that federal mandates against involuntary servitude would allow Navajo women and children to be released from bondage. Demonstrating the impact that Reconstruction-era antislavery legislation would have on the Southwest, Sherman specifically referenced the 1867 congressional Peon Law when explaining to the Indians that "if any Mexican holds a Navajo in peonage," the offending party would be subject to imprisonment in the territorial penitentiary. He assured tribal leaders that military personnel would work to effect the release of captives, promising that the "government is determined that the enslavement of the Navajos shall cease and those who are guilty of holding them as peons shall be punished."[134]

The final treaty, consummated on June 1, 1868, when twenty-nine Navajos and ten federal officers affixed their marks and signatures, contained a clause explicitly addressing the captive trade. The Navajos agreed that they would "never capture or carry off from the settlements women or children." In return, they secured a pledge from the government that American bureaucrats would eradicate the enslavement of Indians.[135] Unlike Mexican leaders prior to 1846, U.S. officials did in fact take action to enforce treaty obligations to the Navajos. On July 27, 1868, Congress adopted a joint resolution that authorized Sherman "to reclaim from peonage the women and children of the Navajo Indians, now held in slavery in the Territory."[136] The infamous leader of the Civil War's "March to the Sea" ordered an investigation in August to determine the extent to which Navajos remained in bondage throughout the settlements. He instructed Major General George W. Getty, commanding the Military District of New Mexico, to ensure that Navajo headmen understood that their people would be permitted to scour the territory in search of captive family members.[137] With Indian slavery thus becoming "pretty much broken up," Sherman informed

Ulysses S. Grant that the previously interminable Navajo Wars had likely come to an end.[138]

These efforts notwithstanding, the stigmatizing effects of captivity lingered. For some Navajos, it would be many years before they reunited with their families in Dinétah, if in fact they ever returned at all. In 1872, a group of approximately one hundred women and children arrived at Fort Defiance, having been emancipated from their life of bondage in the Rio Grande settlements. Even so, an Indian agent named Thomas Varker Keam continued to receive complaints "almost every day from relatives of others, who say they are kept by the citizens against their will." He suggested that a special agent be appointed to accompany Navajo chiefs as they traveled throughout New Mexico's villages in search of captive kinfolk.[139] Despite the cooperation of local and federal officials, it remained difficult, if not impossible, to secure the liberation of all captives, a clear indication that systems of involuntary servitude had a long-lasting impact on southwestern culture.

By the 1860s, more than two hundred years of forced servitude and cultural integration had resulted in an extensive displacement of Indians from their families and of Euro-Americans from theirs. Captives experienced a coerced process of assimilation into their captors' culture, a process that oftentimes involved a psychological transformation of human identity. Masters systematically modified a captive's sense of community and kinship by eliminating vestiges of their former life, including language and religion. The path to freedom for indigenous slaves would be a long and tedious one, inciting controversy and violence throughout the territory much like chattel slavery did in the contemporaneous South. Nuevomexicano slaveholders clung vigorously to their captives, just as Southern masters refused to loosen their grasp on African American slaves. In the process, questions repeatedly arose among easterners as to the exact nature and characteristics of involuntary servitude in the Southwest. Drawing upon reports from military officers, correspondence with New Mexico officials, published travelogues, and mere hearsay in the national capital, lawmakers would further convolute perceptions of Indian slavery and debt peonage in the years following the Mexican-American War. In so doing, they affirmed the importance of New Mexico's involuntary labor systems within the context of abolition, sectionalism, and popular sovereignty, and the discourse surrounding peonage and captivity during the antebellum era would prove critical for post–Civil War reformulations of free labor ideology.

Chapter 3

The Peculiar Institution of Debt Peonage

In November 1846, Lieutenant Richard Smith Elliott of the Laclede Rangers—a Missouri cavalry unit attached to General Kearny's Army of the West—had a revealing conversation with a Mexican teamster in Santa Fe. Asked whether the Hispano population favored American rule, the man told Elliott, "*Los pobres sí, los ricos no*" (the poor yes, the rich no). In explaining this, he stated "that the reason why the rich were dissatisfied, was that they could not oppress the poor as they had heretofore done— frequently requiring the laboring classes to toil from early dawn until dark . . . and giving them scarcely food sufficient to keep body and soul together."[1] Lieutenant A. B. Dyer observed in February 1847 that many of the priests and other wealthy or influential men remained inimical to political change, primarily because they knew it would upend the egregiously inegalitarian social order under which they enjoyed free rein.[2] One soldier put it rather bluntly when remembering that "the lower classes were all peons to the higher," and an unnamed newspaperman echoed that view when explaining that "the lower classes lived too long in a state of abject slavery, dependence, and ignorance, to be at once capable of the benefits conferred on them by the change of government."[3] Most Anglo-American observers lacked complete objectivity when observing social relations in the Hispanic Southwest, due largely to their own racial and religious prejudices. But their descriptions indicate, at the very least, that some New Mexicans were divided in their support of the American conquest, with traditional forms of slavery and dependency being among the primary motivating factors behind divergences in perspectives.

In 1855 a New Mexican peon named Cruz Marqués filed a lawsuit against his master, José Manuel Angel, in the San Miguel County District Court. The debtor servant alleged that Angel had violently taken hold of him and tied him up like a kidnapping victim. The plaintiff's attorney, seeking a guilty verdict against the abusive *patrón* that might result in the liberation of the peon and the forgiveness of his debt, declared that "it is no excuse for Angel that Marques was his servant, for either the assault, or [for] putting the chains upon him." Despite these efforts, a jury ruled in favor of the master and remanded Marqués to his service.[4] Just a decade earlier, when New Mexico was a province of the Mexican republic, such a trial never would have occurred in the first place. The U.S. conquest of New Mexico at midcentury brought with it the implementation of American jurisprudence and the imposition of ideological principles regarding servitude and free labor that counteracted previous Mexican laws. At the same time, American influence in the Southwest placed debt peonage and Indian captivity firmly within national debates over the political, economic, and moral viability of slavery. Although Cruz Marqués lost his case, his efforts elicited important comparisons between chattel slavery and traditional forms of involuntary servitude in the Southwest, ones that would inform political perspectives and legal doctrine during the Civil War and Reconstruction eras.

Hispanic peons fulfilled a variety of chores depending on gender, age, and necessity. Women and children typically performed menial household duties, while men served as herdsmen and, in the more fertile river valleys, as field hands at planting and harvesting time. "Generally they are in the employ of wealthy persons owning the lands, and the peons live upon the lands and cultivate them as serfs," U.S. senator James R. Doolittle explained in 1867.[5] At Lucien B. Maxwell's sprawling ranch along the upper Cimarron River, eyewitnesses in the 1850s and 1860s reported seeing hundreds (one source even claimed thousands) of Hispanic peons and Indian slaves toiling side-by-side in fields spanning miles up and down the valley, making Maxwell's operation one of the largest and most profitable in the territory.[6] Colonel Henry Inman, an army quartermaster, wrote that Maxwell's peons "were as much his thralls as were Gurth and Wamba of Cedric of Rotherwood," but he noted that the famous land baron generally treated them with kindness.[7]

When American troops entered New Mexico in 1846, they also noticed many impoverished Hispanos toiling in the crudely developed gold mines southeast of Santa Fe. At the village of Tuerto, Lieutenant James W. Abert observed that men, women, and children congregated around pools of water at the mining pits, where they used "wooden platters or great horns"

Figure 9. Site of Lucien Maxwell's estate at Cimarron, New
Mexico, as it appeared c. 1905. The three-story mill in the
background was built in the early 1860s, when captives and
peons still toiled there. From the collection of the author.

as makeshift gold pans. He later reported that "even the life of the poor
pastores [herders] is much preferable to these diggers of gold."[8] Contemporaneously in Northern California, Chilean peons fulfilled similar duties,
scrounging gold from placer mines in exchange for passage to the region
and the barest subsistence, and their presence in that purportedly free state
prompted abolitionist complaints as early as 1849.[9]

In the 1840s and 1850s, Nuevomexicanos participating in the burgeoning Comanchero trade took their peons with them to serve during the journey to and from the South Plains, where they met with Comanches, Kiowas,
and Cheyennes to trade for horses, mules, buckskins, and other supplies.
Rafael Chacón, a twenty-three-year-old from a prominent New Mexican
family, recalled that, following a trade fair in 1856, a Comanche Indian
confronted his party and stole a bridle from the horse that his peon rode.[10]
While the nameless servant was unlucky in losing the bridle (which almost
certainly belonged to Chacón and, having been stolen, would have been

added to the peon's mounting debt), he nevertheless ranked among the more fortunate of New Mexico's lower class, inasmuch as his journey to the South Plains—even as a servant—temporarily alleviated him from the monotonous daily routine he experienced while toiling either in one of the settlements or on a hacienda.

One military officer, John C. Reid, traveled through New Mexico in the 1850s and observed that peonage encompassed "the most numerous class of Mexicans."[11] Because of the large number of peons inhabiting the territory—one passerby in the late 1850s described that form of labor as "universal" throughout New Mexico—it would have been hard for visitors to overlook their presence.[12] They could easily be distinguished by their manner of dress, reminiscent of any financially destitute person subjected to a life of peasantry. International Boundary Commissioner John Russell Bartlett wrote in 1852 that peon men, like most New Mexicans at that time, wore short jackets, oversized white pants with slits on both sides, and a serape or blanket over their shoulders.[13] Women exhibited a similar simplicity of dress, as the merchant Josiah Gregg attested to when writing that "the ordinary apparel of the female peasantry" included a flannel petticoat and a *rebozo*, or scarf.[14] In many ways a peon's meager ensemble was not unlike the tattered and dirty clothing that black slaves wore on Southern plantations.

As peons grew older or became ill, their productivity declined and masters no longer had a use for them. "One of the most objectionable features of the system," according to one witness, "is that the master is not obliged to maintain the peon in sickness or old age." Once a servant became too ill or too old to work, many *patrones* simply sent them on their way "like an old horse who is turned out to die" or, as a *Harper's Weekly* correspondent put it in 1859, "turn[ed] him upon the world perfectly helpless."[15] The ability of *hacendados* and rancheros to subvert a servant's kin into bondage for satisfaction of outstanding debts only exacerbated this practice, as creditors could simply impress one's family members into service once the initial debtor became too enfeebled to work. Creditors could also manipulate the system in a manner that ensured that the peon could never earn his or her freedom. According to George Ruxton, advances on wages would be issued to a prospective peon, who then became legally bound to serve the lender until the debt was satisfied, although creditors typically applied interest in such a way that prevented this from happening, meaning that "the debtor remains a bondsman to the day of his death."[16] As Ruxton knew, the law had supported masters in their human property interests since Spanish colonial times, and Mexican edicts passed in the 1820s and 1830s protected the interests of masters by enabling them to hold debtors in servitude and force their subjective obedience.[17] Touring New Mexico in 1856, territorial secretary William Davis pointed out that the decree upholding peonage "is dignified with the title of 'Law regulating contracts between masters and servants.' This is all well enough on paper, as far as it goes, but the statute is found to be all upon the side of the master."[18]

Members of General Kearny's expedition of conquest witnessed the harsh realities of peonage almost everywhere they went. On October 6, 1846, Lieutenant William H. Emory, accompanying the campaign south of Socorro, New Mexico, recorded in his diary that a young boy, serving the troops as a mule driver, "was today claimed by his creditor or master." According to Emory, the lad owed the man $60 and had fallen into forced labor to fulfill the pecuniary obligation. In the 1840s, $60 constituted an enormous debt (about $1,860 today), one that the child could never repay. The entire institution disgusted Emory, an antislavery man who had served in the Union Army during the Civil War. "The poor debtors thus enthralled for life, for a debt of $60," he concluded, "constitute, as a class, the cheapest laborers in the world." He went on to observe that "the price of the labor for life of a man was, in the case we have stated, $60, without any expense of rearing and maintenance in infancy or old age, the wages covering only a sum barely sufficient for the most scanty supply of food and clothing."[19] Emory's colleague, Lieutenant Philip St. George Cooke, could find nothing positive to say about the territory and its engrained systems of servitude. With the addition of New Mexico to the American domain, he lamented that "the great book of American citizenship [is] thus thrust . . . upon eighty thousand mongrels who cannot read,—who are almost heathens,—the great mass reared in real slavery, called peonism."[20]

Peons did sometimes receive compensation for their work, but the meager earnings went toward satisfying the debt owed, with the remainder being so little that, when accompanied by compounding interest, the system ensured permanent bondage. In an 1848 speech to Congress, Representative Richard Donnell of North Carolina noted that masters could release peons from their terms of servitude, but they rarely did so because they managed the debt in such a manner that even a lifetime of labor could not repay the perpetually increasing amount owed.[21] Josiah Gregg wrote that peonage "acts with terrible severity upon the unfortunate poor," whose paltry wages were insufficient even to clothe and feed themselves, much less pay down their debt.[22] This practice continued even beyond the Civil War, when Congress finally addressed the subject. "A very small debt with interest, where the peon has a family to support and the creditor supports him, amounts to a servitude for life," one politician explained in an attempt to convince colleagues to support a new law banning debt bondage.[23]

According to Gregg, some adult male peons earned between $2 and $5 per month, depending on the generosity of their creditor. Women received much less, typically between 50 cents and $2.[24] A number of additional witnesses also reported that peons made anywhere from $1 to $6 each month, "out of which the peon has to support himself and family."[25] These stipends, however, never came in the form of hard currency but were instead issued as "articles of apparel and other necessities at the most exorbitant prices." All food, clothing, and other essential provisions had to be procured from the creditor himself, who often managed a small store where a peon purchased these items, making it "an easy matter to keep him always in debt."[26] In an 1854 Valencia County court case, a master sued his servant, Vicente Ortega, for breach of contract and presented an account book showing that the man owed $194 for various items obtained from the creditor—primarily shoes, shirts, sombreros, and pants, along with an occasional plug of tobacco.[27] As one observer noted of the *ricos*, "The key to their wealth [is] a store of necessaries for their dependent laborers . . . at their own prices they manage to keep the poor peons always in debt, and this legally binds them and their families to endless service and dependence."[28] The proclivity of masters to charge exorbitant prices for goods had the intended consequence of at least maintaining—and oftentimes increasing—a peon's debt and perpetuating the term of servitude.[29]

Some masters occasionally lent a peon's services to others, but the precise extent to which an illicit trade in human servants occurred in the Southwest is impossible to gauge because such transactions went unrecorded. The Taos and Santa Fe marketplaces frequently saw the exchange of Indian slaves, but much less so Hispanic peons. Such dealings occurred with far less regularity than in the American South, where slave auctions were common and individuals made a living out of the practice.[30] Nevertheless, peons did sometimes revert between overseers. Utah's 1852 law relative to masters and servants allowed that "servants may be transferred from one master or mistress to another" with the permission of a local probate court.[31] Similarly, while a creditor in New Mexico could not sell a peon outright, he could still transmit the person "just as he would a mule or a horse," making it a system "of the most wretched and degrading character."[32] Samuel Ellison, who served as both a Supreme Court clerk and a secretary to several territorial governors, recollected that peons constituted "as much an article of trade as a horse or a sheep." A Radical Republican who spent time after the Civil War searching out slaveowners in New Mexico, Ellison drew little distinction between indebted bondsmen and indigenous servants, essentially lumping "Indians taken captive or purchased from wild tribes and held as slaves" into the same class of unfree laborers as indigent debtors.[33] The commodification and transfer of peons did occur periodically, although only on a small scale and usually involving one or two persons at a time in localized transactions rather than in an open marketplace, as was often the case with Indian captives in the Southwest and black slaves in the South.[34]

Owing to its apparent comparability to chattel slavery, discussions about peonage as a source of involuntary labor became increasingly common once New Mexico was admitted to the United States. Because of the slavery issue's resounding importance during the first half of the nineteenth century, Anglo-American travelers and merchants passing through the Southwest almost invariably mentioned the presence of debt bondage, oftentimes associating it with the more familiar system of race slavery. After Mexico gained its independence in 1821, the Santa Fe trade brought an influx of American explorers, fur trappers, and merchants into the province. This occasioned the publication of travelogues and newspaper articles explicating the eccentricities of peonage, providing a lens through which to view the institution as seen through the eyes of witnesses already familiar with similar forms of involuntary servitude in the South. Many such anecdotes stemmed from an ethnocentric nativist rhetoric that mongrelized Nuevomexicanos for their dark physiognomy and polyethnic background, but the descriptions are nonetheless instructive in that they reveal a common Anglo-American mind-set toward inhabitants of the Southwest during the Civil War era.[35]

Debt bondage, according to one New York editorialist, differed from chattel slavery only insofar as "it applies to all colors, shades and complexions, from the pure white to the sooty African." In New Mexico, the writer noted, "The creditor has as much command over the labor of the debtor, as the Southern slaveholder has over that of the negro."[36] One U.S. senator

proclaimed peonage to be nothing more than "modified slavery," prompting his colleague to add that "it is a system of serfdom worse than the
Russian system ever was."[37] When the German doctor and botanist Adolph
Wislizenus passed through the Southwest during the Mexican-American
War, he described the feudalistic aristocracy that prevailed there and pitied
"the great number of human beings attached to these haciendas [who] are,
in fact, nothing more than serfs."[38] Ruxton made a similar comparison
when writing in 1848 that the relationship between Mexican landholders
and laborers "is a species of serfdom, little better than slavery itself."[39] Lieutenant Abert referenced the disparity between "the rico of the village" and
the poor masses when he traveled through New Mexico in 1846, drawing a
direct parallel to the relationship between slaves and plantation owners in
the South and noting of Nuevomexicanos that, aside from the wealthy few,
"no one else owns a single sheep."[40] And when U.S. representative John J.
Hardin of Kentucky described Mexico and its people to a friend just
months before his death at the Battle of Buena Vista in 1847, he disparag-
ingly wrote that "they are a miserable race, with a few intelligent men who
lord it over the rest, ³/₄ of the people or more are Paeons [*sic*] and as much
slaves as the negroes of the South."[41]

In drawing such simplistic comparisons between peonage and other systems of involuntary labor, these observers overlooked the social, racial, and
cultural disparities between geographic regions. Witnesses drew distinctions
between the two systems of servitude and, just as frequently, attempted to
distort their characteristics to fit the political or economic necessity of the
situation at hand. From the moment of American occupation, Anglo newcomers routinely misunderstood debt bondage as it existed in the Southwest. In September 1846, General Kearny, along with Colonel Alexander
W. Doniphan and other assistants, wrote the first set of civil regulations for
New Mexico and modeled it closely off of Missouri's state laws. The drafters
of the document dedicated twenty-two sections to an elaborate explanation of the circumstances whereby a creditor could sue a debtor, clearly
unaware of the true nature of master-servant relations there, as no peon had
ever enjoyed privileges of due process or the right to a fair trial under Mexican law.[42] So too did many easterners misapply notions of chattel slavery to
the Southwest in an attempt to advance sectional ideologies, and in so doing
they misconstrued the debate on slavery in the western territories. Many
Hispanics, in turn, habitually misrepresented their system of servitude to

these outsiders in order to perpetuate their own economic or social aspirations and simultaneously appeal to either pro- or antislavery interests.

The differences between peonage and slavery often depended on the
persons attempting to define them. Sectionalism influenced and skewed
viewpoints, as did economic interests, political persuasions, and moral sen-
sibilities. By New Mexicans' own admission, involuntary servitude—in
both peon and captive forms—had existed since Spanish colonial times,
but it had never been clearly defined, and local residents showed little
urgency in providing a specific description of the two systems.[43] This
changed once the region became a part of the United States. With the slavery issue at the forefront of heated congressional interchange during and
after the Mexican-American War, the admission of new territories incited
tremendous strife among lawmakers. When Americans ventured into New
Mexico, those who expected to see chattel slaves instead found large numbers of Hispanic peons and Indian captives. Between the time of New Mexico's inception as a U.S. possession in 1846 and the outbreak of the Civil
War in 1861, the need to define peonage in unambiguous legal terms, with
an emphasis on its relation to more familiar forms of servitude, became
important at both the local and national levels of government.[44]

Due to the availability of an indigent, socially subordinate class of peon
laborers, racial or chattel slavery never gained a foothold in New Mexico.
One U.S. representative referred to debt bondage as "a most wretched system," expressing his aversion to both "negro slavery" as well as peonage
and requesting that Congress take action to ban both systems throughout
the United States.[45] The assertion that peonage resembled chattel slavery in
principle and practice was nothing new among Northern free-soilers.
Another congressman announced that Hispanic peons "are in a worse condition of slavery than our negroes, and would be happy to change places
with them," a belief that coincided with Lieutenant Abert's observation in
1846 that "the major portion of the people live not one bit better than the
negroes on a plantation in our southern States."[46] One Northerner, writing
pseudonymously as Cora Montgomery, claimed in 1850 that she resided
along the Rio Grande and reported that the average peon's "sad, downcast
air, is in strange contrast with the ever-cheerful buoyancy of the blacks;
even [the peon's] singing has the wail of death in its slow, melancholy
notes."[47] The supposition that peons would happily trade places with those
enslaved in the South met with skepticism on many fronts. It did, however,
indicate a recognition on the part of some politicians that peonage involved

a different race than chattel slavery, which helps to explain why the institution persevered even beyond the emancipation of African American bondpeople in 1865.

The South Carolina senator John C. Calhoun echoed these sentiments when he told Congress that "the Puros [referring to peons and Indian captives collectively] are as much slaves as our negroes, and are less intelligent and well treated."[48] His stance mirrored that of many proslavery citizens inasmuch as he did distinguish between peonage and chattel slavery, but he believed New Mexico's forms of servitude to be far worse than that practiced among his own Southern brethren. The assertion that captives and peons suffered greater hardships than did African American slaves in the East had little basis in fact. During a visit to Santa Fe in the 1860s, James Meline overheard a conversation about slavery between a Hispano and an Anglo-American, whom he did not identify by name. "The official presented their position as we used to be accustomed to hear slave-holders speak of that of their slaves—they were very happy, well cared for, well fed, treated kindly, and all the usual bosh talked south of Mason and Dixon's line," Meline related in his memoirs. The New Mexican replied, "You know as well as I do, sir, that although they are sometimes kindly treated, it is generally the reverse, and, get round the matter as you may, they are, after all, slaves, and nothing but slaves."[49]

According to John Ayers, a Union soldier stationed in New Mexico during the Civil War, peons suffered far more at the hands of their masters than did slaves in the South. If one ran away, for example, they could be punished in a variety of ways. "It was worse than slavery," Ayers opined, "for slaves had a mercantile value, while if a peon died his place was at once filled with no loss but the small debt he was working out."[50] Another observer believed peonage to be "much more repugnant" than the Southern chattel system, while a correspondent for *Harper's Weekly* went even further when writing that "peonage is a state of servitude a thousand times worse than our slavery."[51] Of course, variations between the chattel system and debtor servitude depended on the perception of the beholder; millions of whipped and bleeding black slaves in the antebellum South would likely have refuted the claim that New Mexico's peons had it worse in regards to their abusive treatment.

Reflecting the viewpoints of many people, one U.S. politician believed New Mexico to be composed of "a few thousand Americans, a few thousand Mexicans, and the balance of mixed bloods and peons," or, as another congressman from Pennsylvania derisively put it, "Indians, Mustees and Mexicans."[52] In 1860, district judge John S. Watts announced that the territory contained only a few thousand Anglo-Americans, along with "forty-four thousand peons, and forty-four thousand Indians, about half civilized."[53] According to one New York editorialist, New Mexico was home to a "mongrel population" of "semi-barbarous, half Indian, half Mexican tribes" who could not be trusted to act as loyal American citizens if granted statehood. "The population of New Mexico is in the main ignorant, superstitious, and degraded," another New Yorker raved, proclaiming them to be intellectually inferior and "morally about on a par with the inhabitants of our Fourth or Sixth Ward."[54] In a revealing rhetorical conflation, these authors ascribed peon status to all landless Hispanos, using the idiom of slavery to assert their own ethnic superiority while marginalizing the economically dependent inhabitants of the Southwest.

Some Northerners who staunchly abhorred slavery and agitated for the emancipation of Southern slaves turned a blind eye to captivity and peonage as a result of prejudice toward Indians and Hispanics. Senator Calhoun typified the American mind-set toward southwestern inhabitants. "We have never dreamt of incorporating into our Union any but the Caucasian race," he ranted in 1848, insisting that neither Hispanics nor Indians deserved to be American citizens. Calhoun's speech, laced with bigoted rhetoric, epitomized one of the most common arguments that Anglo-Americans proffered against the admittance of New Mexico into the Union on equal political footing as the eastern states. The elder statesman spoke for many of his peers when expressing an overall aversion to the enfranchisement of nonwhites, especially those living in a state of peonage.[55]

Abolitionist, sectionalist, and ethnocentric ideologies had a profound influence on perceptions of the Southwest and its inhabitants. After the Mexican-American War, varying definitions of slavery and peonage were commonly interjected into national political debates. Representative Richard Donnell claimed in 1848 that the two systems bore little resemblance to one another, declaring "peon slavery" to be a condition of contractual labor between creditors and debtors, a dynamic that did not exist in the South, where slaves could not negotiate the terms of their servitude.[56] The Massachusetts senator Daniel Webster, an ardent opponent of slavery in the territories, likewise distinguished between the two labor regimes, stating in an 1850 congressional speech that he understood peonage to be "a sort of penal servitude" in which a man voluntarily sold himself into slavery by accepting the contractual conditions of the initial loan of goods or money. His point, however, was not to opine on the specifics of peonage, but rather to demonstrate that that preexisting system of servitude would render "African slavery, as we see it among us, as utterly impossible" to exist in the Southwest.[57] On the other side, Miguel A. Otero, a New Mexico congressional representative, forcefully denied all negative connotations of debt bondage. His defense of the institution came in direct response to a newspaper editorial in the antislavery *New-York Daily Tribune* that lambasted both debt servitude as well as New Mexico's predominantly mixed-blood population. "I deny that peonage, as it exists in New Mexico, is a modified slavery, or any slavery at all," he lectured, describing it as "a system of apprenticeship or temporary voluntary servitude" with no degrading or oppressive characteristics whatsoever. Otero deceptively assured critics that peonage had no adverse effect on one's social or political status as a freeman, drawing sharp distinctions between debtor servitude in New Mexico and chattel slavery in the South, which unquestionably did undermine the agency of unfree blacks.[58]

As both Donnell and Otero rightfully claimed, peonage involved citizens holding one another in servitude for fulfillment of a pecuniary debt. That system, arguably voluntary inasmuch as a person willingly placed himself in arrears when becoming a party to such transactions, differed from that in which Euro-American colonists and Native American tribes took captives from one another and subjected them to a lifetime of assimilative bondage, inasmuch as no pecuniary obligations attended the latter method of slaving.[59] It also contrasted sharply with indentured servitude in the early mid-Atlantic colonies. In New Mexico's creditor-debtor system, peons had little hope of ever repaying their debt, nor was there any predetermined length of servitude, and therefore they frequently found themselves bound for life. After spending time in northern New Mexico during the late 1850s, the American journalist Albert D. Richardson observed of peons that "cases where one liquidated his debts and became free were very rare."[60] An army inspector, George A. McCall, noted the frequency with which many a Hispano "inextricably involved himself as the debtor of his employer" and in so doing became "a *peon* for life."[61] Another antebellum military officer explained that, regardless of the amount that a peon owed, masters were entitled to their labor until contented that the debt and all interest had been covered. "Should the debtor die without satisfying the debt, his wife and children are required to assume its payment," he wrote, "and thus generation after generation, are liable for a debt contracted between persons whom they never saw."[62] Of all federal politicians, the antislavery Pennsylvania representative Thaddeus Stevens put it most pithily when he chided those of his colleagues who had "become enamored of peonage . . . which saves the poor man's cow to furnish milk for his children, by selling the father instead of the cow."[63]

As political debates and witness testimony revealed, cultural custom as well as Mexican law upheld the right of a master to exploit a peon's family members by retaining them in bondage after his or her demise, in the common event that a debt remained unpaid. According to Spanish-era statutes, the wife and children of a deceased peon inherited the debt and could be held in servitude to satisfy such obligations.[64] Creditors interpreted this clause loosely in order to apply it to their individual situations. Peonage often emanated from unwritten but mutually understood contracts, which, being legally ambiguous, provided masters with sufficient impetus to apply the law as they saw fit. This also allowed for minors to be bound to labor in repayment of a parent's debt, a common occurrence until antebellum court rulings decreed otherwise.

Foreseeing future legal problems, Governor James S. Calhoun asked the territorial legislature in 1851 to define the relationship between masters and peons in clear terms, hoping to enlighten citizens about their obligations and rights in circumstances of unpaid debt.[65] One month later, New Mexico lawmakers responded by passing the "law regulating contracts between masters and servants," a statute containing eighteen sections covering everything from child servants to runaway peons.[66] Neighboring Utah Territory quickly followed suit, passing an edict in 1852 that sanctioned human bondage for indebtedness, although that decree included a clause forbidding the permanent servitude of one's descendants if they died before satisfying their debt.[67] If a master in New Mexico believed that a peon failed to adequately perform his or her duties, he could have them locked up in the nearest jail. The law also borrowed from the 1850 Fugitive Slave Act by including strict provisions for runaway peons, and local prefects had a statutory obligation to assist in recapturing absconded servants.[68]

New Mexico legislators cleverly designed the 1851 peon law to seem like a benign set of regulations pertaining to any two contracting parties in a business transaction. When read more closely, however, the vague and abstruse provisions gave creditors considerable leeway while providing only minimal protection for debtors. Section five, for example, stated that even abused or otherwise mistreated servants had no legitimate claim to freedom unless they first satisfied the terms of their debt contract.[69] Referencing this section of the law in 1861, Representative Otero blatantly misrepresented the true nature of its purpose and enforcement. The act, he claimed, "gives to the peon the privilege of changing from one temporary owner of his services to another whenever he becomes oppressed or unfairly treated," a supposedly inexpensive and simple process that even illiterate and indigent peons could use as a recourse.[70] The legal process to which Otero referred, however, was mostly inaccessible to peons and captives and, because of the swarthy means whereby masters ensured the continued indebtedness of their servants, it remained nearly impossible for a peon to ever repay the amount owed or to work for another party in the event that a master became physically abusive. While this particular portion of the law appeared to grant servants the right to seek redress if beaten or otherwise injured, it actually provided no assistance in that regard and instead kept them submissive. Even if a peon did manage to repay his or her debt, there was little pressure on a master to grant freedom because no written documentation existed to verify the satisfaction of their dues. In rare instances when the authorities became involved, New Mexican *patrones*, like white Southerners in the Jim Crow era, often contrived new debts or criminal charges to keep the peon in bondage.

Other sections of the law similarly upheld a lifetime of bondage. Upon agreeing to a verbal contract, a peon was obligated to work every day from sunrise to sunset. The code affirmed New Mexico's social hierarchy by mandating that "all male or female servants shall respect their masters as their superior guardians," with any disobedience or aberrant behavior punishable by law.[71] The most pervasive component of the 1851 act, however, involved the capture of fugitive peons, and masters quickly utilized the law to their advantage in that regard. In 1854, José María Gutierres of Santa Ana County filed suit in district court, alleging that his four peons—Pablo Maldonado, Diego Chaves, Juan Lopez, and Alvino Valdes—had fled and taken refuge in nearby San Miguel County. He requested that either the sheriff arrest the men and remand them to his service, or else the court require them to repay their debts, which ranged from $132 to an astronomical $1,630 (approximately $47,400 today). In 1860, Manuel Armijo filed a similar complaint in the Bernalillo County probate court, seeking redress for his runaway peon, Pablo Gamboa. Under such circumstances, the law unequivocally favored creditors and allowed them to reclaim peons through judicial mechanisms.[72]

Owing to such realities, many Anglo-Americans could discern little or no difference between New Mexican peonage and Southern slavery. One traveler noted in 1856 that the only variance he could see between the two systems involved the chattel value of black slaves as opposed to the lack thereof for Hispanic peons, stating that "in other respects I believe the difference is in favor of the negro." He bluntly criticized peonage as "a more charming name for a species of slavery as abject and oppressive as any found upon the American continent."[73] Governor Calhoun corroborated this similarity, informing Commissioner of Indian Affairs Orlando Brown that "*peons . . . is but another name for *slaves*, as that term is understood in our Southern States." To Calhoun, peonage seemed even more pervasive than chattel slavery inasmuch as it had no racial prerogative.[74] Thomas Rusk, a Texas senator, made a similar—albeit somewhat sarcastic, given his staunch proslavery position—statement to Congress on June 6, 1850. "If gentlemen want an object on which to exercise their philanthropy," he declared in reference to peonage, "let me tell them there is now in New Mexico a system of slavery of the most abject and heartrending character."[75] All told, these conditions led to a harsh life of servitude for countless persons, simply because they had fallen into debt. In southwestern society, peonage constituted a veritable debtor's prison from which the unfortunate servant had little hope of ever being liberated. As one army officer observed, "The provisions of this system result in enslaving thousands during their health and manhood, who otherwise would be at least as independent as the insolvent debtors of our land . . . and hence Mexico contains more beggars than any other division of North America."[76]

Following the implementation of a territorial legislature and court system, certain legal privileges became available to New Mexico's captive slaves and debt peons. As is often the situation with matters of law, however, the lower classes seldom possessed the pecuniary resources or empowerment to try a case in court. This held especially true with peons, whose masters took care to ensure that illiterate servants could not broadcast their grievances or enlist a confidante to file the necessary paperwork with a local magistrate. New Mexico residents informed congressional leaders that "peonage is a pernicious system [with] degrading influences," but they also claimed that debtor servitude could not be eradicated because the victims "willingly submit to it and make no effort to avail themselves of the provisions of laws which are passed for the exclusive benefit of persons in their condition."[77] Republican senator James R. Doolittle of Wisconsin spoke of both Hispanic peons and captive Indians when explaining that, "not knowing their rights, not being in a position to go into court to assert their rights, or not having a desire to do so, they were generally remaining in the families of their masters."[78] What these commentators fallaciously assumed, however, was that peons knew the laws and that they possessed the monetary assets to try the case in court—which many lacked, having already spent so many years in financial and social degradation.[79]

Not until the eve of the Civil War would servants begin to achieve some semblance of legal empowerment through America's judicial infrastructures. New Mexico's supreme court heard two cases in 1857 that pertained to peonage, both trials representing the first of their kind in not only the territory, but also the entire United States. One trial, *Marcellina Bustamento v. Juana Analla*, pertained to illegitimate children conceived between masters and servants.[80] The second and more prominent hearing provided the first legal interpretation of peonage. Chief Justice Kirby Benedict wrote the opinion in that case, *Mariana Jaremillo v. Jose de la Cruz Romero*, and in so doing he established important legal precedents on debt bondage that would resonate into the twentieth century and inform rulings in the Jim Crow South as well as by the U.S. Supreme Court.

Born in Connecticut in 1811, Benedict attended law school in Tennessee, where he attained fluency in French and Spanish. He went on to practice law in Illinois, where he met and befriended a young Abraham Lincoln in 1832. As lawyers, Benedict and Lincoln rode circuit together in the state's Eighth Judicial District, visiting various county seats to attend sessions of court. In 1850, a newspaper editorialist condescendingly wrote of Benedict that he "has never been a deep thinker and, in his arguments, he depends almost entirely upon the resources of a rich and powerful imagination."[81] Yet his ruling in 1857 relative to peonage contradicted that assertion, as he diligently researched preexisting Spanish and Mexican laws before rendering a decision. Although not an ardent abolitionist, Benedict did entertain a pro-North, free labor ideology in the years leading up to the Civil War, which he incorporated into his ruling on the case. His longtime personal and professional association with Lincoln also influenced his viewpoints on the issue of human bondage.[82] Several of his decisions while serving on the territorial supreme court were sympathetic to Indian and Hispanic rights,

Figure 10. Kirby Benedict, chief justice of the New Mexico Territorial Supreme Court, who ruled in favor of a young peon girl in a pivotal 1857 hearing. Courtesy Museum of New Mexico, negative #091330.

with *Jaremillo v. Romero* being a prime example. In 1865, Benedict proudly proclaimed that he had ruled in favor of involuntary servants on multiple occasions, specifically citing two proceedings (one in 1855, the other in 1862) involving writs of habeas corpus and explaining his rationale in liberating the slaves in both instances.[83]

The territorial high court, vis-à-vis Benedict, highlighted several of the most controversial issues surrounding peonage, including the applicability of former Spanish and Mexican laws and the legality of subjecting a minor to debt bondage. *Jaremillo v. Romero* arose from relatively simple circumstances that were not at all uncommon in antebellum New Mexico but that rarely ascended to the forefront of public discourse. Benedict began by noting the uniqueness of the situation, understanding that the relationship between masters and servants, as commonly found in the Southwest, had never been examined within the context of American jurisprudence. He foreshadowed the ultimate ruling by drawing a direct parallel between New Mexican peonage and Southern slavery, noting that debt bondage operated upon "similar relations between masters and servants as are found to be established between the master and his slave in different states of the Union."[84]

The plaintiff in the case, Jose de la Cruz Romero, filed suit against his former peon, Mariana Jaremillo, claiming that she owed him $51.75 at the time she "abandoned the work of service to her master" or, in other words, ran away. The initial case appeared before the local justice of the peace in Bernalillo County, with judgment rendered in favor of Romero. Jaremillo had failed to appear in court, at which time the presiding authority sentenced her to twenty-six months of additional servitude in recompense for the unpaid loan plus interest. The case subsequently went to district court, where a judge added court costs to the girl's already mounting debt. If she defaulted, Jaremillo could "be held to serve her said master" until the obligations were repaid in full, with interest continuing to accrue.[85] This final judgment reached the territorial supreme court on appeal in January 1857, eight years after the justice of the peace heard the initial complaint in 1849.[86] The appeal hinged on a technicality—the failure to adhere to due process on the part of the justice of the peace who first heard the case. Jaremillo's counsel attributed her absence at the initial hearing to her not having been notified of the proceedings, thereby rendering nugatory the judgment against her. In the court's decision to entertain the appeal, Benedict emphasized the "unscrupulous disregard which too often prevails . . .

as to the legal rights of the unfortunate, the peon and the feeble, when contesting with the influential and more wealthy."[87]

In the preliminary 1849 hearing, two witnesses testified for the creditor. The first, Francisco Ortíz y Delgado (prefect of Santa Fe County), stated that Romero approached him to help reclaim a servant girl whose father, Jose Jaremillo, had taken her back home. Herein arose one of the primary points of contention, the legitimacy of Mariana—a minor at the time—to serve as a peon in recompense for her father's debt. The second witness was Ambrosio Armijo, justice of the peace in Bernalillo County, before whom Romero had first appeared requesting assistance in the apprehension of his peon. The court reviewed the two witness statements but questioned their validity and scoured previous legal definitions of debt bondage, tracing the documentary record as far back as Spanish colonial times in search of guiding precedent.[88]

When analyzing preexisting laws, the court found that "vassals and vassalage had ceased to exist under the Spanish monarchy," and in subsequent years Mexico's authorities had declined to reinstitute slavery. After a careful examination, the justices failed to locate any Spanish or Mexican provisions relating specifically to peons, although the law books contained numerous measures "clearly marking out the legal rights and duties of masters and servants."[89] In this, Benedict and his colleagues made an important observation about colonial statutes and their validity once New Mexico became a part of the United States. During the Mexican national era, that country's lawmakers had not viewed slavery as being synonymous with debt bondage and frequently distinguished between the two by citing servitude as a voluntary agreement between two parties for the satisfaction of a debt. This explanation, however, neglected to address the widespread system of Indian slavery, which Mexican legislators disregarded in their decrees. Lawmakers almost invariably represented the propertied class of citizens, and some even held servants themselves. Many times, they intentionally omitted debt bondpeople and captive Indians from master-servant laws, as it would have counteracted their own interests to include any such regulatory provisions.

The court proceeded to examine the legislative acts of New Mexico following its inception into the Union. The legislature had approved its first law relative to masters and servants in 1851. The code regulated labor contracts between two or more individuals, mandating that the terms of any agreement between creditor and debtor be enforced by civil officials and stressing that such arrangements stemmed from the "free and voluntary will" of the parties involved. The decree contained numerous provisions governing debt bondage. One directive declared that parents could not contract the services of their children to others in order to satisfy a debt, while another stipulation allowed a master to enlist the aid of authorities in pursuing runaway servants.[90] These final two regulations pertained directly to the case at hand. The defendant had run away, thus willfully abandoning her debt and her bondage and entitling Romero to file suit for recompense. Furthermore, Jaremillo was a minor who had been contracted to work in fulfillment of her father's debt.

The case ultimately hinged upon whether or not the girl's bondage had been legally executed by the creditor, this being a predetermining factor in the legitimacy of Romero's claim for compensation. If Jaremillo had been held illegally in servitude, then the plaintiff would lose his case. In the final judgment, both witness testimonies from the 1849 trial were reviewed and summarily dismissed as inadequate evidence for the legitimacy of Romero's claim. Benedict called attention to the failure of the justice of the peace to notify Jaremillo of the proceedings and therefore concluded that she had been denied her right to due process of law. In further reference to the prefect's dereliction of duty, the court pointed out that a victory for Romero would set a dangerous precedent, one that would allow "whosoever within the territory [to] be made a debtor and sent into servitude, should an unscrupulous man and an ignorant and faithless prefect or probate judge devise mischief together."[91] The judiciary also ruled that Jaremillo, as a minor, "was no party to the transaction" in which the debt had been established between her father and Romero. The court emphasized that the initial debt belonged to her father alone, reiterating that "a child cannot be held bound, without his [or her] own consent, to serve a third person in payment of his father's debt beyond his minority."[92] This outcome countermanded preconceived customs of debt bondage that allowed, and often even encouraged, the pawnship and servitude of younger family members —especially women and girls—who might be more readily coerced into sexual liaisons with their masters and creditors.[93]

By issuing broad statements about the nature of peonage and the discreet cooperation of territorial officials and servantholders in upholding the practice, Benedict engaged in a certain amount of *obiter dictum*, going beyond the necessary explanation of legal precedent to sustain the court's decision and offering sweeping allegations with profound judicial ramifications. In so doing, Benedict mirrored the actions of Chief Justice Roger B.

Taney in the infamous Dred Scott decision of that same year, but in an antithetical way. Whereas Taney's court came down strongly on the side of proslavery interests by opining broadly on the national slavery issue and the meaning of citizenship, Benedict's court established itself as the face of antislavery judicial activism in territorial New Mexico when it spoke of corruption and collusion among peonholders and law officers. Benedict, in a sense, was New Mexico's version of Taney, but from the opposite ideological perspective.[94]

The territorial supreme court's decision in *Marcellina Bustamento v. Juana Analla* accorded with Benedict's ruling on the Jaremillo case, offering further protection for minors and attacking the hereditary nature of peonage. In that trial, Judge C. J. Deavenport ruled that Catalina Bustamento, a child born illegitimately to her master (Carpio Bustamento) and his servant (Juana Analla), could not be held as a peon merely because of the servile status of her mother. His legal spouse, Marcellina Bustamento, claimed that the girl belonged to her as a servant and that she had raised her at the behest of Analla.[95] Deavenport ruled that the biological mother, despite her marginalized status as a peon, retained legal guardianship over her child and that neither the father nor the surrogate mother could claim ownership of the girl as a servant. As the blood father, Bustamento could "maintain and educate" the child in a patriarchal capacity, but he could not do so under the guise of servitude or peonage. The defense countered that the girl had not been asked whether or not she wanted to remain under the charge of Carpio and Marcellina Bustamento, contending that the child's wishes should supersede all other concerns. Recognizing the lopsided power dynamic between authoritative master and subservient child, Deavenport rejected the notion that she could testify as to her own desires, stating that her youth and dependency precluded her as a reliable witness. The ruling granted protection to children conceived through master-servant relationships and prohibited their servitude through ascribed or inherited dependency.[96]

Deavenport had protected the bond between biological mother and child, and in so doing he rendered a stunning blow to a tradition of hereditary servitude and fictive kinship that had proliferated in New Mexico for generations. Because it undermined the transmissible nature of debt peonage, the decision served as a form of gradual emancipation, inasmuch as it prohibited one of the causal factors of dependency and servitude— responsibility for a parent or family member's debt—that led to youngsters becoming peons themselves. Like the congressional abolition of the transatlantic slave trade that became effective in 1808, which U.S. politicians believed would occasion the slow multigenerational decline of chattel slavery in the South, Deavenport's ruling on hereditary dependent status provided a legal framework through which peonage might one day be entirely eliminated from existence.

In rendering these two decisions, the court maintained accordance with preexisting Mexican statutes, one of which held that minors under fourteen years of age could not enter into contracts because of juvenile incapacity.[97] The rulings also reflected a provision in the territory's 1851 master-servant law dictating that parents could not use the labor of their children for the repayment of debt, nor could a son or daughter be held responsible for the unpaid obligations of a deceased mother or father.[98] The master-servant act made inheritable enslavement illegal, but officials seldom enforced that provision of the law until after the 1857 proceedings. Because Jaremillo was underage when coerced into bondage, her contractual obligation to Romero became nugatory based on her legal incapacity to be a party to such an agreement. Similarly, because of Catalina Bustamento's status as a minor, the simple fact that she was born to a peon mother did not automatically condemn her to a life of servility. Prior to the late 1850s, debt peonage worked in such a way that a peon's children often became servile dependents within the same household, and when their parent died, they usually inherited the debt and servitude obligations of their mother or father. Because New Mexico's hierarchical social system left so little room for upward social or economic mobility, the child of a peon was almost invariably born into poverty and, by extension, a state of servitude. In a roundabout way, debt peonage resembled chattel slavery in regards to inheritable status, although in the legal realm the specific conditions allowing for this remained much hazier for peons than for black slaves in the South.

In summarizing the judgment in the Jaremillo case, the court wrote the most concise legal definition of debt bondage in New Mexico up to that time. The justices explicitly noted that the word "peon" had been conveniently avoided in all previous territorial proceedings, which had invariably substituted the less suggestive term "servant" instead. In so doing, public officials avoided the negative connotations associated with certain terminology, acting selfishly to preserve an institution from which they derived economic benefits and social prestige. "Personal interests to a wide extent have been and still continue interwoven with this system," the court acknowledged. "It is seen to be carefully regulated by the legislature."[99] The ruling defined peons as "a class of servants in New Mexico, bound to personal service for the payment of debts due their masters," noting that no existing law specifically referred to this dynamic of servitude and concluding that "the term 'peon' is now used as synonymous with 'servant.' "[100] Under the auspices of the American judicial system, New Mexico's institution of debt bondage finally received a strict legal definition in 1857. Yet this did little to actively regulate or prohibit the practice, nor did it address the altogether separate issue of Indian slavery. It did, however, represent a rare victory for the territory's destitute lower class and provided a basis for future legislative proceedings, which would become more commonplace with the onset of the Civil War, implementation of emancipatory federal laws, and enforcement of Reconstruction policies.

These two cases provided clear definitions of an ambiguous labor regime, highlighting the continuity of debt bondage across time and space while illuminating the most controversial issues surrounding it. In the years that followed, local and even federal officials referred to Benedict's decision when describing peonage, especially those seeking to abolish the practice altogether.[101] The territorial supreme court remained consistent in rulings relative to the subject; ten years after the Jaremillo proceedings, the judiciary found once again in favor of a peon, Tomás Heredia of Doña Ana. Declaring that the 1851 master-servant act "is involuntary servitude in the meaning and intent of the Constitution and the laws of Congress, and [is] therefore prohibited," the territory's highest court struck down any notion that a person could be held in bondage and likened it to the type of false imprisonment that a writ of habeas corpus protects against.[102]

The cases that arose in New Mexico involving peonage, while relatively few in number, marked the development of a more republicanized legal culture that emerged during the early period of American sovereignty, one that became increasingly available to indebted servants as time wore on and free labor ideology gained a stronger foothold in the national consciousness. Like freedmen in the post–Civil War South, who asserted political agency in part through strategic use of local laws and customs, aggrieved peons in the Southwest followed legal mechanisms in pursuit of relief from a servile condition. In so doing, they not only contributed to the legislative processes that eventually propagated their freedom, but also made their cause more broadly known and placed themselves in a position to claim the civil and political rights incumbent upon all Americans following ratification of the Civil War amendments.[103] The enduring importance of Benedict's 1857 ruling can be gleaned from the fact that the first two federal cases involving debt peonage—one in a Georgia district court in 1899 and another in the U.S. Supreme Court in 1905—both cited *Jaremillo v. Romero* in rendering their decisions, specifically referencing New Mexico as the point of origin for peonage in the United States.[104] More than forty years after the fact, territorial rulings on debt bondage resonated in the legal realm and continued to serve as a point of departure for judges when hearing litigation relative to peonage. New Mexico courts had established important standards on debt bondage and involuntary servitude that would inform legal philosophy and free labor ideology in the United States for many years to come.

In the years immediately following the Mexican-American War, senators and representatives attempted to define the forms of involuntary servitude existing throughout the Southwest, invoking a wide array of strategic arguments in support of their respective causes. Slavery in the territories had become a central issue in national politics between 1848 and 1850, thrusting New Mexico into the center of a renewed sectionalist debate that had arisen periodically in Congress since 1820. These deliberations over peonage and captivity would have far-reaching implications for American politics and law in the decades that followed. The very same year that Judges Benedict and Deavenport formulated legal doctrine that seemed to signal an ideological shift toward servant emancipation, however, the territorial legislature took a pronounced step in the opposite direction by passing the first of two antiblack, proslavery codes that placed New Mexico within the rhetorical and political orbit of Southern interests.

Chapter 4

Slave Codes and Sectional Favor

An 1841 West Point graduate twice brevetted for gallantry during the Mexican-American War, Major William Brooks of the Third Infantry received an assignment to serve as commanding officer at Fort Defiance in November 1857. When transferring to his new post in the heart of the Navajo homeland, he brought his personal servant, an African American man about twenty years of age named Jim.[1] On July 12, 1858, Jim stepped outside one of the buildings at Fort Defiance, situated at the mouth of Canyon Bonito a few miles northwest of today's Navajo capital of Window Rock, Arizona. Earlier that day, an Indian arrived at the post and lingered for several hours, soliciting trades among the soldiers and awaiting "the opportunity that finally presented itself." As Jim walked toward the laundress's quarters, Brooks reported that the Navajo man "saw my servant boy, Jim (a slave), coming towards him" and went into premeditated action. As Jim turned away, the Navajo drew a steel-tipped arrow from his quiver and fired it directly into the boy's back, puncturing both of his lungs. "The Indian immediately put his whip to his horse and left over the hill," Brooks wrote, noting the culprit to be a stranger whom nobody at the post could positively identify.[2] The event proved to be Jim's deliverance from bondage, although his death would be a slow and painful one. "The boy, strange to say, never uttered a word or exclamation," his master recalled, "but attempted to pull the arrow out, in doing which he broke it off near the head." The post surgeon, Dr. James Cooper McKee, was unable to extract the arrowhead from Jim's lungs and he died four days later.[3]

From the beginning, Major Brooks seemed less concerned about the death of Jim than about his own pecuniary loss. The department commander reassured the major that, if the murderer was not surrendered, "it will be considered cause for war."[4] The day after Jim's death, an indignant

Brooks sent for Zarcillos Largos, a prominent Navajo headman, and demanded that he turn over the killer and remunerate him for the monetary value of the slave. He threatened to lead a prolonged military campaign against the Navajos, intimating to the chief "the consequences of a war to his people and that it would certainly be made on them did they not give up the murderer."[5] The fallout of this event involved a long-lasting state of hostility between the two groups and ultimately led to the death or captivity of many persons on each respective side. In his annual report, James L. Collins, New Mexico's superintendent of Indian affairs, criticized Brooks for circumventing the civil authorities and appealing directly to the military chain of command for authorization to use force against the Indians. Collins accurately predicted that, in so doing, Brooks had ensured that no peaceful outcome would be reached.[6] Years later, in a letter to Senator Charles Sumner, New Mexicans specifically blamed this incident for inciting "a war of the most bloody nature with the Navajo Indians."[7]

Not surprisingly, the Navajos failed to deliver the murderer; it was wishful thinking on the part of Major Brooks to believe that they would turn over one of their own tribesmen for what promised to be a death sentence. The Navajos' agent played devil's advocate by reasoning that recent events in the Rio Grande settlements, including the "brutal and unprovoked butchery of a defenseless female of the tribe," had driven them to the warpath. He further insinuated that, until the murderer of the captive woman at Albuquerque could be brought to justice, the army should not expect the Indians to turn over Jim's killer.[8] A group of Navajos did, however, come to Fort Defiance some time later with a corpse, which they claimed to be that of the slave's murderer. An autopsy performed at the post revealed that the body belonged to a teenage Mexican boy, almost certainly a captive and not the actual culprit.[9] Through this act, the Navajos sought to bring closure to the issue in what one scholar has termed "blood compensation," but they instead angered the military and Indian departments because of the attempted deceit.[10] Tribal leaders believed that they had fulfilled their obligation to Brooks by killing one of their own slaves in return. U.S. officials, however, did not view the situation in a similar light, exemplifying the differences in cultural expectations and the resulting misunderstandings that arose between the two groups.[11]

Frustrated by the futility of his efforts, and in a further attempt to receive compensation for the loss of Jim, Brooks implored a superior officer, Colonel Dixon S. Miles, to demand payment from the Indians. Miles

Figure 11. Major William Brooks, commanding officer at Fort Defiance and owner of the murdered African American slave Jim. Courtesy United States Military Academy Library.

lacked the authority to pursue such action, recommending instead that Brooks submit a claim for a herd of goats that soldiers recently confiscated from the Navajos.[12] The agent at Fort Defiance, Samuel Yost, wrote to the superintendent of Indian affairs on Brooks's behalf, suggesting that "the boy should be paid for as the destroyed property" and inquiring as to the expediency of using the Navajos' annuity presents to remunerate the officer.[13]

Like many army leaders, Brooks received an annual stipend from the War Department as an "allowance for servants." In 1858 he earned a base salary of $651, along with an additional $226 to cover the expense of a personal servant.[14] Because he utilized the services of an African American slave, Brooks did not spend any of that money on wages. The officer also used surplus government supplies at the fort to feed and clothe Jim, meaning that he pocketed most, if not all, of his yearly payment for servants. Brooks had little reason to request compensation from the government, because he had already been receiving a substantial allowance from the army that far exceeded his valuation of Jim.

These events at Fort Defiance occurred just after the adoption of New Mexico's first slave laws in 1857 and just prior to its implementation of a second and more pervasive slave code in 1859. The murder of Jim therefore contributed to the antiblack, proslavery rhetoric that induced the approval of those measures in the territorial legislature. The antebellum regulation of African Americans—both free and enslaved—has commonly been attributed to the eastern states. Legislators, especially those in the South, frequently promulgated statutory regulations that governed everything from miscegenation to daily mobility, effectively stripping free blacks of most rights. Scholars have largely overlooked the fact that popular sovereignty in the West induced territorial lawmakers to consider similar legislation, often as a symbolic political declaration. This held especially true in New Mexico, where local officials approved numerous measures throughout the 1850s that closely resembled slave laws in the so-called border states as well as some upper Midwest states. By passing two separate slave codes in the years leading up to the Civil War, New Mexicans again thrust themselves into the center of tense debates over slavery and became a pawn for American politicians in that larger ideological and political conflict.

Scholars of slavery have taken their cue from antebellum politicians in misinterpreting the nature of preexisting slave systems in the western territories. Just as congressmen in the 1850s attempted to construe their platforms for sectional debate upon the existence or nonexistence of slavery in the Southwest based solely upon notions of African American servitude, so too have historians perpetuated this misconception. A leading scholar once observed that New Mexico "perversely became the only jurisdiction in American history to enact a slave code for a slaveless society," but this statement presents multiple inaccuracies.[15] First and foremost, New Mexico was far from being slaveless, with thousands of Indian captives and Hispanic debt peons detained in systems of coerced servitude that effectively stripped them of fundamental liberties. Second, the territory did in fact contain a number of black slaves prior to the Civil War. New Mexico's slave code pertained specifically to African Americans and refrained from mentioning either Indian slavery or debt peonage, the two systems of involuntary servitude that flourished in the Southwest.

While historians have acknowledged anti-Hispanic and anti-Catholic sentiment as leading factors in New Mexico's stifled statehood ambitions during the years between the Mexican-American War and the Reconstruction era, the passage of strict slave codes became a tertiary factor in the territory's struggle to gain political recognition among the American public. With rampant strife plaguing discussions about slavery during the two decades following the war with Mexico, the existence of territorial codes became a liability for those seeking some measure of political equality at the national level. Exhibiting revulsion for coercive labor and surprised by the implementation of laws mirroring those already in place throughout the South, many Northerners hesitated to acknowledge New Mexico's residents as their equals, and the territorial legislature's adoption of such measures influenced Americans' moral and ethnic distaste for the newly acquired territory.

As Jim's case demonstrates, peonage and captivity did not exist in total isolation from chattel slavery, as some black bondsmen did reside in New Mexico following the U.S. occupation in 1846. A handful of Anglo-Americans, including several military officers, brought their own servants with them to the territory in the 1850s, introducing a visible black slave population. The sudden presence of African Americans in the Southwest, coupled with intensifying sectional discord throughout the country, led to the adoption of strict slave codes as a symbolic indication of the territory's relationship to the South and to slavery, and this would significantly impact New Mexico's association with the federal government in the years to come. The 1850 U.S. census—the first one conducted in New Mexico under

American sovereignty—reported just twenty-two black persons in the territory; of those, the recordkeepers notated less than half as enslaved. That same year, Utah enumerated fifty African Americans, twenty-four of whom were freemen and twenty-six enslaved, and California, despite representing itself as a free-state, was home to at least 381 black slaves who worked the region's gold mines.[16] Describing New Mexico's racial breakdown to Congress in 1860, district judge John S. Watts estimated there to be "fifty [black] slaves only, mostly servants of army and federal officers."[17] Governor Abraham Rencher similarly pointed out that New Mexico contained just a couple dozen black slaves, all of whom belonged to appointed public officials or military officers who frequently transferred between posts, insinuating that their residency in the territory was just temporary.[18] Under pressure from abolitionist interests in Congress, Representative Miguel A. Otero insisted that the few men who took chattel slaves to New Mexico did so "simply for domestic service, and with no intent of propagating there the institution of slavery."[19]

The first identifiable black slaves to arrive in New Mexico came in 1851 and belonged to Major James H. Carleton of the First U.S. Regiment of Dragoons. He subsequently sold Hannah (twenty-three years old) and Benjamin (twenty-one years old) to Governor William Carr Lane, formerly of Missouri.[20] This pattern of military complicity in the westward spread of chattel slavery originated during the Mexican-American War, and Southerners sometimes based their arguments in support of slavery in the West upon the fact that invading U.S. forces had slaves with them during the war. As one proponent of slavery stressed, "Even General [Zachary] Taylor was attended by slaves whose services he exacted during the whole campaign."[21] Once the conquest of New Mexico had been completed and the Mexican Cession lands appended to the federal domain, Southern slaveholders who fought in the war believed that their right to property in slaves should be protected if they migrated to the new territory.[22]

Throughout the antebellum years, military officers stationed in New Mexico perpetuated involuntary servitude, either by holding slaves themselves or by turning a blind eye to others who held black slaves, Indian captives, or Hispanic peons. The War Department itself unwittingly encouraged its staff to employ servants by issuing annual stipends for that purpose. While these allowances were originally intended to pay, feed, and clothe wage laborers—cooks, maids, or laundresses—officers in New Mexico sometimes employed peons and black slaves instead and pocketed the federal subsidy. The availability of involuntary laborers doubtless contributed to instances of undetected fraud among army personnel, whose allowances amounted to between one-quarter and one-third of their annual salary. In 1851, each officer in the First Dragoons received a servant grant between $94 and $398; several years later, on the eve of the Civil War, such stipends remained mostly unchanged, ranging from $144 to $288 per annum.[23]

Shortly after the Mexican-American War, accusations began to surface that New Mexico's military department commander, Colonel John Munroe, acted with complicity in attempts to "smuggle slavery into the territory against the will of the people." James Cooper, a Pennsylvania senator, cited numerous communications between Munroe and a Texan commissioner, Robert S. Neighbors, in which the former pledged his full support to the latter if Texas attempted to annex New Mexico. Northerners condemned Munroe's open cooperation with officials from a slave state as indicative of his affability toward the Southern cause and feared that, as military commander, he might lend his authority to the sanctioning of chattel slavery in New Mexico. "It is on the side of Texas, and through her exertions and influence, that slavery will obtain a foothold in these Territories, if it obtain such foothold at all," Cooper feared.[24] While Munroe did not openly advocate for the extension of slavery in either practice or ideology, he also did nothing to free the territory's black slaves that his own personnel held in bondage, nor did he provide any assistance to peons or captives.

Following passage of the Compromise of 1850, both Utah and New Mexico legislated on slavery based on the premise of popular sovereignty, and in so doing they brought the first hint of clarity to a vexing topic. With the slave issue demanding attention, lawmakers in both territories enacted measures that essentially upheld the right of citizens to hold slaves and regulated the activities of all black persons.[25] Although the two sets of laws differed substantially in their particulars—owing in part to disparities in religious views on the part of Utah's Mormons and New Mexico's Catholics—they served, in the most fundamental sense, to legalize slavery in both places. By the time New Mexico became an official U.S. territory in September 1850, it had already been under the dominion of the United States for four years, an interval during which the region was governed by laws that General Kearny and his officers enacted after the 1846 conquest. The Kearny Code, however, had neglected to mention slavery in any form. Its authors, mostly lawyers from Missouri serving as officers in Army of the

West volunteer regiments, purposely omitted slavery from the statutes in order to avoid sparking an incendiary issue. They intended the laws to be only temporary until federal officials decided upon either territorial or statehood status for New Mexico. A subsequent congressional report noted that, since the Kearny Code lacked any guidance on involuntary servitude, Mexico's former laws "recognizing the system of peonage" remained in place and Southerners who traveled to New Mexico with slaves were therefore "protected in their possession and enjoyment of them as property."[26] This situation remained unchanged when Congress approved territorial status for New Mexico on September 9, 1850. Southerners utilized the preexistence of debt peonage and captive servitude as a basis for slavery being extended westward, inferring that the status quo remained intact because the Kearny Code did not address the issue. The widespread presence of peonage and Indian captivity therefore provided impetus for debate, both locally and nationally, on sectional issues.

Throughout the 1850s, New Mexico's territorial legislature approved numerous measures regarding involuntary servitude independent of those enacted at the federal level.[27] In so doing, local lawmakers followed in the footsteps of California politicians who, despite their status in the Union as a free state, considered two laws in the early 1850s that would have prohibited the immigration of "Free Negroes" and regulated the daily activities of all African Americans in the same manner as Southern slave codes.[28] In New Mexico, as in California, the edicts mirrored policies that the Spanish crown had instituted centuries earlier in its New World empire. Even before the first Euro-American settlers arrived on the upper Rio Grande in 1598, Spanish laws already prohibited African miscegenation and instituted stringent regulations on all interracial liaisons. As the sixteenth century progressed, additional mandates limited the mobility of blacks and prohibited them from carrying weapons.[29] While these laws primarily targeted Central American colonies with significant numbers of African slaves, New Mexico's status as a Spanish province meant that the regulations likewise applied to any black persons in that region. These provisions would be repeated, almost verbatim, two and a half centuries later in the territorial slave codes. Early territorial legislative maneuverings thus represented the statutory reintroduction of antiblack racism in New Mexico.

When a council of New Mexicans, comprising mostly native Hispanos, petitioned Congress on October 14, 1848, seeking organization as a territorial government, the memorialists specifically stated that "we do not desire to have domestic slavery within our borders" and requested protection from the introduction of slaves until statehood might be granted.[30] Not surprisingly, the petition sparked an uproar among Southerners who hoped to extend slavery into the Mexican Cession lands. The incident initiated two years of continuous debate over slavery in the territories, followed by ten more years of reverberating pro- and antislavery legislation being enacted in Utah and New Mexico.

In May 1850, shortly before its actual admission as a territory, New Mexico's prostatehood bloc produced a constitution and submitted it to Congress.[31] The delegates charged with presenting the document to federal lawmakers had explicit instructions that, during deliberations over the various clauses, they must insert "a provision which shall secure the compliance with contracts between masters and servants," a direct protection of peonage in an otherwise antislavery manifesto.[32] In California that same year, a statehood convention created a constitution that banned African American slavery while leaving unaddressed alternative systems of coercive labor like peonage, Indian apprenticeship, and Chinese coolieism.[33] New Mexico's territorial secretary later pointed out these hypocritical discrepancies when noting that local legislators "declared in unequivocal terms that the people did not desire domestic slavery in their midst, nor did they welcome the introduction of slaves into New Mexico. And yet these same memorialists recognized a system of domestic servitude called 'peonage' which existed at the time throughout New Mexico."[34]

Many people, in fact, were afraid that the chaos arising from political factionalism might instigate a regional acceptance of racial slavery along with peonage. One Northern senator feared in 1850 that "confusion, disorder, and lawlessness" in the territory would enable the introduction of slavery, stating that "advantage may be taken of this condition of things to entail upon the people an institution totally repugnant to their wishes and feelings."[35] Henry Connelly and James L. Collins, both of whom had lived in the Southwest for many years and knew the sentiments of the residents well, foreshadowed the results of New Mexico's constitutional convention in early 1850 when predicting that "there is not the *remotest* probability that any constitutional sanction would be given by our citizens to the introduction of African slavery among us."[36] Their prophetic notion would ultimately prove correct, if only temporarily.

Although New Mexico's statehood constitution became irrelevant once Congress admitted it as a territory, the document attested to the influence of slave debates in local politics at that time. The first article of the proposed constitution explicitly outlawed slavery and mandated that nobody over the age of twenty-one could be held as a servant.[37] Legislators identified peonage as a form of consensual bondage, originating from sheer necessity among debtors who, owing substantial sums of money, had to choose between servitude or incarceration. In allowing individuals "to be bound by their own consent," the law deliberately did nothing to alter the long-standing tradition of debt bondage.[38] Northern newspaper editors were quick to notice this discrepancy and criticized the document's misleading nature. "It may exclude African slavery," observed one New Yorker, "but we are very much mistaken, if the system of slavery which has existed in the whole of Mexico for a great many years, and known as *peonage*, is not tolerated and provided for by that instrument."[39]

The statehood constitution denied Indians and blacks (free or otherwise) the right to vote but reiterated an antislavery objective, noting that involuntary servitude, "wherever it has existed[,] has proved a curse and a blight to the State upon which it has been afflicted,—a moral, social and political evil."[40] Most residents remained indifferent toward this decree because chattel slavery had not previously concerned them. Major Henry Lane Kendrick, stationed in Santa Fe at the time, quipped rather simplistically that only three topics seemed to interest New Mexicans: "Taxation, which they dislike; slavery, which they hate, and Texas, which they most cordially abhor."[41]

New Mexico's statehood constitution contained unmistakably self-contradicting characteristics. It prohibited chattel slavery, yet it left wholly intact the traditional systems of debt peonage and Indian captivity, neglecting to even mention their existence. This political maneuvering failed to deceive abolitionists. A slew of condemnatory newspaper articles appeared, with one editorialist declaring that New Mexico's statehood constitution "not only allows a continuance of *peon* slavery, but of slavery in any and every form."[42] Some of the more politically attuned territorial citizens alluded to this anomaly as evidence of a political double standard. Charles A. Hoppin, a resident of the Mesilla Valley and a sutler for U.S. troops stationed at the village of Doña Ana, pointed out this contradiction in his private correspondence. The constitution, he believed, sought to ensure the political support of Northern free-soilers while simultaneously appealing to the wishes of local voters by not impinging upon their traditional systems of servitude.[43] It likely owed to this nonchalant protection of peonage that

New Mexicans turned out almost unanimously in favor of the measure: In a popular vote on the 1850 constitution, 6,771 residents approved while only thirty-nine cast their ballots in opposition.[44]

Antislavery interests also used New Mexico's constitution in their arguments against the introduction of chattel slavery into the region. In the North, state legislatures adopted resolutions supporting the exclusion of slavery from the new territory, praising the proposed constitution and mandating that congressional representatives ensure that those regions be exempted from involuntary servitude, except as punishment for convicted criminals.[45] The statehood charter came before Congress in May, four months prior to the acceptance of the Compromise of 1850. Because of the timing, the New Mexico constitution had become a focal point of debate. Representative Truman Smith, a Connecticut Whig, thought that public sentiment opposed slavery and also believed that "the American, whether from the free States or slave States, the Spaniard of the full blood, and the mixed Spaniard and Indian race, are all alike opposed to negro bondage."[46] His colleague Daniel Webster concurred by reiterating that territorial inhabitants should be afforded popular sovereignty and commending New Mexicans for having supposedly come out against slavery.[47]

The 1850 statehood constitution reflected only the views of a small portion of territorial inhabitants. Many of New Mexico's Anglo-American citizens, from both the South and the North, promoted racial discrimination through their words and actions. The first territorial governor, James S. Calhoun of Georgia, spoke passionately on the issue during an address to the legislature on June 2, 1851. "Free Negroes are regarded as nuisances in every state and territory in the Union," he ranted, "and where they are tolerated Society is most depraved."[48] Calhoun, who implored the legislature to pass a code prohibiting blacks from even entering the territory, was himself an anomalous figure. As New Mexico's superintendent of Indian affairs, he openly disavowed regional systems of servitude yet simultaneously embraced laws promoting racial discrimination toward African Americans. Such contradictory viewpoints pervaded the dispositions of New Mexico's elite classes (both Anglo and Hispanic), ultimately resulting in the passage of numerous prejudicial laws at the territorial level. Within just five years of Calhoun's speech, the legislature would live up to his expectations. From 1851 until the early months of the Civil War, proceedings in Santa Fe reflected a pronounced shift away from the antislavery sentiment manifested in the original statehood constitution.

The first indication of this ideological turn came on July 20, 1851, when the territorial legislature passed the "master-servant law" pertaining to debt peonage.[49] The mandate defined the relationship between benefactors and their peons and, in so doing, became a catalyst for future legislative measures. Similar edicts had been approved between 1821 and 1846, while the territory remained under Mexican rule, but this represented the first attempt to legally uphold human bondage after the American occupation. Originally intended to regulate only debt-related servitude, the overall ambiguity of the statute resulted in it being widely abused and provided ample legal mechanisms for subjecting people to involuntary labor.[50] The law, however, only regulated peonage in its traditional form and entirely omitted Indian slaves and black persons from its purview.

Two years later, policymakers implemented a measure granting local authorities the power to place servants in public auctions if their master no longer wished to employ and sustain them.[51] Coupled with the 1851 master-servant law, this provided the impetus for additional legislative action that imposed strict regulations on Hispanic peons, Indian captives, and African Americans. For the remainder of the decade, New Mexico's legal directives coincided with the stance of dominant Southern Democrats in Washington, as territorial leaders sought to preserve their interests in captives and peons while appealing to federal legislators on broader sectional issues.

During the 1856 legislative session, New Mexico lawmakers passed "An Act Concerning Free Negroes" that delineated stringent guidelines for any colored person venturing into the territory. Democratic governor David Meriwether, a native of Kentucky, approved the measure on January 29, 1857—less than two months prior to the U.S. Supreme Court's ruling in the Dred Scott case, which affirmed the direction in which the territorial legislature was heading with such enactments.[52] Although it contained only seven short sections, the law confirmed the discriminatory intentions of the legislators. Section 1 mandated that "no free negro nor mulatto of the African race" could remain in the territory for a period of more than thirty days. If such persons attempted to establish permanent residency, they would be subject to a fine of $100 and hard labor for up to two years.[53] This provision clearly contradicted the antislavery sentiment outlined in the null 1850 statehood constitution. The $100 fine also exceeded the repayment capability of such persons and essentially meant that they would be subverted to servitude in fulfillment of the debt, thus ensuring a lifetime of bondage under the guise of criminally imposed peonage.

Even in New Mexico, far removed from the eastern states, antiblack racism proliferated among members of the lawmaking class. Anglo-Americans from the United States as well as New Mexican landholders realized that most residents did not entertain strong ethnocentric sentiments, in part because of their own mixed-blood heritage. The territorial legislature therefore took preemptive action, hoping to minimize the likelihood of miscegenation between the Hispanic population and any newly arrived African Americans by implementing strict punishments for such activity. According to one observer, whose commentary expressed the tendency of outsiders to project overly inclusive stereotypes on the local population, "among the lower classes the Mexicans know no distinction of color, and the women as soon intermarry and cohabit, with a negro as one of their own race." If indeed black slavery did become a permanent fixture in the region, some territorial residents feared that intermarriage would cause "the negro blood [to] be generally diffused through the population."[54]

The 1857 law also contained stipulations that prohibited African Americans from interacting with local inhabitants. Black persons caught cohabiting with white (or Hispanic) women would face up to three years in prison, and any female accomplice to such interaction would likewise be subject to incarceration. Furthermore, any minister who sanctified a biracial liaison would be obliged to pay a hefty fine. Thus, the legislature enacted a veritable no-tolerance policy for interracial relations. In this the lawmakers actually promulgated nothing new; antimiscegenation laws were common throughout the United States and served to reinforce popular notions of a racial hierarchy in which both Americans and Hispanics viewed themselves as superior to blacks.[55] The lawmakers' actions reflected a continuing consciousness of the pervasive desire to retain blood purity among the region's inhabitants by socially denigrating African Americans and imposing strict penalties for those caught in violation of the law.

The act included numerous additional provisions intended to ensure compliance. If he chose to emancipate a slave, a master was obligated to escort the liberated party to the territorial border before setting him or her free. Even black persons merely passing through New Mexico were required to post a bond in the amount of $100 to ensure good behavior.[56] The law regulated the movements and actions of all black persons in New Mexico, but it did nothing to either promote or denounce involuntary servitude in an ideological sense. While peonage and Indian captivity remained in place throughout the territory, black slavery was virtually nonexistent due to its economic impracticality in the region. But Nuevomexicanos could not ignore the issue forever; sectional debates continued to plague Congress, and territorial lawmakers would soon be forced to declare a united stance either for or against slavery—if not in fact, then at least in principle.

Such independent and misleading action on the part of a territory was not without precedent, having already occurred in more easterly regions where the population remained divided over the slavery issue. The creation of Indiana Territory (1803) and Illinois Territory (1809) enabled geographically isolated residents there to adopt local statutes that ignored or contradicted pro- and antislavery federal mandates without much backlash. People in the southerly portions of those two new territories skirted the provision of the Northwest Ordinance that prohibited involuntary servitude by using a variety of tactics, including indentured servitude as a modified form of human bondage. In Illinois, legislators passed laws that upheld indentured servitude but also retained black slave codes in order to give an appearance of compliance with the territorial antislavery provision.[57] In the antebellum era, New Mexicans did much the same when they passed the 1851 master-servant act—which legally affirmed debt peonage in practice—as well as the 1857 and 1859 slave codes, both of which regulated black people and chattel slavery.

Two years after the 1857 sanctions became law, territorial policymakers took an even larger stride toward promoting an antiblack, pro-Southern agenda. On January 22, 1859, Representative Pedro Valdez of Taos County introduced a bill entitled "An Act to Provide for the Protection of Property in Slaves in This Territory."[58] The legislation passed on January 26 by a vote of 23 to 1 and promptly received approval from the thirteen-member council, after which Democratic governor Abraham Rencher signed it into law on February 3.[59] The decree remained in effect until December 10, 1861, and, during almost three years of enforcement, incited repeated controversy at the congressional level.[60] New Mexico's provisions presupposed by a full year the controversial Senate Resolutions that Jefferson Davis proposed on February 2, 1860. Suggesting the adoption of six proslavery decrees, the future Confederate president demanded that territories be forbidden from legislating on slavery until applying for statehood, at which time residents could make that determination on their own under the premise of popular sovereignty. In the interim territorial period, Davis wanted Congress to impose a universal slave code to regulate such areas in the absence of strong local leadership.[61]

Often referred to simply as the "Slave Code," one abolitionist dubbed it "the most cruel, mean and barbarous slave-code that disgraces any State or Colony in the Western hemisphere."[62] New Mexico's new law proved to be a political liability and placed the infant territory at the forefront of public controversy on the eve of the Civil War. The act contained thirty sections and represented the most all-encompassing regulatory device that the territory had yet employed relative to the subject. It no doubt made Jefferson Davis proud and may well have influenced his Senate Resolutions on the matter a year later. With chattel slavery virtually nonexistent in New Mexico, though, the Slave Code was primarily a symbolic gesture. As a testament to the superfluous nature of such legislation, a 1790 Spanish census recorded only eight black (or mulatto) slaves in the province and seventy years later things remained little changed, with the 1860 U.S. census enumerating a mere sixty-four African Americans in the entire territory.[63] To secure support among leading citizens, the code's designers promised that it would have no impact on preexisting institutions of Indian slavery and debt peonage.[64]

The law strictly forbade assistance to runaway slaves, requiring that anybody convicted of aiding and abetting escaped servants be sentenced to at least four years in prison. The most controversial aspect of the Slave Code, however, involved a stipulation that "totally prohibited" the emancipation of any slaves within territorial boundaries.[65] The law itself explicitly stated that it did not apply to peons, who constituted the vast majority of servants in the territory. In effect, it protected debt bondage as an economic and social institution while condemning free black persons based solely on race and political ideology. Antebellum legislatures, composed mostly of New Mexico's elite landholding class, held personal interests in peonage, not chattel slavery. According to a witness in Santa Fe, the family of the legislator J. Francisco Chaves had "beyond the shadow of a doubt the most numerous lot of Mexican peons and Indian slaves of any one family in New Mexico," and his friends and business partners were "the largest holders of this species of property in the country and exert an almost insurmountable influence in behalf of its perpetuation."[66] The composition of the territory's legislative bodies ranged from 55 percent to 95 percent Hispanic in the 1850s; few Anglo-Americans were elected to office there, and outsiders therefore exerted their influence on New Mexican lawmakers in other ways.[67] In order to achieve passage of the Slave Code in a predominantly Hispanic legislature that remained mostly indifferent toward chattel slavery, territorial secretary Alexander M. Jackson had to assure lawmakers that the mandate "would protect their own system of peonage."[68]

The law mirrored legislation that one might have expected to encounter in slaveholding states, and indeed many of the provisions were modeled on similar codes enacted in the South.[69] This caused anxiety among Northern abolitionists and free-soilers, who saw the extension of black slavery westward as an expansion of Southern political power. Remarking on the 1860 census and the comparatively diminutive number of black slaves in New Mexico, one New Yorker editorialized, "True, it would have few slaves, but what of that? Our objection is to widening the base of the Slave Power. Delaware has few slaves; but slavery rules and uses her as thoroughly as though she had twenty times as many."[70]

The code represented the chicanery of leading white citizens, who exerted their proslavery influence on Hispanic civic leaders to advance their own political agendas. One Civil War–era observer, W. W. Mills, observed that most locals "knew but little about the questions involved in secession" and slavery.[71] Another editorialist referred to Nuevomexicanos as "ignorant" when explaining that they voted in favor of the law only after being promised that it "would have no real effect on this Territory," a thinly veiled allusion to peonage and captive slavery.[72] The abolitionist Horace Greeley deplored the Slave Code and wrote a lengthy report in his newspaper, the *New-York Daily Tribune*, in which he stirred up impassioned readers by claiming that "zealous slavery propagandists fill all the important federal offices" in New Mexico. The recent enactment of the Slave Code affirmed these men's fears that the territory had come under the control of proslavery interests.[73]

One individual to whom these men referred was Miguel A. Otero, the territory's delegate to Congress in the years leading up to the Civil War, who manipulated New Mexican legislators into embracing his desired sectional stance. Born in Valencia County on June 21, 1829, Otero studied law in New York and St. Louis before returning to the territory in 1852. He held the distinction of being educated in prestigious American schools, something highly unusual among native New Mexicans of that time. Otero quickly ascended in political prominence and, in 1855, announced his candidacy—as a member of the Democratic Party—for the position of congressional delegate.[74] After being elected, Otero relocated to Washington, D.C., where he courted and later married Mary Josephine Blackwood, a member of an influential proslavery family from Charleston, South

Carolina. Otero's relationship with Blackwood and membership in the Democratic Party exposed him to Southern social circles and helped to shape his ideology on sectional issues.[75] Prior to the Civil War, many people viewed Otero as a man whose sentiments belonged wholeheartedly to the Southern cause, a belief stemming primarily from his advocacy for the Slave Code. Horace Greeley, a nemesis of Otero, lambasted him in a series of 1861 newspaper editorials, calling him a "half-breed Hidalgo" and "an avowed Secessionist" whom he accused of personally authoring New Mexico's Slave Code.[76]

As a congressional delegate and one of the most influential men in the territory, Otero played a significant role in the passage of the Slave Code. In 1861, a Republican representative from Wisconsin accused him of being complicit in the law's approbation, stating that Otero "had something to do with getting up the existing slave code in that Territory, a code which . . . would mantle with blushes the face of Caligula." Otero sprang to his feet and shouted, "I do not own a slave, and have nothing to do with slavery!"[77] Although speaking truthfully in stating that he did not personally possess slaves, he effectively dodged the larger issue of his overall support for the institution in principle. The entire exchange between the two lawmakers emanated from a Washington, D.C. newspaper's recent publication of a letter from Otero praising New Mexico's Slave Code. "I commend the wisdom and applaud the patriotism that prompted the enactment of such a code," he had boasted, "and I denounce as false and malevolent the allegation that said code is one of signal atrocity and inhumanity."[78]

Foreseeing political benefits for his constituents at a time when proslavery Democrats controlled Congress and the White House, Otero vigorously defended New Mexico's slave codes throughout his tenure as territorial representative, but he drew the ire of antislavery colleagues in the process. In private correspondence with the U.S. marshal in New Mexico, Otero admitted that his primary motivation in advocating the Slave Code stemmed from his belief that its passage would be "advantageous to our Territory" and he reiterated that the implementation of a strong slave code would also "direct political attention" toward New Mexico.[79] Two years later, during a heated debate with Pennsylvania representative Thaddeus Stevens on the House floor, Otero once again defended the law and had portions of it read aloud while challenging Stevens on every point he made. Otero's efforts ultimately proved futile and his remarks invoked mirth throughout the chamber, especially when he attempted to recite the law in

Spanish. The shrewd Stevens got the last word in the argument, telling his listeners that "slavery in New Mexico means nothing more than parental admonition." Those in attendance responded with a resounding chorus of laughter, embarrassing the greenhorn representative and bringing closure to the tense oratorical exchange.[80]

While he spoke openly in Congress about his position, Otero also advanced his stance on slavery in private correspondence with civil officials. He wrote to Territorial Secretary Jackson on December 16, 1858, requesting that he "draw up an act for the protection of property in slaves in New Mexico" and do whatever necessary to ensure that it passed in the legislature. He went on to inform Jackson—a staunch Southern sympathizer who would later fight for the Confederacy during the Civil War—that federal laws, the U.S. Constitution, and even the recent Dred Scott case all "establish property in slaves in the territories" and could therefore be used as supporting doctrine when lobbying for the law. Once it passed, Otero instructed Jackson to distribute copies of the code to newspapers throughout the South in a clear attempt to recruit political support in that section.[81]

A Mississippian by birth and an acquaintance of Jefferson Davis, Jackson was amenable to Otero's views on slavery even before he received the letter in December 1858 asking that he "draw up" the measure. Several months earlier, Jackson had indicated that the territorial legislature would likely pass "some kind of slave code" during its next session. "Otero has let it be known," he wrote, "that if New Mexico expects any favors from Washington, a slave code would be a wise move." He assumed that Governor Rencher and other leading officials favored such legislation, lending credence to abolitionist concerns that New Mexico harbored influential Southern ideologues who sought to incite secessionist fervor.[82] Jackson also urged the appointment of fellow Southerners to leading government positions, adding further weight to implications that both he and Otero privately, if not publicly, espoused proslavery interests.[83] The secretary put to rest any lingering uncertainty about his sympathies when he wrote in February 1861—just months prior to the Confederate invasion of New Mexico—that "the mass of Mexicans . . . are decidedly in favor of the institution of Slavery, and this sentiment has been steadily growing ever since the enactment of our Slave Code."[84]

Writing to Commissioner of Indian Affairs Alfred B. Greenwood in June 1859, another resident of the territory warned of Otero's pro-South inclinations, postulating that his influence in Washington relied upon the

Figure 12. Alexander Jackson, New Mexico's territorial secretary
on the eve of the Civil War and staunch Southern supporter.
Courtesy Alexander M. Jackson Papers, McCain Library
and Archives, University of Southern Mississippi.

adoption of a territorial slave law. The informant claimed that Otero and his political cohorts blackmailed local citizens into supporting the slave policy by threatening that any opposition to the code would prompt the military's withdrawal from New Mexico, rendering territorial residents defenseless against debilitating Indian raids.[85] As the letter revealed, antislavery Northerners residing in the territory at that time feared the worst.

The conspiracy theory regarding Southern agents secretly advancing their cause appeared in numerous communiqués just prior to and during the Civil War. One individual well acquainted with the Southwest, Secretary William Davis, observed in the 1850s that only about five hundred Hispanos in the entire territory favored "the introduction of negro slavery" because they already had "a cheaper system of labor in peonage."[86] In 1861, William Need—a Union soldier stationed in New Mexico and a devoted abolitionist—leveled numerous accusations against local officials in this same regard, claiming that their sole objective had been to invoke secessionist sentiment among the inhabitants.[87] "Four-fifths of the voting population of New Mexico are utterly opposed to the incorporation of the slave code," Need wrote to Secretary of War Simon Cameron. "Yet there it is, by virtue of the slave power exercising its influence through the accredited agents (civil and military) of the Federal Government. The officeholders, the tools of Jeff. Davis and company, put the slave code in the statutes of New Mexico and not the people, but in utter violation of their will and desire."[88] As one pseudonymous writer claimed in a New York newspaper article, "For the last eight years the Federal Government has used every effort to promote Slavery in this territory, and nearly all the officers who have been appointed here have been of the ultra-Southern school."[89] New Mexico's first five presidentially appointed territorial governors did indeed hail from Southern states: James S. Calhoun (Georgia), William Carr Lane (Missouri), David Meriwether (Kentucky), Abraham Rencher (North Carolina), and Henry Connelly (Virginia). But not all of these men supported slavery, and in fact one of them, Connelly, received his appointment from Abraham Lincoln and had worked tirelessly to see the Slave Code repealed. Furthermore, of New Mexico's five military department commanders during the decade preceding the Civil War, three hailed from Southern states, although just two went on to fight for the Confederacy.[90]

Northerners advanced these conspiracy theories during the months leading up to the Civil War and, in so doing, placed tremendous pressure on New Mexican lawmakers. Greeley editorialized in December 1860 that "the most insidious and systematic efforts have been made to plant slavery" in New Mexico and expressed concern with the success of such endeavors. "A slave code of signal atrocity and inhumanity has been put through the Territorial Legislature, and is now in full force," he continued, noting that "everything conspires to make New Mexico . . . a slave state."[91] A week later Greeley wrote that many territorial officials had been sent from the South and received their appointments because of "their known devotion to the slavery propaganda," and he also charged military officers who transported slaves when reassigned to duty at southwestern forts with being especially culpable. "Under Pro-Slavery Federal influences," wrote the renowned editor of the *New-York Daily Tribune*, New Mexico "has been transformed from a Free into a Slave Territory."[92] Otero responded quickly, telling the Ohio senator George Pugh in January 1861 that Greeley's allegations "are groundless and untrue" and stressing that the Slave Code "had its origin within the borders of the territory." Otero insisted that the law had passed without any outside encouragement and therefore, as a strictly localized piece of legislation, had not been "trammeled by sectional prejudices, and not [induced] by fanaticism."[93] When it came to slavery, Northern newspapers proved to be an unrelenting antagonist to New Mexicans generally and to Otero specifically. Greeley wrote no fewer than five editorials in the opening months of 1861 relative to slavery in the Southwest, some of which reappeared in territorial newspapers for local distribution in both English and Spanish.[94] While Greeley's abolitionism garnered strong opposition in southern New Mexico—where Texans exercised considerable political sway and had already initiated a movement to create their own pro-South territory of Arizona—it met with mixed feelings in the upper Rio Grande settlements, where the Hispanic population found itself divided on the issue.[95]

Apprehensive of proslavery conspiracies, Need also accused prominent officials of being actively involved in the Southern plot to seize New Mexico. If one took Need for his word, Governor Connelly had "always been a *Pro-Slavery* man" and had even "owned negroes here" until he supposedly took them back to the South and sold them in the years leading up to the Civil War. "He is now a professed *neutral* Union man," Need wrote, "provided the Union cause is the strongest."[96] The diatribe did not end there. The conspiracy theorist believed that, despite being appointees of President Lincoln, both Connelly and Superintendent of Indian Affairs James L. Collins "were the friends of Mr. Pierce, of Buchanan, and Jeff. Davis," making them nothing more than "slavery propagandists" who favored the Slave

Figure 13. Horace Greeley, abolitionist editor of the *New-York Daily Tribune*, who, in his fiery editorials, drew attention to peonage and captivity. Courtesy National Archives and Records Administration, Washington, D.C.

Code, opposed its repeal, and published secessionist rhetoric in the Santa Fe newspaper.[97] Still bitter about the passage of proslavery legislation, another individual claimed that lawmakers rushed the statute through the process without even hesitating to reflect on the gravity of their actions.[98]

Need's accusations were only partially true. In regard to Collins and the *Santa Fe Weekly Gazette*, he was correct in asserting their advancement of the proslavery Democratic platform. When the Slave Code became law in February 1859, Collins had used his newspaper to rally popular support for the new measure.[99] But upon the subject of Connelly, who served as a territorial governor throughout much of the Civil War, Need's accusations proved somewhat misguided. Having resided in the Southwest for the better part of three decades, Connelly did in fact own a considerable number of servants at one time. Writing of his experiences in New Mexico during the 1840s, a merchant named James Josiah Webb recalled a conversation during which Connelly "was boasting of the improved condition of his servants under his liberal management . . . and he flattered himself that he was treating them with great generosity and kindness, and was doing more to improve the condition of his servants than any of his neighbors." According to Webb, Connelly once had 108 servants at his hacienda south of Albuquerque.[100] By the time Need wrote in 1861, however, Connelly had purportedly freed them all and advocated the Northern cause.[101] As governor, he not only called for the immediate repeal of the Slave Code in his inaugural address, but also spoke against secession and devoted himself to thwarting the Confederate invasion of the territory by raising thousands of volunteers and militiamen. Any accusations that he entertained pro-South sentiments or acted as a conspirator therefore had no factual basis, and his previous status as a landowning servantholder had much more to do with traditional forms of coerced servitude in the region than with any ideological devotion to chattel slavery or secession.

Still ranting about the Slave Code, Greeley complained that New Mexico had been "reckoned an easy prey to the gathering forces of the Rebellion," and he pointed out that the territory "had been mainly under the training of Democratic officials of strong pro-slavery sympathies." These officials—whom he did not name—had not only convinced the legislature to approve an act recognizing slavery, but also implanted the necessary safeguards to prevent its repeal.[102] New Mexico's new code, Greeley believed, constituted "the most atrocious Slave law ever known."[103] He clearly targeted Otero in these statements and also implicated Rencher, who remained a quiet proponent of the South during his governorship. In January 1861, a mere five months before the Confederate invasion of the territory, Greeley excoriated New Mexico's territorial officials as secessionists and demanded that Rencher be removed and replaced "by an able and wise Free-State man."[104] Lieutenant Colonel Benjamin S. Roberts, stationed at Fort Craig, was even more succinct in his indictment of local bureaucrats. Writing to the assistant adjutant general in Santa Fe, he accused Rencher, Otero, and Collins of being fully complicit "in this [Southern] conspiracy."[105]

Otero delivered a direct rebuttal to these accusations in a letter that appeared a week later in a Washington, D.C. newspaper. Lambasting Greeley as "an unscrupulous demagogue and a vile calumniator," Otero referenced the situation existing in 1850 when Congress admitted New Mexico into the Union as a territory and insisted that local opinion remained unchanged since that time. Any accusation that Southerners conspired to implant slavery in New Mexico, he contended, bore no basis in fact. He accused the New York publisher of attempting to sway popular opinion in such a way that Northerners would become convinced of a government conspiracy, citing the Democratic presidents Franklin Pierce and James Buchanan as Greeley's scapegoats.[106]

Requests for the repeal of the Slave Code arose almost instantly after its passage. Territorial Speaker of the House Levi Keithly introduced a countermeasure that called for its immediate nullification. He took this action at the behest of Representative John A. Bingham of Ohio, who sponsored a similar bill at the federal level. Keithly's attempt summarily failed in the territorial legislature, owing in large part to his lackluster efforts, he having, according to Bingham, "taken no steps to get backers among the other members of the Legislature, as he believed the bill would pass on its own merits." Antislavery advocates were less than thrilled with the proceedings in New Mexico and attributed the Slave Code's retention to the conniving work of several influential men. The legislature adjourned immediately after Keithly introduced the measure, whereupon advocates of the law supposedly invited voting members to an after-hours party where "John Barleycorn did his work and 'mint drops' were freely administered where other means failed." According to Bingham, "One of the Mexicans was offered the speakership in exchange for his vote."[107]

Supporters of the code pointed to the protection of slave property in New Mexico as a necessity if territorial residents wished to experience any significant economic development or to increase their political standing in the national capital. A special committee composed of five members and chaired by Manuel Salazar y Vigil subsequently convened to review Keithly's nullification measure.[108] In a reflection of the political divide, the committee's report unanimously recommended against the repeal, outlining numerous reasons why the law should be upheld and claiming that it had had no negative impact on rights of person or property. The committee believed that the repeal attempt stemmed directly from Northern abolitionists, rather than from a desire to promote the common welfare. In upholding the property rights of slave owners, committee members cited "the celebrated case of Dred Scott" when explaining that "the citizen whose property consists in slaves has the same right to bring them to and demand protection for his property in them, that any other citizen has." Because New Mexico's Slave Code protected the same property rights as those found in the Constitution, the lawmakers recommended that the nullification bill be voted down.[109]

In a letter to Secretary of War Simon Cameron, William Need advanced the opposing viewpoint, stressing the importance of abrogating the law in its entirety. "Slavery and peonage, twin relics of barbarism and the offspring of an oligarchy, have had sway and are held up as an example of patriarchal observance for the guidance of the masses," he wrote, noting that this condition of things precluded "an enlightened standard of civilization, of progress, and improvement." Need called upon Cameron and his powerful political allies in Lincoln's cabinet to work toward a strategy for eliminating all forms of involuntary servitude in New Mexico. "Why," he asked rhetorically, "should this slave code, more odious and bloody than the code of Draco, be longer suffered to pollute the statute laws of this Territory, where Daniel Webster declared that the ordinances of God had forbidden its introduction?"[110]

Congress ultimately seized control of the issue. When the matter came up for debate in March 1860, the Illinois senator Stephen A. Douglas pointed out that, under the premises of popular sovereignty, New Mexico had every right to enact such a law. "Kansas has adopted a free state; New Mexico has established a slave territory," he declared. "I am content with both. If the people of New Mexico want slavery, let them have it." If the Slave Code was to be repealed, Douglas said, then the territorial legislature must rescind it without congressional intervention.[111] Democratic representative John H. Reagan concurred, referencing the recent Dred Scott decision and rationalizing that "the territorial legislature has passed the necessary laws" for the protection of slavery under its entitlement to popular sovereignty.[112] As a proslavery Texas congressman, Reagan perpetuated the opinion of his predecessor, Senator Thomas J. Rusk, who in 1850 directly referenced servants in New Mexico when proclaiming that, in conformity with the tenets of popular sovereignty, "it seems to me clear that the best plan that we can adopt is to leave this matter to the regulation of the people among whom it exists."[113] Despite these long-running misgivings on congressional interference with territorial self-government, Representative Bingham spearheaded the annulment effort by introducing a bill on May 10, 1860, detailing the particulars of New Mexico's Slave Code. The following day the measure was passed along to the committee on territories, which called for a vote on the code's immediate repeal.[114]

The thirty-eight-page House minority report, written by Representative Miles Taylor of Louisiana, staunchly rebutted the attempted abrogation of the Slave Code and upheld the opinions of Douglas and Reagan regarding popular sovereignty. Opponents cited the Organic Act upon which New Mexico had been admitted to the Union as a territory in 1850, a law stipulating that the legislature could pass its own decrees but that Congress would retain the right to approve or disapprove them. If New Mexico applied for statehood, it would be accepted "with or without slavery, as their constitution may prescribe at the time of their admission." This created a dilemma because the citizens of New Mexico, according to the 1850 act of incorporation, retained the right to legislate on slavery. The same 1850 Organic Act, however, stipulated that any laws passed at the territorial level must be submitted to Congress, which had the authority to nullify them by a majority vote. Thus, according to the minority report, the proposition was one "of the gravest importance," because the outcome had clear implications for congressional power as well as for the rights of U.S. citizens living in the territories.[115]

The report succinctly defined congressional authority relative to New Mexico, explaining that its 1850 Organic Act allowed U.S. senators and representatives to approve or disapprove of laws that the territorial legislature passed. The authors also pointed out a logical fallacy in this argument when noting that "it does not therefore follow . . . that the right to disapprove of *every* law passed by the legislative assembly of the Territory results from it." The committee therefore concluded that "Congress can no more legislate to exclude slavery from a Territory than it can from a State . . . what Congress cannot do directly it certainly cannot do indirectly."[116] Thus, according to Southerners, abrogation of the Slave Code amounted to a question of constitutionality and would have far-reaching legal ramifications.[117]

The minority contingent provided a detailed analysis of the constitutionality question, going as far back as the Declaration of Independence to support their stance on the rights of temporary (territorial) governments and congressional powers. From the time of the nation's founding, Congress had never attempted to exert its authority over municipal laws in a territory, "except under the pressure of a sectional feeling for the prohibition of slavery." The Missouri Compromise and the Wilmot Proviso provided the two most applicable examples of this. Federal repeal of the Slave Code would therefore be "a palpable usurpation of power by Congress," violating the premises of the Compromise of 1850 and constituting "a blow aimed at slavery itself."[118] In making these generalizations, the report did mention peonage, which Southerners acknowledged as both legal and justifiable, asserting that its existence should not be impinged upon. Despite any misgivings, the committee on territories reported the bill to the chamber without amendment, along with a recommendation that "it ought to pass." The House approved it by a vote of 97–90; when it reached the Senate, however, it died in committee, leaving the Slave Code temporarily intact.[119]

Addressing the territorial legislature on December 4, 1861—more than a year after the failed congressional repeal effort—Governor Connelly spoke authoritatively against the law, noting the overall absurdity of its provisions and the potential political ramifications for New Mexico if it remained in effect. He informed his colleagues that most of the Slave Code's contents "are unnecessarily severe and rigorous" and recommended that the edict be "entirely repealed."[120] The legislature responded quickly to Connelly's suggestion; only two days after the gubernatorial address, a bill appeared before the council mandating the immediate abrogation of the law. Unlike the protracted process two years earlier when Levi Keithly introduced a similar nullification measure, this bill passed after only two days, without amendments, and by a unanimous vote of 22–0.[121]

Following the 1861–62 legislative session, Facundo Piño, the president of the council, delivered an address outlining the various proceedings that had taken place. In the resulting manifesto the legislators expressed, for the first time, an aversion toward chattel slavery, seemingly forgetting their previous embracement of the institution. "We are a free people," they declared, "and our fathers ever abhorred negro slaves and slavery."[122] The January 29, 1862, declaration failed to mention debt bondage and Indian captivity, a testament once again to the hypocrisy of many New Mexican lawmakers. The legislature denounced black slavery without condemning peonage or indigenous servitude, recognizing that few easterners—even those counting themselves among abolitionist forces—would notice such an omission.[123]

The repeal of the Slave Code and subsequent legislative proclamation claiming that slavery had always been contrary to New Mexico's interests clearly was meant to appeal to Northerners. New Mexico had long been linked to Missouri (a border state that never seceded) via the Santa Fe Trail, and a lucrative trade benefiting hundreds of merchants on both ends of that road bound the two entities together in commerce. Such incentives influenced some New Mexicans, whose support for the Northern cause stemmed from a desire to preserve economic stability at the local level. Furthermore, at that early stage of the war, New Mexico relied heavily upon continued Union support. By the time Governor Connelly delivered his address on December 4, 1861, Rebel forces already occupied the entire southern portion of New Mexico and had declared the region a Confederate territory. Under such circumstances, policymakers had little choice but to repeal the Slave Code if they wished to retain federal support in thwarting the Texan invasion. As a Union territory, any failure to rescind the law would have been politically damning inasmuch as it would have discouraged the federal government from acting to retain New Mexico as a Northern possession. Indeed, when West Virginia applied for and was eventually granted statehood on June 20, 1863, it first had to abolish slavery in its own constitution, a prerequisite for admission into the Union that would apply to all formerly rebellious states as well as federal territories seeking statehood after the Civil War.[124] If there were any lingering doubts about rescinding the Slave Code, the circumstances surrounding West Virginia's statehood bid reassured New Mexicans that they had pursued the proper course of action.

By 1862, Congress itself had passed an act prohibiting the peculiar institution in New Mexico, declaring that "there shall be neither slavery nor involuntary servitude in any of the Territories of the United States."[125] Serving as a territorial governor in Connelly's absence, William F. M. Arny duly notified the legislature of this act and praised their repeal of the 1859 law, proclaiming New Mexico to be composed of "a free people."[126] Thus, after more than three years, the Slave Code came to an unceremonious end at the hands of both the territorial legislature and the U.S. Congress. Ultimately, it served as a lasting testament to the vacillation of New Mexico's leading officials relative to the appropriate position on slavery. Legislators had attempted to anticipate the sectional stance that would be most politically and economically beneficial to them, and they acted accordingly when considering discriminatory slave laws. When it appeared that Southerners held the political advantage, the legislature, influenced by congressional delegates, passed proslavery legislation. Once it became clear during the Civil War that Union forces would retain control of the region, lawmakers promptly rescinded such laws in order to secure Northern support. In short, New Mexicans sought to stay on the winning side through their political maneuverings on slavery, while simultaneously retaining debt peonage and Indian captivity as regional institutions—ones that they portrayed as falling outside the parameters of involuntary servitude.

Most Nuevomexicanos remained indifferent toward chattel slavery but necessarily took a stance on the issue at the behest of their territorial representatives. In the years leading up to the Civil War, both Northerners and Southerners looked to New Mexico for support and sought to enlist the territory to their respective causes. The outbreak of the war in 1861 and subsequent Confederate invasion of the territory only exacerbated preexisting tensions. Ultimately, the repeal of the Slave Code came about more as a result of the 1862 Union victory over Confederate forces in that territory than the personal sentiments of citizens and public officials. With Rebel troops having been ousted from New Mexico, the legislature had little choice but to overturn the code and hope, at the very least, to retain their long-entrenched systems of peonage and captive Indian servitude. Despite their efforts, however, both of those labor regimes would be outlawed in the aftermath of the Civil War.

The continuing reverberation of territorial law relative to chattel slavery and African Americans, coupled with the retention of debt bondage and Indian slavery, left easterners confused about the political mind-set of New Mexicans. With many Protestant Anglo-Americans already concerned about the prominence of Catholicism among a predominantly Hispanic culture, regional ambiguity on the slave issue exacerbated pessimism toward New Mexico. After the Civil War, when Radical Republicans directed Reconstruction efforts and abolitionism reigned supreme at the federal level, New Mexico's former espousal of a slave code and retention of involuntary servitude made many politicians—especially Northerners—apprehensive about granting the territory equal political representation concomitant with statehood status. In nearby California, lawmakers had recognized the potentially damaging impact of proslavery laws in that state and worked throughout the early 1860s to rescind codes that upheld peonage and Indian apprenticeship.[127] Territorial slave policies and racially motivated discrimination ranked alongside anti-Catholic nativism and anti-Hispanic ethnocentrism as a contributing factor in New Mexico's stymied political aspirations in the mid-nineteenth century, and the retention of peonage and captivity in local communities would play an important role in the nation's postwar transformation to free labor.

Chapter 5

Reconstruction and the Unraveling
of Alternative Slaveries

With the onset of the Civil War, stances on slavery began to take a pronounced shift among New Mexico's occupants, most of whom had
remained ambivalent on the issue prior to 1861. Whereas many territorial
officials previously advocated discriminatory proslavery laws, such a position suddenly became a political liability once the North began to prevail
in the war and regional inhabitants started sympathizing with the Union
cause. Many peons, in fact, enlisted in Union militia and volunteer regiments during the war as a means of freeing themselves from labor obligations, and military service in New Mexico provided an avenue toward self-
emancipation.[1]

In order to promote political interests, local lawmakers and citizens
necessarily adopted a lukewarm antislavery position beginning in 1862—a
shift that, not coincidentally, corresponded with the Confederates' retreat
from the territory after a failed invasion attempt. The legislative repeal of
the controversial 1859 Slave Code foretold of a doomed future for involuntary servitude in New Mexico. The ensuing decade would see the passage
of local and national legislative measures designed to undermine coerced
labor as a sanctioned social, cultural, and economic practice in the Southwest, and the proceedings that brought about the liberation of captives
and peons created legal precedents that contributed to the nation's broader
transition to free labor.

Although legislative emancipation originated with the First Confiscation
Act on August 8, 1861, the first regulatory device that directly impacted
New Mexico came in the form of a congressional mandate on June 19,
1862, that banned all forms of involuntary servitude in U.S. territories. The

edict was meant to apply primarily to black slaves, but it also encompassed Indian captives.[2] Because peonage was represented as voluntary in nature, New Mexicans believed that it did not fall within the parameters of this act. In response to these laws, territorial legislators memorialized congressional leaders in January 1863 informing them that at least six hundred Indian captives lived in New Mexico and claiming that, upon liberation, such persons would "be placed in a far worse condition than they are now." Employing the concept of compensated emancipation that so many Americans—including Abraham Lincoln in the early months of his presidency—advocated as a conciliatory means toward the desired end, they requested that the federal government appropriate funds to reimburse captiveholders and asked that another law be passed outlining the mode whereby indigenous slaves should be freed and repatriated.[3] Fundamentally, territorial officials sought nothing more than to secure pecuniary redress for the liberation of captives while simultaneously understating the total number of Indians held in servitude. Somewhat characteristically, the memorialists neglected to mention indebted peons detained in similar bondage, once again casting a veil over that institution in hopes of perpetuating a system from which landholders and other elites derived increased social standing.

Coinciding with the legislators' memorial, President Lincoln's Emancipation Proclamation became effective on January 1, 1863, symbolically (although not actually) freeing all slaves in the rebellious states.[4] The order had no impact in New Mexico, a Union territory where a mere two dozen black slaves resided at the time, most belonging to military officers who lived there only temporarily. Territorial residents did, however, continue to retain thousands of captured Indians and indigent peons in dependent servitude, constituting two forms of coerced labor similar in principle and only slightly variant in practice from that existing in the South. Northern abolitionists deployed Lincoln's proclamation as a rhetorical tool, applying it to the slavery argument as it pertained to the western territories. The ideology behind the Emancipation Proclamation, they contended, encompassed all persons held involuntarily for servitude, regardless of race or class; by extension, this also included peons and Indian slaves. At the local level, Superintendent of Indian Affairs Michael Steck wrote as early as October 1863 that officials "were endeavoring to abolitionize [sic] the territory."[5] Not until the passage of the Thirteenth Amendment to the U.S. Constitution, however, did some slaves actually receive their freedom.[6]

Ratified on December 6, 1865—well after the Confederate surrender at Appomattox—this amendment sought to liberate all persons subjected to involuntary servitude (except in cases of criminal conviction) in the United States and should have marked the moment at which debt peonage and captive slavery ceased to exist in the Southwest.[7] This, however, proved not to be the case. An expansion of that amendment, in the form of a congressional antipeonage statute stipulating that indebtedness did not constitute a crime punishable by servitude, would ultimately be needed in order to end New Mexico's systems of coercive labor.[8]

Before the country arrived at that point, numerous proceedings played out regarding slavery and servitude in New Mexico. Just as it did following the ratification of the Treaty of Guadalupe Hidalgo in 1848, the slave debate proliferated once again in 1860–61, when Congress heard proposals for New Mexico's promotion to statehood status, along with simultaneous bids to admit neighboring Colorado as a territory. For many ethnocentric U.S. politicians, the question of granting statehood could be summarized as a matter of "whether New Mexico, with its peons, with its wild lands, with its half-breeds and Mexicans, its mixed population, shall be free or slaveholding territory."[9] Once again, New Mexico found itself denigrated because of its systems of servitude and mestizo population. Newcomers from an American nation largely defined by racial and ethnic divisions remained hesitant to grant political equality to nonwhites whose sectional proclivities remained a matter of mystery and reverberation throughout the antebellum era. Colorado did indeed become a territory—one statutorily devoid of slavery—but New Mexico once again failed in its quest to attain statehood. The issue became especially contentious when Congress demarcated the boundaries of Colorado, because the adopted proposal included the northernmost portion of New Mexico (the San Luis Valley of today's south-central Colorado). Since New Mexico existed under the premise of popular sovereignty and at that time retained its territorial slave codes, Northerners unequivocally objected to slave-free Colorado annexing a portion of slaveholding New Mexico.[10]

The Illinois senator Stephen A. Douglas questioned what might become of slaves held in the northernmost reaches of New Mexico upon that region's transfer to free-soil Colorado. Addressing Congress, Douglas asked whether the proposal to detach a portion of New Mexico constituted an attempt to outlaw slavery and make it a free-soil territory. Sectional tension at that critical juncture—just months prior to the Civil War—manifested itself in the ensuing debate, during which the Missouri senator James S. Green stood and proclaimed that the bill admitting Colorado "does not cut off five inhabitants, and not a single nigger."[11] Green might have been correct that no black slaves resided in that region, but many peons and Indian captives occupied the villages near the headwaters of the Rio Grande, which became a part of Colorado once the bill passed. Most of those servants would remain in bondage despite being in free-soil Colorado. Because that new territory's Anglo-American population centers of Boulder and Denver City sat on the faraway Rocky Mountain Front Range, and paranoia surrounding the Confederate invasion of New Mexico was occurring simultaneously to the south, the plight of such involuntary servants went unaddressed. Colorado's admission as a territory did, however, provide an opportunity for proponents of New Mexico statehood to argue in favor of their cause. Ironically, it does not appear that any of New Mexico's political leaders encouraged this action, although some Northerners, including Charles Francis Adams of Massachusetts, endorsed the legislation in hopes of appeasing the South and averting civil war.[12] This sparked renewed angst throughout the chamber as politicians revisited the free-soil debate. Many individuals rejected the notion that New Mexico should be granted statehood, in part because it remained a matter of mystery as to where the native Hispanic population stood relative to slavery and sectional issues.[13]

The Republican representative Cadwallader C. Washburn of Wisconsin voiced opposition to statehood, believing the entire prospect to be a scheme for adding two pro-South senators in Congress and postulating that New Mexico would "give all its influence in favor of the institutions of slavery." Washburn refuted any claim that New Mexico might become slaveless if admitted as a state. "I believe that the same power and the same party which has adopted in that Territory a slave code of the most barbarous character," he proclaimed, "will adopt a pro-slavery constitution."[14] The New Hampshire representative Mason Tappan shared Washburn's concerns, recognizing that the promotion of New Mexico to "an equal footing with the other States" would implicitly sanction the 1859 Slave Code and disrupt sectional balance by admitting another slave state.[15] Many Republicans—and virtually all abolitionists—opposed New Mexico statehood because of its Slave Code, which, they argued, indicated that the territory had already bowed to Southern interests. To Northerners, New Mexico's admission amounted to little more than additional proslavery representation in Congress. Once again, however, politicians remained focused on the potential geographic expansion of chattel slavery, casting aside as tangential the thousands of captives and peons who remained involuntarily bound to their masters.

Even New Mexico's leading officials disagreed with one another over their constituents' sentiments. Their ambiguity sent a confusing message to federal lawmakers, rendering many congressmen hesitant to approve statehood for fear that New Mexico might lean further toward Southern interests. "Let Mr. Lincoln be inaugurated and make his appointments, and we trust all this will soon change for the better," Horace Greeley speculated, condemning New Mexico as unfit for statehood and hypothesizing that "to admit her now is simply to make her over to slavery—the scheme has no other purpose."[16] Attempts to achieve statehood fell flat in 1860–61, and New Mexico would remain a territory for fifty-one more years, its failure to ascend politically once again attributable to the slavery issue and the continuing use of involuntary servants in local villages and haciendas.[17]

Throughout the Civil War, many New Mexico officials publicly denounced their predecessors for having been congenial toward slavery. Abraham Rencher, the last governor to express any proclivity toward the Southern cause, completed his term in office before the war commenced. New Mexico's first wartime governor, Henry Connelly, professed loyalty to the Union, and within a year of the bombardment of Fort Sumter, South Carolina, the territory's Hispanic citizens rose against a Confederate onslaught and turned back the Texan invasion of 1861–62. This nationalistic unity on the part of New Mexicans—which had as much to do with their hatred for Texas as it did any prevailing sense of loyalty to the United States—convinced many easterners by midwar that most Hispanos supported the North.[18] But while New Mexicans did coalesce to repulse the Confederate invasion and uphold the federal Union in principle, they did not necessarily unite for the purpose of advancing the emancipation cause. Coerced labor remained common throughout the settlements, with many people continuing to subject debtors and captured Indians to dependent servitude. Although most residents had renounced race slavery and the legislature repealed the Slave Code, human bondage remained culturally and socially implanted. While the turmoil of the Civil War had little immediate effect on the discontinuance of the practice, the arrival of antislavery Lincoln appointees did bring greater awareness to the matter.

After being selected to serve as territorial secretary in July 1862, William F. M. Arny called direct attention to peonage and involuntary labor during

Figure 14. Abraham Rencher, New Mexico's last territorial governor prior
to the Civil War. Courtesy Museum of New Mexico, negative #010758.

Figure 15. Henry Connelly, pro-Union governor of New Mexico for much of the Civil War. Courtesy Museum of New Mexico, negative #009846.

his time in New Mexico. The forty-nine-year-old arrived in the Southwest intent on advancing the Northern platform of free labor. Although he exhibited little opposition to the institution of slavery early in life, he experienced an ideological transformation during his involvement with the violently sectional Kansas political scene. Exerting a strong Republican influence from the moment of his arrival, Arny helped to initiate a shift away from the Democrat-controlled legislature that dominated territorial politics throughout much of the 1850s. Rumors even swirled in 1864 that Arny and a handful of his friends "were attempting to establish a [political] party upon an abolition basis" in New Mexico.[19] Although those efforts never materialized, he still wielded his civic influence in perpetuation of the abolitionist cause during his five years as a secretary and interim governor.[20]

Acting as temporary head of state during Henry Connelly's illness-induced absence, Arny delivered a message to the territorial legislature on December 2, 1862, in which he openly addressed the continued existence of peonage and alluded to it as a disguised form of slavery. His speech came just months after Confederate forces had been driven from the territory after their defeat at Glorieta Pass in March 1862, and wartime concerns about slavery stood at the forefront of legislative discourse. With New Mexico having remained under Union control, it became imperative that legislators nullify preexisting slave codes and free all involuntary servants, whether they be Indian captives or Hispanics held in debt bondage. Any failure to do so, Arny warned, would have severe political ramifications for the territory if the North won the war. Outlining preexisting territorial slave laws, he noted that such mandates continued to be "misrepresented by many" and therefore deserved careful explanation and consideration. He also pointed out that Chief Justice Kirby Benedict had ruled in favor of a peon plaintiff in the 1857 case *Jaremillo v. Romero* and cited this important decision as a precedent for the appropriate action the legislature should take relative to servitude in general. Arny concluded by recommending that legislators amend the master-servant laws so that "the same course of proceeding was left a master to collect his debt from his servant or Peon as in the ordinary way from any other debtor."[21]

Arny's message was important for several reasons. Legislators had already repealed the 1859 Slave Code, but in so doing they retained elements of earlier peon laws, including the 1851 master-servant act. Predicting that many in the East would interpret peonage as a form of involuntary servitude, Arny implored his colleagues to similarly nullify that measure in

Figure 16. William F. M. Arny, temporary New Mexico governor who staunchly opposed slavery and encouraged territorial legislators to ban involuntary servitude. Library of Congress, Abraham Lincoln Papers, Microfilm Roll 1, W. F. M. Arny to Abraham Lincoln, September 21, 1860. Courtesy Library of Congress.

order to maintain consistency in the abrogation of all laws protecting or promoting coerced labor. He failed, however, to acknowledge the continued existence of Indian slavery, a peculiar oversight considering that his prior service as an agent for the Utes and the Jicarilla Apaches in 1861 exposed him to issues surrounding the captive trade.[22]

Even at the close of 1862, with the symbolic Emancipation Proclamation slated to go into effect on the first day of the new year, New Mexicans continued to resist change on the subjects of peonage and captivity by attempting to ignore their existence altogether. Arny's omission of Indian slavery in his diatribe about peonage typified the territorial politics of that era. Anti-Indian mind-sets prevailed throughout the United States and transcended the ideological boundaries of sectionalism, allowing for captive servitude to proliferate even as legislators began to take aim at eradicating debt peonage. Chattel slavery had mostly been shunned in New Mexico, primarily as a political gesture, but also in recognition of the fact that peons and captives already satisfied regional labor needs. The territory's inhabitants therefore clung to their Indian servants because they believed that that institution would be overlooked by Euro-Americans wishing to incorporate Native peoples through the very types of dependency and assimilation that already characterized the evolution of indigenous slave systems in the Southwest.

Additional evidence that peonage and captivity persevered can be gleaned from the actions of several leading territorial and federal officials near the end of the Civil War. In a proclamation issued May 4, 1864, Governor Connelly warned New Mexicans "against further traffic in captive Indians," because the Interior Department was already in the process of codifying a new policy "to have all Indians surrendered who have been sold into slavery."[23] In California, wartime Republicans had embarked on a similar crusade to repeal an 1860 law that condoned the enslavement of Indians, and by 1863 they succeeded in overturning the measure, although an estimated six thousand California Natives remained in varying conditions of servility for several years thereafter.[24] Just one year after Connelly's proclamation, on June 9, 1865, President Andrew Johnson acknowledged the large number of New Mexico's Indians who had been "seized and reduced into slavery" when he requested that the Executive Branch instigate "the effectual suppression of a practice which is alike in violation of the rights of the Indians and the provisions of the Organic Law" of New Mexico. Johnson's various department heads circulated an order among their subordinates in the field "to take all lawful means to suppress" the enslavement of Indians.[25]

The active involvement of President Johnson, a Tennessee Democrat who became the nemesis of Republicans after the Civil War, indicates that the abolition of captivity and peonage transcended not only the moderate and radical stances among Republicans, but also the ideological chasms separating the two major national parties. The moderate Republican senator James Doolittle, who directed the 1865 investigation of Indian affairs that ultimately prompted legislative action toward captivity, was in fact an occasional ally of Johnson and did not usually side with the radicals in his own party.[26] Despite the many discrepancies in policy objectives between the president and his Republican counterparts during postwar Reconstruction, the two groups shared common ground regarding the eradication of peonage and Indian slavery in the Southwest. Forging a rare partnership on the issue, executive and legislative authorities took concrete action regarding the abolition of those two systems of involuntary servitude during a time when those two branches of government typically found themselves locked in a contentious stalemate with one another. The seemingly incongruous approaches of presidential and congressional Reconstruction actually coalesced in the statutory elimination of southwestern slavery during the years immediately following Lee's surrender at Appomattox.[27]

Pursuant to the president's mandate—which Johnson issued a full six months before ratification of the Thirteenth Amendment—Secretary of the Interior James Harlan mailed a copy of the order to Commissioner of Indian Affairs William P. Dole with instructions to direct all Indian Service personnel in New Mexico "to discontinue the practice" of enslaving Native peoples. Harlan requested that agents report directly to his department on all instances of Indian slavery that came to their attention. "Such violations of the personal liberty of Indians, and the exaction from them of labor, should not be tolerated in a country professing to be free," Harlan lectured, reiterating his determination to use all resources at his command to induce an abrupt end to the practice.[28] Commissioner Dole immediately wrote to Felipe Delgado, New Mexico's superintendent of Indian affairs, forwarding Johnson's executive order and instructing him on how to appropriately comply with the decree.[29] If the Indian slave trade was to be suppressed, it would require collaboration at all levels, beginning in Washington, D.C. and trickling down to individual agents in the field. Without complete cooperation, President Johnson's order could never be enforced, because of the scale on which Indian slavery remained embedded in southwestern society and the extent to which residents attempted to hide and protect the institution.

The level of intragovernmental cooperation necessary to initiate and sustain the emancipation of Indian slaves and debt peons was not immediately forthcoming. In his 1866 annual report, Commissioner of Indian Affairs Dennis N. Cooley insisted that "this office has done all that lay in its power" to eradicate Indian slavery and enforce the president's mandate, yet the practice remained mostly unaffected because captiveholders did everything possible to resist these outside forces and retain their human subjects in bondage.[30] "Those who hold them [captives and peons] are exceedingly sensitive of their supposed interest in them," Judge Kirby Benedict explained just three months after the Civil War ended, noting New Mexico slaveholders to be "easily alarmed at any movements in the civil courts or otherwise to dispossess them of their imagined property." The failure to undermine this long-standing trend owed to the fact that most New Mexicans who held peons or captives "have much popular influence . . . and the exertion of this influence is one of the means by which they hope to retain their grasp upon their Indian slaves."[31]

Steck had alluded to the failures of these legislated emancipation efforts as early as 1864, writing that "the civil authorities could not, for obvious reasons, accomplish the work of liberating the captive Indians at present" and recommending that the military be ordered "to proclaim the immediate and unconditional emancipation of all Indians in this department, and that they be returned to their respective tribes."[32] As Steck noted, military emancipation had become the official Union wartime policy with passage of the First Confiscation Act in August 1861, and the government expanded that measure a year later when it approved the Second Confiscation Act on July 17, 1862, using the war powers clause of the Constitution as justification for freeing slaves within rebellious states.[33]

Marking a shift in Lincoln's wartime objectives, the Second Confiscation Act signified the transition from limited to universal emancipation by using federal troops as a tool for accomplishing that end, with the Emancipation Proclamation officially transforming the Union military into an army of liberation.[34] Just two months after the Second Confiscation Act became law, General Edward R. S. Canby, commanding the Military Department of New Mexico, issued a general order instructing army officers to reclaim any Indian captives "sold into slavery" and quarter them at their posts for protection. Canby also instructed his officers not to return peons to their masters once they had enlisted in the army.[35] At almost the same time, Union officers in Northern California received similar orders requiring them to assist in capturing kidnappers who abducted Indian children into slavelike apprenticeships.[36] Aware that many black bondspeople in the South attained their freedom only with the aid of Union officers and soldiers, Steck suggested that a similar approach be used in New Mexico to buttress otherwise ineffective legislative measures, and indeed Canby issued his orders to that effect. In so doing, both the Indian agent and the department commander applied the logic of universal emancipation—as outlined in the Confiscation Acts and enforced by the U.S military—to New Mexico in furtherance of peon and captive liberation. As late as 1867, however, antislavery men acknowledged policy failures when lamenting to federal officials that "as for the peonage of Mexicans [and the captivity of Indians] neither the military authorities, nor civil authorities, nor the enactments of Congress can reach it except in the cases which are brought to the courts."[37]

In the rare instances when bondsmen did bring their grievances before a judge, they experienced a surprising success rate, as evidenced in the peonage cases heard in the New Mexico Supreme Court. Despite occasional litigation, however, civil and military officials could do little to eradicate peonage and captive slavery unless the oppressed servants could be induced to bring their own cases to trial. Differing personal and political objectives, accompanied by competition of egos at the territorial level, undermined the government's attempts to intervene with Indian captivity. In New Mexico, Interior Department agents believed that orders suppressing Indian slavery had emanated from "greatly exaggerated" reports on the extent of the practice.[38]

Felipe Delgado, who succeeded Steck as superintendent of Indian affairs, replied to Commissioner Dole two days after reading President Johnson's moratorium and defended his superintendency against allegations that he and his cohorts ignored the widespread enslavement of Indians. "It is true," he acknowledged, "there are among the citizens of this country a large number of Indian captives belonging to various tribes, that have been acquired or purchased from the Utah, Navajo, and other tribes." Echoing the ideological and theological views that Brigham Young and other Mormon authorities expressed a decade earlier, Delgado also claimed that "the object in purchasing them has not been to reduce them to slavery, but rather from a Christian piety on the part of the Whites, to obtain them, in order to instruct and educate them in civilization." Delgado invoked the argument of cultural tradition, informing Commissioner Dole that the enslavement of Indian women and children had been common practice in New Mexico "for the last century and a half" and that the Indians had, as a result of their captivity, been entitled to a "favorable, humane and satisfactory" life among their captors. Despite his misgivings, Delgado promised that he would enforce the law and claimed that he had already informed his field agents that "under no pretext whatever" would the capture and exchange of Indians be thereafter tolerated.[39] Perhaps in reference to the seemingly futile efforts of Delgado and his personnel, the commissioner admitted in 1866 that the practice of Indian enslavement "continues to a greater or less extent" in some western departments.[40]

The realization among federal leaders in 1865–66 that captivity and peonage continued mostly unchanged in the Southwest emanated in part from former Superintendent Steck's trip to Washington, D.C. just after the war ended. Once Delgado replaced Steck as New Mexico's leading Indian agent, the longtime territorial resident and bureaucrat traveled to the national capital to settle outstanding accounts with the Interior Department. He also carried laudatory letters introducing him to a number of high-ranking Republican officials, including the radical abolitionist Salmon

P. Chase, who had recently replaced Roger B. Taney as chief justice of the U.S. Supreme Court. The author of one of the letters, the former Indian agent John Greiner, wrote that Steck "is well posted as to the Peon system and its workings, in which I know you have ever manifested deep interest."[41] As an avowed Republican who opposed slavery, Steck was exceptionally familiar with the machinations of New Mexican servantholders after spending more than a decade residing in their midst.[42] While his primary intent on the journey to Washington might have been to settle financial accounts and conduct personal business, he also advanced abolitionist motives and visited GOP officials to enlighten them about the continuing existence of involuntary servitude in the Southwest. The information he provided no doubt helped to influence the ensuing federal mandates that banned Indian captivity and debt peonage in more specific terms.

The issuance of additional antislavery decrees such as those targeting peonage and captivity coincided with a massive shift in national politics immediately following the Civil War, one that afforded incredible control to Northern Republicans who implemented Reconstruction policies. Had those radicals not risen to power at that time, it is improbable that much attention would have been directed toward peonage and Indian slavery in the Southwest. Already demonized by Democrats after the war as a "black man's party," Republicans endeavored to extend legislative emancipation westward to include peons and captives as well.[43] It was not merely the North's increasing momentum in the war effort that drove New Mexican officials to rescind previous peon laws and slave codes—and California legislators to simultaneously nullify implicitly proslavery mandates of their own—but also the ascension of Radical Republicans in Congress at war's end and the subsequent ideological transformation that began at the national level and trickled down to state and local governments.[44]

Under pressure from federal legislators, and recognizing that many antislavery Northerners had taken notice of the institution as one in dire need of reform, the territorial legislature pursued further action relative to involuntary servitude shortly after President Johnson issued his 1865 moratorium on the enterprise. On January 26, 1866, lawmakers amended existing statutes in order to redefine debt peonage as a voluntary form of servitude.[45] They did so in direct response to ratification of the Thirteenth Amendment a month earlier, essentially removing debtor servitude from the purview of constitutional restraint by dropping the two-letter prefix from the word "involuntary" in their definition of peonage. A disappointed Secretary Arny informed government officials that local legislators had "repealed the odious so called 'Free Negro law' . . . and amended the 'Peon Law' so as to make the servitude *voluntary*."[46] This deceptive action failed to trick abolitionists like U.S. representative George P. Marsh, who had demanded that peonage, a "barbaric relic of the ancient Roman law," be explicitly outlawed along the same provisions as chattel slavery.[47] In repealing the 1859 Slave Code, the territorial legislature neglected to take any steps toward suppressing Indian captivity and sidestepped the most important issue entirely, retaining the peonage system by changing their definition of it from involuntary to voluntary servitude. In so doing, they formulated their legislative rhetoric in direct defiance of the recently amended U.S. Constitution. New Mexicans hoped that nullification of the Slave Code might satisfy radical antislavery interests and deflect their attention elsewhere, but ultimately their scheme had an inverse effect and brought about an expansion of the Thirteenth Amendment, vis-à-vis the 1867 Peon Law, that completely undermined debtor servitude.

While Hispano legislators slyly modified preexisting peon laws, they also continued to disregard the rights of Indian captives held as servants. Addressing the legislature in December 1866 as a temporary governor, Arny pointed out that captive slaves could no longer be owned without violating the Constitution, leaving no doubt that the Thirteenth Amendment applied to Indians as well as African Americans held in bondage.[48] Although the practice of enslaving Natives had finally reached its symbolic statutory demise, large numbers of captive women and children continued to await repatriation to their tribes, despite federal mandates requiring that masters manumit all involuntary servants.

Some female captives, having been baptized in the Catholic faith and married into Hispano families, actually wished to remain with their adoptive kinfolk. Many indigenous women had borne children with their male overseers and declined opportunities for repatriation in order to remain with their mestizo offspring. "The question however arises," Arny explained, "whether these Indians who have in former years been taken captive and held in servitude, but who have voluntarily chosen to remain in the families where they have for years lived, come under the above [constitutional] amendment." A serious predicament therefore arose in New Mexico. Federal law required that all slaves, regardless of race or ethnicity, be immediately freed. As Arny pointed out, however, some of them did not wish to return to their Native tribes. With this in mind, he questioned whether it might be "an act of inhumanity" to forcibly remove Indian slaves from the families that fed and clothed them.[49] Just one year earlier, having received the executive order mandating that indigenous servants be liberated and the illicit trade in human flesh halted, a Ute agent named Lafayette Head reported that 148 captives remained in bondage in southern Colorado's San Luis Valley alone.[50] Of those, only one supposedly wanted to return to her natal family. The remainder, according to the agent, "know not their own parents, nor can they speak their mother tongue," prompting him to pose the question already on so many people's minds: "What are we to do with these [captives]?"[51]

Arny and Head both implied that the manumission of Indian slaves might be a greater evil than the perpetuity of their servitude. Many bondspeople had become dependent upon their masters and fictive kin for their own livelihood, a situation that mirrored that of liberated African Americans in the South following the Civil War. The strategy that Nuevomexicanos employed to baptize, marry, and procreate with captives largely succeeded in its purpose, as those coercive tactics fostered strong psychological, familial, and social bonds between servants and masters, the result being that indigenous abductees often declined repatriation and voluntarily perpetuated their own captivity.

Neither President Johnson's order banning Indian slavery nor the territorial legislature's repeal of previous slave codes had the desired effect of unshackling New Mexico's involuntary servants. While both actions did increase national publicity and exposure, they had little impact on the systems as they actually existed in the territory, and the legislators' sneaky tactic of modifying the definition of peonage was purposefully antithetical to federal attempts to eradicate slavery. Much like the South's chattel system, it would ultimately require an act of Congress to unravel peonage in New Mexico. Senator Charles Buckalew of Pennsylvania understood that the institution had become so deeply embedded in southwestern culture that it simply could not die out on its own. "Eventually the courts will weed out this system in that Territory," he prophesized, "but it will remain lingering there for a considerable time unless Congress shall interpose." Once the federal government stepped in, the senator believed that peonage would "fall to the ground at once."[52] Buckalew's oversimplification typified the misinformed manner in which many easterners viewed unfamiliar systems of servitude. While federal legislation during the early Reconstruction period would indeed set in motion the legal processes necessary to disband peonage and Indian slavery, it was by no means a painless process as Buckalew believed it would be. Events over the ensuing three years would prove just how deeply entrenched those systems of servitude had become in the Southwest.

During its autumn 1866 term, the New Mexico Supreme Court heard a case involving Tomás Heredia, a peon held involuntarily in satisfaction of debt at Doña Ana, a farming village along the Rio Grande in the southernmost portion of the territory. Heredia had recently fled from his master, José María García, whereupon the local justice of the peace overtook and remanded him back to the service of his creditor in accordance with the provisions of the 1851 master-servant act. At the district court trial, a jury recognized the validity of unwritten labor contracts and upheld García's right to retain Heredia in bondage.[53] John S. Watts, serving as legal counsel for the aggrieved peon, filed an appeal and the case ultimately went to the territorial Supreme Court, which overturned the earlier decision on grounds that the 1851 statute violated both the 1862 act of Congress banning slavery and involuntary servitude in U.S. territories, as well as the recently ratified Thirteenth Amendment outlawing slavery more broadly. New Mexico's high court reached a unanimous decision, granting Heredia his freedom based on the fact that congressional action superseded that of any territorial legislature. In a blunt assessment, the justices declared that "the system of servitude heretofore prevailing in New Mexico, generally known as *peonage* and attempted to be regulated and enforced by statutory provisions under the title of relations between 'master and servant' [is] *involuntary servitude*—it is clearly prohibited and abolished by the act of Congress and the amendment to the constitution referred to."[54] In rendering this decision and explicitly describing peonage as coerced labor, the court directly overruled the law that legislators passed earlier that year redefining debtor servitude as a voluntary institution. The judges thus foreshadowed congressional action that would sustain that outcome and provide for nationwide enforcement. In the Heredia case, the New Mexico Supreme Court built upon the 1857 Jaremillo trial and strengthened the judicial foundation for an expansion of the Thirteenth Amendment to include debtor servitude; their local action would have national implications for decades to come.

At the same time that judges on the territorial Supreme Court passed down their decision in January 1867, debates on peonage at the federal level also proliferated, largely due to the Civil War amendments to the Constitution banning all forms of involuntary servitude and granting political agency to the formerly enslaved. Yet despite these laws, the practice remained mostly intact throughout New Mexico because of its secluded geographic position, which concealed the prominence of coerced labor from everybody except those individuals who had traveled to the Southwest and witnessed the situation firsthand. The legislature's renunciation of the 1859 Slave Code notwithstanding, Hispano landholders and civic leaders continued to detain Indians and indebted citizens as servants. On January 3, 1867, Radical Republican senator Charles Sumner informed Congress that all available evidence implicated New Mexicans in the retention of a variation of slavery that "a proclamation of the President has down to this day been unable to root out," clearly referencing Andrew Johnson's recent executive order. "During the life of Mr. Lincoln I more than once appealed to him to exercise his power as the head of the executive, to root this evil out of the Territory of New Mexico," Sumner claimed, but the more urgent demands of the Civil War had prevented the president from doing so prior to the assassination, and it thus fell to Johnson to issue the order in June 1865.[55]

Although Lincoln did not take forceful action prior to his death, Sumner's repeated inquiries into southwestern slavery had led Commissioner Dole to solicit advice from his subagent in New Mexico, Michael Steck, about the most appropriate policy for effecting "the liberation and disposition of such Indians as are now held in bondage," with specific reference to the Navajo tribe.[56] Citing reports from Bureau of Indian Affairs officials as corroborating evidence, Sumner himself conceded following the Civil War that "this abuse has continued, and according to the official evidence it seems to have increased."[57] To advance his argument, Sumner read aloud from the report of a special agent named Julius K. Graves, who a year earlier had conducted investigations throughout New Mexico. "In spite of the stringent orders of the Government, the system continues, and nearly every Federal officer held peons in service," Graves observed, noting that even the superintendent of Indian affairs "had half a dozen."[58] The special agent recommended that the government adopt "a definite policy relative to this remaining blot upon the otherwise fair scroll of freedom," lest peonage continue to exist in a nation professing to be democratic. Graves also suggested that the government establish a branch of the Freedmen's Bureau in New Mexico to provide educational opportunities to children born to peon parents and redistribute small parcels of land to men held in debt bondage.[59] In response to Graves's damaging indictment, territorial legislators once again dismissed peonage as a form of voluntary servitude. They also swore that the enslavement of Indians stemmed from "ancient custom" and that Hispanos who adopted captives treated them "as members of their own legal family," granting them all of the rights and privileges incumbent upon "legitimate children."[60] Many lawmakers continued to use these cultural and filial considerations of dependency to justify the retention of Indian captives in New Mexico households.

Graves cited several specific incidents proving that territorial officials generally, and military officers particularly, held personal interests in slavery and peonage. One such reference pertained to Assistant Inspector General of the Army Nelson H. Davis. In August 1865, Davis ordered Captain James H. Whitlock, the commanding officer at Fort Selden in southern New Mexico, to "allow and assist" Don Pedro García in reclaiming a fugitive peon named Antonio Rodriguez. In light of recent legislative developments relative to slavery and servitude, Whitlock immediately questioned the legality of such an order. "The laws of the Territory, according to my recollection, have made it a penal offense to return a man to another claiming him as his own," Whitlock wrote, noting that the federal government had already abolished involuntary servitude and that such an order contradicted that mandate. Furthermore, an article of war passed by Congress on March 13, 1862, prohibited military officers from using either their troops or their authority "for the purpose of returning fugitives from service or labor" to their masters, a decree applying primarily to escaped black slaves but that, by literal definition, also encompassed peons and captives.[61] Mindful of these legal underpinnings and their implications in transforming Union forces into an army of liberation, Whitlock boldly informed Davis that his order to capture and return peons to their owners "is directly contrary to my opinion of law and justice, and I will only do it on positive and unmistakable orders." Hesitant to break the law, he requested further affirmation before taking any action.[62]

Captain Whitlock's fortitude ultimately succumbed to the dictates of the military chain of command. As a subordinate officer, he had little choice but to comply with the order, a fact that his superiors reiterated to him in no uncertain terms. Inspector Davis (ironically a native of Massachusetts, the bastion of abolitionist ideology) defended his order and upheld peonage as a legal institution. In conformity with the 1851 master-servant law, he defined it as voluntary servitude, describing peonage as an apprenticeship agreement between two contracting parties. "Not only can the master arrest and take his servant peon," he wrote, "but the civil authorities are commanded to arrest and deliver the peon to his master when deserting him." Davis reproached Whitlock for his insubordinate rebuke of the initial order. "You ask for explicit instructions, and make use of disrespectful and threatening language," he scolded. "The first will be granted, and the latter this time overlooked." He ordered Whitlock "to aid in the rendition of peons when claimed by their masters" and concluded his admonition by naming Major James H. Carleton, commander of the New Mexico military department, as his authority for issuing the order and the person to whom Whitlock would be held accountable if he failed to comply.[63]

Accusations that military officers acted with complicity in perpetuating involuntary servitude had arisen periodically throughout the 1850s and 1860s, and the Davis-Whitlock incident affirmed the veracity of such claims. Indeed it had been military leaders who initially took chattel slaves to the territory after the 1846 American conquest, and army personnel owned most of New Mexico's approximately two dozen black slaves enumerated in the 1850 census. Congressional resolutions eventually prohibited officers from taking action relative to peonage or slavery in New Mexico, nor could they directly aid in the efforts of civil officials to force the emancipation of servants, although the Confiscation Acts did grant some leeway and allowed for indirect military emancipation if and when runaway captives or peons arrived at an army post. As Davis's order to Whitlock suggests, however, some officers paid little attention to statutory requirements and intervened in master-servant relations as they deemed appropriate. Government resolutions notwithstanding, the army did occasionally confront slaveholders, especially Indian groups retaining Hispanos in bondage. In this the U.S. military perpetuated the double standard that originated with Spanish and Mexican officials, who continuously demanded that tribes surrender their captives while failing to require the same of settlers who held Indians in captivity. Attempting to induce the manumission of slaves represented a conflict of interest according to some Civil War–era lawmakers, because the military officers making these demands sometimes remained amenable to the Southern proslavery cause, and their efforts, therefore, were often lackadaisical at best.[64]

Finding it difficult to spur New Mexicans to action, Senator Sumner invoked the aid of Congress "to stop the practice" of peonage and captivity altogether and called upon the War Department to initiate an inquiry into Major Carleton's issuance of orders that upheld institutions of bondage. "The administration of military affairs in the Territory of New Mexico has been a standing disgrace to this Government," one senator from California roared in an open indictment of Carleton's policies and morality.[65] Unfortunately for Sumner and his Radical Republican colleagues, the ambivalent sentiment toward peonage that characterized men like Davis and Carleton represented the norm rather than the exception in New Mexico. As seen in the case of Captain Whitlock, some officers did question the issuance of seemingly proslavery orders, aware that they contradicted federal laws prohibiting involuntary servitude. As the correspondence between Davis and Whitlock revealed, however, lower-ranking army personnel simply could not sustain an argument in the face of orders from their commanding officers in Santa Fe and Washington. As long as Carleton continued to allow the recapture of runaway servants through military force, the practice of holding peons would remain unimpeded. As a staunch authoritarian, Carleton imposed martial law and presided over a veritable monarchy in New Mexico's military and civil affairs during the Civil War, until repeated complaints about his overextended authority prompted the War Department to transfer him to another theater in 1868. For the five years that he spent in command of New Mexico, however, his unspoken support of peonage trickled down the military ranks and undermined the attempts of outsiders to uproot it.

A month after Sumner's tirade in the Capitol Building, Republican senator Henry Wilson of Massachusetts implored his colleagues to consider an act "to abolish and forever prohibit the system of peonage," not only in New Mexico but throughout the United States. If approved, the law would supplement both President Johnson's 1865 executive order forbidding the enslavement of Indians as well as the 1866 Civil Rights Bill, which stated in part that all Americans, regardless of "race, religion, or previous condition of servitude," would be assured their basic rights.[66] Taken collectively, the three decrees provided the legislative framework necessary to unravel all systems of coerced labor in the Southwest. Although the Thirteenth Amendment, the Civil Rights Bill, and other Reconstruction legislation were all conceived with African Americans and Southerners foremost in mind—Supreme Court justice Samuel Miller admitted as much when ruling on the famous *Slaughter-House Cases* (1873)—reformers utilized those edicts to assert the rights of captive Indians and indebted peons, marking the beginning of a crusade to liberate all involuntary servants in the Southwest.[67]

Senator Wilson met with considerable resistance from the moderate wing of the Republican Party, members of which demanded that he specifically define "what this thing called peonage is." After more than two decades of deliberation on captivity and debt bondage, a four-year Civil War, and ratification of the Thirteenth Amendment, federal lawmakers had yet to reach a consensus on what exactly constituted involuntary servitude. Kentucky senator Garrett Davis proclaimed that he had "seen a great deal of general statement about peonage" yet admitted to having little understanding of how it operated or who it affected. Colleagues enlightened him by describing it as "a system of modified servitude which is carried on to a great extent in New Mexico, and especially to a lamentable extent with the Indians," specifically mentioning the use of force in holding such persons in long-term bondage.[68] In so defining the institution, congressmen echoed previous explanations that had been forgotten or disregarded over the preceding twenty years. The respondents exhibited a similar naiveté concerning peonage, in that they conflated debt bondage and Indian slavery as one and the same thing.

After hearing several descriptions of peonage, all of which represented it as a form of involuntary servitude, Senator Davis snidely remarked, "I have been for a good many years of my life in about the same state of slavery that . . . peons of [New] Mexico have been." He told onlookers that he had accrued significant debts earlier in life, "and I have worked mighty hard to repay them." As Davis saw it, his condition had been worse than that of peons, in that his creditors never supported him or provided food, shelter, and clothing while he worked elsewhere for wages to pay them off.[69] He thus likened himself to having endured slavery simply by accruing debts, failing to distinguish between owing money and repaying it without any hindrance on one's liberty and mobility, and being subverted to a lifetime of involuntary labor, as in the case of New Mexico's peons.

The Senate bill addressed the issue of New Mexican peonage, but it also cast a larger shadow by precluding involuntary servitude, in its various forms, from all parts of the United States. By abolishing peonage, proponents of the new law assured skeptics that they sought to do nothing more than limit creditors to customary methods of collecting debts without holding "the peon in slavery."[70] After striking out a section of the bill that would have unilaterally voided every peon's debt and eliminated all liability, the

Senate approved the revised measure on February 19 and submitted it to President Johnson, who signed it into law on March 2, 1867—the same day that he approved a landmark bankruptcy act that codified additional debtor protections.[71] From a legislative standpoint, this symbolized the end of peonage, although it would be some time before its implementation actually liberated involuntary servants in the southwestern territories.

The Peon Law, as it came to be known, explicitly forbade any individual from holding another person "to service or labor under the system known as peonage," specifically referencing Nuevomexicanos as the most egregious offenders. All previous laws and regulations that "established, maintained, or enforced" involuntary servitude, including persons being held in satisfaction of debt, became null and void. It further mandated that anybody convicted of holding persons against their will or detaining former servants would be subject to punishment in the form of a fine ranging from $1,000 to $5,000 or imprisonment for a period of up to five years, at the discretion of the judiciary.[72] The new statute also addressed the problem that Senator Sumner highlighted—that of the military department's complicity in promoting and perpetuating debt bondage. Congress charged all military and civil officers in New Mexico with the responsibility of enforcement, ordering strict sanctions for anybody caught obstructing or interfering with the authorities when carrying out these duties. Any federal officer failing to uphold the law would face court martial and dishonorable discharge if convicted.[73] The Peon Law provided strict and unambiguous consequences for anybody holding persons in bondage and showed no tolerance for federal and territorial officials who did not enforce the act.

On April 14, five weeks after President Johnson signed the Peon Law, New Mexico governor Robert B. Mitchell circulated a proclamation informing government officials and citizens of the provisions contained in the new edict. "In pursuance of the foregoing act of Congress," Mitchell declared, "I do hereby proclaim all persons free within the Territory of New Mexico, who are held to service or labor by any statute or custom heretofore in force." The governor promised strict compliance, warning that anybody continuing to hold captives or peons in a condition of slavery "will be severely dealt with" by the U.S. district attorney.[74] With this congressional action and gubernatorial assurance that it would be enforced, it seemed that finally, after three centuries, New Mexico would be rid of its traditional systems of servitude. Peons and Indian captives were thus among the last involuntary laborers in the United States to be liberated by federal mandate, their emancipation coming a full two years after that of African American slaves in the South.

Even after Congress outlawed debt bondage in 1867, however, the institution did not immediately disappear in the Southwest. The Peon Law was little more than a duplication of the Emancipation Proclamation, inasmuch as it served almost exclusively as a symbolic measure and did little, if anything, to actively liberate servants. Just four months after the edict went into effect, Superintendent of Indian Affairs A. B. Norton circulated a memorandum stressing the importance of compliance. Realizing that some Pueblo leaders held peons, Norton instructed an Indian agent named John Ward to ensure that those in authority understood "that all persons retained as peons . . . [must] be immediately released & set free from said bondage."[75] Norton's order doubtless liberated some bondsmen but certainly did not have a universal effect.

Prompted by the persistence of slaveholders and well attuned to the fact that few peons had actually been freed, Governor Herman M. Heath circulated a proclamation on June 10, 1868, condemning slavery "in every name and form." As an avowed abolitionist, Heath declared the system of peonage to be "at variance with the principles of a Republican Government and repugnant to the moral, social and political advancement of the victims" and reiterated that "peonage and every other class of involuntary servitude" were forbidden in New Mexico. In a final attempt to ensure enforcement, the governor implored his colleagues to aid him in "utterly destroying the system of peonage in this Territory."[76]

Despite forceful declarations and the continuing efforts of government agents, many households retained servants long after the Peon Law went into effect. This was especially true in northern New Mexico, where the system had become more culturally ingrained than in other regions. The counties of Rio Arriba and Taos, along with southern Colorado's San Luis Valley, exemplified this citizen resistance.[77] In the seventeenth and eighteenth centuries, that portion of New Mexico had been among the first places that Spanish colonists settled. Involuntary servitude had existed in those regions the longest, having originated there before spreading to other areas as the population gradually dispersed. Just as the northern sector of New Mexico was the first to implement captive slavery, so too did it become the last to eradicate it. During the 1860s—two decades after New Mexico became a part of the United States—the Catholic Church recorded 849 captive baptisms, of which almost half (413) took place in Taos and Rio

Arriba counties. Even as indigenous slavery came under scrutiny during the Civil War years, baptism continued to be viewed as a form of spiritual salvation for Indians, allowing for their legal adoption into New Mexican families under moral pretenses.[78]

The federal government responded swiftly to reports of residents in these two counties who continued to hold hundreds of servants against their will. Indian Commissioner William W. Griffin, a Radical Republican and staunch antislavery man, conducted a full-scale investigation in 1868.[79] His probe revealed that many New Mexicans did indeed retain servants within their households, although most field laborers had been liberated by that point. This likely owed to the fact that domestic slaves could be more easily concealed indoors. According to Griffin, 87 percent of northern New Mexico households with peons had only one under their charge at that time, with most families having therefore liberated at least some bonds-people.[80]

Griffin's investigation resulted in 363 cases being brought against citizens who illegally held servants after implementation of the Thirteenth Amendment and subsequent 1867 Peon Law. The majority of those were Indian captives, with relatively few individuals remaining in debt bondage at that time. This suggests that peonage succumbed to abolitionist pressure first, while Indian slaves remained in servitude longer. The ability of New Mexicans to retain captives with minimal public opposition owed largely to rampant anti-Indian sentiments during the post–Civil War years, as both U.S. troops and civilian settlers continued to suffer disastrous defeats at the hands of nomadic tribes in the West. With news of hostile engagements between Anglo-Americans and Indians continuing to trickle eastward, civilians felt little remorse for such "savages" and fewer humanitarians took up their cause to advocate for the enforcement of Indian captivity laws.[81]

When Griffin arrived in New Mexico, he immediately ordered that all persons held as slaves be brought before him, whereupon he notified them of recent federal mandates prohibiting servitude and informed them that "they were strictly and absolutely free to live where and work for whom they desired." From that moment on, peons and captives would be "at perfect liberty to go where and when they pleased," although many of them chose to remain among the families with whom they had been residing as dependents for much if not all of their lives.[82] Their behavior mirrored that of some emancipated African American slaves in the South who became sharecroppers; many of New Mexico's landless Indian and Hispano servants could not sustain themselves financially, and therefore they opted to stay with their former masters and benefactors.

Griffin produced a detailed report on the extent to which involuntary servitude lingered as late as 1868. Of the 363 servants that he identified, a mere 70 claimed Hispanic ancestry as peons held in debt bondage, while 293 were Indian captives. Peons comprised only 19 percent of the cases, while indigenous slaves represented 81 percent, indicating the extent to which captivity superseded debt bondage at that point in time. All but 11 of the 363 persons received their freedom in the legal proceedings that followed. In Taos County, 2,280 households sheltered a total of 176 peons, and thus a mere 7 percent of homes appeared to defy the federal peonage law. Santa Fe and Rio Arriba counties had a combined 4,438 households, of which 48 held servants (5 peons and 43 captives), implicating those three counties as the last bastions of peonage. Unfortunately, territorial officials never recorded the number of homes with involuntary laborers prior to the passage of the 1867 law, so it is impossible to accurately determine how many families originally housed servants.[83] It is also unlikely that the investigation revealed the true number of slaves held in those households, as masters could have easily concealed their servants before the inquisitors arrived or, even more likely, coached their captives and peons on what to say in order to deflect suspicion.

Nearly three hundred Nuevomexicanos were subsequently arrested for violating federal law by holding peons and captives. Ultimately, only 171 defendants appeared before the New Mexico District Court. A number of prominent and influential territorial officials, as well as Catholic priests, could be counted among that number.[84] Juan Jose Santistevan of Taos County testified before a federal grand jury and attempted to exonerate himself and his fellow slaveholders of any wrongdoing. Santistevan assured the jurors that all of the servants remained with their masters of their own free will. "I know as long as I can remember that the Indians have been as servants," he explained, alluding to the slave raids that had become so common and asserting that the long-standing captive trade between Hispanos and Indians justified the holding of servants.[85] Santistevan's testimony indicated the hereditary nature of coerced labor in the territory, with servility and dependency sometimes passing from parents to children to grandchildren within the same household. It came as little surprise to those present when the grand jury failed to return a single indictment in any of the cases. Drawn from residents of Taos County, the jury consisted of Hispanos who supported the institution of peonage and would have never convicted their fellow citizens and friends for engaging in a practice that many of the jurors themselves had likely partaken at some point in their lives.[86]

Just as New Mexicans continued to hold involuntary servants, so too did the region's nomadic tribes retain a significant number of Hispanic captives. In 1883, nearly twenty years after passage of the laws prohibiting slavery, the Navajo agent Dennis Riordan reported that the tribe possessed as many as three hundred captives, most of whom had been abducted during intertribal warfare before the Long Walk. "A regular slave system has been in active operation amongst these Indians from time immemorial," Riordan explained. "The slaves are descendents of war captives and of persons sold into slavery from other tribes," many having been mere infants at the time of their abduction. He specifically named the Ute, Comanche, Apache, Moqui (Hopi), and Jemez groups as being complicit in the ongoing trafficking of captives. Riordan worked to free some twenty of those slaves, but he found it difficult and at times even impossible to dislodge servants from the Navajo tribe, which assimilated them into their families and culture.[87] A year later his successor, Agent John H. Bowman, explained in his annual report that "the Navajos still hold some slaves" but admitted that he could not think of an effective way to emancipate them. "Mr. Riordan, while agent here, brought some of them away from their owners and set them free," Bowman wrote, but he noted that most of those liberated quickly returned to their Navajo masters.[88]

Debt bondage in New Mexico did not persist to any significant degree after the 1870s, nor did the enslavement of Indians last much beyond that decade, but many of those already held in captivity and dependency would remain in that condition for the rest of their lives. The family of Lucien B. Maxwell, who at one time owned the biggest land grant in New Mexico and employed a large number of captives and peons on his vast estate at Cimarron, retained fifteen servants in 1870, seven of them Indian children.[89] In northern New Mexico communities, the 1870 census listed a considerable number of persons whose birthplace was either "Navajo Indian Country" or "Pah-Ute Indian Country." By that time, however, they comprised an extreme minority: 6 percent of Abiquiú's population; 5 percent of Tierra Amarilla's occupants; and a mere 3 percent of the inhabitants at Ojo

Caliente admitted to having been born Indian. The manner in which indigenous captives continued to be subjugated, however, came through in the census records, where their occupations invariably appeared as "domestic servants." Contrarily, New Mexico–born persons of similar social status listed their occupation as "keeping house," a much less suggestive term than that of servant.[90] The same discrepancy in occupational descriptions occurred during the 1860s, when the recent federal investigations and indictments, along with the Peon Law, induced residents to substitute the words "laborer" and "housekeeper" in place of "servant" when reporting their household data for census records.[91]

The perseverance of involuntary servitude after the Civil War can be traced directly to the long-running entrenchment of those institutions in regional society and culture. Perhaps nowhere in the United States had human bondage resulted in a more thoroughly amalgamated crucible of race and ethnicity than in the Southwest, where more than three centuries of continuous miscegenation between Euro-American colonists and indigenous captives produced a society altogether contingent upon systems of coercive labor and fictive kinship. Beginning in 1846, and lasting into the early 1870s, Anglo-Americans habitually misperceived the interconnectedness of human bondage with family and community structures. As a newly acquired entity of the United States, New Mexico found itself fully enthralled—albeit as a mere pawn—in the antebellum sectionalism that ultimately drove the nation to internecine conflict. After the culmination of the Civil War, Hispanos resisted efforts to eliminate debt peonage and Indian captivity despite black slaves having already received their statutory freedom in 1865. Consequently, New Mexicans would suffer the hamstringing political effects of their noncompliance during an era in which Reconstruction policies and Republican abolitionists reigned supreme at the federal level of governance. That defiance of federal law also left a permanent imprint on American democratic philosophy regarding involuntary servitude and free labor. The persistence of Indian captivity and debt peonage after 1865 resulted in federal legislation that specifically banned both forms of coercive labor and, in so doing, expanded the parameters of the Thirteenth Amendment by broadening legal definitions of involuntary servitude in the Reconstruction and Jim Crow eras.

Conclusion

The famous escaped slave Harriet Jacobs, whose twenty-seven years of traumatic bondage in the South mirrored the untold tales of countless captives and servants in the Southwest, wrote of slavery that "only by experience can anyone realize how deep, and dark, and foul is that pit of abominations."[1] Over many generations, thousands of men, women, and children in the Southwest shared the similarly stigmatizing experiences of captivity and debt peonage. Colonial and territorial New Mexico became a borderlands of human bondage wherein almost anybody, at any moment, might be swept away into captivity or coerced into a lifetime of debtor servitude. This harsh reality remained just as true in the 1850s as it had been in the 1750s or even the 1650s, demonstrating just how difficult it was to eliminate systems of slavery and involuntary servitude throughout North America.

While captivity and peonage gradually met their demise in the years following the Civil War, the legacy of those systems manifested itself in the lives of many New Mexicans, whose genealogy and culture reflect the institutions of human bondage that for centuries characterized personal and communal interaction in the region. Social and ethnic continuities demonstrate that such cultural distinctions remain firmly implanted in northern New Mexico's villages. The most well-known public display of that heritage is *Los Comanches*, a ritualized performance involving a Comanche chief and a captive girl in a *rescate* (redemption) ceremony.[2] Nuevomexicano oral histories also relate tales of grandparents or other distant relatives being taken captive by Apaches or Comanches in the 1800s. Señor Don R. Casados remembered a story that his father often told about one Teofilo Cordova, who had been abducted by Jicarilla Apaches and held captive for over seven years before making his escape. After describing the ordeal that the young man endured, Casados admitted that "the Spanish-speaking natives of the Territory many years back used to do the same things. They used to steal young Indian women and kept them to work as maids. Later, some joined in marriage." Many others told similar stories of ancestors carried into captivity, often while herding livestock or attending to chores in the fields, a testament to the lasting impression that enslavement left on the collective memory of New Mexican society.[3]

Among New Mexico's *genízaros*, individual families and entire communities continue to perform rituals and ceremonies that celebrate a multiethnic legacy, the annual feast of Santo Tomás in the town of Abiquiú being one of the more well-known examples. In many instances, however, this cultural consciousness is not outwardly expressed. Describing his twentieth-century upbringing as a *genízaro* in the Chama River Valley, Gilberto Benito Córdova remembered the difficulty that he encountered when attempting to learn about his ethnic heritage. Family members dismissed his inquiries, telling the curious youngster that the people of Abiquiú were all Indians, "it's just that they don't talk about it . . . they are secret Indians, masquerading as Mejicanos."[4] After reaching adulthood, Córdova preserved and perpetuated cherished customs through published renditions of oral tradition and folklore. He explained in 1973 that "present day Abiquiu is a Hispano village three hundred and sixty three days of the year. The remaining two days the villagers are actively conscious of their Genízaro origin. . . . Hispano culture is put aside and the Indian heritage of Abiquiu, which on other days is scarcely evident, receives its tribute."[5] Throughout northern New Mexico, Catholic descendants of eighteenth-century *genízaros* continue to perform ritualistic observances of their multifaceted ethnic and cultural backgrounds.[6] In 2007, the legislature passed a memorial "recognizing the role of genizaros in New Mexico history and their legacy" and proclaimed them a state-recognized tribe, highlighting the continuity and perseverance of ethnic identity and tradition in local Hispanic communities.[7] The cultural hybridity of New Mexico's *genízaros* exemplifies the far-reaching impact of the captive slave trade. As Córdova himself proclaimed, "The truth is that the genizaros are both Indian and Hispano. Genizaros are living bridges between the Indian and Hispano worlds. . . . Since many genizaros came from Plains tribes, genizaros are also cultural bridges between the Pueblo and Non-Pueblo worlds. This is what it is to be a genizaro."[8]

Peonage also retains a place in the consciousness of New Mexicans. In 1921, an elderly man named Donaciano Sandoval related a story about his lifetime of servitude at the homestead of former New Mexico governor Donaciano Vigil. Sandoval had been a servant to Vigil since the age of sixteen, and he remained in that condition after the Civil War. Toiling alongside several other bondsmen, he recalled that "they did not feel like slaves and were not treated as such by the Governor, but rather as members of his family to be reared into manhood for some purpose." Vigil's mind-set revealed the extent to which *patrones* succeeded in asserting power and cultivating feelings of security and loyalty simply by placing a roof over the heads of their peons. In response to federal enforcement of the 1867 Peon Law, Vigil offered Sandoval and the others their freedom, but they declined the opportunity. The elderly *patrón* assured his subjects that they need not continue working in repayment of their debt and were "free to go." None-theless, all but one of the peons elected to remain with their master, a testament to the pervasiveness of fictive kinship and patriarchal bonds of dependency that developed through captivity and peonage.[9]

The issue of New Mexican peonage caught public attention once again during the tumultuous 1960s, when political protest movements among Chicanos, Indians, African Americans, women, and other underrepresented groups precipitated social reform throughout the United States. In 1967—exactly one hundred years after Congress approved the Peon Law—the *Albuquerque Journal* featured a front-page headline reading "Suit Says Man Held in Peonage 33 Years." Abernicio Gonzales, a ranch hand near the rural town of Cabezón in northern New Mexico, filed a lawsuit against Joe Montoya, the son of a deceased rancher who negotiated a verbal labor con-tract with Gonzales in 1933. Illiterate and unaware of his rights, the thirteen-year-old peon's mother had sent him to work in repayment of a $50 debt at the height of the Great Depression. Although the mother's pecuniary obligation was to be satisfied after just eighty days of her son's labor, the ambiguous nature of their unwritten arrangement kept Abernicio bound for the next three decades. As the owner of the ranch, Elias Montoya verbally agreed to pay the boy 50 cents per day "plus food, clothing, and shelter," if he would continue working there, and he assured the unsus-pecting lad that the wages would be deposited into the bank for him. When Gonzales began asking for his money in the 1960s, the Montoya family demurred, and when the now middle-aged man sought employment else-where, the landowners "forcibly returned him to the ranch" and "beat Gon-zales on different occasions."[10]

The case seemed as though it had been pulled directly from an 1850s territorial court file. In almost every particular, it matched the plight of New Mexican peons a century earlier. Just like Mariana Jaremillo in 1857, Gonzales had been sent to work in repayment of a parent's debt, and a simple verbal agreement had ensured that the young man would remain in a state of servitude for much of his life. Montoya provided food and shelter for Gonzales—as did most *patrones* in order to increase one's sense of dependency—but when it came time to collect his wages for many years of hard labor, the peon found that the assets did not even exist. When the aggrieved Gonzales decided to terminate his spoken agreement and seek employment elsewhere, Montoya remanded him to service at the Cabezón ranch and resorted to physical force in order to keep him there. Most aspects of the 1851 master-servant act and the 1857 New Mexico Supreme Court rulings—including minors in bondage, verbal contracts, corporal punishment, and the recapture of runaways—were reflected in the suit that Gonzales brought against Montoya in 1967.

In Albuquerque, United States District Attorney John Quinn and FBI special agent Leonard Blaylock sent details about the case to their superiors in the Civil Rights Division of the Department of Justice and awaited instructions on how to proceed. In the meantime, the Albuquerque attorney Ed Parham, who handled the case for Gonzales, told newspaper correspondents that "almost half the Spanish-American or ranch workers in the northern New Mexico counties are laboring in semi-peonage." Such individuals, he claimed, worked from sunup to sundown in exchange for food and housing, under the false assumption that wages were being deposited into bank accounts to provide for their welfare in old age. "Abernicio is not alone," Parham insisted, estimating 40 to 50 percent of northern New Mexicans to be "in a state of semi-peonage" despite the federal minimum wage law having been recently extended to encompass agricultural workers and ranch hands. Just as they had done in the antebellum era, New Mexican landholders skirted ambiguous laws and manipulated verbal contracts in order to retain cheap dependent labor. By the 1960s, according to Parham, some ranchers even threatened to inform the Internal Revenue Service of any peon's failure to report years of income whenever one complained about their situation or asked that their wages be delivered to them.[11] One hundred years after the fact, residual elements of debtor servitude continued to exist in northern New Mexico, operating within a system of labor that relied upon cultural tradition, geographic isolation, and a certain amount of salutary neglect in order to retain workers in bondage. The fact that Gonzales's claims about his condition and treatment so closely resembled those of peons a century earlier suggests that, while debt bondage declined in prominence and visibility, it remained little changed in practice where it did continue to exist.

Peonage also assumed an active presence in modern Hispano culture and oral tradition. As a ten-year-old boy growing up near Belen, New Mexico, in the 1950s, Anthony Romero recalls trips with his grandfather to visit "Don Silvestre," from whom locals would purchase bottles of wine. As they quibbled over details of the transaction, the elderly winemaker would motion toward the child while asking the grandfather, "*Cuánto por el peón?*" (How much for the peon?). "I assumed as a young boy that if my grandfather sold me to Don Silvestre, he would put me straight to work in his vineyards," Romero says, recalling that the dynamics of the situation made a strong impression on him. The circumstances surrounding the seemingly harmless question are compelling for their perpetuation of inegalitarian social relationships revolving around largely defunct systems of coerced labor and dependency. According to Romero, Don Silvestre and other locals used the phrase only in reference to children, thus denoting status and authority in terms of age and servility.

The fact that many nineteenth-century parents contracted their children into peonage for repayment of debt suggests a more sinister element to Don Silvestre's question, which also inferred leverage over Romero's grandfather in the deal that was about to occur. The implication was that the young boy could be exchanged for the wine, should the man lack sufficient funds to buy the product outright. The insinuation that the lad (or at least his labor) could be purchased indicated a sense of ownership over him in much the same way that a *patrón* owned the labor of a peon in the 1800s, or that an eighteenth-century master might trade an Indian captive for a horse or a gun in the Taos marketplace. While the question "*Cuánto por el peón?*" was no doubt posed in jest—a grandfather in the 1950s would not have sold his grandson into peonage at the local vineyards, nor could Don Silvestre have simply bought a child without violating the law—the language used and the circumstances surrounding the event speak volumes about the cultural legacy of peonage and dependency as markers of social status and authority in New Mexico.[12]

The two systems of coerced servitude that evolved during the colonial period changed drastically throughout the nineteenth century, yet they remained an important element of the Hispano and Indian experiences and continue to resonate in the modern era. While the cultural and ethnic components of peonage and captivity are known throughout northern New Mexico, their impact on judicial and political ideology in the United States remains much more obscure in the historiography of American slavery.

Just as this narrative had two strands—one cultural and social, the other political and ideological—so too did the twentieth-century legacies of captivity and peonage diverge in both directions. While those systems of unwaged labor persevered in the oral traditions and cultural practices of Hispanos in the Southwest, debt peonage also attained newfound judicial importance in many Southern states during the Jim Crow era.

While debt peonage was largely eradicated in New Mexico, where expanding merchant capitalism and the arrival of the railroad in 1879 brought the proliferation of wage labor and free markets, the system shifted to the South and became a mechanism whereby rural plantations and farms, as well as corporate mining operations, retained African Americans in a modified form of labor bondage.[13] During the Jim Crow era, kaleidoscopic modes of oppressive social relations proliferated throughout the South, with criminal lessees, female convicts, chain gangs, peons, and sharecroppers filling the labor void that emancipation created.[14]

The primary operational difference between the forms of peonage that existed in New Mexico and in the South involved the manner whereby a person came into debt. Criminal conviction provided the chief method for Southern corporations and white farmers wishing to secure cheap black labor. A nefarious petty charge—usually vagrancy, theft, gambling, or even cursing—was sufficient for local sheriffs to arrest anybody they wished and place them on immediate trial, the purpose being to impose a fine and court costs, which forced the accused individual (almost invariably a black man of working age) into a debt that he or she could not afford to repay. A nearby farmer or mining superintendent, acting as a sort of bail bondsman, would then cover the fines and fees for the unfortunate convicts in exchange for a prefigured duration of labor, typically several months to one year. Once a "convict" neared the completion of that term, new charges would often be levied, with masters and creditors accusing the peon of attempted escape, sexual assault, or some other contrived crime in order to prolong the servitude. In the South, debt peonage and convict labor became virtually synonymous within a penal system that perpetuated a sort of neo-slavery into the twentieth century.[15]

In New Mexico, by contrast, little evidence exists to suggest that criminality was used as a method for creating a debt obligation, nor did a criminal lessee system develop there to any significant extent, although the 1859 Slave Code did include a provision to allow for black convict labor through the imposition of large fines. Instead, Nuevomexicanos in rural areas came into financial arrears simply by borrowing or purchasing consumer goods on credit, with the understanding that the amount owed would be repaid through an unwritten labor contract with the *hacendado* or landowner from whom they acquired the items or received the loan. In a system that resembled Southern sharecropping, many of New Mexico's peons also worked as herdsmen on sheep ranches, where a *patrón* advanced them a certain number of animals to raise and shear in exchange for a predetermined portion of the wool harvest. Aside from the initial causes of indebtedness, however, the two regional systems of peonage operated similarly in that they permanently bound the indebted subject and provided strict punishments for those who attempted to escape or otherwise deviated from the terms of their labor contract. For this reason, the form of peonage that developed in nineteenth-century New Mexico, the political debates surrounding it throughout the Civil War era, and the laws passed to end it during Reconstruction all became critical precedents for twentieth-century judicial proceedings that abolished debtor servitude in the Deep South.

Writing in 1888, Booker T. Washington lamented that the issuance of credit and concomitant debt servitude had already become a technique whereby "colored people on these plantations are held in a kind of slavery that is in one sense as bad as the slavery of antebellum days."[16] The famed African American sociologist and political activist W. E. B. DuBois later wrote of the postbellum era that "the wage of the Negro worker, despite the war amendments, was to be reduced to the level of bare subsistence by taxation, peonage, caste, and every method of discrimination."[17] The same form of coercive labor that Congress banned in New Mexico thus appeared in the South within two decades of the Peon Law being passed and persisted there into the twentieth century. In this sense, southwestern peonage served as an operational prototype for the systems of involuntary servitude that developed in the New South, a fact that many district and federal judges of the Jim Crow era explicitly recognized when tracing the precedent of oppressive labor regimes to the form of debt bondage that existed in territorial New Mexico.

Despite Booker T. Washington's pleas for action, another decade would pass before the first major peonage case was brought before a judge. A Georgia district court heard a suit in 1899 charging the defendant with holding "persons of African descent" in bondage as peons. The prosecutor relied upon the 1867 congressional ban on peonage in New Mexico as the basis for criminality. District judge William T. Newman ruled that the system of debtor servitude in New Mexico, upon which the 1867 law had been formulated, never existed in Georgia and that all allegations of wrongdoing were therefore ill-conceived. "It would be the merest perversion of this act to attempt to apply it to an ordinary case of restraint of personal liberty," he declared, "and the case is not strengthened by the charge that the person so restrained is of African descent."[18] Several judges in Florida, Alabama, and Georgia disagreed with this ruling, which implicitly found the 1867 Peon Law to be inapplicable because, according to Judge Newman's rationale, a law forbidding peonage could not be used if peonage did not exist in the first place.[19]

In 1904, a similar case involving Samuel Clyatt of Florida and two runaway African American peons, Will Gordon and Mose Ridley, reached the U.S. Supreme Court and resulted in a ruling that upheld the constitutionality of the 1867 Peon Law. That landmark decision, written by Associate Justice David J. Brewer, specifically alluded to the 1857 case *Jaremillo v. Romero*, in which New Mexico Supreme Court judge Kirby Benedict provided the first judicial precedent on peonage in the United States. In 1901, the circuit court for the northern district of Florida passed down a conviction in the initial case, finding that the defendant forcibly returned the two peons, Gordon and Ridley, to a condition of bondage and therefore sentenced Clyatt to a somewhat ironic punishment of four years of hard labor. The appeal argued that the 1867 Peon Law, upon which the 1901 ruling had been formulated, pertained only to U.S. territories and had no legal bearing in the states. Furthermore, the appellants contended that the Thirteenth Amendment did not apply to peonage because that system did not constitute involuntary servitude—the exact same argument that New Mexico legislators advanced in the 1860s when amending territorial master-servant codes to define peonage as strictly voluntary.

Regarding the charge that peonage had been variously classified as voluntary or involuntary in nature, the court decided that such a distinction emanated simply from the origin of the servitude in either debt or criminal conviction. Aside from the point of derivation, the characteristics of the actual labor were identical and therefore the court concluded that "peonage, however created, is compulsory service—involuntary servitude." Justice Brewer described peonage as "a status or condition of compulsory service, based upon the indebtedness of the peon to the master," and he stressed that "the basal fact is indebtedness." Using New Mexico's *Jaremillo v. Romero* case as precedent and the 1867 Peon Law as supporting legal doctrine, the court recognized the applicability of the Thirteenth Amendment's ban on involuntary labor to cases involving peonage, therefore declining to reverse the conviction of Samuel Clyatt.[20] The Supreme Court thus affirmed the far-reaching implications of New Mexican peonage for America's judicial and political institutions.

Three years later, South Carolina district judge William H. Brawley, who lost an arm fighting for the Confederate Army during the Civil War, employed the U.S. Supreme Court decision when ruling on a similar case involving peonage. The South Carolina state legislature had passed a law in 1904 that recognized both written and verbal labor contracts, allowing for prosecution and imprisonment via chain gang for defaulted debtors, "the great body of [whom], as is well known, are negroes." The law provided that conviction and chain-gang service only satisfied the legal requirement for punishment and did not release debtors from their contractual obligation, effectively perpetuating servitude even after the guilty party satisfied court-mandated sentencing. The case involved Enoch and Elijah Drayton, African American twin brothers, who allegedly failed to complete the tasks assigned to them by their creditor, R. Lebby Clement of Charleston County. The petitioners and their counsel alleged that the 1904 South Carolina statute "constituted an attempt to secure compulsory service in payment of a debt" and thus violated both the Thirteenth Amendment and the 1867 Peon Law.[21]

Like the U.S. Supreme Court before him, Judge Brawley invoked mid-nineteenth-century southwestern peonage as a judicial measuring stick when formulating his decision in the case. He quoted the former territorial secretary William Davis's 1857 book *El Gringo; or, New Mexico and Her People* at length in order to describe the nature of debtor servitude "as it existed in New Mexico," with the specific intent of demonstrating that a system of veritable slavery might result if South Carolina's 1904 master-servant law remained in effect. The judge used the 1867 Peon Law and the 1904 Supreme Court ruling in the Clyatt case to support his opinion that the South Carolina statute's only purpose had been to "secure compulsory service" and, in so doing, "provide a coercive weapon to be used by the employer." In ruling the law unconstitutional, Brawley condemned peonage as a mechanism of social and physical oppression and declared that "to compel one person to labor for another against his will is legalized thralldom." Based on his understanding of New Mexico peonage in the antebellum era, and in conformity with the legal doctrine that had been established over the preceding four decades in response to that Hispano labor system, Brawley discharged the two brothers as free men and affirmed unequivocally that any type of coerced labor "is as degrading as that of slavery."[22]

Even with the Clyatt and Drayton decisions, salutary neglect toward peonage prevailed throughout the South for decades to come. The attorney general's 1907 annual report noted eighty-three peonage complaints pending with the Department of Justice at that time. Prompted by the increasing prevalence of such lawsuits and widespread noncompliance with the Supreme Court ruling, U.S. Assistant Attorney General Charles W. Russell conducted a four-month investigation of debtor servitude in several Southern states. He submitted a formal report recommending "that an incessant fight be made against peonage," pointing out that Congress must amend the legal definition to encompass "the holding of persons in servitude whether in liquidation of an indebtedness or otherwise." Directly referencing the recent decision of Judge Brawley in South Carolina, Russell explained that Southern states used a variety of fraudulent methods to force blacks into a contrived debt, including laws pertaining to contract labor, vagrancy, and even basic unemployment. Such statutes, he said, "should all be wiped out or so amended as to be harmless for the purpose of enslaving workmen."[23]

Although a 1911 court case overturned Alabama's debtor servitude laws, most residents—and even some local and state judges—ignored that ruling just as they had cast aside the U.S. Supreme Court decision six years earlier, and much like many New Mexicans had done following passage of the federal Peon Law in 1867. Over the first four decades of the twentieth century, hundreds of cases were heard throughout the nation relative to debt peonage; in the vast majority of instances, the hearings pertained to black persons of lower socioeconomic status who had become veritable slaves on the basis of an imposed debt.[24] Not until the World War II era—when the Supreme Court heard two cases involving repayment of advance wages and breach of contract in Florida and Georgia—did the federal judiciary authoritatively preclude peonage in practice. The effectiveness of those two rulings, however, had less to do with a newfound dedication to compliance or enforcement on the part of Southerners than with the fact that industrialized mining and mechanized farming had begun to render peonage obsolete and unprofitable.[25]

The systems of coerced labor that first developed in Spanish New Mexico played an important role in the reformulation of political and legal thought during the Civil War, Reconstruction, and Jim Crow eras, and the legislative and judicial precedents set in the Southwest continued to influence American democracy and jurisprudence well into the twentieth century. Although chattel slavery dominated everyday discourse in the antebellum United States, and federal mandates during the Civil War—including the First and Second Confiscation Acts, the Emancipation Proclamation, and the Thirteenth Amendment—aimed primarily to liberate black slaves in the rebellious South, debt peonage and Indian slavery also played an important role in the nation's nineteenth-century ideological transformations.[26]

Just as many American lawmakers, judges, public officials, and humanitarian reformers came to understand in their own time that slavery was not confined to the South's chattel system, so too must we as citizens begin to think about peonage and captivity within the paradigm of slavery, as they both significantly impacted the expansion of democratic free labor ideology in the post–Civil War United States. Without the political and legal understandings of New Mexican peonage and captivity established during the antebellum and Reconstruction eras, federal district court judges and U.S. Supreme Court justices would have lacked the necessary precedents to attack similar systems of involuntary servitude that developed in the Jim Crow South. In order to fully understand American slavery and the changes in social, political, and legal institutions wrought by the Civil War, debt peonage and Indian captivity must be accorded their rightful place in historical discussions about the nation's second democratic revolution and its legacy in shaping evolving American identities ever since.

Notes

Prologue

1. Michael Steck to William P. Dole, January 13, 1864, RG75, OIA, M234, LR, NMS, Roll 552. See also John Greiner to Luke Lea, May 19, 1852, in Annie Heloise Abel, ed., *The Official Correspondence of James S. Calhoun While Indian Agent at Santa Fe and Superintendent of Indian Affairs in New Mexico, 1849–1852* (Washington, DC: Government Printing Office, 1915), 537.

2. Timothy G. Baugh, "Ecology and Exchange: The Dynamics of Plains-Pueblo Interaction," in Katherine A. Spielmann, ed., *Farmers, Hunters, and Colonists: Interaction Between the Southwest and the Southern Plains* (Tucson: University of Arizona Press, 1991), 107–27; Laura Bayer, *Santa Ana: The People, the Pueblo, and the History of Tamaya* (Albuquerque: University of New Mexico Press, 1994), 101–4; Albert H. Schroeder, "Rio Grande Ethnohistory," in Alfonso Ortiz, ed., *New Perspectives on the Pueblos* (Albuquerque: University of New Mexico Press, 1972), esp. 50–70; James F. Brooks, *Captives & Cousins: Slavery, Kinship, and Community in the Southwest Borderlands* (Chapel Hill: University of North Carolina Press, 2002), 71; Colin G. Calloway, *One Vast Winter Count: The Native American West Before Lewis and Clark* (Lincoln: University of Nebraska Press, 2003), 205.

3. George P. Hammond and Agapito Rey, eds., *Narratives of the Coronado Expedition 1540–1542* (Albuquerque: University of New Mexico Press, 1940), 219.

4. For an excellent analysis of Indian slaves in New Spain's silver mines, see Andrés Reséndez, *The Other Slavery: The Uncovered Story of Indian Enslavement in America* (New York: Houghton Mifflin Harcourt, 2016), 100–124.

5. On pre-Revolt relations between Pueblos and Spaniards, see Reséndez, *Other Slavery*, 116–23; James A. Vlasich, *Pueblo Indian Agriculture* (Albuquerque: University of New Mexico Press, 2005), 17–30; Schroeder, "Rio Grande Ethnohistory," 41–56. For a comparison of Spanish labor systems throughout the New World, see Thomas D. Hall, "The Rio de la Plata and the Greater Southwest," in Donna J. Guy and Thomas E. Sheridan, eds., *Contested Ground: Comparative Frontiers on the Northern and Southern Edges of the Spanish Empire* (Tucson: University of Arizona Press, 1998), 155–66; Howard Lamar, "From Bondage to Contract: Ethnic Labor in the American West,

1600–1890," in Steven Hahn and Jonathan Prude, eds., *The Countryside in the Age of Capitalist Transformation* (Chapel Hill: University of North Carolina Press, 1985), 296.

6. Pekka Hämäläinen, "The Shapes of Power: Indians, Europeans, and North American Worlds from the Seventeenth to the Nineteenth Century," in Juliana Barr and Edward Countryman, eds., *Contested Spaces of Early America* (Philadelphia: University of Pennsylvania Press, 2014), 62; Thomas D. Hall, *A World-Systems Reader: New Perspectives on Gender, Urbanism, Cultures, Indigenous Peoples, and Ecology* (Boulder, CO: Rowman and Littlefield, 2000), 35. For the development of New Mexico's economy during the colonial period, see Ross Frank, *From Settler to Citizen: New Mexican Economic Development and the Creation of Vecino Society, 1750–1820* (Berkeley: University of California Press, 2000); Heather B. Trigg, *From Household to Empire: Society and Economy in Early Colonial New Mexico* (Tucson: University of Arizona Press, 2005).

7. James F. Brooks, " 'This Evil Extends Especially . . . to the Feminine Sex': Negotiating Captivity in the New Mexico Borderlands," *Feminist Studies* 22 (Summer 1996): 279–309.

8. See H. Allen Anderson, "The Encomienda in New Mexico, 1598–1680," *New Mexico Historical Review* 60 (October 1985): 353–73; David H. Snow, "A Note on Encomienda Economics in Seventeenth-Century New Mexico," in Marta Weigle, ed., *Hispanic Arts and Ethnohistory in the Southwest* (Santa Fe, NM: Ancient City Press, 1983), 347–57; Lesley Byrd Simpson, *The Encomienda in New Spain: The Beginnings of Spanish Mexico* (Berkeley: University of California Press, 1966).

9. See María Elena Martínez, *Genealogical Fictions: Limpieza de Sangre, Religion, and Gender in Colonial Mexico* (Stanford, CA: Stanford University Press, 2008), 154–55; J. H. Elliott, *Empires of the Atlantic World: Britain and Spain in America, 1492–1830* (New Haven, CT: Yale University Press, 2006), 81; Martha Menchaca, *Recovering History, Constructing Race: The Indian, Black, and White Roots of Mexican Americans* (Austin: University of Texas Press, 2001), 53–57. See also Fray Francisco Atanasio Domínguez, *The Missions of New Mexico, 1776: A Description by Fray Francisco Atanasio Domínguez, with Other Contemporary Documents*, edited and translated by Eleanor B. Adams and Fray Angelico Chavez (Albuquerque: University of New Mexico Press, 1956), 99.

10. For Spanish policy on indigenous slavery, see David J. Weber, *Bárbaros: Spaniards and Their Savages in the Age of Enlightenment* (New Haven, CT: Yale University Press, 2005), 234–35, 239; Robert Archibald, "Assimilation and Acculturation in Colonial New Mexico," *New Mexico Historical Review* 53 (July 1978): 206–7; John Francis Maxwell, *Slavery and the Catholic Church: The History of Catholic Teaching Concerning the Moral Legitimacy of the Institution of Slavery* (Chichester, UK: Barry Rose, 1975), esp. 68–71. On the "New Laws," see Reséndez, *Other Slavery*, 67–68, 74–75.

11. Virginia's Just-War Doctrine (1676), quoted in Ira Berlin, *Generations of Captivity: A History of African-American Slaves* (Cambridge, MA: Belknap Press of Harvard University Press, 2003), 55. See also James F. Brooks, " 'Lest We Go in Search of Relief

to Our Lands and Our Nation': Customary Justice and Colonial Law in the New Mexico Borderlands, 1680–1821," in Christopher L. Tomlins and Bruce H. Mann, eds., *The Many Legalities of Early America* (Chapel Hill: University of North Carolina Press, 2001), 156–57; Alan Gallay, *The Indian Slave Trade: The Rise of the English Empire in the American South, 1670–1717* (New Haven, CT: Yale University Press, 2002), 46–47.

12. "Petition of Father Juan de Prada," September 26, 1638, in Charles Wilson Hackett, ed., *Historical Documents Relating to New Mexico, Nueva Vizcaya, and Approaches Thereto, to 1773*, vol. 3 (Washington, DC: Carnegie Institution, 1923–37), 111.

13. Brooks, *Captives & Cousins*, 50; Reséndez, *Other Slavery*, 116–23, 149–71; James F. Brooks, *Mesa of Sorrows: A History of the Awat'ovi Massacre* (New York: W. W. Norton, 2016), 62–81; Lamar, "From Bondage to Contract," 297–98.

14. "Report of Serrano," in Hackett, *Historical Documents Relating to New Mexico*, 3:487; Report of Nicolás Ortíz, October 3, 1707, New Mexico State Records Center and Archives, SANM II, Reel 4, Frames 24–26; "Declaration of Captain Andrés Hurtado," in Hackett, *Historical Documents Relating to New Mexico*, 3:191–92; "Reply of Mendizábal," in Hackett, *Historical Documents Relating to New Mexico*, 3:216. For the role of Spanish friars, see Archives of the Archdiocese of Santa Fe, Loose Documents 1680–1743, Microfilm #51, Loose Documents Missions 1715 No. 1, Frame 847; John L. Kessell, *Kiva, Cross, and Crown: The Pecos Indians and New Mexico, 1540–1840* (Washington, DC: National Park Service, 1979), 367. See also Elizabeth A. H. John, *Storms Brewed in Other Men's Worlds: The Confrontation of Indians, Spanish, and French in the Southwest, 1540–1795* (College Station: Texas A&M University Press, 1975), 3–97; Ramón A. Gutiérrez, *When Jesus Came, the Corn Mothers Went Away: Marriage, Sexuality, and Power in New Mexico, 1500–1846* (Stanford, CA: Stanford University Press, 1991), 150–52; Calloway, *One Vast Winter Count*, 134–63; Charles Montgomery, *The Spanish Redemption: Heritage, Power, and Loss on New Mexico's Upper Rio Grande* (Berkeley: University of California Press, 2002), 27.

15. For indigenous slave systems in North America's eastern colonies, see Daniel H. Usner Jr., *Indians, Settlers, and Slaves in a Frontier Exchange Economy: The Lower Mississippi Valley Before 1783* (Chapel Hill: University of North Carolina Press, 1992); Alan Gallay, *The Indian Slave Trade: The Rise of the English Empire in the American South, 1670–1717* (New Haven, CT: Yale University Press, 2002); Christina Snyder, *Slavery in Indian Country: The Changing Face of Captivity in Early America* (Cambridge, MA: Harvard University Press, 2010); Brett Rushforth, *Bonds of Alliance: Indigenous and Atlantic Slaveries in New France* (Chapel Hill: University of North Carolina Press, 2012). For an analysis of all three countries' slave systems, see Robin W. Winks, ed., *Slavery: A Comparative Perspective* (New York: New York University Press, 1972), 23, 67.

16. See Kessell, *Kiva, Cross, and Crown*, 366; Pierre Bourdieu, *Outline of a Theory of Practice*, translated by Richard Nice (Cambridge: Cambridge University Press, 1977), 171–83.

17. On the scarcity of money, see Marc Simmons, ed. and trans., *Father Juan Agustín de Morfí's Account of Disorders in New Mexico, 1778* (Isleta Pueblo: Historical Society of New Mexico, 1977), 15; Frank, *From Settler to Citizen*, 139–51.

18. "Declaration of Captain Andrés Hurtado," September 1661, in Hackett, *Historical Documents Relating to New Mexico*, 3:186–87.

19. Angélico Chávez, *Archives of the Archdiocese of Santa Fe, 1678–1900* (Washington, DC: Academy of American Franciscan History, 1957), 198–219; Gutiérrez, *When Jesus Came*, 92–94. For Spanish approaches to the religious indoctrination of Indians, see Elliott, *Empires of the Atlantic World*, 66–72.

20. David M. Brugge, *Navajos in the Catholic Church Records of New Mexico, 1694–1875* (Tsaile, AZ: Navajo Community College Press, 1985), 30; Brian DeLay, *War of a Thousand Deserts: Indian Raids and the U.S.-Mexican War* (New Haven, CT: Yale University Press, 2008), 167; Gutiérrez, *When Jesus Came*, 200.

21. Three Comanches baptized at San Juan Pueblo in 1780 were listed as being "about" five or six years old. San Juan Baptisms 1774–1798, Archives of the Archdiocese of Santa Fe, Microfilm #9, Frame 900. The padre at that pueblo baptized no fewer than nine Comanche children between the ages of three and eight that year; the following year he baptized an additional six Comanches. Ibid., Frames 899–923. See Pecos Baptisms 1726–1774, Archives of the Archdiocese of Santa Fe, Microfilm #6, Frame 240 for the baptism of four "Jumana" children of various estimated ages. On the symbolic significance of renaming slaves, see Orlando Patterson, *Slavery and Social Death: A Comparative Study* (Cambridge, MA: Harvard University Press, 1982), 54–58.

22. Santa Clara Baptisms 1728–1845, Archives of the Archdiocese of Santa Fe, Microfilm #12, Frame 463. Only these six infants were baptized because "so many Comanches were ransomed" recently at nearby Ojo Caliente that it became impractical to anoint them all at once. Ibid.

23. For Hispanic perspectives on the baptism of captives, see Greiner to Lea, May 19, 1852, in Abel, *Official Correspondence of James S. Calhoun*, 537; Sondra Jones, *The Trial of Don Pedro León Luján: The Attack Against Indian Slavery and Mexican Traders in Utah* (Salt Lake City: University of Utah Press, 2000), 36; Jacqueline Dorgan Meketa, ed., *Legacy of Honor: The Life of Rafael Chacón, a Nineteenth-Century New Mexican* (Albuquerque: University of New Mexico Press, 1986), 230, 388n8. On the concept of othering, see Edward Said, *Orientalism* (New York: Vintage, 1978).

24. Santa Clara Baptisms 1728–1845, Archives of the Archdiocese of Santa Fe, Microfilm #12, Frames 464–65; Laguna Baptisms 1720–1776, ibid., Microfilm #5, Frames 1036–39; Santa Fe Baptisms 1747–1814, ibid., Microfilm #15, Frame 101.

25. Stuart B. Schwartz, *All Can Be Saved: Religious Tolerance and Salvation in the Iberian Atlantic World* (New Haven, CT: Yale University Press, 2008), 130–32.

26. Brooks, "'This Evil Extends Especially,'" 296–97.

27. See, for example, Cochiti Baptisms 1736–1827, Archives of the Archdiocese of Santa Fe, Microfilm #4, Frames 478–96, in which a representative cross-section of all three notations appears in the registry.

28. Gutiérrez, *When Jesus Came*, 153–54, 295; Brooks, *Captives & Cousins*, 35; Chávez, *Archives of the Archdiocese of Santa Fe*, 220–30; Estévan Rael-Galvéz, "Identifying Captivity and Capturing Identity: Narratives of American Indian Slavery, Colorado and New Mexico, 1776–1934" (PhD diss., University of Michigan, 2002), 171.

29. Brugge, *Navajos in the Catholic Church Records*, 101–2. See also Charles Kenner, *A History of New Mexican-Plains Indian Relations* (Norman: University of Oklahoma Press, 1969), 38.

30. Dedra S. McDonald, "Intimacy and Empire: Indian-African Interaction in Spanish Colonial New Mexico, 1500–1800," *American Indian Quarterly* 22 (Winter and Spring 1998): 148; Alicia V. Tjarks, "Demographic, Ethnic and Occupational Structure of New Mexico, 1790," *Americas* 35 (July 1978): 45, 67, 81; Virginia Langham Olmsted, *Spanish and New Mexican Censuses of New Mexico: 1750–1830* (Albuquerque: New Mexico Genealogical Society, 1981), ii.

31. See, for example, Alfred Barnaby Thomas, ed. and trans., "Governor Mendinueta's Proposals for the Defense of New Mexico, 1772–1778," *New Mexico Historical Review* 6 (January 1931): 21–39, esp. 26–35; Juan Joseph Lobato to Tomas Vélez Cachupín, August 28, 1752, in Alfred Barnaby Thomas, ed. and trans., *The Plains Indians and New Mexico, 1751–1778: A Collection of Documents Illustrative of the History of the Eastern Frontier of New Mexico* (Albuquerque: University of New Mexico Press, 1940), 116.

32. Brian DeLay, ed., *North American Borderlands* (New York: Routledge, 2013), 3. See also Pekka Hämäläinen and Samuel Truett, "On Borderlands," *Journal of American History* 98 (September 2011): 338–61.

33. L. R. Bailey, *Indian Slave Trade in the Southwest* (Los Angeles: Westernlore, 1966), 136. See also Fernando de la Concha to Conde de Revilla Gigedo, May 6, 1793, New Mexico State Records Center and Archives, Frank McNitt Collection, Serial #10678, Folder 26; Herbert Eugene Bolton, ed. and trans., *Anza's California Expeditions: Font's Complete Diary of the Second Anza Expedition*, vol. 4 (Berkeley: University of California Press, 1930), 102.

34. For slave raiding among Plains tribes, see Carl Coke Rister, *Border Captives: The Traffic in Prisoners by Southern Plains Indians, 1835–1875* (Norman: University of Oklahoma Press, 1940), 38–59. For the Comanche captive trade, see Pekka Hämäläinen, *The Comanche Empire* (New Haven, CT: Yale University Press, 2008), esp. 223–38; DeLay, *War of a Thousand Deserts*, 35–138; Reséndez, *Other Slavery*, 176–86. On core societies, see Hall, *World-Systems Reader*, 30.

35. For trade fairs, see S. Lyman Tyler and H. Darrel Taylor, "The Report of Fray Alonso de Posada in Relation to Quivira and Teguayo," *New Mexico Historical Review* 33 (October 1958): 301; Declaration of Juan Tindé et al., July 8, 1711, quoted in Kessell, *Kiva, Cross, and Crown*, 364; "Report of Melchon de Pexamás," October 27, 1775, New Mexico State Records Center and Archives, Archivo General de las Indias Photocopy Collection, Serial #15825, Folder 1; Tomás Vélez Cachupín to Conde de Revilla Gigedo, November 27, 1751, in Thomas, *Plains Indians and New Mexico, 1751–*

1778, 68; Pedro Fermín de Mendinueta to Viceroy Bucareli, September 30, 1774, in ibid., 172; Eleanor B. Adams, ed., "Bishop Tamarón's Visitation of New Mexico, 1760," *New Mexico Historical Review* 28 (July 1953): 216; Fernando de la Concha to Fernando Chacón, June 28, 1794, in Donald E. Worcester, ed. and trans., "Notes and Documents: Advice on Governing New Mexico, 1794," *New Mexico Historical Review* 24 (July 1949): 246. For secondary accounts, see Kessell, *Kiva, Cross, and Crown*, 134–38, 364–70; Gary Clayton Anderson, *The Indian Southwest, 1580–1830: Ethnogenesis and Reinvention* (Norman: University of Oklahoma Press, 1999), 206–7, 332n8; Frances Levine, "Economic Perspectives on the Comanchero Trade," in Spielmann, *Farmers, Hunters, and Colonists*, 155–69, esp. 156–58; Kenner, *History of New Mexican-Plains Indian Relations*, 78–97; Thomas W. Kavanagh, *Comanche Political History: An Ethnohistorical Perspective, 1706–1875* (Lincoln: University of Nebraska Press, 1996), 278–80; Hämäläinen, *Comanche Empire*, 211–12.

36. Fray Andrés Varo, "Informe del estado de la Nuevo México," January 28, 1749, quoted in Frank, *From Settler to Citizen*, 14; "Report of Serrano," in Hackett, *Historical Documents Relating to New Mexico*, 3:486–87; Conde de Revilla Gigedo to the Marqués de Ensenada, June 28, 1753, in Thomas, *Plains Indians and New Mexico*, 112; Marc Simmons, ed., "The Chacón Economic Report of 1803," *New Mexico Historical Review* 60 (January 1985): 87. See also Lawrence Kinniard, ed., *The Frontiers of New Spain: Nicolás de Lafora's Description, 1766–1768* (Berkeley, CA: Quivira Society, 1958), 94. For Indian slave valuations in the Old South, see Gallay, *Indian Slave Trade*, 311–14.

37. "Declaration of Fray Miguel de Menchero," May 10, 1744, in Hackett, *Historical Documents Relating to New Mexico*, 3:401.

38. Proclamation of Gervasio Cruzat y Gongora, December 6, 1732, New Mexico State Records Center and Archives, SANM II, Reel 6, Frames 1243–45.

39. Alfred Barnaby Thomas, ed. and trans., *Teodoro de Croix and the Northern Frontier of New Spain, 1776–1783: From the Original Document in the Archives of the Indies, Seville* (Norman: University of Oklahoma Press, 1968), 111–14. For a firsthand account of the 1786 peace accord, see Alfred Barnaby Thomas, ed. and trans., *Forgotten Frontiers: A Study of the Spanish Indian Policy of Don Juan Bautista de Anza, Governor of New Mexico, 1777–1787* (Norman: University of Oklahoma Press, 1969), 294–321. On the treaty, see Hämäläinen, *Comanche Empire*, 119–23; Brooks, *Captives & Cousins*, 162–69. On Anza's Indian policies, see Carlos R. Herrera, *Juan Bautista de Anza: The King's Governor in New Mexico* (Norman: University of Oklahoma Press, 2015), esp. 95–120. For oral histories about the Comanche accord, see Ruth Roessel, ed., *Navajo Stories of the Long Walk Period* (Chinle, AZ: Navajo Community College Press, 1973), 181–82.

40. Ugarte to Juan Bautista de Anza, October 5, 1786, in Thomas, *Forgotten Frontiers*, 335–36, 386n130; Juan Joseph Lobato to Tomás Vélez Cachupín, August 28, 1752, in Thomas, *Plains Indians and New Mexico*, 115–16; "Diary of the Expedition

[of Don Juan Bautista de Anza]," November 9–11, 1780, in Thomas, *Forgotten Frontiers*, 197; Silvio Zavala, *Los Esclavos Indios in Nueva España* (México: El Colegio Nacional, 1967), 250–57.

41. Brooks, *Captives & Cousins*, 366. For Spanish policy on captives, see Malcolm Ebright and Rick Hendricks, *The Witches of Abiquiu: The Governor, the Priest, the Genízaro Indians, and the Devil* (Albuquerque: University of New Mexico Press, 2006), 20–23, 69–87. For *indios de rescate*, see James F. Brooks, "Served Well by Plunder: *La Gran Ladronería* and Producers of History Astride the Río Grande," *American Quarterly* 52 (March 2000): 36; Brooks, "'This Evil Extends Especially,'" 282–83, 303–4; Brooks, *Captives & Cousins*, 50, 125, 143–46.

42. Weber, *Bárbaros*, 240; Brooks, *Captives & Cousins*, 123–38, 374; Ebright and Hendricks, *Witches of Abiquiu*, 4, 30–32; James F. Brooks, "We Betray Our Nation: Indian Slavery and Multi-Ethnic Communities in the Southwest Borderlands," in Alan Gallay, ed., *Indian Slavery in Colonial America* (Lincoln: University of Nebraska Press, 2009), 319–51; Brooks, "'Lest We Go,'" 150–80.

43. Fernando de la Concha to Fernando Chacón, June 28, 1794, in Worcester, "Notes and Documents," 240–41.

44. Domínguez, *Missions of New Mexico*, 42, 126, 208. See also "Declaration of Fray Miguel de Menchero," May 10, 1744, in Hackett, *Historical Documents Relating to New Mexico*, 3:401–2; Adams, "Bishop Tamarón's Visitation of New Mexico," 205; Donald C. Cutter, trans., "An Anonymous Statistical Report on New Mexico in 1765," *New Mexico Historical Review* 50 (October 1975): 351.

45. Decree of Governor Mendinueta, March 31, 1760, New Mexico State Records Center and Archives, SANM I, Item #656, Microfilm Translations, Roll 3; Simmons, *Father Juan Agustín de Morfi's Account of Disorders in New Mexico*, 35.

46. Ugarte to Conde de Revilla Gigedo, December 11, 1789, quoted in Mark Santiago, *The Jar of Severed Hands: Spanish Deportation of Apache Prisoners of War, 1770–1810* (Norman: University of Oklahoma Press, 2011), 90; Ugarte to Juan Bautista de Anza, October 5, 1786, in Thomas, *Forgotten Frontiers*, 335–36. See also Ana María Alonso, *Thread of Blood: Colonialism, Revolution, and Gender on Mexico's Northern Frontier* (Tucson: University of Arizona Press, 1995), 37–39, 44–46, 96; Edwin R. Sweeney, *Mangas Coloradas: Chief of the Chiricahua Apaches* (Norman: University of Oklahoma Press, 1998), 27–136; H. Henrietta Stockel, *Salvation Through Slavery: Chiricahua Apaches and Priests on the Spanish Colonial Frontier* (Albuquerque: University of New Mexico Press, 2008), 111–27.

47. Weber, *Bárbaros*, 238.

48. See Brooks, *Captives & Cousins*; Weber, *Bárbaros*; Ned Blackhawk, *Violence over the Land: Indians and Empires in the Early American West* (Cambridge, MA: Harvard University Press, 2006); Juliana Barr, *Peace Came in the Form of a Woman: Indians and Spaniards in the Texas Borderlands* (Chapel Hill: University of North Carolina Press, 2007), esp. 7–15; Hämäläinen, *Comanche Empire*; Reséndez, *Other Slavery*.

49. Ira Berlin, *Generations of Captivity: A History of African-American Slaves* (Cambridge, MA: Belknap Press of Harvard University Press, 2003), 100.

50. For population figures in Spanish colonial New Mexico between 1750 and 1830, see Olmsted, *Spanish and Mexican Censuses of New Mexico*; Oakah L. Jones Jr., *Los Paisanos: Spanish Settlers on the Northern Frontier of New Spain* (Norman: University of Oklahoma Press, 1979), 120–35. For a case study using these censuses, see Brooks, " 'This Evil Extends Especially,' " 294–95. For populations at the various missions in northern New Mexico, see the 1795 Mission Census, Archives of the Archdiocese of Santa Fe, Loose Documents, Mission, 1790–1817, Microfilm #53, Frame 139.

51. Quoted in David J. Weber, *The Mexican Frontier, 1821–1846: The American Southwest Under Mexico* (Albuquerque: University of New Mexico Press, 1982), 211. See also Dwight L. Clarke, ed., *The Original Journals of Henry Smith Turner: With Stephen Watts Kearny to New Mexico and California, 1846–1847* (Norman: University of Oklahoma Press, 1966), 164. On indigenous labor in Alta California, see Albert L. Hurtado, *Intimate Frontiers: Sex, Gender, and Culture in Old California* (Albuquerque: University of New Mexico Press, 1999), 1–29; Kent G. Lightfoot, *Indians, Missionaries, and Merchants: The Legacy of Colonial Encounters on the California Frontiers* (Berkeley: University of California Press, 2005), esp. 24–26, 186–88; Stephen W. Hackel, *Children of Coyote, Missionaries of Saint Francis: Indian-Spanish Relations in Colonial California, 1769–1850* (Chapel Hill: University of North Carolina Press, 2005); Stacey L. Smith, *Freedom's Frontier: California and the Struggle over Unfree Labor, Emancipation, and Reconstruction* (Chapel Hill: University of North Carolina Press, 2013), 182–92; Weber, *Bárbaros,* 237; Jones, *Los Paisanos,* 199–233; Reséndez, *Other Slavery,* 246–63.

52. See Charles H. Harris III, *The Sánchez Navarros: A Socio-Economic Study of a Cohuilan Latifundio, 1846–1853* (Chicago: Loyola University Press, 1964), esp. 35–40; Charles Gibson, *The Aztecs Under Spanish Rule: A History of the Indians of the Valley of Mexico, 1519–1810* (Stanford, CA: Stanford University Press, 1964), 253–56; François Chevalier, *Land and Society in Colonial Mexico: The Great Hacienda,* translated by Alvin Eustis, edited by Lesley Byrd Simpson (Berkeley: University of California Press, 1970), 265, 277–88; William B. Taylor, *Landlord and Peasant in Colonial Oaxaca* (Stanford, CA: Stanford University Press, 1972), 147–52; Charles H. Harris III, *A Mexican Family Empire: The Latifundio of the Sánchez Navarros, 1765–1867* (Austin: University of Texas Press, 1975), esp. 70–74, 205–30; Patterson, *Slavery and Social Death,* 125; Joseph C. Miller, *The Problem of Slavery as History: A Global Approach* (New Haven, CT: Yale University Press, 2012), esp. 125; Elizabeth Terese Newman, *Biography of a Hacienda: Work and Revolution in Rural Mexico* (Tucson: University of Arizona Press, 2014), 13, 15–16. For a description of peonage as it existed in Mexico before and during the Porfiriato, see A. de Iturbide, "Mexican Haciendas: The Peon System," *North American Review* 168 (April 1899): 424–32.

53. Statement of Brigadier General James H. Carleton, July 3, 1865, in *Condition of the Indian Tribes,* 39th Cong., 2nd Sess., Senate Report No. 156 (Washington, DC:

Government Printing Office, 1867), 325 (emphasis in original). See also James S. Calhoun to Luke Lea, August 27, 1851, in Abel, *Official Correspondence of James S. Calhoun*, 406.

54. James Josiah Webb, *Adventures in the Santa Fe Trade, 1844–1847*, edited by Ralph P. Bieber (Glendale, CA: Arthur H. Clark, 1931), 102; Josiah Gregg, *Commerce of the Prairies*, edited by Max L. Moorhead (Norman: University of Oklahoma Press, 1954), 182–84; "Inland Trade with New Mexico," in Reuben Gold Thwaites, ed., *The Personal Narrative of James O. Pattie of Kentucky* (Cleveland, OH: Arthur H. Clark, 1905), 355. See also Harris, *Sánchez Navarros*, 36–37; Harris, *Mexican Family Empire*, 71–74, 219–20.

55. Simmons, *Father Juan Agustín de Morfi's Account of Disorders in New Mexico*, 15–16, 27.

56. See Vlasich, *Pueblo Indian Agriculture*, 24–25. On debt peonage in Spain's New World colonies, see Chevalier, *Land and Society in Colonial Mexico*, 69, 277–85; Magnus Morner, "The Spanish American Hacienda: A Survey of Recent Research and Debate," *Hispanic American Historical Review* 53 (May 1973): 183–216; Arnold J. Bauer, "Rural Workers in Spanish America: Problems of Peonage and Oppression," *Hispanic American Historical Review* 59 (February 1979): 34–63; Reséndez, *Other Slavery*, 238–39. On peonage in nineteenth-century New Mexico and Texas, see Weber, *Mexican Frontier*, 211–12; David Montejano, *Anglos and Mexicans in the Making of Texas, 1836–1986* (Austin: University of Texas Press, 1987), 76–82; William B. Taylor and Elliott West, "Patrón Leadership at the Crossroads: Southern Colorado in the Late Nineteenth Century," in Norris Hundley Jr., ed., *The Chicano* (Santa Barbara, CA: Clio, 1975), 75–78. On hacienda labor in nineteenth-century and early twentieth-century Mexico, with an emphasis on peonage, see John Kenneth Turner, *Barbarous Mexico* (Chicago: C. H. Kerr, 1911), esp. 5–10; Alan Knight, *The Mexican Revolution, Volume 1: Porfirians, Liberals, and Peasants* (Cambridge: Cambridge University Press, 1986), 85–90; Michael C. Meyer, William L. Sherman, and Susan M. Deeds, *The Course of Mexican History*, 6th ed. (New York: Oxford University Press, 1999), 446–49.

57. Simmons, *Father Juan Agustín de Morfi's Account of Disorders in New Mexico*, 15–16. On slavery and master-servant relationships in colonial Mexico, see Harris, *Mexican Family Empire*, 217–18; Ben Vinson III and Matthew Restall, eds., *Black Mexico: Race and Society from Colonial to Modern Times* (Albuquerque: University of New Mexico Press, 2009); Frank T. Proctor III, *"Damned Notions of Liberty": Slavery, Culture, and Power in Colonial Mexico, 1640–1769* (Albuquerque: University of New Mexico Press, 2010); K. Russell Lohse, "Mexico and Central America," in Robert L. Paquette and Mark M. Smith, eds., *The Oxford Handbook of Slavery in the Americas* (Oxford: Oxford University Press, 2010), 46–67; Newman, *Biography of a Hacienda*, 48–49.

58. See John O. Baxter, *Las Carneradas: Sheep Trade in New Mexico, 1700–1860* (Albuquerque: University of New Mexico Press, 1987), esp. 42–44; William J. Parish, *The Charles Ilfeld Company: A Study of the Rise and Decline of Mercantile Capitalism in*

New Mexico (Cambridge, MA: Harvard University Press, 1961), 151–71; Montgomery, *Spanish Redemption*, 35–36; Thomas D. Hall, *Social Change in the Southwest: 1350–1880* (Lawrence: University Press of Kansas, 1989), 156.

59. Weber, *Mexican Frontier*, 211; Susan Calafate Boyle, *Los Capitalistas: Hispano Merchants and the Santa Fe Trade* (Albuquerque: University of New Mexico Press, 1997); Montgomery, *Spanish Redemption*, 34–39; Max L. Moorhead, *New Mexico's Royal Road: Trade and Travel on the Chihuahua Trail* (Norman: University of Oklahoma Press, 1958), 55–75; Frances Leon Swadesh, "The Social and Philosophical Context of Creativity in Hispanic New Mexico," *Rocky Mountain Social Science Journal* 9 (January 1972): 12.

60. Brooks, *Captives & Cousins*, 208–57, esp. 215–16.

61. U.S. Congress, *Petition of Sundry Inhabitants of the State of Missouri*, February 14, 1825, 18th Cong., 2nd Sess., House Exec. Doc. No. 79, p. 6; U.S. Congress, *Memorial of the Legislature of Missouri*, January 26, 1829, 20th Cong., 2nd Sess., Senate Exec. Doc. No. 52, p. 1. On the Santa Fe trade generally, see Stephen G. Hyslop, *Bound for Santa Fe: The Road to New Mexico and the American Conquest, 1806–1848* (Norman: University of Oklahoma Press, 2002).

62. Gregg, *Commerce of the Prairies*, 332.

63. U.S. Congress, *Trade and Intercourse Between Missouri and the Internal Provinces of Mexico*, January 3, 1825, 18th Cong., 2nd Sess., Senate Exec. Doc. No. 7, p. 10. On the impacts of Southern slavery on the Northern economy, see Walter Johnson, *River of Dark Dreams: Slavery and Empire in the Cotton Kingdom* (Cambridge, MA: Belknap Press of Harvard University Press, 2013), 285.

64. Brooks, *Captives & Cousins*, 222–23, 239.

65. U.S. Congress, *Trade and Intercourse*, 10; Hyslop, *Bound for Santa Fe*, 50.

Introduction

1. Executive Order of Andrew Johnson, June 9, 1865, RG75, OIA, T21, LR, NMS, Roll 6.

2. "An Act to abolish and forever prohibit the System of Peonage in the Territory of New Mexico and other Parts of the United States," United States *Statutes at Large*, 39th Cong., 2nd Sess., Ch. 187, p. 546.

3. Andrés Reséndez, *The Other Slavery: The Uncovered Story of Indian Enslavement in America* (New York: Houghton Mifflin Harcourt, 2016).

4. See James Oakes, *Freedom National: The Destruction of Slavery in the United States, 1861–1865* (New York: W. W. Norton, 2012), chap. 1, for the origins and meaning of the phrase.

5. James F. Brooks, *Captives & Cousins: Slavery, Kinship, and Community in the Southwest Borderlands* (Chapel Hill: University of North Carolina Press, 2002), 145; Don E. Fehrenbacher, *The Slaveholding Republic: An Account of the United States Government's Relations to Slavery* (New York: Oxford University Press, 2001), 15. For statistics on Indian slaves, see Reséndez, *Other Slavery*, 324.

6. Joseph C. Miller, *The Problem of Slavery as History: A Global Approach* (New Haven, CT: Yale University Press, 2012), 151. See also David Eltis and Stanley L. Engerman, "Dependence, Servility, and Coerced Labor in Time and Space," in Eltis and Engerman, eds., *The Cambridge World History of Slavery*, vol. 3 (Cambridge: Cambridge University Press, 2011), 1.

7. Howard Lamar, "From Bondage to Contract: Ethnic Labor in the American West, 1600–1890," in Steven Hahn and Jonathan Prude, eds., *The Countryside in the Age of Capitalist Transformation* (Chapel Hill: University of North Carolina Press, 1985), 294; Reséndez, *Other Slavery*. See also Stacey L. Smith, *Freedom's Frontier: California and the Struggle over Unfree Labor, Emancipation, and Reconstruction* (Chapel Hill: University of North Carolina Press, 2013), esp. 5–7; William S. Kiser, "A 'Charming Name for a Species of Slavery': Political Debate on Debt Peonage in the Southwest, 1840s–1860s," *Western Historical Quarterly* 45:2 (Summer 2014): 169–89.

8. For definitions and explanations of peonage, see Robin W. Winks, ed., *Slavery: A Comparative Perspective* (New York: New York University Press, 1972), 51–57, 71, 165; Arnold J. Bauer, "Rural Workers in Spanish America: Problems of Peonage and Oppression," *Hispanic American Historical Review* 59 (February 1979): 36; Alan Knight, "Mexican Peonage: What Was It and Why Was It?" *Journal of Latin American Studies* 18 (May 1986): 41–74; Alan Knight, *The Mexican Revolution, Volume 1: Porfirians, Liberals, and Peasants* (Cambridge: Cambridge University Press, 1986), 85–90; Claude Meillassoux, *The Anthropology of Slavery: The Womb of Iron and Gold*, translated by Alide Dasnois (London: Athlone, 1991), 343.

9. For global contextualizations of slavery and debt bondage, see Toyin Falola and Paul E. Lovejoy, "Pawnship in Historical Perspective," in Falola and Lovejoy, eds., *Pawnship in Africa: Debt Bondage in Historical Perspective* (Boulder, CO: Westview, 1994); Elizabeth Dore, *Myths of Modernity: Peonage and Patriarchy in Nicaragua* (Durham, NC: Duke University Press, 2006); Eltis and Engerman, "Dependence, Servility, and Coerced Labor in Time and Space," 1–22.

10. Fabiola Cabeza de Baca, *We Fed Them Cactus* (Albuquerque: University of New Mexico Press, 1954), 6. On the use of the term "feudal" to describe New Mexico, see Thomas D. Hall, *Social Change in the Southwest: 1350–1880* (Lawrence: University Press of Kansas, 1989), 157–59, 179. In a work of historical fiction, José Ortiz y Pino III portrays New Mexico's *patrón*-peon relationship as one based on "respect for authority and loyalty to those whom they served." Ortiz y Pino, *Don José: The Last Patrón* (Santa Fe, NM: Sunstone, 1981), unpaginated foreword. One of the earliest scholarly analyses of New Mexican peonage takes a romantic tone and describes it as a utopian relationship of mutual respect. See Clark S. Knowlton, "Patrón-Peon Pattern Among the Spanish Americans of New Mexico," *Social Forces* 41 (October 1962): 12–17. For the importance of honor in New Mexico society and custom, see Brooks, *Captives & Cousins*, 8–9.

11. Brooks, *Captives & Cousins*; Reséndez, *Other Slavery*; Ned Blackhawk, *Violence over the Land: Indians and Empires in the Early American West* (Cambridge, MA: Harvard University Press, 2006); Brian DeLay, *War of a Thousand Deserts: Indian Raids*

and the U.S.-Mexican War (New Haven, CT: Yale University Press, 2008); Pekka Hämä-
läinen, *The Comanche Empire* (New Haven, CT: Yale University Press, 2008); Gary
Clayton Anderson, *The Indian Southwest, 1580–1830: Ethnogenesis and Reinvention*
(Norman: University of Oklahoma Press, 1999); Thomas W. Kavanagh, *Comanche
Political History: An Ethnohistorical Perspective, 1706–1875* (Lincoln: University of
Nebraska Press, 1996), 23, 63–132.

   12. Ramón A. Gutiérrez, *When Jesus Came, the Corn Mothers Went Away: Marriage, Sexuality, and Power in New Mexico, 1500–1846* (Stanford, CA: Stanford Univer-
sity Press, 1991); David J. Weber, *Bárbaros: Spaniards and Their Savages in the Age of
Enlightenment* (New Haven, CT: Yale University Press, 2005); Juliana Barr, *Peace Came
in the Form of a Woman: Indians and Spaniards in the Texas Borderlands* (Chapel Hill:
University of North Carolina Press, 2007); Juliana Barr, "From Captives to Slaves:
Commodifying Indian Women in the Borderlands," *Journal of American History* 92
(June 2005): 19–46.

   13. See Brooks, *Captives & Cousins,* 123–38; Weber, *Bárbaros,* 240–41; John M.
Nieto-Phillips, *The Language of Blood: The Making of Spanish-American Identity in
New Mexico, 1880s–1930s* (Albuquerque: University of New Mexico Press, 2004); Malcolm Ebright and Rick Hendricks, *The Witches of Abiquiu: The Governor, the Priest,
the Genízaro Indians, and the Devil* (Albuquerque: University of New Mexico Press,
2006), esp. 27–47.

   14. Seth Rockman, *Scraping By: Wage Labor, Slavery, and Survival in Early Baltimore* (Baltimore, MD: Johns Hopkins University Press, 2009).

   15. Gavin Wright, *Slavery and American Economic Development* (Baton Rouge:
Louisiana State University Press, 2006), 60.

   16. See Calvin Schermerhorn, *Money over Mastery, Family over Freedom: Slavery
in the Antebellum Upper South* (Baltimore, MD: Johns Hopkins University Press,
2011), 17–18; Sven Beckert, *Empire of Cotton: A Global History* (New York: Alfred A.
Knopf, 2014). On the colonial New Mexican economy, see Ross Frank, *From Settler to
Citizen: New Mexican Economic Development and the Creation of Vecino Society, 1750–
1820* (Berkeley: University of California Press, 2000); Susan Calafate Boyle, *Los Capitalistas: Hispano Merchants and the Santa Fe Trade* (Albuquerque: University of New
Mexico Press, 1997), 7–12. On the integration of the Southwest into America's capitalist economy, see William G. Robbins, *Colony and Empire: The Capitalist Transformation of the American West* (Lawrence: University Press of Kansas, 1994), esp. 22–39.

   17. Rhys Isaac, *The Transformation of Virginia, 1740–1790* (Chapel Hill: University of North Carolina Press, 1999), 21, 132–33.

   18. On the importance of Mexican law as it pertained to involuntary servitude in
California, see Smith, *Freedom's Frontier,* 65–66.

   19. See *Laws of the Territory of New Mexico, Sixth Legislative Assembly, 1856–1857*
(Santa Fe, NM: Office of the Democrat, 1857) and "An Act to Provide for the Protec-
tion of Property in Slaves in This Territory," in *Laws of the Territory of New Mexico,
Eighth Legislative Assembly, 1858–1859* (Santa Fe, NM: A. DeMarle, 1859).

20. Brooks, *Captives & Cousins*, 34; Edmund S. Morgan, *American Slavery, American Freedom: The Ordeal of Colonial Virginia* (New York: W. W. Norton, 1975), 314–38; Brenda Stevenson, *Life in Black and White: Family and Community in the Slave South* (New York: Oxford University Press, 1996), 7; Ira Berlin, *Generations of Captivity: A History of African-American Slaves* (Cambridge, MA: Belknap Press of Harvard University Press, 2003), 10–12.

21. John Higham, *Strangers in the Land: Patterns of American Nativism, 1860–1925* (New Brunswick, NJ: Rutgers University Press, 1955), esp. 3–12. On New Mexico specifically, see Loomis M. Ganaway, *New Mexico and the Sectional Controversy, 1846–1861* (Albuquerque: University of New Mexico Press, 1944); Robert W. Larson, *New Mexico's Quest for Statehood, 1846–1912* (Albuquerque: University of New Mexico Press, 1968); Mark J. Stegmaier, *Texas, New Mexico, and the Compromise of 1850: Boundary Dispute and Sectional Crisis* (Kent, OH: Kent State University Press, 1996); Howard R. Lamar, *The Far Southwest, 1846–1912: A Territorial History* (Albuquerque: University of New Mexico Press, 2000); Laura E. Gómez, *Manifest Destinies: The Making of the Mexican American Race* (New York: New York University Press, 2007); Anthony Mora, *Border Dilemmas: Racial and National Uncertainties in New Mexico, 1848–1912* (Durham, NC: Duke University Press, 2011); David V. Holtby, *Forty-Seventh Star: New Mexico's Struggle for Statehood* (Norman: University of Oklahoma Press, 2012).

22. Pete Daniel, *The Shadow of Slavery: Peonage in the South, 1901–1969* (Urbana: University of Illinois Press, 1972), esp. ix–xi, 15–16; Douglas A. Blackmon, *Slavery by Another Name: The Re-Enslavement of Black Americans from the Civil War to World War II* (New York: Anchor, 2009), esp. 172–75.

Chapter 1

1. *Message from the President of the United States, December 5, 1848*, 30th Cong., 2nd Sess., House Exec. Doc. No. 1, pp. 13–16, quotations on 13.

2. Horace Mann to James Richardson et al., May 3, 1850, in Horace Mann, *Slavery: Letters and Speeches by Horace Mann* (Boston: B. B. Mussey, 1851), 259, 277–81.

3. James K. Polk, *The Diary of James K. Polk*, vol. 2, edited by Milo Milton Quaife (Chicago: A. C. McClurg, 1910), 289.

4. John J. Farrell, ed., *James K. Polk, 1795–1849: Chronology—Documents—Bibliographic Aides* (Dobbs Ferry, NY: Oceana, 1970), 32. See also Michael A. Morrison, *Slavery and the American West: The Eclipse of Manifest Destiny and the Coming of the Civil War* (Chapel Hill: University of North Carolina Press, 1997), 66–70; Christopher Childers, *The Failure of Popular Sovereignty: Slavery, Manifest Destiny, and the Radicalization of Southern Politics* (Lawrence: University Press of Kansas, 2012), 112.

5. Speech of President Polk, 30th Cong., 1st Sess., Senate Exec. Doc. No. 1, p. 11.

6. See Michael F. Holt, *The Political Crisis of the 1850s* (New York: W. W. Norton, 1978); Morrison, *Slavery and the American West*, esp. 96–156.

7. Childers, *Failure of Popular Sovereignty*, 9–16.

8. Ibid., 15; Stacey L. Smith, *Freedom's Frontier: California and the Struggle over Unfree Labor, Emancipation, and Reconstruction* (Chapel Hill: University of North Carolina Press, 2013), 64–65.

9. On slavery in the territories, see David M. Potter, *The Impending Crisis, 1848–1861* (New York: Harper and Row, 1973), 51–62; Morrison, *Slavery and the American West*, 96–125.

10. See, for example, the exchange between pro- and antislavery senators in *Congressional Globe*, 31st Cong., 1st Sess., June 5, 1850, p. 1135. On congressional debates over slavery in the Mexican Cession, see Morrison, *Slavery and the American West*, 109–25.

11. For the treaty, see Hunter Miller, ed., *Treaties and Other International Acts of the United States of America*, vol. 5 (Washington, DC: Government Printing Office, 1931–48), 207–36.

12. William R. Brock, *Parties and Political Conscience: American Dilemmas, 1840–1850* (Millwood, NY: KTO, 1979), 276–84.

13. Richard K. Cralle, ed., *Speeches of John C. Calhoun, Delivered in the House of Representatives and in the Senate of the United States*, vol. 4 (New York: Russell and Russell, 1968), 481.

14. For the court case, see *Dred Scott v. John F. A. Sandford*, 60 U.S. (1857).

15. *Congressional Globe*, 31st Cong., 1st Sess., February 12, 1850, Appendix, p. 207.

16. Eric Foner, *The Fiery Trial: Abraham Lincoln and American Slavery* (New York: W. W. Norton, 2010), 45.

17. The seminal work is Don E. Fehrenbacher, *The Dred Scott Case: Its Significance in American Law and Politics* (New York: Oxford University Press, 1978). On judicial activism and the Supreme Court, see Michael Klarman, *From Jim Crow to Civil Rights: The Supreme Court and the Struggle for Racial Equality* (New York: Oxford University Press, 2004). For the impact of the case in the territories, see Childers, *Failure of Popular Sovereignty*, 250–56; and Earl M. Maltz, *Slavery and the Supreme Court, 1825–1861* (Lawrence: University Press of Kansas, 2009), 210–77.

18. Paul Finkelman, *Dred Scott v. Sandford: A Brief History with Documents* (New York: Bedford, 1997), 55–126. For Taney's personal convictions on slavery, see Timothy S. Huebner, "Roger B. Taney and the Slavery Issue: Looking Beyond—and Before—*Dred Scott*," *Journal of American History* 97 (June 2010): 17–38.

19. Northwest Ordinance, July 13, 1787, NA, RG360, M332, Roll 9. See also Vincent C. Hopkins, *Dred Scott's Case* (New York: Russell and Russell, 1967), 111.

20. *Congressional Globe*, 30th Cong., 1st Sess., August 3, 1848, Appendix, p. 1077.

21. Ibid., 31st Cong., 1st Sess., March 4, 1850, pp. 451–52. See also Edward E. Baptist, *The Half Has Never Been Told: Slavery and the Making of American Capitalism* (New York: Basic Books, 2014), 324.

22. Childers, *Failure of Popular Sovereignty*, 27–28. For a statistical analysis of the compromise, see Sean M. Theriault and Barry R. Weingast, "Agenda Manipulation,

Strategic Voting, and Legislative Details in the Compromise of 1850," in David W. Brady and Mathew D. McCubbins, eds., *Party, Process, and Political Change in Congress: New Perspectives on the History of Congress* (Stanford, CA: Stanford University Press, 2002), 343–91.

23. Quoted in Cralle, *Speeches of John C. Calhoun*, 4:548.

24. Ibid., 4:497; *Congressional Globe*, 29th Cong., 2nd Sess., February 19, 1847, pp. 453–55; *Congressional Globe*, 30th Cong., 2nd Sess., December 19, 1848, pp. 33–34. On Calhoun's arguments generally, see Baptist, *Half Has Never Been Told*, 329–32.

25. Thomas Hart Benton, *Thirty Years' View, or, A History of the Working of the American Government for Thirty Years, from 1820 to 1850*, vol. 2 (New York: D. Appleton, 1856), 696.

26. *Congressional Globe*, 31st Cong., 1st Sess., July 8, 1850, Appendix, p. 1177.

27. Ibid., March 13, 1850, Appendix, p. 371.

28. Benton, *Thirty Years' View*, 2:697.

29. For New Mexico's role in the Compromise of 1850, see Mark J. Stegmaier, *Texas, New Mexico, and the Compromise of 1850: Boundary Dispute and Sectional Crisis* (Kent, OH: Kent State University Press, 1996).

30. *Congressional Globe*, 31st Cong., 1st Sess., March 7, 1850, p. 480.

31. Ibid., March 13, 1850, Appendix, p. 366.

32. The arable valley of the Chama River extends for approximately 130 miles from southern Colorado to its confluence with the Rio Grande near Espanola, New Mexico. The Pecos River, while flowing for over nine hundred miles from its source in the mountains east of Santa Fe to its confluence with the Rio Grande in southwest Texas, was only farmed and settled for a distance of less than one hundred miles from its source during the early 1800s. The longest and largest of these three rivers, the Rio Grande, flows from south-central Colorado to the Gulf of Mexico, a distance of almost 1,900 miles. Much of its course through New Mexico was (and still is) agriculturally productive.

33. See Daniel H. Usner Jr., *Indians, Settlers, and Slaves in a Frontier Exchange Economy: The Lower Mississippi Valley Before 1783* (Chapel Hill: University of North Carolina Press, 1992).

34. See Ross Frank, *From Settler to Citizen: New Mexican Economic Development and the Creation of Vecino Society, 1750–1820* (Berkeley: University of California Press, 2000).

35. See Alvin M. Josephy Jr., *The Civil War in the American West* (New York: Alfred A. Knopf, 1991), 11–12; Donald Frazier, *Blood and Treasure: Confederate Empire in the Southwest* (College Station: Texas A&M University Press, 1995); Megan Kate Nelson, "Death in the Distance: Confederate Manifest Destiny and the Campaign for New Mexico, 1861–1862," in Adam Arenson and Andrew R. Graybill, eds., *Civil War Wests: Testing the Limits of the United States* (Berkeley: University of California Press, 2015), 33–52.

36. *Congressional Globe*, 30th Cong., 1st Sess., August 3, 1848, Appendix, p. 1074. See also "The Slave Code of New Mexico," *New-York Daily Tribune*, April 16, 1861; Mark Stegmaier, "'An Imaginary Negro in an Impossible Place'? The Issue of New Mexico Statehood in the Secession Crisis, 1860–1861," *New Mexico Historical Review* 84 (Spring 2009): 271.

37. *Congressional Globe*, 31st Cong., 1st Sess., July 8, 1850, Appendix, p. 1178. Senator Thomas Hart Benton likewise mentioned the Wilmot Proviso: "The dogma of '47 became an impediment to the territorial extension of slavery . . . [but] a new dogma was invented to fit the case—that of the transmigration of the constitution— (the slavery part of it)—into the territories, overriding and overruling all the anti-slavery laws which it found there." Benton, *Thirty Years' View*, 2:713.

38. *Congressional Globe*, 31st Cong., 1st Sess., July 8, 1850, Appendix, pp. 1180– 82. Other sources that Smith cited included Lieutenant W. H. Emory, Lieutenant Abert, Lieutenant Peck, George Wilkins Kendall, and George F. Ruxton.

39. Ross Calvin, ed., *Lieutenant Emory Reports: Notes of a Military Reconnaissance from Fort Leavenworth, in Missouri, to San Diego, in California* (Albuquerque: University of New Mexico Press, 1951), 60.

40. *Congressional Globe*, 31st Cong., 1st Sess., February 5, 1850, Appendix, p. 119. See also Brock, *Parties and Political Conscience*, 290–94; Childers, *Failure of Popular Sovereignty*, 168–69.

41. *Congressional Globe*, 31st Cong., 1st Sess., February 28, 1850, pp. 436–39.

42. Ibid., June 29, 1850, Appendix, p. 1005.

43. Hugh N. Smith to Daniel Webster, April 9, 1850, in Charles M. Wiltse and Michael J. Birkner, eds., *The Papers of Daniel Webster: Correspondence*, 7 vols. (Hanover, NH: University Press of New England, 1986), 7:62; R. H. Weightman to H. S. Foote, December 16, 1851, in *Speech of Hon. Richard H. Weightman of New Mexico* (Washington, DC: Congressional Globe Office, 1852), 4.

44. Charles M. Wiltse and Alan R. Berolzheimer, eds., *The Papers of Daniel Webster: Speeches and Formal Writings, Volume 2, 1834–1852* (Hanover, NH: University Press of New England, 1988), 563.

45. "New-Mexico," *New-York Daily Tribune*, December 31, 1860.

46. Brock, *Parties and Political Conscience*, 296–300.

47. Wiltse and Berolzheimer, *Papers of Daniel Webster*, 2:576.

48. Webster to Perkins, April 9, 1850, in Wiltse and Birkner, *Papers of Daniel Webster*, 7:59.

49. Webster to R. H. Gardiner, June 17, 1850, in Daniel Webster, *The Works of Daniel Webster*, 18 vols. (Boston: Charles C. Little and James Brown, 1851), 6:572–73. On Webster's speeches regarding the compromise measures, see Brock, *Parties and Political Conscience*, 296–300.

50. "New Mexico—Slavery Recognized in Her Constitution," *Daily Albany Argus*, July 24, 1850; "Important from New Mexico—Slavery and Peonage," *New York Herald*, July 18, 1850; "Peon Slavery on the Rio Grande—Letter from the Border," *New-York Daily Tribune*, July 15, 1850.

51. "Shall We Give Up New Mexico?" *New-York Daily Tribune*, February 25, 1861.

52. Weightman to Foote, December 16, 1851, in *Congressional Globe*, 32nd Cong., 1st Sess., March 17, 1852, p. 755 (emphasis in original). Weightman pointed out that "the popular mind will . . . remain calm on this point, and the question of prohibiting, admitting, or remaining silent, concerning slavery, will be treated simply as a matter of policy in reference to being admitted to the Union." Ibid.

53. Response to Richard Weightman, *National Era*, January 1, 1852.

54. Joab Houghton to John M. Clayton, October 16, 1848, quoted in Loomis M. Ganaway, *New Mexico and the Sectional Controversy, 1846–1861* (Albuquerque: University of New Mexico Press, 1944), 21.

55. Henry Connelly et al. to Truman Smith, May 18, 1850, in *Congressional Globe*, 31st Cong., 1st Sess., July 8, 1850, Appendix, p. 1180.

56. Abraham Rencher to William H. Seward, April 14, 1861, RG59, T17, New Mexico Territorial Papers, Roll 1. In personal correspondence with a family member, Rencher described his "pro-slavery sentiments" and declared soon after the Civil War began that he would leave New Mexico for his home state of North Carolina. Abraham Rencher to J. Grant Rencher, June 30, 1861, Abraham Rencher Papers, University of North Carolina at Chapel Hill, Southern Historical Collections #627.

57. See James David Nichols, "The Line of Liberty: Runaway Slaves and Fugitive Peons in the Texas-Mexico Borderlands," *Western Historical Quarterly* 44:4 (Winter 2013): 413–33.

58. *Congressional Globe*, 31st Cong., 1st Sess., July 8, 1850, Appendix, p. 1180.

59. Connelly et al. to Smith, in ibid., May 18, 1850.

60. Jack D. Rittenhouse, *The Constitution of the State of New Mexico, 1850* (Santa Fe, NM: Stagecoach, 1965), 45.

61. Ganaway, *New Mexico and the Sectional Controversy*, 50.

62. Connelly et al. to Smith, May 18, 1850, in *Congressional Globe*, 31st Cong., 1st Sess., July 8, 1850, Appendix, p. 1180 (emphasis in original).

63. Ibid.

64. *Congressional Globe*, 30th Cong., 1st Sess., August 3, 1848, Appendix, p. 1074.

65. Mann to Richardson et al., May 3, 1850, in Mann, *Slavery: Letters and Speeches by Horace Mann*, 251.

66. *Congressional Globe*, 31st Cong., 1st Sess., July 8, 1850, Appendix, p. 1177.

67. 30th Cong., 1st Sess., House Exec. Doc. No. 41, pp. 98–99.

68. *Congressional Globe*, 31st Cong., 1st Sess., July 8, 1850, Appendix, p. 1180.

69. For slave narratives in the print media, see Jeannine Marie DeLombard, *Slavery on Trial: Law, Abolitionism, and Print Culture* (Chapel Hill: University of North Carolina Press, 2007), esp. 101–98.

70. Joe Lockard, *Watching Slavery: Witness Texts and Travel Reports* (New York: Peter Lang, 2008), xviii.

71. Message on Slavery, *Santa Fe Weekly Gazette*, July 20, 1852 (emphasis in original).

72. Report of Assistant Surgeon J. F. Hammond, in Richard H. Coolidge, *Statistical Report on the Sickness and Mortality in the Army of the United States . . . from January 1839 to January 1855* (34th Cong., 1st Sess., Senate Exec. Doc. 96), 423.

73. Anthony Mora, *Border Dilemmas: Racial and National Uncertainties in New Mexico, 1848–1912* (Durham, NC: Duke University Press, 2011), 43–65.

74. Quintard Taylor, *In Search of the Racial Frontier: African Americans in the American West, 1528–1990* (New York: W. W. Norton, 1998), 74.

75. John Ayers, "A Soldier's Experience in New Mexico," *New Mexico Historical Review* 24 (October 1949): 260.

76. Taylor, *In Search of the Racial Frontier*, 74.

77. Ayers, "Soldier's Experience in New Mexico," 261.

78. James Josiah Webb, *Adventures in the Santa Fe Trade 1844–1847*, edited by Ralph Bieber (Glendale, CA: Arthur H. Clark, 1931), 101.

79. *Organic Law of the Territory of New Mexico, November 23, 1846*, 30th Cong., 1st Sess., House Exec. Doc. No. 60, p. 179.

80. William W. H. Davis, *El Gringo; or, New Mexico and Her People* (Santa Fe, NM: Rydal, 1938), 98.

81. "Slavery in the Territory of New Mexico," 36th Cong., 1st Sess., House Report No. 508, p. 32.

82. *Congressional Globe*, 31st Cong., 1st Sess., February 12, 1850, Appendix, p. 208. See also Childers, *Failure of Popular Sovereignty*, 108–9, 145–46; Morrison, *Slavery and the American West*, 103.

83. Smith to Webster, April 9, 1850, in Wiltse and Birkner, *Papers of Daniel Webster*, 7:62.

84. *Messages of the President of the United States, April 28, 1848*, 30th Cong., 1st Sess., House Exec. Doc. 60, p. 170.

85. *Congressional Globe*, 31st Cong., 1st Sess., February 13, 1850, Appendix, p. 151.

86. Ibid.

87. Ibid., February 12, 1850, Appendix, p. 208.

88. Ibid., July 1, 1850, Appendix, p. 1010.

89. Ibid., February 13, 1850, p. 151.

90. Ibid., February 12, 1850, Appendix, p. 208.

91. Ibid., July 1, 1850, Appendix, p. 1011.

92. *American Insurance Company v. Canter*, 26 U.S. 542 (1828).

93. Ibid.

94. Cralle, *Speeches of John C. Calhoun*, 4:499.

95. *Congressional Globe*, 30th Cong., 1st Sess., July 29, 1848, Appendix, pp. 1060–61.

96. Benton, *Thirty Years' View*, 2:697, 759, quotation on 695.

97. *Congressional Globe*, 31st Cong., 1st Sess., July 8, 1850, Appendix, p. 1180 (emphasis in original).

98. Ibid., p. 1085.

99. Ibid., 30th Cong., 1st Sess., August 3, 1848, Appendix, p. 1073.

100. Ibid. (emphasis in original).

101. Ibid., pp. 1072–73.

102. Quoted in Benton, *Thirty Years' View*, 2:713. In response to Calhoun, Benton wrote, "History cannot class higher than as a vagary of a diseased imagination this imputed self-acting and self-extension of the Constitution." Ibid., 2:714.

103. *Congressional Globe*, 31st Cong., 1st Sess., February 13, 1850, Appendix, p. 151.

104. Quoted in ibid. (emphasis in original).

105. Ibid.

106. *Mariana Jaremillo v. Jose de la Cruz Romero*, January 1857, in Charles H. Gildersleeve, *Reports of Cases Argued and Determined in the Supreme Court of the Territory of New Mexico from January Term 1852 to January Term 1879*, vol. 1 (San Francisco: A. L. Bancroft, 1881), 195–97.

107. Ibid., 197.

108. Quoted in *Congressional Globe*, 30th Cong., 1st Sess., August 3, 1848, pp. 1073–74.

109. *Jaremillo v. Romero*, in Gildersleeve, *Reports of Cases*, 1:198.

110. Ibid., 1:201.

111. Dr. A. Wislizenus, *Memoir of a Tour to Northern Mexico, Connected with Col. Doniphan's Expedition, in 1846 and 1847* (Washington, DC: Tippin and Streeper, 1848), 24.

112. James S. Calhoun to Orlando Brown, March 15, 1850, in Annie Heloise Abel, ed., *The Official Correspondence of James S. Calhoun While Indian Agent at Santa Fe and Superintendent of Indian Affairs in New Mexico, 1849–1852* (Washington, DC: Government Printing Office, 1915), 161–62 (emphasis in original).

113. "A Few Questions About New Mexico," *New-York Daily Tribune*, January 23, 1861.

114. Webster to Hugh N. Smith, April 8, 1850, in Webster, *Works of Daniel Webster*, 6:548–49.

115. Hugh N. Smith to Webster, April 9, 1850, in Wiltse and Birkner, *Papers of Daniel Webster*, 7:62.

116. John Bassett Moore, ed., *The Works of James Buchanan, Comprising His Speeches, State Papers, and Private Correspondence*, 10 vols. (New York: Antiquarian Press, 1960), 1:202; 7:387.

117. For an analysis of race as a factor in western annexation, see Thomas R. Hietala, *Manifest Design: Anxious Aggrandizement in Late Jacksonian America* (Ithaca, NY: Cornell University Press, 1985), 26–40.

118. "The New Mexican Delegate," *Daily Albany Argus*, July 26, 1850.

119. *Address to the Inhabitants of New Mexico and California on the Omission by Congress to Provide Them with Territorial Governments and on the Social and Political*

Evils of Slavery (New York: American and Foreign Anti-Slavery Society, 1849), 55; Ganaway, *New Mexico and the Sectional Controversy*, 25.

120. Quoted in Lawrence R. Murphy, "Antislavery in the Southwest: William G. Kephart's Mission to New Mexico, 1850–1853," *Southwestern Studies* 54 (1978): 5.

121. Ibid., 21.

122. Ganaway, *New Mexico and the Sectional Controversy*, 54.

123. Weightman to Foote, December 16, 1851, in *Congressional Globe*, 32nd Cong., 1st Sess., March 17, 1852, p. 755 (emphasis in original); Spruce M. Baird to Sam Houston, September 28, 1851, in *Speech of Hon. Richard H. Weightman of New Mexico*, 16.

124. *Speech of Hon. Richard H. Weightman of New Mexico*, 1 (emphasis in original); Weightman to Foote, December 16, 1851, in *Congressional Globe*, 32nd Cong., 1st Sess., March 17, 1852, p. 755.

125. Murphy, "Antislavery in the Southwest," 6–7.

126. Kephart to Rev. George Whipple, February 20, 1851, quoted in Murphy, "Antislavery in the Southwest," 22.

127. Brock, *Parties and Political Conscience*, 276–316; Martin H. Quitt, *Stephen A. Douglas and Antebellum Democracy* (Cambridge, MA: Cambridge University Press, 2012), 113–18.

128. *Congressional Globe*, 31st Cong., 1st Sess., June 5, 1850, p. 1135.

129. Ibid.

Chapter 2

1. *Condition of the Indian Tribes*, 39th Cong., 2nd Sess., Senate Report No. 156 (Washington, DC: Government Printing Office, 1867).

2. On abolitionists and the Doolittle report, see Andrés Reséndez, *The Other Slavery: The Uncovered Story of Indian Enslavement in America* (New York: Houghton Mifflin Harcourt, 2016), 296–99.

3. Statement of Brigadier General James H. Carleton, July 3, 1865, in 39th Cong., 2nd Sess., Senate Report No. 156, 323–25.

4. Statement of Chief Justice Kirby Benedict, July 4, 1865, in ibid., 326.

5. Statement of Henry Connelly, July 4, 1865, in ibid., 332.

6. Undated statement of James L. Collins, in ibid., 332.

7. Undated statement of Christopher Carson, in ibid., 97.

8. See Stephen G. Hyslop, *Bound for Santa Fe: The Road to New Mexico and the American Conquest, 1806–1848* (Norman: University of Oklahoma Press, 2002), 33–51, 229–74. For an early account of the Santa Fe trade, see Josiah Gregg, *Commerce of the Prairies*, edited by Max L. Moorhead (Norman: University of Oklahoma Press, 1954).

9. See David M. Brugge, ed., "Vizcarra's Navajo Campaign of 1823," *Journal of the Southwest* 6 (Autumn 1964): 223–44; James F. Brooks, *Captives & Cousins: Slavery, Kinship, and Community in the Southwest Borderlands* (Chapel Hill: University of

North Carolina Press, 2002), 250; Frank McNitt, *Navajo Wars: Military Campaigns, Slave Raids, and Reprisals* (Albuquerque: University of New Mexico Press, 1972), 52–91.

10. New Mexico State Records Center and Archives, Frank McNitt Collection, Serial #10678, Folder 29, Military Papers, Santa Fe Presidial Company, Enlistment Papers, 1821–1845.

11. Report of Governor Manuel Armijo, November 25, 1838, ibid.

12. Donaciano Vigil, "Arms, Indians, and the Mismanagement of New Mexico," edited and translated by David J. Weber, *Southwestern Studies* 77 (1986): 7.

13. February 1855 monthly report of Michael Steck, Center for Southwest Research, Inventory of the Michael Steck Papers, Series 2, Roll 1; report of Michael Steck, May 18, 1855, ibid.; report of Michael Steck, January 27, 1859, ibid.

14. James H. Carleton to W. A. Nichols, October 1, 1855, NA, RG393, M1120, LR, DNM, Roll 4. For similar examples, see transcription of Henry Lane Kendrick, June 22, 1854, NA, RG75, OIA, T21, LR, NMS, Roll 2; Kendrick to W. S. Messervy, June 22, 1854, ibid.; Carleton to Messervy, July 11, 1854, ibid.; James H. Whitlock to George W. Bowie, March 1, 1864, in *The War of the Rebellion: A Compilation of the Official Records of the Union and Confederate Armies*, Series 1, vol. 34, pt. 1 (Washington, DC: Government Printing Office, 1880), 122–23.

15. Daniel W. Jones, *Forty Years Among the Indians* (Los Angeles: Westernlore, 1960), 47–48; James A. Bennett, *Forts and Forays: A Dragoon in New Mexico, 1850–1856* (Albuquerque: University of New Mexico Press, 1948), 19; statement of Chief Justice Kirby Benedict, July 4, 1865, in *Condition of the Indian Tribes*, 326; Julius K. Graves to Dennis N. Cooley, undated report of January 1866, in *1866 Annual Report of the Commissioner of Indian Affairs* (Washington, DC: Government Printing Office, 1866), 136. See also Sondra Jones, "'Redeeming' the Indian: The Enslavement of Indian Children in New Mexico and Utah," *Utah Historical Quarterly* 67 (June 1999): 220–41, esp. 223–25. Observers frequently used animal metaphors to describe the means by which captives and peons were regarded in the marketplace. See, for example, Reuben Gold Thwaites, ed., *The Personal Narrative of James O. Pattie of Kentucky* (Cleveland, OH: Arthur H. Clark, 1905), 113. Lieutenant William Woods Averell described a transaction in which an Indian man offered him "pretty much everything he possessed of cows, sheep, goats, and other personal property" for a young Mexican girl who had formerly been a captive among the Kiowas and Cheyennes. William Woods Averell, *Ten Years in the Saddle: The Memoir of William Woods Averell, 1851–1862*, edited by Edward K. Eckert and Nicholas J. Amato (San Rafael, CA: Presidio, 1978), 118. See also James S. Calhoun to Orlando Brown, March 31, 1850, in Annie Heloise Abel, ed., *The Official Correspondence of James S. Calhoun While Indian Agent at Santa Fe and Superintendent of Indian Affairs in New Mexico, 1849–1852* (Washington, DC: Government Printing Office, 1915), 181–83, in which Calhoun describes the items, which included knives, tobacco, corn, cloth, blankets, and bullets, that Mexican citizens at the village of Mora traded to various Indian tribes for captives.

16. Greiner to Lea, May 19, 1852, in Abel, *Official Correspondence of James S. Calhoun*, 537.

17. Michael Steck to William Dole, January 13, 1864, NA, RG75, OIA, M234, LR, NMS, Roll 552.

18. Calhoun to Brown, March 15, 1850, in Abel, *Official Correspondence of James S. Calhoun*, 161–62.

19. T. J. Farnham, *Life, Adventures and Travels in California* (New York: Nafis and Cornish, 1849), 377; T. J. Farnham, "Travels in the Great Western Prairies," pt. 1, in R. G. Thwaites, *Early Western Travels, 1748–1846*, vol. 28 (Cleveland, OH: Arthur H. Clark, 1906), 249. New Mexico's superintendent of Indian affairs, Michael Steck, noted in 1864 that Indian slaves usually sold for "about $100," but he also stated that "frequently after becoming domesticated, they sell much higher." Steck to William, January 13, 1864, NA, RG75, OIA, M234, LR, NMS, Roll 552. For Indian slave prices in 1850s Utah, see Brian Q. Cannon, "Adopted or Indentured, 1850–1870: Native Children in Mormon Households," in Robert W. Walker and Doris R. Dant, eds., *Nearly Everything Imaginable: The Everyday Life of Utah's Mormon Pioneers* (Provo, UT: Brigham Young University Press, 1999), 342. Lofty as they might seem, these prices still paled in comparison to what African American slaves might fetch at a Southern slave auction; typically, blacks in the mid-nineteenth-century Cotton Belt sold for five to six times the amount of an Indian slave in New Mexico. Sondra Jones, *The Trial of Don Pedro León Luján: The Attack Against Indian Slavery and Mexican Traders in Utah* (Salt Lake City: University of Utah Press, 2000), 142n50.

20. Statement of Chief Justice Kirby Benedict, July 4, 1865, in *Condition of the Indian Tribes*, 326. See also Jones, *Forty Years Among the Indians*, 47–48.

21. Edward E. Baptist, *The Half Has Never Been Told: Slavery and the Making of American Capitalism* (New York: Basic Books, 2014), 240–42. For similar slaving practices in California, see Stacey L. Smith, *Freedom's Frontier: California and the Struggle over Unfree Labor, Emancipation, and Reconstruction* (Chapel Hill: University of North Carolina Press, 2013), 11–12.

22. Calvin Schermerhorn, *Money over Mastery, Family over Freedom: Slavery in the Antebellum Upper South* (Baltimore, MD: Johns Hopkins University Press, 2011), 13–16.

23. John Ward to A. B. Norton, February 10, 1867, NA, RG75, OIA, M234, LR, NMS, Roll 552.

24. For the full text of the Kearny Code, see *Organic Law of the Territory of New Mexico, November 23, 1846*, 30th Cong., 1st Sess., House Exec. Doc. No. 60, pp. 177–229. On the Kearny Code generally, see William A. Keleher, *Turmoil in New Mexico, 1846–1868* (Santa Fe, NM: Rydal, 1952), 118n25.

25. David Meriwether, *My Life in the Mountains and on the Plains*, edited by Robert A. Griffen (Norman: University of Oklahoma Press, 1965), 157.

26. William Carr Lane to Michael Steck, February 12, 1853, Center for Southwest Research, Inventory of the Michael Steck Papers, Series 1, Roll 1.

27. Sumner undertook this reorganization pursuant to orders from the secretary of war, who instructed him to "revise the whole system of defense . . . and rigidly enforce all regulations having reference to the economy of service." Charles M. Conrad to Edwin V. Sumner, April 1, 1851, in Abel, *Official Correspondence of James S. Calhoun*, 383.

28. H. L. Kendrick to W. A. Nichols, November 13, 1853, NA, RG393, M1102, LR, DNM, Roll 7.

29. "Greely's [*sic*] Article on New Mexico—Reply of Hon. M. A. Otero," *Mesilla Times*, March 2, 1861; William W. H. Davis, *El Gringo; or, New Mexico and Her People* (Santa Fe, NM: Rydal, 1938), 84–85.

30. Undated 1851 memorial to Congress, NA, RG46, Territorial Papers of the U.S. Senate, Roll 14 (New Mexico, 1840–1854).

31. Journal of the Convention of the Territory of New Mexico (1849), p. 11, in William Jenkins Skinner, ed. and comp., *Records of the States of the United States of America, New Mexico, 1849–1910*, Class C, Constitutional Records, Microfilm Roll 1.

32. Territorial Legislature Joint Resolution, January 6, 1852, in ibid.

33. Brooks, *Captives & Cousins*, 379–80, 382–83.

34. *Congressional Globe*, 31st Cong., 1st Sess., June 6, 1850, p. 1144.

35. On the strength of the Santa Fe garrison, see Don Pedro Fermín de Mendinueta to Viceroy Bucareli, March 26, 1772, in Alfred Barnaby Thomas, ed. and trans., "Governor Mendinueta's Proposals for the Defense of New Mexico, 1772–1778," *New Mexico Historical Review* 6 (January 1931): 27–28; Eleanor B. Adams, ed., "Bishop Tamarón's Visitation of New Mexico, 1760," *New Mexico Historical Review* 28 (July 1953): 206; Alfred Barnaby Thomas, ed. and trans., *Teodoro de Croix and the Northern Frontier of New Spain, 1776–1783: From the Original Document in the Archives of the Indies, Seville* (Norman: University of Oklahoma Press, 1968), 106; Fernando de la Concha to Fernando Chacón, June 28, 1794, in Donald E. Worcester, ed. and trans., "Notes and Documents: Advice on Governing New Mexico, 1794," *New Mexico Historical Review* 24 (July 1949): 250. On the Santa Fe presidio generally, see Max L. Moorhead, *The Presidio: Bastion of the Spanish Borderlands* (Norman: University of Oklahoma Press, 1975), 173–76.

36. Ross Calvin, ed., *Lieutenant Emory Reports: Notes of a Military Reconnaissance from Fort Leavenworth, in Missouri, to San Diego, in California* (Albuquerque: University of New Mexico Press, 1951), 50. See also Philip St. George Cooke, *The Conquest of New Mexico and California: An Historical and Personal Narrative* (New York: G. P. Putnam's Sons, 1878), 34–38; Ralph Emerson Twitchell, *The History of the Military Occupation of the Territory of New Mexico from 1846 to 1851 by the Government of the United States* (Chicago: Rio Grande, 1963), 65–67.

37. Cooke, *Conquest of New Mexico and California*, 42; Calvin, *Lieutenant Emory Reports*, 68; "Report of Lieut. J. W. Abert of His Examination of New Mexico in the Years 1846–47," in *Report of the Secretary of War, February 10, 1848*, 30th Cong., 1st Sess., Senate Exec. Doc. 23, p. 46.

38. Archives of the Archdiocese of Santa Fe, Taos Baptisms, Microfilm #21, Frame 765; Sterling Price to Roger Jones, February 15, 1847, in *Report of the Secretary of War*, 30th Cong., 1st Sess., Senate Exec. Doc. No. 1, p. 527.

39. Hunter Miller, ed., *Treaties and Other International Acts of the United States of America*, vol. 5 (Washington, DC: Government Printing Office, 1931), 219–22; *Treaty of Guadalupe Hidalgo—Indian Incursions, April 24, 1850*, 31st Cong., 1st Sess., House Report No. 280. The adjutant general of the army issued a circular instructing officers near the Mexican border of the obligation and furnishing each with a copy of the treaty. Roger Jones to W. J. Worth, March 24, 1849, NA, RG393, M1102, LR, DNM, Roll 1.

40. *Treaty of Amity, Commerce, and Navigation, Between the United States of America and the United Mexican States, Concluded on the 5th of April, 1831*, 22nd Cong., 1st Sess., Senate Exec. Doc. No. 11.

41. See Brian DeLay, *War of a Thousand Deserts: Indian Raids and the U.S.-Mexican War* (New Haven, CT: Yale University Press, 2008), esp. 294–303.

42. B. L. Beall to J. H. Dickerson, March 12, 1849, NA, RG393, M1102, LR, DNM, Roll 1; Thomas Fitzpatrick to Beall, February 24, 1849, ibid.

43. For attempts to return captives, see Calhoun to Orlando Brown, March 15, 1850, in Abel, *Official Correspondence of James S. Calhoun*, 161–62; Calhoun to Brown, March 31, 1850, in ibid., 181–83; Calhoun to John Munroe, April 18, 1850, in ibid., 184–85; Calhoun to Luke Lea, July 28, 1851, in ibid., 390–91; Calhoun to Lea, August 22, 1851, in ibid., 401. For Calhoun's tenure as an Indian agent in New Mexico with an emphasis on slavery, see Reséndez, *Other Slavery*, 242–46.

44. Enoch Steen to Lafayette McLaws, December 9, 1849, NA, RG393, M1102, LR, DNM, Roll 2.

45. Steen to McLaws, September 4, 1850, ibid.; "Manuel Martinez Sr. to Commander of the State," *El Sonorense*, April 23, 1850; Edwin R. Sweeney, *Mangas Coloradas: Chief of the Chiricahua Apaches* (Norman: University of Oklahoma Press, 1998), 205–6.

46. Shortly afterward, Bartlett reclaimed a third Mexican captive, Inez González, whom he later returned to her family in Santa Cruz, Sonora. See John Russell Bartlett, *Personal Narrative of Explorations and Incidents in Texas, New Mexico, California, Sonora and Chihuahua, 1850–1853*, vol. 1 (New York: D. Appleton, 1854), 303–12; John C. Cremony, *Life Among the Apaches* (San Francisco: A. Roman, 1868), 53–61; Bartlett to Alexander Stuart, February 19, 1852, NA, RG75, OIA, M234, LR, NMS, Roll 546; Sweeney, *Mangas Coloradas*, 234–35; William S. Kiser, *Dragoons in Apacheland: Conquest and Resistance in Southern New Mexico, 1846–1861* (Norman: University of Oklahoma Press, 2012), 83. When Apache chief Mangas Coloradas negotiated a treaty with Colonel Edwin V. Sumner and Indian agent John Greiner at Acoma Pueblo on July 11, 1852, he traded at least one captive (Jesús Arvisu, taken in a raid at Bacoachi, Sonora, in 1851) to the Navajos en route to the rendezvous point, anticipating that

American officials would demand that he relinquish claim to the boy upon arrival. Sweeney, *Mangas Coloradas*, 258.

47. Sweeney, *Mangas Coloradas*, 295.

48. Dixon S. Miles to Steck, April 3, 1855, Center for Southwest Research, Inventory of the Michael Steck Papers, Series 2, Roll 1.

49. James Gadsden to John Garland, October 8, 1853, NA, RG393, M1102, LR, DNM, Roll 7.

50. David Meriwether to James Smith, October 30, 1853, ibid.; Meriwether to Smith, December 5, 1853, Center for Southwest Research, Inventory of the Michael Steck Papers, Series 1, Roll 1.

51. Israel B. Richardson to Nichols, December 19, 1853, NA, RG393, M1102, LR, DNM, Roll 7; Nichols to Richardson, December 15, 1853, ibid.; Garland to Gadsden, December 25, 1853, ibid.

52. Steck to Lane, August 13, 1853, Center for Southwest Research, Inventory of the Michael Steck Papers, Series 1, Roll 1.

53. Bartlett, *Personal Narrative of Explorations and Incidents*, 1:268; Edwin R. Sweeney, " 'I Had Lost All': Geronimo and the Carrasco Massacre of 1851," *Journal of Arizona History* 27 (Spring 1986): 45–49; Sweeney, *Mangas Coloradas*, 218–19, 223; William B. Griffen, *Utmost Good Faith: Patterns of Apache-Mexican Hostilities in Northern Chihuahua Border Warfare, 1821–1848* (Albuquerque: University of New Mexico Press, 1988), 238–42. See also L. R. Bailey, *Indian Slave Trade in the Southwest* (Los Angeles: Westernlore, 1966), 28–37. On the strategic geographic dislocation of Apache captives, see Matthew Babcock, "Blurred Borders: North America's Forgotten Apache Reservations," in Juliana Barr and Edward Countryman, eds., *Contested Spaces of Early America* (Philadelphia: University of Pennsylvania Press, 2014), 172–73.

54. S. M. Barrett, ed., *Geronimo's Story of His Life* (New York: Duffield, 1906), 75–83.

55. Calhoun to Orlando Brown, March 31, 1850, in Abel, *Official Correspondence of James S. Calhoun*, 183.

56. Brooks, *Captives & Cousins*, 367.

57. Article 2 of the Gadsden Treaty, signed December 30, 1853, and ratified several months later, nullified Article 11 of the Treaty of Guadalupe Hidalgo. Miller, *Treaties and Other International Acts*, 6:296.

58. Richard S. Ewell to Nichols, August 10, 1858, NA, RG393, M1120, LR, DNM, Roll 7. Ewell specifically referred to the captive as a "peon." Both Anglo-Americans and Mexicans often used the terms "captive" and "peon" interchangeably because of the close functional relationship between the two systems of servitude. Rafael Chacón, a New Mexican involved in the Comanchero trade, stated that his trading expeditions included "Pueblo Indians, the Utes, or the Navajoes, [which] we were in the habit of carrying with us as peons." Jacqueline Dorgan Meketa, ed., *Legacy of Honor: The Life of Rafael Chacón, a Nineteenth-Century New Mexican* (Albuquerque: University of New Mexico Press, 1986), 115.

59. Electus Backus to John D. Wilkins, January 18, 1859, NA, RG393, M1120, LR, DNM, Roll 9.

60. John H. Bowman to Commissioner of Indian Affairs, undated correspondence (1880s), quoted in Bailey, *Indian Slave Trade in the Southwest*, 136.

61. Sumner to Jones, November 20, 1851, in Abel, *Official Correspondence of James S. Calhoun*, 445.

62. For advocacy of militias, see Calhoun to William L. Marcy, November 25, 1848, in ibid., 13; Calhoun to Sumner, February 11, 1852, NA, RG393, M1102, LR, DNM, Roll 4; Sumner to Calhoun, March 21, 1852, in Abel, *Official Correspondence of James S. Calhoun*, 492–93; Bailey, *Indian Slave Trade in the Southwest*, 107–8. The secretary of war denied Calhoun's initial request to raise a militia, but the territorial legislature passed resolutions condoning it and future governors David Meriwether and Abraham Rencher likewise voiced support for such a strategy. See Marcy to Calhoun, December 7, 1848, in Abel, *Official Correspondence of James S. Calhoun*, 13; "Proclamation of Governor David Meriwether," January 24, 1855, New Mexico State Records Center and Archives, William G. Ritch Collection, Microfilm Roll 6; Abraham Rencher to Col. B. L. E. Bonneville, December 4, 1858, NA, RG393, M1120, LR, DNM, Roll 8; "Militia Law of the Territory of New Mexico," in 1851 laws and resolutions of the territorial legislature, NA, RG46, Territorial Papers of the U.S. Senate, Roll 14 (New Mexico, 1840–1854); "An Act Amendatory to the Militia Law of the Territory of New Mexico," in *Laws of the Territory of New Mexico Passed by the Legislative Assembly, Session of 1859–1860* (Santa Fe, NM: O. P. Hovey, 1860), 8–10.

63. Proclamation of Governor Henry Connelly, May 4, 1864, in *Condition of the Indian Tribes*, 333.

64. See Kiser, *Dragoons in Apacheland*, esp. 3–12.

65. For Calhoun's views on Comanche slave trading, see Carl Coke Rister, *Border Captives: The Traffic in Prisoners by Southern Plains Indians, 1835–1875* (Norman: University of Oklahoma Press, 1940), 53–58; Thomas W. Kavanagh, *Comanche Political History: An Ethnohistorical Perspective, 1706–1875* (Lincoln: University of Nebraska Press, 1996), 338–43, 381, 383. Calhoun temporarily housed William G. Kephart, an agent for the American and Foreign Anti-Slavery Society, at his home in 1850. Had Calhoun been a proslavery man, it seems unlikely he would have allowed an abolitionist to stay with him. See Lawrence R. Murphy, "Antislavery in the Southwest: William G. Kephart's Mission to New Mexico, 1850–1853," *Southwestern Studies* 54 (1978): 15.

66. Calhoun to Brown, March 15, 1850, in Abel, *Official Correspondence of James S. Calhoun*, 161–62.

67. Calhoun to William Medill, October 1, 1849, 31st Cong., 1st Sess., House Exec. Doc. No. 17, pp. 204–5. For additional examples of ransomed Mexican captives, see Abel, *Official Correspondence of James S. Calhoun*, 183, 226–27, 390–91.

68. Joaquín Real Alencaster to Nemesio Salcedo, May 15, 1805, in New Mexico State Records Center and Archives, Frank McNitt Collection, Serial #10678, Folder 8; Fernando Chacon Treaty Proposals, March 27, 1805, ibid. For a Navajo oral history

recounting the massacre, see Ruth Roessel, ed., *Navajo Stories of the Long Walk Period* (Chinle, AZ: Navajo Community College Press, 1973), 188–89.

69. Treaty with the Navajos, November 11, 1822, New Mexico State Records Center and Archives, Frank McNitt Collection, Serial #10678, Folder 29.

70. Governor Manuel Armijo to Minister of War and Navy, October 3, 1840, ibid., Folder 10.

71. Rural Commandancy of Jemez to Manuel Armijo, March 14, 1841, ibid., Folder 26.

72. Mariano Martinez to Señor Governor, February 26, 1844, ibid., Folder 10. On the incongruities in legal responsibilities and captive exchanges between Navajos and Euro-Americans, see Brian DeLay, "Blood Talk: Violence and Belonging in the Navajo-New Mexican Borderland," in Barr and Countryman, *Contested Spaces of Early America*, 234–35, 247, 250. For Navajo oral tradition, see Roessel, *Navajo Stories of the Long Walk Period*, 151–52, 181, 199, 232, 253–59.

73. Navajo Treaty, February 5, 1823, New Mexico State Records Center and Archives, Frank McNitt Collection, Serial #10678, Folder 29.

74. Brooks, *Captives & Cousins*, 235. For post-1846 Indian baptisms, see ibid., 332, 336n47; Brugge, *Navajos in the Catholic Church Records*, 37.

75. Jones, *Forty Years Among the Indians*, 47–48; Lorenzo Labadi to Meriwether, February 18, 1855, NA, RG75, OIA, T21, LR, NMS, Roll 1.

76. "Report of Lieut. J. W. Abert of His Examination of New Mexico in the Years 1846–47," in *Report of the Secretary of War, February 10, 1848*, 30th Cong., 1st Sess., Senate Exec. Doc. 23, p. 92.

77. "Treaty with the Navajos," in Charles J. Kappler, *Indian Affairs: Laws and Treaties*, vol. 2 (Washington, DC: Government Printing Office, 1904), 583–85; 1858 treaty with the Navajos, in RG75, OIA, NMS, T21, Roll 3. See also McNitt, *Navajo Wars*, 88–89.

78. Medill to Calhoun, April 7, 1849, 31st Cong., 1st Sess., House Exec. Doc. No. 17, p. 195.

79. Medill to Adam Johnston, April 14, 1849, ibid., p. 188.

80. John W. Whitfield to Meriwether, September 29, 1854, NA, RG75, OIA, T21, LR, NMS, Roll 2.

81. Christopher Carson to James L. Collins, December 8, 1858, ibid., Roll 1.

82. Carson to Collins, January 12, 1859, ibid. On Carson's Indian captives, see Tom Dunlay, *Kit Carson and the Indians* (Lincoln: University of Nebraska Press, 2000), 200–204.

83. For Calhoun's proclamation on Indian trading licenses, see Abel, *Official Correspondence of James S. Calhoun*, 105. See also D. V. Whiting to McLaws, March 28, 1851, NA, RG393, M1102, LR, DNM, Roll 3.

84. *Deseret News Weekly*, quoted in *Congressional Globe*, 32nd Cong., 1st Sess., March 15, 1852, p. 754.

85. "Scoundrelism in Our Territories: Kidnapping Under a Governor's License," *National Era*, February 26, 1852. See also *Speech of Hon. Richard H. Weightman of New Mexico, Delivered in the House of Representatives, March 15, 1852* (Washington, DC: Congressional Globe Office, 1852), 3.

86. *Congressional Globe*, 32nd Cong., 1st Sess., March 15, 1852, p. 754. See also Jones, *Trial of Don Pedro León Luján*, 121–23.

87. Jones, *Trial of Don Pedro León Luján*, 53–59.

88. Ned Blackhawk, *Violence over the Land: Indians and Empires in the Early American West* (Cambridge, MA: Harvard University Press, 2006), 106–13; Reséndez, *Other Slavery*, 186–94; Jones, *Trial of Don Pedro León Luján*, 28, 47–49; Jared Farmer, *On Zion's Mount: Mormons, Indians, and the American Landscape* (Cambridge, MA: Harvard University Press, 2008), 30–34. On Spanish excursions into the Great Basin, see Joseph P. Sánchez, *Explorers, Traders, and Slavers: Forging the Old Spanish Trail, 1678–1850* (Salt Lake City: University of Utah Press, 1997), esp. 91–102.

89. Will Bagley, ed., *The Pioneer Camp of the Saints: The 1846 and 1847 Mormon Trail Journals of Thomas Bullock* (Spokane, WA: Arthur H. Clark, 1997), 212. See also James G. Bleak, 1854 journal entry, quoted in Leland Hargrave Creer, "Spanish-American Slave Trade in the Great Basin, 1800–1853," *New Mexico Historical Review* 24 (July 1949): 180; Farnham, *Life, Adventures and Travels in California*, 377; Howard Louis Conard, *Uncle Dick Wootton: The Pioneer Frontiersman of the Rocky Mountain Region* (Chicago: W. E. Dibble, 1890), 187.

90. J. Forney to A. B. Greenwood, September 29, 1859, in *1859 Annual Report of the Commissioner of Indian Affairs*, 365–67. See also P. J. De Smet, *Letters and Sketches: With a Narrative of a Year's Residence Among the Indian Tribes of the Rocky Mountains*, in Thwaites, *Early Western Travels*, 27:166–67.

91. Garland Hurt to James H. Simpson, May 2, 1860, in James H. Simpson, *Report of Explorations Across the Great Basin in 1859* (Reno: University of Nevada Press, 1983), 461–62. Hurt noted that "the Py-eeds are perhaps the most timid and dejected of all the tribes west of the Rocky Mountains, being regarded by the Utahs [Utes] as their slaves. They not infrequently take their children from them by force." Ibid., 462. See also De Smet, "Letters and Sketches," in Thwaites, *Early Western Travels*, 27:167. On Ute captive taking, see Lieut. J. W. Gunnison, *The Mormons, or, Latter-Day Saints, in the Valley of the Great Salt Lake* . . . (Philadelphia: Lippincott, Grambo, 1852), 148–49.

92. George W. Armstrong to Brigham Young, June 30, 1856, in *1856 Annual Report of the Commissioner of Indian Affairs*, 234–35.

93. Virginia McConnell Simmons, *The Ute Indians of Utah, Colorado, and New Mexico* (Boulder: University Press of Colorado, 2000), 128.

94. Greiner to Lea, May 19, 1852, in Abel, *Official Correspondence of James S. Calhoun*, 536–37.

95. For the Paiute slave trade, see Martha C. Knack, *Boundaries Between: The Southern Paiutes, 1775–1995* (Lincoln: University of Nebraska Press, 2001), 35–38; Stephen P. Van Hoak, "And Who Shall Have the Children? The Indian Slave Trade in

the Southern Great Basin, 1800–1865," *Nevada Historical Society Quarterly* 41 (1998): 3–25; Blackhawk, *Violence over the Land*, 141, 148. On the Shoshones, see Colin G. Calloway, "Snake Frontiers: The Eastern Shoshones in the Eighteenth Century," *Annals of Wyoming* 63 (Summer 1991): 82–93, esp. 89.

96. Jones, *Trial of Don Pedro León Luján*, 7–8, 64–66.

97. Jones, *Forty Years Among the Indians*, 50–53. The author, Daniel Jones, served as an interpreter during the initial trial.

98. Greiner to Lea, May 19, 1852, in Abel, *Official Correspondence of James S. Calhoun*, 536. See also Jones, *Trial of Don Pedro León Luján*, 67–69.

99. "An act to regulate trade and intercourse with the Indian tribes," June 30, 1834, U.S. *Statutes at Large*, chap. 161, 23rd Cong., 1st Sess., pp. 729–35.

100. Greiner to Lea, May 19, 1852, in Abel, *Official Correspondence of James S. Calhoun*, 536.

101. The original legal proceedings are contained in *United States v. Pedro Leon et al.*, Doc. 1533 (microfiche), First Judicial Court of Utah. See also Jones, *Trial of Don Pedro León Luján*, 70–92.

102. *Acts, Resolutions, and Memorials, Passed at the Several Annual Sessions of the Legislative Assembly of the Territory of Utah* (Great Salt Lake City, UT: Joseph Cain, 1855), 173–74.

103. Jones, *Trial of Don Pedro León Luján*, 61.

104. Proclamation of Brigham Young, April 23, 1853, NA, RG59, M12, U.S. State Department, Territorial Papers of Utah, Roll 1.

105. Greiner to Lea, May 19, 1852, in Abel, *Official Correspondence of James S. Calhoun*, 536.

106. *Congressional Globe*, 32nd Cong., 1st Sess., March 15, 1852, p. 754.

107. Ibid., pp. 754–55.

108. On Calhoun's failing health, see Greiner to Lea, May 19, 1852, in Abel, *Official Correspondence of James S. Calhoun*, 537; Greiner to Lea, April 30, 1852, NA, RG75, OIA, M234, LR, NMS, Roll 546.

109. See Blackhawk, *Violence over the Land*, 239–41; Jones, *Trial of Don Pedro León Luján*, 100–104.

110. Jones, *Trial of Don Pedro León Luján*, 42–44, 145n9.

111. Farmer, *On Zion's Mount*, 55–57.

112. John Simonson to John D. Wilkins, September 25, 1859, NA, RG393, M1120, LR, DNM, Roll 10.

113. On the nature of these laws, see Cannon, "Adopted or Indentured," in Walker and Dant, *Nearly Everything Imaginable*, 341–42.

114. "Brigham Young's Address to the Utah Legislature," *Deseret News Weekly*, January 10, 1852. For early Mormon-Paiute relations, see Knack, *Boundaries Between*, 48–94, esp. 56–59. On Indian slavery among the Mormons generally, see Cannon, "Adopted or Indentured," in Walker and Dant, *Nearly Everything Imaginable*, 341–57; Reséndez, *Other Slavery*, 266–77.

115. Smith, *Freedom's Frontier*, 11, 182–92.

116. Solomon Nunes Carvalho, *Incidents of Travel and Adventure in the Far West*, edited by Bertram Wallace Korn (Philadelphia: Jewish Publication Society of America, 1954), 260. Chief Walkara was a renowned Ute slave trader until his death in 1855. See Bailey, *Indian Slave Trade in the Southwest*, 150–52, 163; Farmer, *On Zion's Mount*, 34.

117. George Armstrong to Brigham Young, June 30, 1857, in *1857 Annual Report of the Commissioner of Indian Affairs*, 309. During his time as the superintendent of Indian affairs in Utah, Young's official reports made no mention of purchasing Indian children, and even his agents in the field were careful to avoid such terminology when referring to Indian children serving in Mormon households.

118. Fourth Annual Message of Governor Abraham Rencher, December 6, 1860, NA, RG59, T17, New Mexico Territorial Papers, Roll 2. See also 1861 Executive Journal of Abraham Rencher, ibid.; *Santa Fe Weekly Gazette*, December 6, 1860. On the legislature's attempt to pass the Indian slavery amendment, see Mark Stegmaier, "A Law That Would Make Caligula Blush? New Mexico Territory's Unique Slave Code, 1859–1861," *New Mexico Historical Review* 87 (Spring 2012): 219–20. During the Confederate invasion of 1861–62, Brigadier General Henry Hopkins Sibley suggested that his government legalize the enslaving of Indians. Had New Mexico fallen to Rebel forces, the legislature's previous attempt to sanction Indian slavery might have become a reality under the auspices of the Confederate government. Sibley to Samuel Cooper, May 4, 1862, *War of the Rebellion*, Series 1, 9:512.

119. *Congressional Globe*, 39th Cong., 2nd Sess., February 19, 1867, p. 1571.

120. Statements of Henry Connelly and Chief Justice Kirby Benedict, July 4, 1865, in *Condition of the Indian Tribes*, 332, 326; James F. Meline, *Two Thousand Miles on Horseback: Santa Fe and Back* (Albuquerque, NM: Horn and Wallace, 1966), 120.

121. Quoted in Laura E. Gómez, "Off-White in an Age of White Supremacy: Mexican Elites and the Rights of Indians and Blacks in Nineteenth Century New Mexico," in Michael A. Olivas, ed., *Colored Men and Hombres Aquí: Hernandez v. Texas and the Emergence of Mexican-American Lawyering* (Houston, TX: Arte Público, 2006), 30.

122. "Peonage in New Mexico," *Santa Fe Weekly Gazette*, February 2, 1867.

123. Thwaites, *Personal Narrative of James O. Pattie of Kentucky*, 113.

124. Sumner to Jones, November 20, 1851, NA, RG393, M1072, LS, DNM, Roll 1.

125. Miles to Steck, August 12, 1855, Center for Southwest Research, Inventory of the Michael Steck Papers, Series 2, Roll 1.

126. Greiner to Calhoun, January 31, 1852, in Abel, *Official Correspondence of James S. Calhoun*, 468.

127. Kendrick to S. D. Sturgis, June 14, 1853, NA, RG393, M1102, LR, DNM, Roll 7.

128. Steck to Charles E. Mix, June 4, 1864, Center for Southwest Research, Inventory of the Michael Steck Papers, Series 2, Roll 3.

129. On Navajo-Ute enmity, see Joaquín Real Alencaster to Nemesio Salcedo, May 15, 1805, New Mexico State Records Center and Archives, Frank McNitt Collection, Serial #10678, Folder 8; Kendrick to Nichols, February 11, 1857, NA, RG393,

M1120, LR, DNM, Roll 6; Kendrick to Nichols, July 12, 1856, ibid., Roll 5; Lorenzo Labadi to Meriwether, October 20, 1856, NA, RG75, OIA, T21, LR, NMS, Roll 2; John Ward to Samuel M. Yost, April 9, 1858, ibid., Roll 3; Yost to James L. Collins, November 23, 1858, ibid.; Roessel, *Navajo Stories of the Long Walk Period*, esp. 28–30, 218–19, 226. For the effects of the Navajo campaign with an emphasis on the enslavement of tribe members, see Reséndez, *Other Slavery*, 266–77.

130. Christopher Carson to AAG, July 24, 1863, *War of the Rebellion*, Series 1, vol. 26, pt. 1, pp. 233–34; Carson to James H. Carleton, July 24, 1863, ibid., 234; see also statement of Colonel Kit Carson, in *Condition of the Indian Tribes*, 97.

131. McNitt, *Navajo Wars*, 442–46; Clifford E. Trafzer, *The Kit Carson Campaign: The Last Great Navajo War* (Norman: University of Oklahoma Press, 1982), 80–82; Roessel, *Navajo Stories of the Long Walk Period*, 226–27.

132. E. Butler to Cyrus DeForrest, May 5, 1867, NA, RG75, OIA, T21, LR, NMS, Roll 8. This Fort Wingate should not be confused with the later Fort Wingate located thirteen miles east of Gallup at Ojo del Oso (Bear Spring). The first Fort Wingate, established as a base of operations during Carson's Navajo campaigns, was near Gallinas Springs about five miles south of the present town of Grants, New Mexico. Robert Julyan, *The Place Names of New Mexico* (Albuquerque: University of New Mexico Press, 1996), 137. Navajo oral histories are replete with stories of women and children being taken or sold into captivity during the Long Walk. See Roessel, *Navajo Stories of the Long Walk Period*.

133. See Gerald Thompson, *The Army and the Navajo: The Bosque Redondo Reservation Experiment, 1863–1868* (Tucson: University of Arizona Press, 1976), 47–48, 80–81, 98–99, 128–29.

134. "Proceedings of Council, May 28, 29, 30, 1868," in J. Lee Correll, *Through White Men's Eyes: A Contribution to Navajo History . . .* , vol. 6 (Window Rock, AZ: Navajo Heritage Center, 1979), 137–38. See also Report on Navajo Indians, *Santa Fe New Mexican*, August 6, 1868. Like many Anglo-Americans, Sherman conflated the term "peon," which applied to indebted Mexicans, with an Indian captive. Recent scholars have perpetuated this conflation, adding to the confusion surrounding the two systems of slavery. See, for example, Laura E. Gómez, *Manifest Destinies: The Making of the Mexican American Race* (New York: New York University Press, 2007), 111, where the author writes that "Congress in 1867 directly prohibited Indian slavery and the practice of Indian peonage."

135. Correll, *Through White Men's Eyes*, 6:95. On the treaty generally, see Peter Iverson, *Diné: A History of the Navajos* (Albuquerque: University of New Mexico Press, 2002), 63–65. For Navajo accounts of the treaty, see Roessel, *Navajo Stories of the Long Walk Period*.

136. "Joint Resolution to aid in relieving from peonage women and children of the Navajo Indians," July 27, 1868, in *Acts and Resolutions of the United States of America Passed at the Second Session of the Fortieth Congress* (Washington, DC: Government Printing Office, 1868), 331.

137. "William T. Sherman to George W. Getty," *Santa Fe New Mexican*, September 26, 1868.

138. Sherman to Ulysses S. Grant, June 7, 1868, in Correll, *Through White Men's Eyes*, 6:45.

139. Thomas V. Keam to Nathaniel Pope, September 9, 1872, in *1872 Annual Report of the Commissioner of Indian Affairs*, 304.

Chapter 3

1. Mark L. Gardner and Marc Simmons, eds., *The Mexican War Correspondence of Richard Smith Elliott* (Norman: University of Oklahoma Press, 1997), 106.

2. A. B. Dyer to Col. Talcott, February 17, 1847, New Mexico State Records Center and Archives, Misc. Letters and Diaries, Box 1, File 5.

3. John Ayers, "A Soldier's Experience in New Mexico," *New Mexico Historical Review* 24 (October 1949): 260–61; "Later from New Mexico," *New-York Daily Tribune*, March 3, 1847.

4. *Cruz Marqués v. José Manuel Angel*, October 3, 1855, New Mexico State Records Center and Archives, San Miguel County District Court Records, Serial #13533, Folder 1, Case #24. On corporal punishment of peons, see Charles H. Harris III, *A Mexican Family Empire: The Latifundio of the Sánchez Navarros, 1765–1867* (Austin: University of Texas Press, 1975), 223–25.

5. *Congressional Globe*, 39th Cong., 2nd Sess., February 19, 1867, p. 1572.

6. William H. Ryus, *The Second William Penn: Treating with Indians on the Santa Fe Trail, 1860–66* (Kansas City, MO: Frank T. Riley, 1913), 108; Lawrence R. Murphy, *Lucien Bonaparte Maxwell: Napoleon of the Southwest* (Norman: University of Oklahoma Press, 1983), 111–12; Lawrence R. Murphy, *Philmont: A History of New Mexico's Cimarron Country* (Albuquerque: University of New Mexico Press, 1972), 101; María E. Montoya, *Translating Property: The Maxwell Land Grant and the Conflict over Land in the American West, 1840–1900* (Berkeley: University of California Press, 2002), 68–73. On "thousands" of peons, see Irving Howbert, *Memories of a Lifetime in the Pikes Peak Region* (Glorieta, NM: Rio Grande, 1970), 169. Another observer placed the number of peons on Maxwell's estate at about five hundred. Henry Inman, *The Old Santa Fe Trail: The Story of a Great Highway* (Topeka, KS: Crane, 1916), 374.

7. Inman, *Old Santa Fe Trail*, 374.

8. "Report of Lieut. J. W. Abert of his Examination of New Mexico in the years 1846–47," in *Report of the Secretary of War, February 10, 1848*, 30th Cong., 1st Sess., Senate Exec. Doc. 23, p. 35.

9. Stacey L. Smith, *Freedom's Frontier: California and the Struggle over Unfree Labor, Emancipation, and Reconstruction* (Chapel Hill: University of North Carolina Press, 2013), 24–30, 82–95.

10. Jacqueline Dorgan Meketa, ed., *Legacy of Honor: The Life of Rafael Chacón, a Nineteenth-Century New Mexican* (Albuquerque: University of New Mexico Press, 1986), 107; see also Josiah Gregg, *Commerce of the Prairies*, edited by Max L. Moorhead (Norman: University of Oklahoma Press, 1954), 257.

11. John C. Reid, *Reid's Tramp, or a Journal of the Incidents of Ten Months' Travel Through Texas, New Mexico, Arizona, Sonora and Chihuahua* (Austin, TX: Steck, 1935), 143.

12. Albert D. Richardson, *Beyond the Mississippi: From the Great River to the Great Ocean, Life and Adventure on the Prairies, Mountains, and Pacific Coast . . . 1857–1867* (Hartford, CT: American Publishing, 1867), 239.

13. John Russell Bartlett, *Personal Narrative of Explorations and Incidents in Texas, New Mexico, California, Sonora and Chihuahua, 1850–1853*, vol. 1 (New York: D. Appleton, 1854), 192.

14. Gregg, *Commerce of the Prairies*, 152.

15. William W. H. Davis, *El Gringo; or, New Mexico and Her People* (Santa Fe, NM: Rydal, 1938), 98–99; "Incidents of Travel on the Tehuantepec Route," *Harper's Weekly*, January 15, 1859. See also Philip St. George Cooke, *The Conquest of New Mexico and California: An Historical and Personal Narrative* (New York: G. P. Putnam's Sons, 1878), 61.

16. George F. Ruxton, *Adventures in Mexico and the Rocky Mountains* (New York: Harper and Brothers, 1848), 116.

17. *Jaremillo v. Romero*, in Charles H. Gildersleeve, *Reports of Cases Argued and Determined in the Supreme Court of the Territory of New Mexico from January Term 1852 to January Term 1879*, vol. 1 (San Francisco: A. L. Bancroft, 1881), 198.

18. Davis, *El Gringo*, 98.

19. Ross Calvin, ed., *Lieutenant Emory Reports: Notes of a Military Reconnaissance from Fort Leavenworth, in Missouri, to San Diego, in California* (Albuquerque: University of New Mexico Press, 1951), 87.

20. Cooke, *Conquest of New Mexico and California*, 34–35.

21. *Congressional Globe*, 30th Cong., 1st Sess., July 29, 1848, Appendix, p. 1061.

22. Gregg, *Commerce of the Prairies*, 166.

23. *Congressional Globe*, 39th Cong., 2nd Sess., February 19, 1867, p. 1571. On peon wages, see Harris, *Mexican Family Empire*, 216–18; Elizabeth Terese Newman, *Biography of a Hacienda: Work and Revolution in Rural Mexico* (Tucson: University of Arizona Press, 2014), 47–48.

24. Gregg, *Commerce of the Prairies*, 166.

25. Davis, *El Gringo*, 98. See also *Congressional Globe*, 31st Cong., 1st Sess., July 8, 1850, Appendix, p. 1180; *Jaremillo v. Romero*, in Gildersleeve, *Reports of Cases*, 1:194.

26. Gregg, *Commerce of the Prairies*, 166. See also Lewis H. Garrard, *Wah-To-Yah and the Taos Trail* (Palo Alto, CA: American West Publishing, 1968), 138–39; Dr. A. Wislizenus, *Memoir of a Tour to Northern Mexico, Connected with Col. Doniphan's Expedition, in 1846 and 1847* (Washington, DC: Tippin and Streeper, 1848), 23. During the Jim Crow era, white Southerners used similar methods of perpetuating the debts of black peons. See Douglas A. Blackmon, *Slavery by Another Name: The Re-Enslavement of Black Americans from the Civil War to World War II* (New York: Anchor, 2009), 67–68.

27. *Lorenzo Labadi v. Vicente Ortega*, July 26, 1854, New Mexico State Records Center and Archives, Records of the District Court of Valencia County.

28. Cooke, *Conquest of New Mexico and California*, 61. See also Susan Calafate Boyle, *Los Capitalistas: Hispano Merchants and the Santa Fe Trade* (Albuquerque: University of New Mexico Press, 1997), 7–8.

29. Harris, *Mexican Family Empire*, 70–74.

30. See Walter Johnson, *Soul by Soul: Life Inside the Antebellum Slave Market* (Cambridge, MA: Harvard University Press, 1999); Calvin Schermerhorn, *The Business of Slavery and the Rise of American Capitalism, 1815–1860* (New Haven, CT: Yale University Press, 2015).

31. "An Act in Relation to Service," Section 7, in *Acts, Resolutions and Memorials Passed by the Sessions of the Legislative Assembly of the Territory of Utah* (Great Salt Lake City, UT: B. R. Young, 1852).

32. *Congressional Globe*, 39th Cong., 2nd Sess., February 19, 1867, p. 1571. See also Alan Knight, *The Mexican Revolution, Volume 1: Porfirians, Liberals, and Peasants* (Cambridge: Cambridge University Press, 1986), 88.

33. J. Manuel Espinosa, "Memoir of a Kentuckian in New Mexico, 1848–1884," *New Mexico Historical Review* 13 (January 1938): 5–6; Lawrence R. Murphy, "Reconstruction in New Mexico," *New Mexico Historical Review* 43 (April 1968): 103–4.

34. For a firsthand account of Mexican peon trading, see "Peon Slavery on the Rio Grande—Letter from the Border," *New-York Daily Tribune*, July 15, 1850. For a comparison of slave-market prices in New Mexico and the South, see Sondra Jones, *The Trial of Don Pedro León Luján: The Attack Against Indian Slavery and Mexican Traders in Utah* (Salt Lake City: University of Utah Press, 2000), 142n50. On the transfer of peons between masters, see Harris, *Mexican Family Empire*, 218.

35. Anthony Mora, *Border Dilemmas: Racial and National Uncertainties in New Mexico, 1848–1912* (Durham, NC: Duke University Press, 2011), 43–46.

36. "Important from New Mexico—Slavery and Peonage," *New York Herald*, July 18, 1850. The article referred to New Mexico's proposed 1850 statehood constitution, which stated that the rights of citizenship should be conferred on all "free, white, male inhabitants," a phrase that only thinly veiled its true intention of omitting all slaves and peons from full rights as citizens. See Journal of the Convention of the Territory of New Mexico (1849), p. 9, in William Jenkins Skinner, ed. and comp., *Records of the States of the United States of America, New Mexico, 1849–1910*, Class C, Constitutional Records, Microfilm Roll 1.

37. *Congressional Globe*, 39th Cong., 2nd Sess., February 19, 1867, p. 1571.

38. Wislizenus, *Memoir of a Tour to Northern Mexico*, 23–24.

39. Ruxton, *Adventures in Mexico and the Rocky Mountains*, 116. See also Brantz Mayer, *Mexico, as It Was and as It Is* (Philadelphia: G. B. Zieber, 1847), 201–2.

40. "Report of Lieut. J. W. Abert of His Examination of New Mexico in the Years 1846–47," in *Report of the Secretary of War, February 10, 1848*, 30th Cong., 1st Sess., Senate Exec. Doc. 23, p. 66.

41. John Hardin to David Smith, December 10, 1846, quoted in Amy S. Greenberg, *A Wicked War: Polk, Clay, Lincoln, and the 1846 U.S. Invasion of Mexico* (New York: Alfred A. Knopf, 2012), 151. On American comparisons of chattel slavery and Mexican peonage during the war, see Smith, *Freedom's Frontier*, 84–85.

42. *Organic Law of the Territory of New Mexico, November 23, 1846*, 30th Cong., 1st Sess., House Exec. Doc. No. 60, pp. 185–88.

43. See, for example, "Peonage in New Mexico," *Santa Fe Weekly Gazette*, February 2, 1867.

44. A similar need to define the system occurred contemporaneously in California's gold mines, where Latin American peons arrived during the Gold Rush and elicited comparisons to chattel slavery. See Smith, *Freedom's Frontier*, 10.

45. *Congressional Globe*, 30th Cong., 1st Sess., Appendix, February 12, 1850, p. 208; ibid., 39th Cong., 2nd Sess., February 19, 1867, quotation on p. 1571.

46. Ibid., 30th Cong., 1st Sess., January 31, 1848, Appendix, p. 144; "Report of Lieut. J. W. Abert," in *Report of the Secretary of War, February 10, 1848*, 30th Cong., 1st Sess., Senate Exec. Doc. 23, p. 66.

47. "Peon Slavery on the Rio Grande—Letter from the Border," *New-York Daily Tribune*, July 15, 1850. Montgomery's real name was Jane McManus Cazneau, a Democratic New York journalist who frequently wrote in support of Manifest Destiny. Edward E. Baptist, *The Half Has Never Been Told: Slavery and the Making of American Capitalism* (New York: Basic Books, 2014), 356.

48. Richard K. Cralle, ed., *Speeches of John C. Calhoun, Delivered in the House of Representatives and in the Senate of the United States*, vol. 4 (New York: Russell and Russell, 1968), 499.

49. James F. Meline, *Two Thousand Miles on Horseback: Santa Fe and Back* (Albuquerque, NM: Horn and Wallace, 1966), 120–21.

50. Ayers, "Soldier's Experience in New Mexico," 261.

51. "Peon Slavery on the Rio Grande—Letter from the Border," *New-York Daily Tribune*, July 15, 1850; "Incidents of Travel on the Tehuantepec Route," *Harper's Weekly*, January 15, 1859.

52. *Congressional Globe*, 36th Cong., 2nd Sess., February 16, 1861, pp. 623, 972.

53. "The Disunion Troubles," *New York Times*, December 27, 1860.

54. "A Few Questions About New Mexico," *New-York Daily Tribune*, January 23, 1861; "Shall We Give Up New Mexico?," ibid., February 25, 1861.

55. *Congressional Globe*, 30th Cong., 1st Sess., January 4, 1848, p. 98.

56. Ibid., July 29, 1848, Appendix, pp. 1060–61.

57. Ibid., 31st Cong., 1st Sess., March 7, 1850, p. 480.

58. Miguel A. Otero to the editor of the Washington, D.C., *Constitution*, January 12, 1861, reprinted in the *Santa Fe Weekly Gazette*, February 16, 1861 (emphasis in original). On the Otero-Greeley feud, see Mark Stegmaier, "New Mexico's Delegate in the Secession Winter Congress, Part 1: Two Newspaper Accounts of Miguel Otero in 1861," *New Mexico Historical Review* 86 (Summer 2011): 385–92; Mark Stegmaier,

"New Mexico's Delegate in the Secession Winter Congress, Part 2: Miguel A. Otero Responds to Horace Greeley, and Greeley Takes Revenge," *New Mexico Historical Review* 86 (Fall 2011): 513–23.

59. Alvin R. Sunseri, *Seeds of Discord: New Mexico in the Aftermath of the American Conquest, 1846–1861* (Chicago: Nelson-Hall, 1979), 39.

60. Richardson, *Beyond the Mississippi*, 239.

61. Robert W. Frazer, ed., *New Mexico in 1850: A Military View* (Norman: University of Oklahoma Press, 1968), 85 (emphasis in original).

62. Reid, *Reid's Tramp*, 144.

63. *Congressional Globe*, 36th Cong., 2nd Sess., January 29, 1861, p. 623.

64. Gustavus Schmidt, *The Civil Law of Spain and Mexico* (New Orleans, LA: T. Rea, 1851), 96. See also Newman, *Biography of a Hacienda*, 45–46.

65. James S. Calhoun, "Message to the Legislature of the Territory of New Mexico," June 2, 1851, NA, RG59, T17, New Mexico Territorial Papers, Roll 1.

66. The act was passed on July 20, 1851. For the complete version, see the laws and resolutions of the 1851 territorial legislature, in NA, RG46, Territorial Papers of the U.S. Senate, Roll 14 (New Mexico, 1840–1854).

67. "An Act in Relation to Service," Section 2, in *Acts, Resolutions and Memorials Passed by the Sessions of the Legislative Assembly of the Territory of Utah.*

68. *Jaremillo v. Romero*, in Gildersleeve, *Reports of Cases*, 1:194. The military sometimes assisted in recovering runaway peons and slaves. See, for example, "Fatal Accident—A Soldier Shot Himself," *Santa Fe Weekly Gazette*, June 17, 1854. On fugitive peons, see Harris, *Mexican Family Empire*, 225–30.

69. Laws and resolutions of the territorial legislature, 1851, NA, RG46, Territorial Papers of the U.S. Senate, Roll 14 (New Mexico, 1840–1854).

70. Miguel A. Otero to the editor of the Washington, D.C., *Constitution*, January 12, 1861, reprinted in the *Santa Fe Weekly Gazette*, February 16, 1861.

71. Laws and resolutions of the territorial legislature, 1851, in NA, RG46, Territorial Papers of the U.S. Senate, Roll 14 (New Mexico, 1840–1854).

72. *José María Gutierres v. Pablo Maldonado et al.*, April 5, 1854, New Mexico State Records Center and Archives, San Miguel County District Court Records, Serial #13533, Folder 1, Case #21; "Complaint Brought by Manuel Armijo," August 25, 1860, ibid., Bernalillo County Probate Court, Serial #13734, Folder 51.

73. Davis, *El Gringo*, 98–99.

74. James S. Calhoun to Orlando Brown, March 15, 1850, in Annie Heloise Abel, ed., *The Official Correspondence of James S. Calhoun While Indian Agent at Santa Fe and Superintendent of Indian Affairs in New Mexico, 1849–1852* (Washington, DC: Government Printing Office, 1915), 161 (emphasis in original).

75. *Congressional Globe*, 31st Cong., 1st Sess., June 6, 1850, p. 1144.

76. Reid, *Reid's Tramp*, 144–45.

77. "Peonage in New Mexico," *Santa Fe Weekly Gazette*, February 2, 1867.

78. *Congressional Globe*, 39th Cong., 2nd Sess., February 19, 1867, p. 1572.

79. Ruxton, *Adventures in Mexico and the Rocky Mountains*, 116.

80. See *Marcellina Bustamento v. Juana Analla*, January 1857, in Gildersleeve, *Reports of Cases,* 1:255–62.

81. Quoted in Aurora Hunt, *Kirby Benedict: Frontier Federal Judge* (Glendale, CA: Arthur H. Clark, 1961), 39–40. Benedict was appointed an associate justice in the New Mexico Supreme Court by President Franklin Pierce in 1853 and served as chief justice from 1858 to 1866. He continued to practice law until 1871 and died in Santa Fe in 1874 at the age of sixty-three. On Benedict's judicial career in New Mexico, see Arie W. Poldevaart, *Black-Robed Justice: A History of the Administration of Justice in New Mexico from the American Occupation in 1846 Until Statehood in 1912* (Holmes Beach, FL: Gaunt, 1999), 49–66.

82. For Lincoln's evolving views on slavery, see Eric Foner, *The Fiery Trial: Abraham Lincoln and American Slavery* (New York: W. W. Norton, 2010).

83. Statement of Chief Justice Kirby Benedict, July 4, 1865, in *Condition of the Indian Tribes*, 39th Cong., 2nd Sess., Senate Report No. 156 (Washington, DC: Government Printing Office, 1867), 326.

84. *Jaremillo v. Romero*, January 1857, in Gildersleeve, *Reports of Cases*, 1:195. Emphasis added.

85. Ibid., 192–93.

86. Hunt, *Kirby Benedict*, 109–11.

87. *Jaremillo v. Romero*, in Gildersleeve, *Reports of Cases*, 1:193.

88. Ibid., 200–201.

89. Ibid., 192–95.

90. Ibid., 198–99.

91. Ibid.

92. Ibid., 191–204.

93. Toyin Falola and Paul E. Lovejoy, "Pawnship in Historical Perspective," in Falola and Lovejoy, eds., *Pawnship in Africa: Debt Bondage in Historical Perspective* (Boulder, CO: Westview, 1994), 3–8.

94. On Taney's judicial activism, see Don E. Fehrenbacher, *The Dred Scott Case: Its Significance in American Law and Politics* (New York: Oxford University Press, 1978).

95. The practice of a master assuming custody of a servant's children for the purpose of passing them down as property to his own heirs long predated this court ruling. See, for example, Ralph Emerson Twitchell, *Spanish Archives of New Mexico*, vol. 1 (Cedar Rapids, IA: Torch, 1914), document no. 344.

96. *Bustamento v. Analla*, in Gildersleeve, *Reports of Cases*, 1:255–61.

97. Schmidt, *Civil Law of Spain and Mexico*, 107.

98. "Law regulating contracts between masters and servants," in NA, RG46, Territorial Papers of the U.S. Senate, Roll 14 (New Mexico, 1840–1854).

99. *Jaremillo v. Romero*, in Gildersleeve, *Reports of Cases*, 1:206–7.

100. Ibid., 190.

101. See, for example, executive message of Acting Governor William F. M. Arny, December 2, 1862, NA, RG59, T17, New Mexico Territorial Papers, Roll 2 (emphasis in original), p. 14.

102. *Tomás Heredia v. José María García*, December 4, 1865, in the Third Judicial District Court of New Mexico, and appeal, January 26, 1867, in the New Mexico Territorial Supreme Court, all contained at New Mexico State Records Center and Archives, U.S. Territorial and New Mexico Supreme Court Records, Box 3, No. 36. See also "The Supreme Court on Peonage," *Santa Fe Weekly Gazette*, February 2, 1867.

103. Laura F. Edwards, "Status Without Rights: African Americans and the Tangled History of Law and Governance in the Nineteenth-Century U.S. South," *American Historical Review* 112 (April 2007): 365–93, esp. 365–67. See also Steven Hahn, *A Nation Under Our Feet: Black Political Struggles in the Rural South from Slavery to the Great Migration* (Cambridge, MA: Belknap Press of Harvard University Press, 2003).

104. *United States v. Eberhart*, 127 F. 252 (February 24, 1899); *Clyatt v. United States*, 197 U.S. 207 (March 13, 1905). See also Pete Daniel, *The Shadow of Slavery: Peonage in the South, 1901–1969* (Urbana: University of Illinois Press, 1972), 3–18.

Chapter 4

1. "The Killing of Jim," *Santa Fe Weekly Gazette*, July 24, 1858; William Brooks to AAG, November 30, 1857, NA, RG393, M1120, LR, DNM, Roll 6.

2. Brooks to W. A. Nichols, July 15, 1858, NA, RG393, M1120, LR, DNM, Roll 7; Samuel M. Yost to James L. Collins, August 31, 1858, NA, RG75, OIA, T21, LR, NMS, Roll 3.

3. Brooks to Nichols, July 15, 1858, NA, RG393, M1120, LR, DNM, Roll 7. On the lasting importance of the incident, see statements by Kirby Benedict, John Greiner, and James L. Collins, July 4, 1865, in *Condition of the Indian Tribes*, 39th Cong., 2nd Sess., Senate Report No. 156 (Washington, DC: Government Printing Office, 1867), pp. 325, 328, 331.

4. John Garland to Brooks, July 26, 1858, NA, RG393, M1072, LS, DNM, Roll 2.

5. Brooks to Nichols, July 15, 1858, NA, RG393, M1120, LR, DNM, Roll 7.

6. Collins to Charles E. Mix, September 27, 1858, in *Annual Report of the Commissioner of Indian Affairs* (Washington, DC: Wm. A. Harris, 1858), 190–91.

7. "Peonage in New Mexico," *Santa Fe Weekly Gazette*, February 2, 1867.

8. "Death of Jim at Fort Defiance," *Santa Fe Weekly Gazette*, August 21, 1858.

9. James C. McKee to Yost, September 9, 1858, in J. Lee Correll, *Through White Men's Eyes: A Contribution to Navajo History . . .* , vol. 2 (Window Rock, AZ: Navajo Heritage Center, 1979), 156.

10. James F. Brooks, *Captives & Cousins: Slavery, Kinship, and Community in the Southwest Borderlands* (Chapel Hill: University of North Carolina Press, 2002), 246.

11. Ibid., 310–13.

12. Dixon S. Miles to Lt. Wilkins, December 1, 1858, quoted in Frank McNitt, *Navajo Wars: Military Campaigns, Slave Raids, and Reprisals* (Albuquerque: University

of New Mexico Press, 1972), 359. Correspondence relating to the murder of Jim and subsequent hostilities in Dinétah is found in Correll, *Through White Men's Eyes*, 2:133–56.

13. Yost to Collins, September 9, 1858, NA, RG75, OIA, T21, LR, NMS, Roll 3.

14. *Official Army Register*, 1858, 35th Cong., 2nd Sess., House Exec. Doc. No. 58, p. 42.

15. Don E. Fehrenbacher, *Slavery, Law, and Politics: The Dred Scott Case in Historical Perspective* (Oxford: Oxford University Press, 1981), 84.

16. Seventh United States Census (1850); Stacey L. Smith, *Freedom's Frontier: California and the Struggle over Unfree Labor, Emancipation, and Reconstruction* (Chapel Hill: University of North Carolina Press, 2013), 40. In an 1852 report to Congress, Richard Weightman noted that "there are in New Mexico a few negroes, in all, as shown by the census . . . and of this number there may be as many as five or six slaves—house servants of officers of the Army and others." *Congressional Globe*, 32nd Cong., 1st Sess., March 15, 1852, p. 755.

17. "The Disunion Troubles," *New York Times*, December 27, 1860.

18. Abraham Rencher to William H. Seward, April 14, 1861, NA, RG59, T17, New Mexico Territorial Papers, Roll 1; Miguel A. Otero to the editor of the Washington, D.C. *Constitution*, January 12, 1861, reprinted in the *Santa Fe Weekly Gazette*, February 16, 1861. Hubert Howe Bancroft, one of New Mexico's earliest historians, noted in his 1889 monograph that many U.S. officials in New Mexico held black slaves, Indian slaves, or both. Bancroft, *History of Arizona and New Mexico, 1530–1888* (San Francisco: History Company, 1889), 681.

19. Otero to the editor of the Washington, D.C. *Constitution*, January 12, 1861, reprinted in the *Santa Fe Weekly Gazette*, February 16, 1861.

20. William A. Keleher, *Turmoil in New Mexico, 1846–1868* (Santa Fe, NM: Rydal, 1952), 279–80; Aurora Hunt, *Kirby Benedict: Frontier Federal Judge* (Glendale, CA: Arthur H. Clark, 1961), 112. In 1851, Carleton received an annual allowance for servants of $116.41 in addition to his base salary of $690. Whether or not he used any of this money to feed and clothe his two slaves is not known, but he certainly did not pay them any wages. *Official Army Register*, 1851, 32nd Cong., 2nd Sess., House Exec. Doc. No. 48.

21. *Congressional Globe*, 31st Cong., 1st Sess., July 1, 1850, Appendix, p. 1012.

22. "Slavery in the Territory of New Mexico," 36th Cong., 1st Sess., House Report No. 508, p. 30.

23. *Official Army Register*, 1851, 32nd Cong., 2nd Sess., House Exec. Doc. No. 48; *Official Army Register*, 1860, 36th Cong., 2nd Sess., House Exec. Doc. No. 54.

24. *Congressional Globe*, 31st Cong., 1st Sess., June 29, 1850, Appendix, p. 1009.

25. For slave codes in the western territories, see Eugene H. Berwanger, *The Frontier Against Slavery: Western Anti-Negro Prejudice and the Slavery Extension Controversy* (Urbana: University of Illinois Press, 1967), esp. 118–20.

26. 36th Cong., 1st Sess., House Report No. 508 to accompany H.R. Bill 64, p. 31.

27. New Mexico passed laws in 1851, 1857, and 1859 regulating peons as well as both free and enslaved black persons. For Utah's 1852 servant law, see *Acts, Resolutions and Memorials Passed by the Sessions of the Legislative Assembly of the Territory of Utah* (Great Salt Lake City, UT: B. R. Young, 1852).

28. Smith, *Freedom's Frontier*, 61–63, quotation on 61.

29. Dedra S. McDonald, "Intimacy and Empire: Indian-African Interaction in Spanish Colonial New Mexico, 1500–1800," *American Indian Quarterly* 22 (Winter and Spring 1998): 138–39.

30. *Petition of the People of New Mexico, October 14, 1848*, 30th Cong., 2nd Sess., Senate Misc. Doc. 5.

31. On the factionalizing of statehood and territorial blocs in New Mexico, see Howard R. Lamar, *The Far Southwest, 1846–1912: A Territorial History* (Albuquerque: University of New Mexico Press, 2000), 65–70.

32. NA, RG59, T17, New Mexico Territorial Papers, Roll 1, "Instructions to the Convention Delegates," pp. 20–22.

33. Smith, *Freedom's Frontier*, 86–88.

34. William W. H. Davis, *El Gringo; or, New Mexico and Her People* (Santa Fe, NM: Rydal, 1938), 98. See also Robert W. Larson, *New Mexico's Quest for Statehood, 1846–1912* (Albuquerque: University of New Mexico Press, 1968), 15–16; Mark J. Stegmaier, *Texas, New Mexico, and the Compromise of 1850: Boundary Dispute and Sectional Crisis* (Kent, OH: Kent State University Press, 1996), 53, 66.

35. *Congressional Globe*, 31st Cong., 1st Sess., June 3, 1850, Appendix, p. 1010.

36. Henry Connelly et al. to Truman Smith, May 18, 1850, *Congressional Globe*, 31st Cong., 1st Sess., July 8, 1850, Appendix, p. 1180 (emphasis in original).

37. Jack D. Rittenhouse, *The Constitution of the State of New Mexico, 1850* (Santa Fe, NM: Stagecoach, 1965), 14.

38. Ibid.

39. "Important from New Mexico—Slavery and Peonage," *New York Herald*, July 18, 1850 (emphasis in original).

40. Rittenhouse, *Constitution of the State of New Mexico*, 34, 45.

41. Quoted by Stegmaier, *Texas, New Mexico, and the Compromise of 1850*, 66.

42. "New Mexico—Slavery Recognized in Her Constitution," *Daily Albany Argus*, July 24, 1850 (emphasis in original).

43. Stegmaier, *Texas, New Mexico, and the Compromise of 1850*, 119.

44. Laura E. Gómez, "Off-White in an Age of White Supremacy: Mexican Elites and the Rights of Indians and Blacks in Nineteenth-Century New Mexico," in Michael A. Olivas, ed., *Colored Men and Hombres Aquí: Hernandez v. Texas and the Emergence of Mexican-American Lawyering* (Houston, TX: Arte Público, 2006), 26.

45. *Resolutions of the Legislature of New York, January 17, 1849*, 30th Cong., 2nd Sess., House Misc. Doc. No. 6, p. 1.

46. *Congressional Globe*, 31st Cong., 1st Sess., July 8, 1850, Appendix, p. 1180.

47. Charles M. Wiltse and Alan R. Berolzheimer, eds., *The Papers of Daniel Webster: Speeches and Formal Writings, Volume 2, 1834–1852* (Hanover, NH: University Press of New England, 1988), 563.

48. James S. Calhoun, "Message to the Legislature of the Territory of New Mexico," June 2, 1851, NA, RG59, T17, New Mexico Territorial Papers, Roll 1.

49. For the entire text of the law, see NA, RG46, Territorial Papers of the U.S. Senate, Roll 14 (New Mexico, 1840–1854).

50. William F. M. Arny, executive message of December 2, 1862, NA, RG59, T17, New Mexico Territorial Papers, Roll 2 (emphasis in original). Evidence of the law being somewhat malleable is found in a letter from Representative Miguel A. Otero in which he misconstrues several sections, making peonage appear to be a benign system. See Otero to the editor of the Washington, D.C. *Constitution*, January 12, 1861, reprinted in the *Santa Fe Weekly Gazette*, February 16, 1861.

51. *Laws of the Territory of New Mexico, Fourth Legislative Assembly, 1852–1853* (Santa Fe, NM: Gazette Printing, 1853).

52. Executive Journal of the Territory of New Mexico, 1856–1857, NA, RG59, T17, New Mexico Territorial Papers, Roll 1.

53. *Laws of the Territory of New Mexico, Sixth Legislative Assembly, 1856–1857* (Santa Fe, NM: Office of the Democrat, 1857), 48.

54. Statement of W. W. H. Davis, quoted in Alvin R. Sunseri, *Seeds of Discord: New Mexico in the Aftermath of the American Conquest, 1846–1861* (Chicago: Nelson-Hall, 1979), 117.

55. Rachel F. Moran, *Interracial Intimacy: The Regulation of Race and Romance* (Chicago: University of Chicago Press, 2001), 17. Moran notes that while thirty-eight states at one time banned black-white relationships, none had ever forbade Latino-white relationships because "treaty protections accorded former Spanish and Mexican citizens the status of white persons." Ibid.

56. *Laws of the Territory of New Mexico, Sixth Legislative Assembly*, 48–50. Connelly addressed this law in an 1865 speech: "The law regulating free negroes is in discord with the legislation of Congress [as well as] the proclamation of the President abolishing slavery and restoring to civil rights the freedmen of the African race." He encouraged his colleagues to nullify the law, noting that statutes "should be made to conform to the status now occupied by that race, under the laws of Congress." "The Fourth Annual Message of Governor Connelly," December 1865, NA, RG59, T17, New Mexico Territorial Papers, Roll 3.

57. Christopher Childers, *The Failure of Popular Sovereignty: Slavery, Manifest Destiny, and the Radicalization of Southern Politics* (Lawrence: University Press of Kansas, 2012), 27–28. Senator Stephen A. Douglas referenced Illinois slavery statutes in a speech on the Compromise of 1850 and noted the relevance to the Mexican Cession lands. See *Congressional Globe*, 31st Cong., 1st Sess., March 13, 1850, Appendix, p. 369.

58. Mark Stegmaier, "A Law That Would Make Caligula Blush? New Mexico Territory's Unique Slave Code, 1859–1861," *New Mexico Historical Review* 87 (Spring

2012): 209–42; Loomis M. Ganaway, *New Mexico and the Sectional Controversy, 1846–1861* (Albuquerque: University of New Mexico Press, 1944), 69.

59. Frank D. Reeve, *History of New Mexico*, vol. 2 (New York: Lewis Historical Publishing, 1961), 73; Stegmaier, "A Law That Would Make Caligula Blush?," 213–14, 236n16.

60. *Congressional Globe*, 36th Cong., 2nd Sess., February 5, 1861, p. 761.

61. Ibid., 36th Cong., 1st Sess., February 2, 1860, pp. 658–59.

62. "A Few Questions About New Mexico," *New-York Daily Tribune*, January 23, 1861.

63. Alicia V. Tjarks, "Demographic, Ethnic and Occupational Structure of New Mexico, 1790," *Americas* 35 (July 1978): 74; Eighth United States Census (1860). Neighboring Utah Territory was home to fifty-nine African Americans in 1860, of whom twenty-nine were categorized as slaves. Ibid.

64. "An Act to Provide for the Protection of Property in Slaves in This Territory," *Laws of the Territory of New Mexico, Eighth Legislative Assembly, 1858–1859* (Santa Fe, NM: A. DeMarle, 1859), 80.

65. Ibid., 64–66. In the event that a reward was not offered, the person delivering the runaway slave back to their master was entitled to "demand and recover from such owner or master the sum of twenty dollars, besides ten cents for each mile of travel to and from the place where such apprehension was made."

66. "Peonage in New Mexico," *Santa Fe Weekly Gazette*, February 2, 1867. Chaves was serving as New Mexico's delegate to Congress at the time the piece appeared in print.

67. Laura E. Gómez, *Manifest Destinies: The Making of the Mexican American Race* (New York: New York University Press, 2007), 89; Lamar, *Far Southwest*, 80–81.

68. Quoted by Gómez, "Off-White," 25.

69. Brooks, *Captives & Cousins*, 329.

70. "Shall We Give Up New Mexico?" *New-York Daily Tribune*, February 25, 1861.

71. W. W. Mills, *Forty Years at El Paso, 1858–1898* (El Paso, TX: Carl Hertzog, 1962), 37.

72. "Interesting Letter from New Mexico," *Montpelier Watchman and State Journal*, June 10, 1859.

73. "New-Mexico," *New-York Daily Tribune*, December 31, 1860; Ganaway, *New Mexico and the Sectional Controversy*, 81–83.

74. Gómez, *Manifest Destinies*, 98–99; Larson, *New Mexico's Quest for Statehood*, 64. On Otero's activities relative to statehood and slavery during his time as a congressional representative, see Mark Stegmaier, "New Mexico's Delegate in the Secession Winter Congress, Part 1: Two Newspaper Accounts of Miguel Otero in 1861," *New Mexico Historical Review* 86 (Summer 2011): 385–92.

75. William Need to Simon Cameron, undated, quoted in Ganaway, *New Mexico and the Sectional Controversy*, 90.

76. "Governor of New-Mexico," *New-York Daily Tribune*, July 15, 1861.

77. *Congressional Globe*, 36th Cong., 2nd Sess., January 22, 1861, p. 515.

78. The letter appeared in the January 12, 1861, issue of the Washington, D.C. *Constitution* and was reprinted a month later in the *Santa Fe Weekly Gazette*. See also Mark Stegmaier, "New Mexico's Delegate in the Secession Winter Congress, Part 2: Miguel A. Otero Responds to Horace Greeley, and Greeley Takes Revenge," *New Mexico Historical Review* 86 (Fall 2011): 513–23.

79. Miguel A. Otero to Charles P. Cleaver, December 24, 1858, quoted in Stegmaier, "A Law That Would Make Caligula Blush?," 212.

80. *Congressional Globe*, 36th Cong., 2nd Sess., January 29, 1861, p. 623.

81. Otero to Alexander Jackson, December 16, 1858, quoted in Hunt, *Kirby Benedict*, 113; "The Slave Code of New Mexico," *New-York Daily Tribune*, April 16, 1861. See also Stegmaier, "A Law That Would Make Caligula Blush?," 212. Otero's term as a congressional delegate ended March 3, 1861, and he was subsequently appointed as secretary of state for New Mexico on June 19 of that year, but the Senate declined his appointment. Otero attributed his rejection to "the malicious and false representations made against me by my unprincipled personal and political enemies in the States." Otero to William H. Seward, September 1, 1861, NA, RG59, T17, New Mexico Territorial Papers, Roll 2; Stegmaier, "New Mexico's Delegate in the Secession Winter Congress, Part 1," 390, 391n11.

82. Jackson to Robert Downs, August 16, 1858, NA, RG59, T17, New Mexico Territorial Papers, Roll 1.

83. Ganaway, *New Mexico and the Sectional Controversy*, 67; Martin Hardwick Hall, *Sibley's New Mexico Campaign* (Austin: University of Texas Press, 1960), 14–16.

84. Alexander Jackson to Orlando Davis, February 17, 1861, in John P. Wilson, *When the Texans Came: Missing Records from the Civil War in the Southwest, 1861–1862* (Albuquerque: University of New Mexico Press, 2001), 19.

85. E. P. Walton to A. B. Greenwood, June 9, 1859, NA, RG75, OIA, M234, LR, NMS, Roll 549.

86. Quoted in Sunseri, *Seeds of Discord*, 118.

87. William Need joined Company C, First Regiment of New Mexico Volunteers, on July 16, 1861. For his complete service record, see New Mexico State Records Center and Archives, Frank McNitt Collection, Serial #10680, Folder 27.

88. William Need to Simon Cameron, September 27, 1861, in *The War of the Rebellion: A Compilation of the Official Records of the Union and Confederate Armies*, Series 1, vol. 50, pt. 1 (Washington, DC: Government Printing Office, 1880), 635. On alleged Southern conspiracies, see Michael Steck to Col. Pulston, January 22, 1865, Center for Southwest Research, Inventory of the Michael Steck Papers, Series 2, Roll 4.

89. "The Slave Code of New Mexico," *New-York Daily Tribune*, April 16, 1861.

90. Ganaway, *New Mexico and the Sectional Controversy*, 87.

91. "New Mexico," *New-York Daily Tribune*, December 31, 1860. For Greeley's role in abolition movements, see Adam Tuchinsky, *Horace Greeley's New York Tribune:*

Civil War–Era Socialism and the Crisis of Free Labor (Ithaca, NY: Cornell University Press, 2009).

92. "Mr. Robinson's Proposition," *New-York Daily Tribune,* January 5, 1861.

93. "Miguel A. Otero to Senator G. E. Pugh," *Memphis Daily Appeal,* January 20, 1861.

94. See "New-Mexico," *New-York Daily Tribune,* December 30, 1860; "Mr. Robinson's Proposition," ibid., January 5, 1861; "A Few Questions About New Mexico," ibid., January 23, 1861; "Shall We Give Up New Mexico?" ibid., February 25, 1861; "Governor of New-Mexico," ibid., July 15, 1861.

95. See, for example, "The Slave Code of New Mexico," *New-York Daily Tribune,* April 16, 1861, in which the writer claimed that the territory's "native population know absolutely nothing of slavery; that they seldom read a paper; that they know little of the national irritability upon this subject."

96. Need to Seward, August 8, 1861, quoted in Ganaway, *New Mexico and the Sectional Controversy,* 95–96 (emphasis in original). While Connelly did have a considerable number of peons at one time, there is no evidence that he ever owned black slaves in New Mexico.

97. Need to Cameron, September 27, 1861, in *War of the Rebellion,* vol. 50, pt. 1, p. 638.

98. Walton to Greenwood, June 9, 1859, NA, RG75, OIA, M234, LR, NMS, Roll 549.

99. New Mexico Slave Code, *Santa Fe Weekly Gazette,* January 29, 1859.

100. James Josiah Webb, *Adventures in the Santa Fe Trade 1844–1847,* edited by Ralph Bieber (Glendale, CA: Arthur H. Clark, 1931), 102–3.

101. While virtually all records indicate Connelly to have been an antislavery man by the time of the Civil War, at least one source suggests that he continued to retain servants. Testifying before a federal investigative committee, Judge Kirby Benedict claimed, "As to federal officers holding this description of persons [captive Indians] or trafficking in them, I can only say that I see them attending the family of Governor Connelly, but whether claimed by his wife, himself, or both, I know not." Statement of Chief Justice Kirby Benedict, July 4, 1865, in *Condition of the Indian Tribes,* 326.

102. Horace Greeley, *The American Conflict: A History of the Great Rebellion in the United States of America, 1860–1865* (Hartford, CT: O. D. Case, 1881), 20.

103. "Mr. Robinson's Proposition," *New-York Daily Tribune,* January 5, 1861.

104. Ibid.

105. Benjamin S. Roberts to A. L. Anderson, August 21, 1861, in Wilson, *When the Texans Came,* 121.

106. Otero to the editor of the Washington, D.C. *Constitution,* January 12, 1861. The letter was reprinted in the *Santa Fe Weekly Gazette* on February 16, 1861, and in the *Mesilla Times* on March 2, 1861.

107. Letter of John A. Bingham entitled "Report and Vote on the Repeal of the New Mexico Slave Code," quoted in Hunt, *Kirby Benedict,* 115–16. See also "The Slave

Code of New Mexico," *New-York Daily Tribune*, April 16, 1861. The historian Mark Stegmaier attributes this story to a letter written by a New Mexico rancher, Samuel B. Watrous, dated March 8, 1860. See Stegmaier, "A Law That Would Make Caligula Blush?," 216–18, 237n29.

108. The other four committee members were Miguel A. Lobato, Candelario García, Antonio Tafoya, and Matías Medina. See *Report of the Special Committee Upon the Bill to Repeal the Act of February 3, 1859*, NA, RG59, T17, New Mexico Territorial Papers, Roll 2.

109. Ibid.

110. Need to Cameron, September 27, 1861, in *War of the Rebellion*, vol. 50, pt. 1, p. 638.

111. *Congressional Globe*, 36th Cong., 1st Sess., March 1, 1860, p. 916.

112. Ibid., p. 928.

113. Ibid., 31st Cong., 1st Sess., June 6, 1850, p. 1144.

114. Ibid., 36th Cong., 1st Sess., May 11, 1860, p. 2059. The full title of Bingham's bill (H.R. 64) was "A bill to disapprove and declare null and void all territorial acts and parts of acts heretofore passed by the Legislative Assembly of New Mexico, which establish, protect, or legalize involuntary servitude within said territory, except as punishment for crime upon due conviction." 36th Cong., 1st Sess., House Exec. Docs., Report No. 508 to accompany Bill H.R. No. 64, May 10, 1860, p. 1; Stegmaier, "A Law That Would Make Caligula Blush?," 220–21.

115. 36th Cong., 1st Sess., House Exec. Report No. 508, p. 1.

116. Ibid., pp. 33–35. Emphasis added.

117. Ibid., pp. 8–9.

118. Ibid., pp. 27, 34–35.

119. *Senate Journal*, May 11, 1860, p. 459.

120. First annual message of Governor Henry Connelly, December 4, 1861, NA, RG59, T17, New Mexico Territorial Papers, Roll 2.

121. Stegmaier, "A Law That Would Make Caligula Blush?," 225.

122. This statement relative to New Mexicans being against black slavery is corroborated by earlier commentary printed in a Vermont newspaper. According to E. P. Walton, "The people [of New Mexico] have always expressed themselves on the subject of Slavery in the most unequivocal manner, and I shall never believe their views have undergone a change until there is further evidence of it than the fraudulent passage of these laws." See "Interesting Letter from New Mexico," *Montpelier Watchman and State Journal*, June 10, 1859.

123. Address of the Legislative Assembly of New Mexico, January 29, 1862, NA, RG59, T17, New Mexico Territorial Papers, Roll 2.

124. James Oakes, *Freedom National: The Destruction of Slavery in the United States, 1861–1865* (New York: W. W. Norton, 2012), 257.

125. Executive message of acting governor William F. M. Arny, December 2, 1862, NA, RG59, T17, New Mexico Territorial Papers, Roll 2.

126. Ibid.

127. Smith, *Freedom's Frontier*, 177.

Chapter 5

1. Jerry D. Thompson, *A Civil War History of the New Mexico Volunteers and Militia* (Albuquerque: University of New Mexico Press, 2015), 19–20.

2. "An Act to Secure Freedom to all Persons Within the Territories of the United States," U.S. *Statutes at Large*, 36th Cong., 2nd Sess., Ch. 112, p. 432.

3. Territorial Legislature, Memorial to Congress, January 29, 1863, NA, RG46, Territorial Papers of the U.S. Senate, Roll 14 (New Mexico, 1840–1854). On compensated emancipation, see Eric Foner, *The Fiery Trial: Abraham Lincoln and American Slavery* (New York: W. W. Norton, 2010), esp. 195–96.

4. Brooks D. Simpson, *The Reconstruction Presidents* (Lawrence: University Press of Kansas, 1998), 33–35.

5. Informal personal note, October 15, 1863, Center for Southwest Research, Inventory of the Michael Steck Papers, Series 2, Roll 3.

6. See Michael Vorenberg, *Final Freedom: The Civil War, the Abolition of Slavery, and the Thirteenth Amendment* (Cambridge: Cambridge University Press, 2001); Alexander Tsesis, *The Thirteenth Amendment and American Freedom: A Legal History* (New York: New York University Press, 2004); Simpson, *Reconstruction Presidents*, 55–57.

7. For President Johnson's role in Reconstruction, see Simpson, *Reconstruction Presidents*, 67–130. For the seminal work on Reconstruction, see Eric Foner, *Reconstruction: America's Unfinished Revolution, 1863–1877* (New York: Harper and Row, 1988).

8. Vorenberg, *Final Freedom*, 241.

9. *Congressional Globe*, 36th Cong., 2nd Sess., January 18, 1861, p. 455.

10. Mark Stegmaier, "'An Imaginary Negro in an Impossible Place?' The Issue of New Mexico Statehood in the Secession Crisis, 1860–1861," *New Mexico Historical Review* 84 (Spring 2009): 281–83.

11. Quoted by Robert W. Larson, *New Mexico's Quest for Statehood, 1846–1912* (Albuquerque: University of New Mexico Press, 1968), 83.

12. Stegmaier, "'Imaginary Negro in an Impossible Place?,'" 271–73.

13. Anthony Mora, *Border Dilemmas: Racial and National Uncertainties in New Mexico, 1848–1912* (Durham, NC: Duke University Press, 2011), 88–94.

14. *Congressional Globe*, 36th Cong., 2nd Sess., January 22, 1861, pp. 514–15.

15. Ibid.

16. "New-Mexico," *New-York Daily Tribune*, December 31, 1860.

17. On the 1860–61 New Mexico statehood bill and the political maneuverings surrounding it, see Stegmaier, "'An Imaginary Negro in an Impossible Place?,'" 263–90.

18. On Hispano-Texan enmity, see Charles Montgomery, *The Spanish Redemption: Heritage, Power, and Loss on New Mexico's Upper Rio Grande* (Berkeley: University of California Press, 2002), 40–41.

19. Michael Steck to Col. Pulston, January 22, 1865, Center for Southwest Research, Inventory of the Michael Steck Papers, Series 2, Roll 4.

20. William Frederick Milton Arny was born in Washington, D.C. on May 9, 1813. At the age of nineteen he joined the Disciples of Christ and became a devoutly religious man, which influenced his stance on the slavery issue. Lawrence R. Murphy, *Frontier Crusader: William F. M. Arny* (Tucson: University of Arizona Press, 1972), 3–19; Lawrence R. Murphy, "Reconstruction in New Mexico," *New Mexico Historical Review* 43 (April 1968): 99–100.

21. Executive message of acting governor William F. M. Arny, December 2, 1862, NA, RG59, T17, New Mexico Territorial Papers, Roll 2.

22. Lawrence R. Murphy, "William F. M. Arny: Secretary of New Mexico Territory, 1862–1867," *Arizona and the West* 8 (Winter 1966): 324. Arny succeeded Kit Carson as the agent to the Utes and Jicarilla Apaches.

23. Proclamation of Governor Henry Connelly, May 4, 1864, in *1866 Annual Report of the Commissioner of Indian Affairs* (Washington, DC: Government Printing Office, 1867), 333.

24. Stacey L. Smith, *Freedom's Frontier: California and the Struggle over Unfree Labor, Emancipation, and Reconstruction* (Chapel Hill: University of North Carolina Press, 2013), 182–92.

25. Executive Order of Andrew Johnson, June 9, 1865, RG75, OIA, T21, LR, NMS, Roll 6. On the legal abolition of Indian slavery during the Civil War era, see Andrés Reséndez, *The Other Slavery: The Uncovered Story of Indian Enslavement in America* (New York: Houghton Mifflin Harcourt, 2016), 295–313.

26. See George F. Milton, *The Age of Hate: Andrew Johnson and the Radicals* (New York: Coward-McCann, 1930), 180, 221, 338; Foner, *Reconstruction*, 222–23, 247.

27. On Johnson's relationship with Radical and moderate Republicans, see Foner, *Reconstruction*, esp. 228–80.

28. James Harlan to William P. Dole, June 12, 1865, RG75, OIA, T21, LR, NMS, Roll 6.

29. Dole to Felipe Delgado, June 14, 1865, RG75, OIA, T21, LR, NMS, Roll 6.

30. D. N. Cooley to O. H. Browning, October 22, 1866, in *1866 Annual Report of the Commissioner of Indian Affairs*, 33.

31. Statement of Chief Justice Kirby Benedict, July 4, 1865, in *Condition of the Indian Tribes*, 39th Cong., 2nd Sess., Senate Report No. 156 (Washington, DC: Government Printing Office, 1867), 326.

32. Steck to Dole, January 13, 1864, NA, RG75, OIA, M234, LR, NMS, Roll 552.

33. "An Act to Confiscate Property Used for Insurrectionary Purposes," August 6, 1861, *U.S. Statutes at Large, Treaties, and Proclamations of the United States of America*, vol. 12 (Boston: Little, Brown, 1863), 319; "An Act to Suppress Insurrection, to Punish Treason and Rebellion, to Seize and Confiscate the Property of Rebels, and for Other Purposes," July 17, 1862, ibid., 12:589–92.

34. James Oakes, *Freedom National: The Destruction of Slavery in the United States, 1861–1865* (New York: W. W. Norton, 2012), 143, 236–42, 344–45.

35. Edward R. S. Canby, General Orders No. 81, September 9, 1862, NA, RG75, OIA, M234, LR, NMS, Roll 552; Thompson, *Civil War History*, 19–20, 225.

36. Smith, *Freedom's Frontier*, 201.

37. "Peonage in New Mexico," *Santa Fe Weekly Gazette*, February 2, 1867.

38. Delgado to Dole, June 16, 1865, NA, RG75, OIA, M234, LR, NMS, Roll 552.

39. Ibid.

40. D. N. Cooley to O. H. Browning, October 22, 1866, in *1866 Annual Report of the Commissioner of Indian Affairs*, 33.

41. John Greiner to Salmon P. Chase, June 11, 1865, Center for Southwest Research, Inventory of the Michael Steck Papers, Series 2, Roll 4.

42. On Steck's loyalties to the Republican Party, see Steck to Col. Pulston, January 22, 1865, ibid.

43. Steven Hahn, *A Nation Under Our Feet: Black Political Struggles in the Rural South from Slavery to the Great Migration* (Cambridge, MA: Belknap Press of Harvard University Press, 2003), 375.

44. See Murphy, "Reconstruction in New Mexico," 99–110; Smith, *Freedom's Frontier*, 177.

45. Journal of the Legislative Assembly, December 4, 1865, to February 1, 1866, New Mexico State Records Center and Archives, Territorial Archives of New Mexico, Microfilm Reel 3.

46. W. F. M. Arny to Benjamin F. Wade, January 1866, NA, RG59, T17, New Mexico Territorial Papers, Roll 3 (emphasis in original).

47. *Congressional Globe*, 30th Cong., 1st Sess., August 3, 1848, pp. 1072–73.

48. Second annual address of Governor Arny, December 1866, NA, RG59, T17, New Mexico Territorial Papers, Roll 3.

49. Ibid.

50. Of the 148 captives, only 49 were male. The vast majority (113) claimed Navajo origin. Frank McNitt, *Navajo Wars: Military Campaigns, Slave Raids, and Reprisals* (Albuquerque: University of New Mexico Press, 1972), 442–46.

51. Lafayette Head to John Evans, July 1865, NA, RG75, OIA, NMS, Microcopy 234, Roll 553.

52. *Congressional Globe*, 39th Cong., 2nd Sess., February 19, 1867, p. 1572.

53. *Tomás Heredia v. José María García*, December 4, 1865, Third Judicial District Court of New Mexico, New Mexico State Records Center and Archives, U.S. Territorial and New Mexico Supreme Court Records, Box 3, No. 36.

54. *Tomás Heredia v. José María García*, January 26, 1867, New Mexico Territorial Supreme Court, Third Judicial District Court of New Mexico, New Mexico State Records Center and Archives, U.S. Territorial and New Mexico Supreme Court Records, Box 3, No. 36; "The Supreme Court on Peonage," *Santa Fe Weekly Gazette*, February 2, 1867. Emphasis added.

55. *Congressional Globe*, 39th Cong., 2nd Sess., January 3, 1867, pp. 239–40; Murphy, "Reconstruction in New Mexico," 104.

56. Dole to Steck, December 23, 1863, Center for Southwest Research, Inventory of the Michael Steck Papers, Series 2, Roll 3.

57. *Congressional Globe*, 39th Cong., 2nd Sess., January 3, 1867, pp. 239–40; Murphy, "Reconstruction in New Mexico," 104.

58. Undated report of Special Agent J. K. Graves, in *Annual Report of the Secretary of the Interior, 1866* (Washington, DC: Government Printing Office, 1866), 137. On the Graves report, see Reséndez, *Other Slavery*, 299–300.

59. Julius K. Graves to Dennis N. Cooley, undated report of January 1866, in *1866 Annual Report of the Commissioner of Indian Affairs*, 133–34.

60. New Mexico Territorial Legislature to Julius Graves, January 30, 1866, NA, RG59, T17, New Mexico Territorial Papers, Roll 3.

61. "An Act to Make an Additional Article of War," in U.S. *Statutes at Large*, 37th Cong., 1st Sess., vol. 12, chap. 15, p. 354.

62. Undated report of Special Agent J. K. Graves, in *Annual Report of the Secretary of the Interior, 1866*, 137.

63. Ibid.

64. See, for example, "Peonage in New Mexico," *Santa Fe Weekly Gazette*, February 2, 1867, which describes the actions of James H. Carleton relative to Indian slavery; Murphy, "Reconstruction in New Mexico," 101.

65. *Congressional Globe*, 39th Cong., 2nd Sess., January 3, 1867, p. 240.

66. Formally called "An act to protect all persons in the United States in their civil rights, and furnish the means for their vindication," the bill was eventually declared unconstitutional by the U.S. Supreme Court. U.S. *Statutes at Large*, 39th Cong., 1st Sess., chap. 31, pp. 27–29.

67. Murphy, "Reconstruction in New Mexico," 102. Miller wrote, "Undoubtedly, while negro slavery alone was in the mind of the Congress which passed the 13th Article, it forbids any other kind of slavery, now or hereafter." Quoted in Douglas A. Blackmon, *Slavery by Another Name: The Re-Enslavement of Black Americans from the Civil War to World War II* (New York: Anchor, 2009), 253.

68. *Congressional Globe*, 39th Cong., 2nd Sess., February 19, 1867, p. 1571. Senator Davis continually referred to peonage in Mexico—not New Mexico—suggesting that he misunderstood the situation. This theory is supported by his subsequent statement: "I think we are about to legislate on a subject that we know very little about." Davis failed to differentiate between New Mexico (a U.S. territory) and Mexico (a sovereign nation).

69. Ibid.

70. Ibid.

71. For the bill as originally proposed, see "A bill to abolish and forever prohibit the system of peonage in the Territory of New Mexico and other parts of the United States," January 26, 1867, 39th Cong., 2nd Sess., Senate Exec. Doc. No. 543. For the

bankruptcy act, see "An Act to Establish a Uniform System of Bankruptcy Throughout the United States," U.S. *Statutes at Large*, 39th Cong., 2nd Sess., vol. 14, chap. 176, pp. 517–41. See also Edward J. Balleisen, "Bankruptcy and Bondage: The Ambiguities of Economic Freedom in the Civil War Era," in Steven Mintz and John Stauffer, eds., *The Problem of Evil: Slavery, Freedom, and the Ambiguities of American Reform* (Amherst: University of Massachusetts Press, 2007), 276–86.

72. "An Act to Abolish and Forever Prohibit the System of Peonage in the Territory of New Mexico and Other Parts of the United States," U.S. *Statutes at Large*, 39th Cong., 2nd Sess., chap. 187, p. 546. For a legal perspective on the law's significance, see Aviam Soifer, "Federal Protection, Paternalism, and the Virtually Forgotten Prohibition of Voluntary Peonage," *Columbia Law Review* 112 (June 2012): 1607–29.

73. "An Act to Abolish and Forever Prohibit the System of Peonage," U.S. *Statutes at Large*, 39th Cong., 2nd Sess., chap. 187, p. 546. The law is also quoted in a proclamation by the governor of the Territory of New Mexico, April 14, 1867, NA, RG59, T17, New Mexico Territorial Papers, Roll 3. In 1869, Congress amended the bill to retroactively allow for compensation of territorial officials for services rendered in compliance with the peonage law. Senate Bill 962, 40th Cong., 3rd Sess., February 19, 1869, p. 2.

74. Proclamation of Robert B. Mitchell, April 14, 1867, NA, RG59, T17, New Mexico Territorial Papers, Roll 3

75. A. B. Norton to John Ward and the Governors of the Pueblos of New Mexico, August 6, 1867, NA, RG75, OIA, T21, NMS, Roll 8.

76. Proclamation of Herman M. Heath, June 10, 1868, NA, RG59, T17, New Mexico Territorial Papers, Roll 3.

77. In 1865 Indian agent Lafayette Head counted eighty-eight Indian captives being held in the San Luis Valley and an additional sixty-five in Costilla County, Colorado. Head himself continued to hold captive Indian children at that time. Pedro León, a former slave trader, likewise held at least two Paiute captives as late as 1870. See Sondra Jones, *The Trial of Don Pedro León Luján: The Attack Against Indian Slavery and Mexican Traders in Utah* (Salt Lake City: University of Utah Press, 2000), 95.

78. Estévan Rael-Galvéz, "Identifying Captivity and Capturing Identity: Narratives of American Indian Slavery, Colorado and New Mexico, 1776–1934" (PhD diss., University of Michigan, 2002), 215.

79. Murphy, "Reconstruction in New Mexico," 106–9.

80. It was rare for any New Mexico household to contain more than two peons at any given time. Only the wealthiest landowners held more than half a dozen servants. About 75 percent of New Mexican families had only one servant and 89 percent held two or fewer. James F. Brooks, *Captives & Cousins: Slavery, Kinship, and Community in the Southwest Borderlands* (Chapel Hill: University of North Carolina Press, 2002), 240.

81. Murphy, "Reconstruction in New Mexico," 106.

82. William W. Griffin to Stephen B. Elkins, September 28, 1868, NA, RG46, Territorial Papers of the U.S. Senate, Roll 14 (New Mexico, 1840–1854).

83. Brooks, *Captives & Cousins*, 351–52, 403.

84. Murphy, "Reconstruction in New Mexico," 106.

85. "Additional Evidence," Grand Jury Proceedings, NA, RG46, Territorial Papers of the U.S. Senate, Roll 14 (New Mexico, 1840–1854).

86. Laura E. Gómez, "Off-White in an Age of White Supremacy: Mexican Elites and the Rights of Indians and Blacks in Nineteenth-Century New Mexico," in Michael A. Olivas, ed., *Colored Men and Hombres Aquí: Hernandez v. Texas and the Emergence of Mexican-American Lawyering* (Houston, TX: Arte Público, 2006), 36. More than 80 percent of jurors in these northern New Mexico trials were of Mexican descent. Laura E. Gómez, *Manifest Destinies: The Making of the Mexican American Race* (New York: New York University Press, 2007), 89.

87. Dennis Riordan to Hiram Price, August 14, 1883, in *1883 Annual Report of the Commissioner of Indian Affairs* (Washington, DC: Government Printing Office, 1884), 121. At any given time in the nineteenth century, Navajos held between three hundred and five hundred slaves, composing about 5 percent of the tribal population. Brooks, *Captives & Cousins*, 249.

88. John H. Bowman to Price, September 3, 1884, in *1884 Annual Report of the Commissioner of Indian Affairs* (Washington, DC: Government Printing Office, 1885), 135–36.

89. María E. Montoya, *Translating Property: The Maxwell Land Grant and the Conflict over Land in the American West, 1840–1900* (Berkeley: University of California Press, 2002), 69.

90. 1870 U.S. Census. At Abiquiú, the census listed 44 of 728 persons as being ethnically Indian; at Tierra Amarilla, 22 of 399; and at Ojo Caliente, 9 of 258. With the census having occurred only a year after the federal investigations of 1868–69, it is plausible that many households would have been wary of informing the census taker that they held captives and thus the record may not be an accurate representation of how many Indian-born persons inhabited northern New Mexico communities at that time.

91. Censuses taken at the New Mexico village of El Cerrito reflect this changing nomenclature for servants and slaves. In the records for 1850 and 1860, the term "servant" appears under the occupational category for some residents, whereas in the post-1870 censuses, only the words "laborer" and "housekeeper" are used. Richard L. Nostrand, *El Cerrito, New Mexico: Eight Generations in a Spanish Village* (Norman: University of Oklahoma Press, 2003), 183–204.

Conclusion

1. Harriet A. Jacobs, *Incidents in the Life of a Slave Girl Written by Herself,* edited by Jean Fagan Yellin (Cambridge, MA: Harvard University Press, 1987), 2.

2. James F. Brooks, *Captives & Cousins: Slavery, Kinship, and Community in the Southwest Borderlands* (Chapel Hill: University of North Carolina Press, 2002), 1–10;

Bernardo P. Gallegos, " 'Dancing the Comanches': The *Santo Niño, La Virgen* (of Gua-dalupe), and the Genizaro Indians of New Mexico," in Kathleen J. Martin, ed., *Indige-nous Symbols and Practices in the Catholic Church: Visual Culture, Missionization and Appropriation* (Farnham, UK: Ashgate, 2010), 203–24. For continuity in Hispano com-munities, see Abe M. Peña, *Memories of Cíbola: Stories from New Mexico Villages* (Albuquerque: University of New Mexico Press, 1997), 51–53; Miguel Gandert et al., *Nuevo México Profundo: Rituals of an Indo-Hispano Homeland* (Santa Fe: Museum of New Mexico Press, 2000), 1–78.

3. Alfonso Griego, *Voices of the Territory of New Mexico: An Oral History of People of Spanish Descent and Early Settlers Born During the Territorial Days* (Published by the author, 1985), 39, 55, 99, quotation on 55.

4. Gilberto Benito Córdova, "The Genizaros" (unpublished conference paper pre-sented at Taos, New Mexico, 1999), 6–7.

5. Gilberto Benito Córdova, *Abiquiú and Don Cacahuate: A Folk History of a New Mexican Village* (Los Cerrillos, NM: San Marcos, 1973), 63; Cordova, "Genizaros," 2–3. See also Curtis Marez, "Signifying Spain, Becoming Comanche, Making Mexi-cans: Indian Captivity and the History of Chicana/o Popular Performance," *American Quarterly* 53 (June 2001): 267–307.

6. Malcolm Ebright and Rick Hendricks, *The Witches of Abiquiu: The Governor, the Priest, the Genízaro Indians, and the Devil* (Albuquerque: University of New Mexico Press, 2006), 47; Gallegos, " 'Dancing the Comanches,' " 203–13.

7. House Memorial 40, State of New Mexico, 48th Legislature, 1st Sess., 2007; Senate Memorial 59, State of New Mexico, 48th Legislature, 1st Sess., 2007.

8. Córdova, "Genizaros," 16–17.

9. New Mexico State Records Center and Archives, WPA Collection, Folder 82, Donaciano Vigil Oral Histories, Testimony of Refugio Vigil, June 30, 1939.

10. "Suit Says Man Held in Peonage 33 Years," *Albuquerque Journal*, March 23, 1967.

11. Ibid.; "Peonage Claim to be Probed by Justice Department," *Albuquerque Journal*, March 24, 1967; "Workers in Peonage, Says Attorney," ibid., March 28, 1967; "Rancher Answers Charge of Peonage," ibid., April 26, 1967. I thank David Holtby for informing me about the existence of these newspaper articles.

12. Author interview with Anthony Romero, Santa Clara, NM, September 16, 2014.

13. On nineteenth-century wage labor in New Mexico, see William J. Parish, *The Charles Ilfeld Company: A Study of the Rise and Decline of Mercantile Capitalism in New Mexico* (Cambridge, MA: Harvard University Press, 1961); Hal K. Rothman, *On Rims and Ridges: The Los Alamos Area Since 1880* (Lincoln: University of Nebraska Press, 1992), 20–38; Susan Calafate Boyle, *Los Capitalistas: Hispano Merchants and the Santa Fe Trade* (Albuquerque: University of New Mexico Press, 1997); David V. Holtby, *Forty-Seventh Star: New Mexico's Struggle for Statehood* (Norman: University of Oklahoma Press, 2012), 134–35. On economic change in the Southwest, see Charles

Montgomery, *The Spanish Redemption: Heritage, Power, and Loss on New Mexico's Upper Rio Grande* (Berkeley: University of California Press, 2002), 33–53. For the impact of merchant capitalism on New Mexican women, see Deena J. González, *Refusing the Favor: The Spanish-Mexican Women of Santa Fe, 1820–1880* (New York: Oxford University Press, 1999).

14. Steven Hahn, *A Nation Under Our Feet: Black Political Struggles in the Rural South from Slavery to the Great Migration* (Cambridge, MA: Belknap Press of Harvard University Press, 2003), 441–42. See also Douglas A. Blackmon, *Slavery by Another Name: The Re-Enslavement of Black Americans from the Civil War to World War II* (New York: Anchor, 2009); Alex Lichtenstein, *Twice the Work of Free Labor: The Political Economy of Convict Labor in the New South* (New York: Verso, 1996), esp. 3–5; Talitha L. LeFlouria, *Chained in Silence: Black Women and Convict Labor in the New South* (Chapel Hill: University of North Carolina Press, 2015), esp. 25–26.

15. See Blackmon, *Slavery by Another Name*, esp. 402.

16. Quoted in Pete Daniel, *The Shadow of Slavery: Peonage in the South, 1901–1969* (Urbana: University of Illinois Press, 1972), ix.

17. W. E. B. DuBois, *Black Reconstruction: An Essay Toward a History of the Part Which Black Folk Played in the Attempt to Reconstruct Democracy in America, 1860–1880* (New York: Harcourt, Brace, 1935), 670. On DuBois and neoslavery, see LeFlouria, *Chained in Silence*, 54–56.

18. *United States v. Eberhart*, 127 F. 252 (February 24, 1899). See also Blackmon, *Slavery by Another Name*, 172–73.

19. For a similar case that utilized this argument, see Blackmon, *Slavery by Another Name*, 226.

20. *Samuel M. Clyatt v. United States*, 197 U.S. 207 (March 13, 1905). See also Daniel, *Shadow of Slavery*, 3–18, esp. 15–16; William Cohen, *At Freedom's Edge: Black Mobility and the Southern White Quest for Racial Control, 1861–1915* (Baton Rouge: Louisiana State University Press, 1991), 276–81; Blackmon, *Slavery by Another Name*, 174–75, 264.

21. *The Federal Reporter: Cases Argued and Determined in the Circuit Courts of Appeals and Circuit District Courts of the United States*, vols. 153–54 (St. Paul, MN: West Publishing, 1907), 986–97, quotations on 986 and 988.

22. Ibid., quotations on 988, 992, 996.

23. "Report of Hon. Charles W. Russell, Assistant Attorney General, Relative to Peonage Matters," October 10, 1907, in *Annual Report of the Attorney-General of the United States for the Year 1907*, vol. 1 (Washington, DC: Government Printing Office, 1907), 207–15, quotations on 207.

24. For peonage cases after 1901, see Pete Daniel, ed., *The Peonage Files of the Department of Justice, 1901–1945: A Guide to the Microfilm Edition of Black Studies Research Sources* (Bethesda, MD: University Publications of America, 1989).

25. Michael Klarman, *From Jim Crow to Civil Rights: The Supreme Court and the Struggle for Racial Equality* (New York: Oxford University Press, 2004), 233–35. For a

brief synthesis of early 1900s peonage cases in the South, see Cohen, *At Freedom's Edge*, 275–92.

26. See Stacey L. Smith, *Freedom's Frontier: California and the Struggle over Unfree Labor, Emancipation, and Reconstruction* (Chapel Hill: University of North Carolina Press, 2013), 234.

Bibliography

─────────

Manuscript Collections and Unpublished Documents

Archives of the Archdiocese of Santa Fe.

Center for Southwest Research, University of New Mexico, Albequerque, NM
    Inventory of the Michael Steck Papers, Series 1, 1839–1853, Microcopy E93; Series
        2, Microcopy E93.

New Mexico State Records Center and Archives. Santa Fe, NM.
    Archivo General de las Indias Photocopy Collection.
    Bernalillo County Records Series 7, Probate Court Subseries 7.1.
    Frank McNitt Collection.
    Mexican Archives of New Mexico I.
    Mexican Archives of New Mexico II.
    Misc. Letters and Diaries.
    Spanish Archives of New Mexico I.
    Spanish Archives of New Mexico II.
    Territorial Archives of New Mexico.
    U.S. Territorial and New Mexico Supreme Court Records.
    William G. Ritch Collection (Microfilm from Huntington Library).
    WPA Oral History Collection.

Skinner, Williams Jenkins, ed. and comp. *Records of the States of the United States
    of America, New Mexico, 1849–1910*. Class C, Constitutional Records. Microfilm
    Roll 1.

United States, National Archives and Records Center, Washington, DC, Record Group
    46 (RG46), Territorial Papers of the United States Senate, New Mexico 1840–1854.

———, Record Group 59 (RG59), U.S. State Department, New Mexico Territorial
    Papers, 1851–1872. Microfilm T17.

———, Record Group 59 (RG59), U.S. State Department, Utah Territorial Papers,
    1853–1873. Microfilm M12.

———, Record Group 75 (RG75), Records of the Bureau of Indian Affairs, Microcopy
    234, Letters Received, 1824–1880, New Mexico Superintendency, 1849–1880.

————, Record Group 75 (RG75), Records of the Bureau of Indian Affairs, Microcopy T17, Records of the New Mexico Superintendency of Indian Affairs, 1849–1880.

————, Record Group 75 (RG75), Records of the Bureau of Indian Affairs, Microcopy T21, Records of the New Mexico Superintendency, 1849–1880.

————, Record Group 360 (RG360), Miscellaneous Papers of the Continental Congress, 1774–1789, Records of the Continental and Confederation Congresses and the Constitutional Convention, 1774–1789. Microcopy 332.

————, Record Group 393 (RG393), U.S. War Department, Letters Sent, Ninth Military Department, Department of New Mexico, and District of New Mexico, 1849–1890. Microcopy 1072.

————, Record Group 393 (RG393), U.S. War Department, Records of the United States Army Continental Commands, 1821–1920. Registers of Letters Received by Headquarters, Department of New Mexico, 1849–53. Microcopy 1102.

————, Record Group 393 (RG393), U.S. War Department, Records of the United States Army Continental Commands, 1821–1920. Registers of Letters Received by Headquarters, Department of New Mexico, 1854–1865. Microcopy 1120.

University of North Carolina. Louis Round Wilson Special Collections Library. Chapel Hill, NC. Abraham Rencher Papers, Southern Historical Collection #627.

Government Publications

Abel, Annie Heloise, ed. *The Official Correspondence of James S. Calhoun While Indian Agent at Santa Fe and Superintendent of Indian Affairs in New Mexico, 1849–1852.* Washington, DC: Government Printing Office, 1915.

Acts and Resolutions of the United States of America Passed at the Second Session of the Fortieth Congress. Washington, DC: Government Printing Office, 1868.

Acts, Resolutions, and Memorials, Passed at the Several Annual Sessions of the Legislative Assembly of the Territory of Utah. Great Salt Lake City, UT: Joseph Cain, 1855.

Acts, Resolutions and Memorials Passed by the Sessions of the Legislative Assembly of the Territory of Utah. Great Salt Lake City, UT: B. R. Young, 1852.

Annual Report of the Attorney-General of the United States for the Year 1907. Vol. 1. Washington, DC: Government Printing Office, 1907.

Annual Report of the Secretary of the Interior, 1866. Washington, DC: Government Printing Office, 1866.

Annual Reports of the Commissioner of Indian Affairs, 1849–1884. Washington, DC: Government Printing Office (various dates).

Cases Argued and Decided in the Supreme Court of the United States, October Terms, 1903, 1904, in 195, 196, 197, 198 U.S., Book 49, Lawyers' Edition. Rochester, NY: Lawyers' Co-operative Publishing Company, 1905.

Condition of the Indian Tribes. 39th Cong., 2nd Sess., Senate Report No. 156. Washington, DC: Government Printing Office, 1867.

Coolidge, Richard H. *Statistical Report on the Sickness and Mortality in the Army of the*

United States . . . from January 1839 to January 1855. 34th Cong., 1st Sess., Senate Exec. Doc. No. 96.

Eighth United States Census (1860). Washington, DC: National Archives.

Journal of the Executive Proceedings of the Senate of the United States of America. 37th Cong., 1st Sess.

Kappler, Charles J. *Indian Affairs: Laws and Treaties.* 7 vols. Washington, DC: Government Printing Office, 1904.

Laws of the Territory of New Mexico, Eighth Legislative Assembly, 1858–1859. Santa Fe, NM: A. DeMarle, 1859.

Laws of the Territory of New Mexico, Fourth Legislative Assembly, 1852–1853. Santa Fe, NM: Gazette Printing, 1853.

Laws of the Territory of New Mexico Passed by the Legislative Assembly, Session of 1859–1860. Santa Fe, NM: O. P. Hovey, 1860.

Laws of the Territory of New Mexico, Sixth Legislative Assembly, 1856–1857. Santa Fe, NM: Office of the Democrat, 1857.

Miller, Hunter, ed. *Treaties and Other International Acts of the United States of America.* 8 vols. Washington, DC: Government Printing Office, 1931–48.

Ninth United States Census (1870). Washington, DC: National Archives.

Official Army Register. 1851: 32nd Cong., 2nd Sess., House Exec. Doc. #48; 1858: 35th Cong., 2nd Sess., House Exec. Doc. #58; 1860: 36th Cong., 2nd Sess., House Exec. Doc. #54.

Seventh United States Census (1850). Washington, DC: National Archives.

Speech of Hon. Richard H. Weightman of New Mexico, Delivered in the House of Representatives, March 15, 1852. Washington, DC: Congressional Globe Office, 1852.

U.S. Congress. House. *Message from the President of the United States, December 5, 1848.* 30th Cong., 2nd Sess., House Exec. Doc. 1.

———. *Message of the President of the United States, August 2, 1848.* 30th Cong., 1st Sess., House Exec. Doc. 76.

———. *Messages of the President of the United States, April 28, 1848.* 30th Cong., 1st Sess., House Exec. Doc. 60.

———. *Organic Law of the Territory of New Mexico, November 23, 1846.* 30th Cong., 1st Sess., House Exec Doc. 60.

———. *Petition of Sundry Inhabitants of the State of Missouri, February 14, 1825.* 18th Cong., 2nd Sess., House Exec. Doc. 79.

———. *Resolutions of the Legislature of New York, January 17, 1849.* 30th Cong., 2nd Sess., House Misc. Doc. 6.

———. *Treaty of Guadalupe Hidalgo—Indian Incursions, April 24, 1850.* 31st Cong., 1st Sess., House Report 280.

U.S. Congress. Senate. *Memorial of the Legislature of Missouri, January 26, 1829.* 20th Cong., 2nd Sess., Senate Exec. Doc. 52.

———. *Petition of the People of New Mexico, October 14, 1848.* 30th Cong., 2nd Sess., Senate Misc. Doc. 5.

———. "Report of Lieut. J. W. Abert of His Examination of New Mexico in the Years 1846–47." In *Report of the Secretary of War, February 10, 1848*. 30th Cong., 1st Sess., Senate Exec. Doc. 23.

———. *Report of the Secretary of War*. 30th Cong., 1st Sess., S. Exec. Doc. 1.

———. *Trade and Intercourse Between Missouri and the Internal Provinces of Mexico, January 3, 1825*. 18th Cong., 2nd Sess., Senate Exec. Doc. 7.

———. *Treaty of Amity, Commerce, and Navigation, Between the United States of America and the United Mexican States, Concluded on the 5th of April, 1831*. 22nd Cong., 1st Sess., Senate Exec. Doc. 11.

United States *Congressional Globe*, 1846–73.

United States Constitution.

U.S. *Statutes at Large*. Vol. 4, Organization of the Government in 1789 to March 3, 1845. Boston: Charles C. Little and James Brown, 1850.

———. 37th Congress. Vol. 12, March 1861 to March 1863. Boston: Little, Brown, 1863.

———. 39th Congress. Vol. 14, March 1865 to March 1867. Boston: Little, Brown, 1868.

The War of the Rebellion: A Compilation of the Official Records of the Union and Confederate Armies. Series 1, 53 vols. Washington, DC: Government Printing Office, 1880–1901.

Published Primary Sources

Address to the Inhabitants of New Mexico and California on the Omission by Congress to Provide Them with Territorial Governments and on the Social and Political Evils of Slavery. New York: American and Foreign Anti-Slavery Society, 1849.

Averell, William Woods. *Ten Years in the Saddle: The Memoir of William Woods Averell, 1851–1862*. Edited by Edward K. Eckert and Nicholas J. Amato. San Rafael, CA: Presidio, 1978.

Bagley, Will, ed. *The Pioneer Camp of the Saints: The 1846 and 1847 Mormon Trail Journals of Thomas Bullock*. Spokane, WA: Arthur H. Clark, 1997.

Barrett, S. M., ed. *Geronimo's Story of His Life*. New York: Duffield, 1906.

Bartlett, John Russell. *Personal Narrative of Explorations and Incidents in Texas, New Mexico, California, Sonora and Chihuahua, 1850–1853*. 2 vols. New York: D. Appleton, 1854.

Bennett, James A. *Forts and Forays: A Dragoon in New Mexico, 1850–1856*. Albuquerque: University of New Mexico Press, 1948.

Benton, Thomas Hart. *Thirty Years' View, or, A History of the Working of the American Government for Thirty Years, from 1820 to 1850*. 2 vols. New York: D. Appleton, 1856.

Bolton, Herbert Eugene, ed. and trans. *Anza's California Expeditions: Font's Complete Diary of the Second Anza Expedition*. Vol. 4. Berkeley: University of California Press, 1930.

Calvin, Ross, ed. *Lieutenant Emory Reports: Notes of a Military Reconnaissance from Fort Leavenworth, in Missouri, to San Diego, in California.* Albuquerque: University of New Mexico Press, 1951.

Carvalho, Solomon Nunes. *Incidents of Travel and Adventure in the Far West.* Edited by Bertram Wallace Korn. Philadelphia: Jewish Publication Society of America, 1954.

Clarke, Dwight L., ed. *The Original Journals of Henry Smith Turner: With Stephen Watts Kearny to New Mexico and California, 1846–1847.* Norman: University of Oklahoma Press, 1966.

Cooke, Philip St. George. *The Conquest of New Mexico and California: An Historical and Personal Narrative.* New York: G. P. Putnam's Sons, 1878.

Correll, J. Lee. *Through White Men's Eyes, A Contribution to Navajo History: A Chronological Record of the Navajo People from Earliest Times to the Treaty of June 1, 1868.* 6 vols. Window Rock, AZ: Navajo Heritage Center, 1979.

Cralle, Richard K., ed. *Speeches of John C. Calhoun, Delivered in the House of Representatives and in the Senate of the United States.* Vol. 4. New York: Russell and Russell, 1968.

Cremony, John C. *Life Among the Apaches.* San Francisco: A. Roman, 1868.

Davis, William W. H. *El Gringo; or, New Mexico and Her People.* Santa Fe, NM: Rydal, 1938.

De Smet, P. J. *Letters and Sketches: With a Narrative of a Year's Residence Among the Indian Tribes of the Rocky Mountains.* In R. G. Thwaites, *Early Western Travels, 1748–1846.* Vol. 27. Cleveland, OH: Arthur H. Clark, 1906.

Domínguez, Fray Francisco Atanasio. *The Missions of New Mexico, 1776: A Description by Fray Francisco Atanasio Domínguez, with Other Contemporary Documents.* Edited and translated by Eleanor B. Adams and Fray Angelico Chavez. Albuquerque: University of New Mexico Press, 1956.

Farnham, T. J. *Life, Adventures and Travels in California.* New York: Nafis and Cornish, 1849.

———. "Travels in the Great Western Prairies," part 1. In R. G. Thwaites, *Early Western Travels, 1748–1846.* Vol. 28. Cleveland, OH: Arthur H. Clark, 1906.

Farrell, John J., ed. *James K. Polk, 1795–1849: Chronology—Documents—Bibliographic Aides.* Dobbs Ferry, NY: Oceana, 1970.

The Federal Reporter: Cases Argued and Determined in the Circuit Courts of Appeals and Circuit District Courts of the United States. Vols. 153–54. St. Paul, MN: West Publishing, 1907.

Finkelman, Paul. *Dred Scott v. Sanford: A Brief History with Documents.* New York: Bedford, 1997.

Frazer, Robert W., ed. *New Mexico in 1850: A Military View.* Norman: University of Oklahoma Press, 1968.

Gardner, Mark L., and Marc Simmons, eds. *The Mexican War Correspondence of Richard Smith Elliott.* Norman: University of Oklahoma Press, 1997.

Garrard, Lewis H. *Wah-To-Yah and the Taos Trail*. Palo Alto, CA: American West Publishing, 1968.

Gildersleeve, Charles H. *Reports of Cases Argued and Determined in the Supreme Court of the Territory of New Mexico, from January Term 1852 to January Term 1879*. Vol. 1. San Francisco: A. L. Bancroft, 1881.

Gregg, Josiah. *Commerce of the Prairies*. Edited by Max L. Moorhead. Norman: University of Oklahoma Press, 1954.

Griego, Alfonso. *Voices of the Territory of New Mexico: An Oral History of People of Spanish Descent and Early Settlers Born During the Territorial Days*. Published by the author, 1985.

Gunnison, Lieut. J. W. *The Mormons, or, Latter-Day Saints, in the Valley of the Great Salt Lake: A History of Their Rise and Progress, Peculiar Doctrines, Present Condition, and Prospects, Derived from Personal Observation, During a Residence Among Them*. Philadelphia: Lippincott, Grambo, 1852.

Hackett, Charles Wilson, ed. *Historical Documents Relating to New Mexico, Nueva Vizcaya, and Approaches Thereto, to 1773*. 3 vols. Washington, DC: Carnegie Institution, 1923–37.

Hammond, George P., and Agapito Rey, eds. *Narratives of the Coronado Expedition 1540–1542*. Albuquerque: University of New Mexico Press, 1940.

Howard, Benjamin C., ed. *United States Reports: Cases Argued and Adjudged in the Supreme Court of the United States*. Washington, DC, 1857.

Howbert, Irving. *Memories of a Lifetime in the Pikes Peak Region*. Glorieta, NM: Rio Grande, 1970.

Inman, Henry. *The Old Santa Fe Trail: The Story of a Great Highway*. Topeka, KS: Crane, 1916.

Jacobs, Harriet A. *Incidents in the Life of a Slave Girl Written by Herself*. Edited by Jean Fagan Yellin. Cambridge, MA: Harvard University Press, 1987.

Jones, Daniel W. *Forty Years Among the Indians*. Los Angeles: Westernlore, 1960.

Kinniard, Lawrence, ed. *The Frontiers of New Spain: Nicolás de Lafora's Description, 1766–1768*. Berkeley, CA: Quivira Society, 1958.

Mann, Horace. *Slavery: Letters and Speeches by Horace Mann*. Boston: B. B. Mussey, 1851.

Mayer, Brantz. *Mexico, as It Was and as It Is*. Philadelphia: G. B. Zieber, 1847.

Meketa, Jacqueline Dorgan, ed. *Legacy of Honor: The Life of Rafael Chacón, a Nineteenth-Century New Mexican*. Albuquerque: University of New Mexico Press, 1986.

Meline, James F. *Two Thousand Miles on Horseback: Santa Fe and Back*. Albuquerque, NM: Horn and Wallace, 1966.

Meriwether, David. *My Life in the Mountains and on the Plains*. Edited by Robert A. Griffen. Norman: University of Oklahoma Press, 1965.

Mills, W. W. *Forty Years at El Paso, 1858–1898*. El Paso, TX: Carl Hertzog, 1962.

Moore, John Bassett, ed. *The Works of James Buchanan, Comprising His Speeches, State Papers, and Private Correspondence.* 10 vols. New York: Antiquarian Press, 1960.

Polk, James K. *The Diary of James K. Polk.* Edited by Milo Milton Quaife. 4 vols. Chicago: A. C. McClurg, 1910.

Reid, John C. *Reid's Tramp, or a Journal of the Incidents of Ten Months' Travel Through Texas, New Mexico, Arizona, Sonora, and California.* Austin, TX: Steck, 1935.

Richardson, Albert D. *Beyond the Mississippi: From the Great River to the Great Ocean, Life and Adventure on the Prairies, Mountains, and Pacific Coast . . . 1857–1867.* Hartford, CT: American Publishing, 1867.

Rittenhouse, Jack D. *The Constitution of the State of New Mexico, 1850.* Santa Fe, NM: Stagecoach, 1965.

Roessel, Ruth, ed. *Navajo Stories of the Long Walk Period.* Chinle, AZ: Navajo Community College Press, 1973.

Ruxton, George F. *Adventures in Mexico and the Rocky Mountains.* New York: Harper and Brothers, 1848.

Ryus, William H. *The Second William Penn: Treating with Indians on the Santa Fe Trail, 1860–66.* Kansas City, MO: Frank T. Riley, 1913.

Schmidt, Gustavus. *The Civil Law of Spain and Mexico.* New Orleans, LA: T. Rea, 1851.

Simmons, Marc, ed. and trans. *Father Juan Agustín de Morfi's Account of Disorders in New Mexico, 1778.* Isleta Pueblo: Historical Society of New Mexico, 1977.

Simpson, James H. *Report of Explorations Across the Great Basin in 1859.* Reno: University of Nevada Press, 1983.

Thomas, Alfred Barnaby, ed. and trans. *Forgotten Frontiers: A Study of the Spanish Indian Policy of Don Juan Bautista de Anza, Governor of New Mexico, 1777–1787.* Norman: University of Oklahoma Press, 1969.

———, ed. and trans. *The Plains Indians and New Mexico, 1751–1778: A Collection of Documents Illustrative of the History of the Eastern Frontier of New Mexico.* Albuquerque: University of New Mexico Press, 1940.

———, ed. and trans. *Teodoro de Croix and the Northern Frontier of New Spain, 1776–1783: From the Original Document in the Archives of the Indies, Seville.* Norman: University of Oklahoma Press, 1968.

Thwaites, Reuben Gold, ed. *The Personal Narrative of James O. Pattie of Kentucky.* Cleveland, OH: Arthur H. Clark, 1905.

Twitchell, Ralph Emerson. *Spanish Archives of New Mexico.* 2 vols. Cedar Rapids, IA: Torch, 1914.

Webb, James Josiah. *Adventures in the Santa Fe Trade, 1844–1847.* Edited by Ralph Bieber. Glendale, CA: Arthur H. Clark, 1931.

Webster, Daniel. *The Works of Daniel Webster.* 18 vols. Boston: Charles C. Little and James Brown, 1851.

Wilson, John P. *When the Texans Came: Missing Records from the Civil War in the Southwest, 1861–1862.* Albuquerque: University of New Mexico Press, 2001.

Wiltse, Charles M., and Alan R. Berolzheimer, eds. *The Papers of Daniel Webster: Speeches and Formal Writings, Volume 2, 1834–1852*. Hanover, NH: University Press of New England, 1988.

Wiltse, Charles M., and Michael J. Birkner, eds. *The Papers of Daniel Webster: Correspondence*. 7 vols. Hanover, NH: University Press of New England, 1986.

Wislizenus, Dr. A. *Memoir of a Tour to Northern Mexico, Connected with Col. Doniphan's Expedition, in 1846 and 1847*. Washington, DC: Tippin and Streeper, 1848.

Secondary Sources: Books

Alonso, Ana María. *Thread of Blood: Colonialism, Revolution, and Gender on Mexico's Northern Frontier*. Tucson: University of Arizona Press, 1995.

Anderson, Gary Clayton. *The Indian Southwest, 1580–1830: Ethnogenesis and Reinvention*. Norman: University of Oklahoma Press, 1999.

Bailey, L. R. *Indian Slave Trade in the Southwest*. Los Angeles: Westernlore, 1966.

Bancroft, Hubert Howe. *History of Arizona and New Mexico, 1530–1888*. San Francisco: History Company, 1889.

Baptist, Edward E. *The Half Has Never Been Told: Slavery and the Making of American Capitalism*. New York: Basic Books, 2014.

Barr, Juliana. *Peace Came in the Form of a Woman: Indians and Spaniards in the Texas Borderlands*. Chapel Hill: University of North Carolina Press, 2007.

Baxter, John O. *Las Carneradas: Sheep Trade in New Mexico, 1700–1860*. Albuquerque: University of New Mexico Press, 1987.

Bayer, Laura, with Floyd Montoya and the Pueblo of Santa Ana. *Santa Ana: The People, the Pueblo, and the History of Tamaya*. Albuquerque: University of New Mexico Press, 1994.

Beckert, Sven. *Empire of Cotton: A Global History*. New York: Alfred A. Knopf, 2014.

Berlin, Ira. *Generations of Captivity: A History of African-American Slaves*. Cambridge, MA: Belknap Press of Harvard University Press, 2003.

Berwanger, Eugene H. *The Frontier Against Slavery: Western Anti-Negro Prejudice and the Slavery Extension Controversy*. Urbana: University of Illinois Press, 1967.

Blackhawk, Ned. *Violence over the Land: Indians and Empires in the Early American West*. Cambridge, MA: Harvard University Press, 2006.

Blackmon, Douglas A. *Slavery by Another Name: The Re-Enslavement of Black Americans from the Civil War to World War II*. New York: Anchor, 2009.

Bourdieu, Pierre. *Outline of a Theory of Practice*. Translated by Richard Nice. Cambridge: Cambridge University Press, 1977.

Boyle, Susan Calafate. *Los Capitalistas: Hispano Merchants and the Santa Fe Trade*. Albuquerque: University of New Mexico Press, 1997.

Brock, William R. *Parties and Political Conscience: American Dilemmas, 1840–1850*. Millwood, NY: KTO, 1979.

Brooks, James F. *Captives & Cousins: Slavery, Kinship, and Community in the Southwest Borderlands*. Chapel Hill: University of North Carolina Press, 2002.

———. *Mesa of Sorrows: A History of the Awat'ovi Massacre*. New York: W. W. Norton, 2016.

Brugge, David M. *Navajos in the Catholic Church Records of New Mexico, 1694–1875*. Tsaile, AZ: Navajo Community College Press, 1985.

Cabeza de Baca, Fabiola. *We Fed Them Cactus*. Albuquerque: University of New Mexico Press, 1954.

Calloway, Colin G. *One Vast Winter Count: The Native American West Before Lewis and Clark*. Lincoln: University of Nebraska Press, 2003.

Chávez, Angélico. *Archives of the Archdiocese of Santa Fe, 1678–1900*. Washington, DC: Academy of American Franciscan History, 1957.

Chevalier, François. *Land and Society in Colonial Mexico: The Great Hacienda*. Translated by Alvin Eustis. Edited by Lesley Byrd Simpson. Berkeley: University of California Press, 1963.

Childers, Christopher. *The Failure of Popular Sovereignty: Slavery, Manifest Destiny, and the Radicalization of Southern Politics*. Lawrence: University Press of Kansas, 2012.

Cohen, William. *At Freedom's Edge: Black Mobility and the Southern White Quest for Racial Control, 1861–1915*. Baton Rouge: Louisiana State University Press, 1991.

Conard, Howard Louis. *Uncle Dick Wootton: The Pioneer Frontiersman of the Rocky Mountain Region*. Chicago: W. E. Dibble, 1890.

Córdova, Gilberto Benito. *Abiquiú and Don Cacahuate: A Folk History of a New Mexican Village*. Los Cerrillos, NM: San Marcos, 1973.

Daniel, Pete, ed. *The Peonage Files of the Department of Justice, 1901–1945: A Guide to the Microfilm Edition of Black Studies Research Sources*. Bethesda, MD: University Publications of America, 1989.

———. *The Shadow of Slavery: Peonage in the South, 1901–1969*. Urbana: University of Illinois Press, 1972.

DeLay, Brian, ed. *North American Borderlands*. New York: Routledge, 2013.

———. *War of a Thousand Deserts: Indian Raids and the U.S.-Mexican War*. New Haven, CT: Yale University Press, 2008.

DeLombard, Jeannine Marie. *Slavery on Trial: Law, Abolitionism, and Print Culture*. Chapel Hill: University of North Carolina Press, 2007.

Dore, Elizabeth. *Myths of Modernity: Peonage and Patriarchy in Nicaragua*. Durham, NC: Duke University Press, 2006.

DuBois, W. E. B. *Black Reconstruction: An Essay Toward a History of the Part Which Black Folk Played in the Attempt to Reconstruct Democracy in America, 1860–1880*. New York: Harcourt, Brace, 1935.

Dunlay, Tom. *Kit Carson and the Indians*. Lincoln: University of Nebraska Press, 2000.

Ebright, Malcolm, and Rick Hendricks. *The Witches of Abiquiu: The Governor, the Priest, the Genízaro Indians, and the Devil*. Albuquerque: University of New Mexico Press, 2006.

Elliott, J. H. *Empires of the Atlantic World: Britain and Spain in America, 1492–1830.* New Haven, CT: Yale University Press, 2006.

Farmer, Jared. *On Zion's Mount: Mormons, Indians, and the American Landscape.* Cambridge, MA: Harvard University Press, 2008.

Fehrenbacher, Don E. *The Dred Scott Case: Its Significance in American Law and Politics.* New York: Oxford University Press, 1978.

———. *The Slaveholding Republic: An Account of the United States Government's Relations to Slavery.* Completed and edited by Ward M. McAfee. New York: Oxford University Press, 2001.

———. *Slavery, Law, and Politics: The Dred Scott Case in Historical Perspective.* Oxford: Oxford University Press, 1981.

Foner, Eric. *The Fiery Trial: Abraham Lincoln and American Slavery.* New York: W. W. Norton, 2010.

———. *Reconstruction: America's Unfinished Revolution, 1863–1877.* New York: Harper and Row, 1988.

Frank, Ross. *From Settler to Citizen: New Mexican Economic Development and the Creation of Vecino Society, 1750–1820.* Berkeley: University of California Press, 2000.

Frazier, Donald S. *Blood and Treasure: Confederate Empire in the Southwest.* College Station: Texas A&M University Press, 1995.

Gallay, Alan. *The Indian Slave Trade: The Rise of the English Empire in the American South, 1670–1717.* New Haven, CT: Yale University Press, 2002.

Ganaway, Loomis M. *New Mexico and the Sectional Controversy, 1846–1861.* Albuquerque: University of New Mexico Press, 1944.

Gandert, Miguel (photographer) with Enrique R. Lamadrid, Ramón A. Gutiérrez, Lucy R. Lippard, and Chris Wilson. *Nuevo México Profundo: Rituals of an Indo-Hispano Homeland.* Santa Fe: Museum of New Mexico Press, 2000.

Gibson, Charles. *The Aztecs Under Spanish Rule: A History of the Indians of the Valley of Mexico, 1519–1810.* Stanford, CA: Stanford University Press, 1964.

Gómez, Laura E. *Manifest Destinies: The Making of the Mexican American Race.* New York: New York University Press, 2007.

González, Deena J. *Refusing the Favor: The Spanish-Mexican Women of Santa Fe, 1820–1880.* New York: Oxford University Press, 1999.

Greeley, Horace. *The American Conflict: A History of the Great Rebellion in the United States of America 1860–65.* Hartford, CT: O. D. Case, 1881.

Greenberg, Amy S. *A Wicked War: Polk, Clay, Lincoln, and the 1846 U.S. Invasion of Mexico.* New York: Alfred A. Knopf, 2012.

Griffen, William B. *Utmost Good Faith: Patterns of Apache-Mexican Hostilities in Northern Chihuahua Border Warfare, 1821–1848.* Albuquerque: University of New Mexico Press, 1988.

Gutiérrez, Ramón A. *When Jesus Came, the Corn Mothers Went Away: Marriage, Sexuality, and Power in New Mexico, 1500–1846.* Stanford, CA: Stanford University Press, 1991.

Hackel, Stephen W. *Children of Coyote, Missionaries of Saint Francis: Indian-Spanish Relations in Colonial California, 1769–1850*. Chapel Hill: University of North Carolina Press, 2005.

Hahn, Steven. *A Nation Under Our Feet: Black Political Struggles in the Rural South from Slavery to the Great Migration*. Cambridge, MA: Belknap Press of Harvard University Press, 2003.

Hall, Martin Hardwick. *Sibley's New Mexico Campaign*. Austin: University of Texas Press, 1960.

Hall, Thomas D. *Social Change in the Southwest: 1350–1880*. Lawrence: University Press of Kansas, 1989.

———. *A World-Systems Reader: New Perspectives on Gender, Urbanism, Cultures, Indigenous Peoples, and Ecology*. Boulder, CO: Rowman and Littlefield, 2000.

Hämäläinen, Pekka. *The Comanche Empire*. New Haven, CT: Yale University Press, 2008.

Harris, Charles H., III. *A Mexican Family Empire: The Latifundio of the Sánchez Navarros, 1765–1867*. Austin: University of Texas Press, 1975.

———. *The Sánchez Navarros: A Socio-Economic Study of a Cohuilan Latifundio, 1846–1853*. Chicago: Loyola University Press, 1964.

Herrera, Carlos R. *Juan Bautista de Anza: The King's Governor in New Mexico*. Norman: University of Oklahoma Press, 2015.

Hietala, Thomas R. *Manifest Design: Anxious Aggrandizement in Late Jacksonian America*. Ithaca, NY: Cornell University Press, 1985.

Higham, John. *Strangers in the Land: Patterns of American Nativism, 1860–1925*. New Brunswick, NJ: Rutgers University Press, 1955.

Holt, Michael F. *The Political Crisis of the 1850s*. New York: W. W. Norton, 1978.

Holtby, David V. *Forty-Seventh Star: New Mexico's Struggle for Statehood*. Norman: University of Oklahoma Press, 2012.

Hopkins, Vincent C. *Dred Scott's Case*. New York: Russell and Russell, 1967.

Hunt, Aurora. *Kirby Benedict: Frontier Federal Judge*. Glendale, CA: Arthur H. Clark, 1961.

Hurtado, Albert L. *Intimate Frontiers: Sex, Gender, and Culture in Old California*. Albuquerque: University of New Mexico Press, 1999.

Hyslop, Stephen G. *Bound for Santa Fe: The Road to New Mexico and the American Conquest, 1806–1848*. Norman: University of Oklahoma Press, 2002.

Isaac, Rhys. *The Transformation of Virginia, 1740–1790*. Chapel Hill: University of North Carolina Press, 1999.

Iverson, Peter. *Diné: A History of the Navajos*. Albuquerque: University of New Mexico Press, 2002.

John, Elizabeth A. H. *Storms Brewed in Other Men's Worlds: The Confrontation of Indians, Spaniards, and French in the Southwest, 1540–1795*. College Station: Texas A&M University Press, 1975.

Johnson, Walter. *River of Dark Dreams: Slavery and Empire in the Cotton Kingdom.* Cambridge, MA: Belknap Press of Harvard University Press, 2013.

———. *Soul by Soul: Life Inside the Antebellum Slave Market.* Cambridge, MA: Harvard University Press, 1999.

Jones, Oakah L., Jr. *Los Paisanos: Spanish Settlers on the Northern Frontier of New Spain.* Norman: University of Oklahoma Press, 1979.

Jones, Sondra. *The Trial of Don Pedro León Luján: The Attack Against Indian Slavery and Mexican Traders in Utah.* Salt Lake City: University of Utah Press, 2000.

Josephy, Alvin M., Jr. *The Civil War in the American West.* New York: Alfred A. Knopf, 1991.

Julyan, Robert. *The Place Names of New Mexico.* Albuquerque: University of New Mexico Press, 1996.

Kavanagh, Thomas W. *Comanche Political History: An Ethnohistorical Perspective, 1706–1875.* Lincoln: University of Nebraska Press, 1996.

Keleher, William A. *Turmoil in New Mexico, 1846–1868.* Santa Fe, NM: Rydal, 1952.

Kenner, Charles. *A History of New Mexican-Plains Indian Relations.* Norman: University of Oklahoma Press, 1969.

Kessell, John L. *Kiva, Cross, and Crown: The Pecos Indians and New Mexico, 1540–1840.* Washington, DC: National Park Service, 1979.

Kiser, William S. *Dragoons in Apacheland: Conquest and Resistance in Southern New Mexico, 1846–1861.* Norman: University of Oklahoma Press, 2012.

Klarman, Michael. *From Jim Crow to Civil Rights: The Supreme Court and the Struggle for Racial Equality.* New York: Oxford University Press, 2004.

Knack, Martha C. *Boundaries Between: The Southern Paiutes, 1775–1995.* Lincoln: University of Nebraska Press, 2001.

Knight, Alan. *The Mexican Revolution, Volume 1: Porfirians, Liberals, and Peasants.* Cambridge: Cambridge University Press, 1986.

Lamar, Howard R. *The Far Southwest, 1846–1912: A Territorial History.* Albuquerque: University of New Mexico Press, 2000.

Larson, Robert W. *New Mexico's Quest for Statehood, 1846–1912.* Albuquerque: University of New Mexico Press, 1968.

LeFlouria, Talitha L. *Chained in Silence: Black Women and Convict Labor in the New South.* Chapel Hill: University of North Carolina Press, 2015.

Lichtenstein, Alex. *Twice the Work of Free Labor: The Political Economy of Convict Labor in the New South.* New York: Verso, 1996.

Lightfoot, Kent G. *Indians, Missionaries, and Merchants: The Legacy of Colonial Encounters on the California Frontiers.* Berkeley: University of California Press, 2005.

Lockard, Joe. *Watching Slavery: Witness Texts and Travel Reports.* New York: Peter Lang, 2008.

Maltz, Earl M. *Slavery and the Supreme Court, 1825–1861.* Lawrence: University Press of Kansas, 2009.

Martínez, María Elena. *Genealogical Fictions: Limpieza de Sangre, Religion, and Gender in Colonial Mexico*. Stanford, CA: Stanford University Press, 2008.

Maxwell, John Francis. *Slavery and the Catholic Church: The History of Catholic Teaching Concerning the Moral Legitimacy of the Institution of Slavery*. Chichester, UK: Barry Rose, 1975.

McNitt, Frank. *Navajo Wars: Military Campaigns, Slave Raids, and Reprisals*. Albuquerque: University of New Mexico Press, 1972.

Meillassoux, Claude. *The Anthropology of Slavery: The Womb of Iron and Gold*. Translated by Alide Dasnois. London: Athlone, 1991.

Menchaca, Martha. *Recovering History, Constructing Race: The Indian, Black, and White Roots of Mexican Americans*. Austin: University of Texas Press, 2001.

Meyer, Michael C., William L. Sherman, and Susan M. Deeds. *The Course of Mexican History*. 6th ed. New York: Oxford University Press, 1999.

Miller, Joseph C. *The Problem of Slavery as History: A Global Approach*. New Haven, CT: Yale University Press, 2012.

Milton, George F. *The Age of Hate: Andrew Johnson and the Radicals*. New York: Coward-McCann, 1930.

Montejano, David. *Anglos and Mexicans in the Making of Texas, 1836–1986*. Austin: University of Texas Press, 1987.

Montgomery, Charles. *The Spanish Redemption: Heritage, Power, and Loss on New Mexico's Upper Rio Grande*. Berkeley: University of California Press, 2002.

Montoya, María E. *Translating Property: The Maxwell Land Grant and the Conflict over Land in the American West, 1840–1900*. Berkeley: University of California Press, 2002.

Moorhead, Max L. *New Mexico's Royal Road: Trade and Travel on the Chihuahua Trail*. Norman: University of Oklahoma Press, 1958.

———. *The Presidio: Bastion of the Spanish Borderlands*. Norman: University of Oklahoma Press, 1975.

Mora, Anthony. *Border Dilemmas: Racial and National Uncertainties in New Mexico, 1848–1912*. Durham, NC: Duke University Press, 2011.

Moran, Rachel F. *Interracial Intimacy: The Regulation of Race and Romance*. Chicago: University of Chicago Press, 2001.

Morgan, Edmund S. *American Slavery, American Freedom: The Ordeal of Colonial Virginia*. New York: W. W. Norton, 1975.

Morrison, Michael A. *Slavery and the American West: The Eclipse of Manifest Destiny and the Coming of the Civil War*. Chapel Hill: University of North Carolina Press, 1997.

Murphy, Lawrence R. *Frontier Crusader: William F. M. Arny*. Tucson: University of Arizona Press, 1972.

———. *Lucien Bonaparte Maxwell: Napoleon of the Southwest*. Norman: University of Oklahoma Press, 1983.

————. *Philmont: A History of New Mexico's Cimarron Country*. Albuquerque: University of New Mexico Press, 1972.

Newman, Elizabeth Terese. *Biography of a Hacienda: Work and Revolution in Rural Mexico*. Tucson: University of Arizona Press, 2014.

Nieto-Phillips, John M. *The Language of Blood: The Making of Spanish-American Identity in New Mexico, 1880s–1930s*. Albuquerque: University of New Mexico Press, 2004.

Nostrand, Richard L. *El Cerrito, New Mexico: Eight Generations in a Spanish Village*. Norman: University of Oklahoma Press, 2003.

Oakes, James. *Freedom National: The Destruction of Slavery in the United States, 1861–1865*. New York: W. W. Norton, 2012.

Olmsted, Virginia Langham. *Spanish and Mexican Censuses of New Mexico: 1750–1830*. Albuquerque: New Mexico Genealogical Society, 1981.

Ortiz y Pino, José, III. *Don José: The Last Patrón*. Santa Fe, NM: Sunstone, 1981.

Paquette, Robert L., and Mark M. Smith, eds. *The Oxford Handbook of Slavery in the Americas*. Oxford: Oxford University Press, 2010.

Parish, William J. *The Charles Ilfeld Company: A Study of the Rise and Decline of Mercantile Capitalism in New Mexico*. Cambridge, MA: Harvard University Press, 1961.

Patterson, Orlando. *Slavery and Social Death: A Comparative Study*. Cambridge, MA: Harvard University Press, 1982.

Peña, Abe M. *Memories of Cíbola: Stories from New Mexico Villages*. Albuquerque: University of New Mexico Press, 1997.

Poldevaart, Arie W. *Black-Robed Justice: A History of the Administration of Justice in New Mexico from the American Occupation in 1846 Until Statehood in 1912*. Holmes Beach, FL: Gaunt, 1999.

Potter, David M. *The Impending Crisis, 1848–1861*. New York: Harper and Row, 1973.

Proctor, Frank T., III. *"Damned Notions of Liberty": Slavery, Culture, and Power in Colonial Mexico, 1640–1769*. Albuquerque: University of New Mexico Press, 2010.

Quitt, Martin H. *Stephen A. Douglas and Antebellum Democracy*. Cambridge, MA: Cambridge University Press, 2012.

Reeve, Frank D. *History of New Mexico*. 2 vols. New York: Lewis Historical Publishing, 1961.

Reséndez, Andrés. *The Other Slavery: The Uncovered Story of Indian Enslavement in America*. New York: Houghton Mifflin Harcourt, 2016.

Rister, Carl Coke. *Border Captives: The Traffic in Prisoners by Southern Plains Indians, 1835–1875*. Norman: University of Oklahoma Press, 1940.

Robbins, William G. *Colony and Empire: The Capitalist Transformation of the American West*. Lawrence: University Press of Kansas, 1994.

Rockman, Seth. *Scraping By: Wage Labor, Slavery, and Survival in Early Baltimore*. Baltimore, MD: Johns Hopkins University Press, 2009.

Rothman, Hal K. *On Rims and Ridges: The Los Alamos Area Since 1880*. Lincoln: University of Nebraska Press, 1992.

Rushforth, Brett. *Bonds of Alliance: Indigenous and Atlantic Slaveries in New France*. Chapel Hill: University of North Carolina Press, 2012.

Said, Edward. *Orientalism*. New York: Vintage, 1978.

Sánchez, Joseph P. *Explorers, Traders, and Slavers: Forging the Old Spanish Trail, 1678–1850*. Salt Lake City: University of Utah Press, 1997.

Santiago, Mark. *The Jar of Severed Hands: Spanish Deportation of Apache Prisoners of War, 1770–1810*. Norman: University of Oklahoma Press, 2011.

Schermerhorn, Calvin. *The Business of Slavery and the Rise of American Capitalism, 1815–1860*. New Haven, CT: Yale University Press, 2015.

———. *Money over Mastery, Family over Freedom: Slavery in the Antebellum Upper South*. Baltimore, MD: Johns Hopkins University Press, 2011.

Schwartz, Stuart B. *All Can Be Saved: Religious Tolerance and Salvation in the Iberian Atlantic World*. New Haven, CT: Yale University Press, 2008.

Simmons, Virginia McConnell. *The Ute Indians of Utah, Colorado, and New Mexico*. Boulder: University Press of Colorado, 2000.

Simpson, Brooks D. *The Reconstruction Presidents*. Lawrence: University Press of Kansas, 1998.

Simpson, Lesley Byrd. *The Encomienda in New Spain: The Beginnings of Spanish Mexico*. Berkeley: University of California Press, 1966.

Smith, Stacey L. *Freedom's Frontier: California and the Struggle over Unfree Labor, Emancipation, and Reconstruction*. Chapel Hill: University of North Carolina Press, 2013.

Snyder, Christina. *Slavery in Indian Country: The Changing Face of Captivity in Early America*. Cambridge, MA: Harvard University Press, 2010.

Stegmaier, Mark J. *Texas, New Mexico, and the Compromise of 1850: Boundary Dispute and Sectional Crisis*. Kent, OH: Kent State University Press, 1996.

Stevenson, Brenda. *Life in Black and White: Family and Community in the Slave South*. New York: Oxford University Press, 1996.

Stockel, H. Henrietta. *Salvation Through Slavery: Chiricahua Apaches and Priests on the Spanish Colonial Frontier*. Albuquerque: University of New Mexico Press, 2008.

Sunseri, Alvin R. *Seeds of Discord: New Mexico in the Aftermath of the American Conquest, 1846–1861*. Chicago: Nelson-Hall, 1979.

Sweeney, Edwin R. *Mangas Coloradas: Chief of the Chiricahua Apaches*. Norman: University of Oklahoma Press, 1998.

Taylor, Quintard. *In Search of the Racial Frontier: African Americans in the American West, 1528–1990*. New York: W. W. Norton, 1998.

Taylor, William B. *Landlord and Peasant in Colonial Oaxaca*. Stanford, CA: Stanford University Press, 1972.

Thompson, Gerald. *The Army and the Navajo: The Bosque Redondo Reservation Experiment, 1863–1868*. Tucson: University of Arizona Press, 1976.

Thompson, Jerry D. *A Civil War History of the New Mexico Volunteers and Militia.* Albuquerque: University of New Mexico Press, 2015.

Trafzer, Clifford E. *The Kit Carson Campaign: The Last Great Navajo War.* Norman: University of Oklahoma Press, 1982.

Trigg, Heather B. *From Household to Empire: Society and Economy in Early Colonial New Mexico.* Tucson: University of Arizona Press, 2005.

Tsesis, Alexander. *The Thirteenth Amendment and American Freedom: A Legal History.* New York: New York University Press, 2004.

Tuchinsky, Adam. *Horace Greeley's New York Tribune: Civil War–Era Socialism and the Crisis of Free Labor.* Ithaca, NY: Cornell University Press, 2009.

Turner, John Kenneth. *Barbarous Mexico.* Chicago: C. H. Kerr, 1911.

Twitchell, Ralph Emerson. *The History of the Military Occupation of the Territory of New Mexico from 1846 to 1851 by the Government of the United States.* Chicago: Rio Grande, 1963.

Usner, Daniel H., Jr. *Indians, Settlers, and Slaves in a Frontier Exchange Economy: The Lower Mississippi Valley Before 1783.* Chapel Hill: University of North Carolina Press, 1992.

Vinson, Ben, III, and Matthew Restall, eds. *Black Mexico: Race and Society from Colonial to Modern Times.* Albuquerque: University of New Mexico Press, 2009.

Vlasich, James A. *Pueblo Indian Agriculture.* Albuquerque: University of New Mexico Press, 2005.

Vorenberg, Michael. *Final Freedom: The Civil War, the Abolition of Slavery, and the Thirteenth Amendment.* Cambridge: Cambridge University Press, 2001.

Weber, David J. *Bárbaros: Spaniards and Their Savages in the Age of Enlightenment.* New Haven, CT: Yale University Press, 2005.

———. *The Mexican Frontier, 1821–1846: The American Southwest Under Mexico.* Albuquerque: University of New Mexico Press, 1982.

Winks, Robin W., ed. *Slavery: A Comparative Perspective.* New York: New York University Press, 1972.

Wright, Gavin. *Slavery and American Economic Development.* Baton Rouge: Louisiana State University Press, 2006.

Zavala, Silvio. *Los Esclavos Indios en Nueva España.* México: El Colegio Nacional, 1967.

Secondary Sources: Journal Articles and Book Chapters

Adams, Eleanor B., ed. "Bishop Tamarón's Visitation of New Mexico, 1760." *New Mexico Historical Review* 28 (July 1953): 192–221.

Anderson, H. Allen. "The Encomienda in New Mexico, 1598–1680." *New Mexico Historical Review* 60 (October 1985): 353–73.

Archibald, Robert. "Acculturation and Assimilation in Colonial New Mexico." *New Mexico Historical Review* 53 (July 1978): 205–17.

Ayers, John. "A Soldier's Experience in New Mexico." *New Mexico Historical Review* 24 (October 1949): 259–66.

Babcock, Matthew. "Blurred Borders: North America's Forgotten Apache Reservations." In *Contested Spaces of Early America*, edited by Juliana Barr and Edward Countryman, 163–83. Philadelphia: University of Pennsylvania Press, 2014.

Balleisen, Edward J. "Bankruptcy and Bondage: The Ambiguities of Economic Freedom in the Civil War Era." In *The Problem of Evil: Slavery, Freedom, and the Ambiguities of American Reform*, edited by Steven Mintz and John Stauffer, 276–86. Amherst: University of Massachusetts Press, 2007.

Barr, Juliana. "From Captives to Slaves: Commodifying Indian Women in the Borderlands." *Journal of American History* 92 (June 2005): 19–46.

Bauer, Arnold J. "Rural Workers in Spanish America: Problems of Peonage and Oppression." *Hispanic American Historical Review* 59 (February 1979): 34–63.

Baugh, Timothy G. "Ecology and Exchange: The Dynamics of Plains-Pueblo Interaction." In *Farmers, Hunters, and Colonists: Interaction Between the Southwest and the Southern Plains*, edited by Katherine A. Spielmann, 107–27. Tucson: University of Arizona Press, 1991.

Brooks, James F. "'Lest We Go in Search of Relief to Our Lands and Our Nation': Customary Justice and Colonial Law in the New Mexico Borderlands, 1680–1821." In *The Many Legalities of Early America*, edited by Christopher L. Tomlins and Bruce H. Mann, 150–80. Chapel Hill: University of North Carolina Press, 2001.

———. "Served Well by Plunder: *La Gran Ladronería* and Producers of History Astride the Río Grande." *American Quarterly* 52 (March 2000): 23–58.

———. "'This Evil Extends Especially . . . to the Feminine Sex': Negotiating Captivity in the New Mexico Borderlands." *Feminist Studies* 22 (Summer 1996): 279–309.

———. "We Betray Our Nation: Indian Slavery and Multi-Ethnic Communities in the Southwest Borderlands." In *Indian Slavery in Colonial America*, edited by Alan Gallay, 319–52. Lincoln: University of Nebraska Press, 2009.

Brugge, David M., ed. "Vizcarra's Navajo Campaign of 1823." *Journal of the Southwest* 6 (Autumn 1964): 223–44.

Calloway, Colin G. "Snake Frontiers: The Eastern Shoshones in the Eighteenth Century." *Annals of Wyoming* 63 (Summer 1991): 82–93.

Cannon, Brian Q. "Adopted or Indentured, 1850–1870: Native Children in Mormon Households." In *Nearly Everything Imaginable: The Everyday Life of Utah's Mormon Pioneers*, edited by Robert W. Walker and Doris R. Dant, 341–57. Provo, UT: Brigham Young University Press, 1999.

Creer, Leland Hargrave. "Spanish-American Slave Trade in the Great Basin, 1800–1853." *New Mexico Historical Review* 24 (July 1949): 171–83.

Cutter, Donald C., trans. "An Anonymous Statistical Report on New Mexico in 1765." *New Mexico Historical Review* 50 (October 1975): 347–52.

de Iturbide, A. "Mexican Haciendas: The Peon System." *North American Review* 168 (April 1899): 424–32.

DeLay, Brian. "Blood Talk: Violence and Belonging in the Navajo-New Mexican Borderland." In *Contested Spaces of Early America*, edited by Juliana Barr and Edward Countryman, 229–56. Philadelphia: University of Pennsylvania Press, 2014.

Edwards, Laura F. "Status Without Rights: African Americans and the Tangled History of Law and Governance in the Nineteenth-Century U.S. South." *American Historical Review* 112 (April 2007): 365–93.

Eltis, David, and Stanley L. Engerman. "Dependence, Servility, and Coerced Labor in Time and Space." In *The Cambridge World History of Slavery*, vol. 3, edited by David Eltis and Stanley L. Engerman, 1–22. Cambridge: Cambridge University Press, 2011.

Espinosa, J. Manuel. "Memoir of a Kentuckian in New Mexico, 1848–1884." *New Mexico Historical Review* 13 (January 1938): 1–13.

Falola, Toyin, and Paul E. Lovejoy. "Pawnship in Historical Perspective." In *Pawnship in Africa: Debt Bondage in Historical Perspective*, edited by Toyin Falola and Paul E. Lovejoy, 1–26. Boulder, CO: Westview, 1994.

Gallegos, Bernardo P. " 'Dancing the Comanches': The *Santo Niño, La Virgen* (of Guadalupe), and the Genizaro Indians of New Mexico." In *Indigenous Symbols and Practices in the Catholic Church: Visual Culture, Missionization and Appropriation*, edited by Kathleen J. Martin, 203–24. Farnham, UK: Ashgate, 2010.

Gómez, Laura E. "Off-White in an Age of White Supremacy: Mexican Elites and the Rights of Indians and Blacks in Nineteenth-Century New Mexico." In *Colored Men and Hombres Aquí: Hernandez v. Texas and the Emergence of Mexican-American Lawyering*, edited by Michael A. Olivas, 1–40. Houston, TX: Arte Público, 2006.

Hall, Thomas D. "The Rio de la Plata and the Greater Southwest." In *Contested Ground: Comparative Frontiers on the Northern and Southern Edges of the Spanish Empire*, edited by Donna J. Guy and Thomas E. Sheridan, 150–66. Tucson: University of Arizona Press, 1998.

Hämäläinen, Pekka, and Samuel Truett. "On Borderlands." *Journal of American History* 98 (September 2011): 338–61.

Hämäläinen, Pekka. "The Shapes of Power: Indians, Europeans, and North American Worlds from the Seventeenth to the Nineteenth Century." In *Contested Spaces of Early America*, edited by Juliana Barr and Edward Countryman, 31–68. Philadelphia: University of Pennsylvania Press, 2014.

Huebner, Timothy S. "Roger B. Taney and the Slavery Issue: Looking Beyond—and Before—*Dred Scott*." *Journal of American History* 97 (June 2010): 17–38.

Jones, Sondra. " 'Redeeming' the Indian: The Enslavement of Indian Children in New Mexico and Utah." *Utah Historical Quarterly* 67 (June 1999): 220–41.

Kiser, William S. "A 'Charming Name for a Species of Slavery': Political Debate on Debt Peonage in the Southwest, 1840s–1860s." *Western Historical Quarterly* 45:2 (Summer 2014): 169–89.

Knight, Alan. "Mexican Peonage: What Was It and Why Was It?" *Journal of Latin American Studies* 18 (May 1986): 41–74.

Knowlton, Clark S. "Patrón-Peon Pattern Among the Spanish Americans of New Mexico." *Social Forces* 41 (October 1962): 12–17.

Lamar, Howard. "From Bondage to Contract: Ethnic Labor in the American West, 1600–1890." In *The Countryside in the Age of Capitalist Transformation*, edited by Steven Hahn and Jonathan Prude, 293–326. Chapel Hill: University of North Carolina Press, 1985.

Levine, Frances. "Economic Perspectives on the Comanchero Trade." In *Farmers, Hunters, and Colonists: Interaction Between the Southwest and the Southern Plains*, edited by Katherine A. Spielmann, 155–70. Tucson: University of Arizona Press, 1991.

Lohse, K. Russell. "Mexico and Central America." In *The Oxford Handbook of Slavery in the Americas*, edited by Robert L. Paquette and Mark M. Smith, 46–67. Oxford: Oxford University Press, 2010.

Marez, Curtis. "Signifying Spain, Becoming Comanche, Making Mexicans: Indian Captivity and the History of Chicana/o Popular Performance." *American Quarterly* 53 (June 2001): 267–307.

McDonald, Dedra S. "Intimacy and Empire: Indian-African Interaction in Spanish Colonial New Mexico, 1500–1800." *American Indian Quarterly* 22 (Winter and Spring 1998): 134–56.

Morner, Magnus. "The Spanish American Hacienda: A Survey of Recent Research and Debate." *Hispanic American Historical Review* 53 (May 1973): 183–216.

Murphy, Lawrence R. "Antislavery in the Southwest: William G. Kephart's Mission to New Mexico, 1850–1853." *Southwestern Studies* 54 (1978): 1–56.

———. "Reconstruction in New Mexico." *New Mexico Historical Review* 43 (April 1968): 99–115.

———. "William F. M. Arny: Secretary of New Mexico Territory, 1862–1867." *Arizona and the West* 8 (Winter 1966): 323–38.

Nelson, Megan Kate. "Death in the Distance: Confederate Manifest Destiny and the Campaign for New Mexico, 1861–1862." In *Civil War Wests: Testing the Limits of the United States*, edited by Adam Arenson and Andrew R. Graybill, 33–52. Berkeley: University of California Press, 2015.

Nichols, James David. "The Line of Liberty: Runaway Slaves and Fugitive Peons in the Texas-Mexico Borderlands." *Western Historical Quarterly* 44:4 (Winter 2013): 413–33.

Schroeder, Albert H. "Rio Grande Ethnohistory." In *New Perspectives on the Pueblos*, edited by Alfonso Ortiz, 41–70. Albuquerque: University of New Mexico Press, 1972.

Simmons, Marc, ed. "The Chacón Economic Report of 1803." *New Mexico Historical Review* 60 (January 1985): 81–88.

Snow, David H. "A Note on Encomienda Economics in Seventeenth-Century New Mexico." In *Hispanic Arts and Ethnohistory in the Southwest*, edited by Marta Weigle, 347–58. Santa Fe, NM: Ancient City Press, 1983.

Soifer, Aviam. "Federal Protection, Paternalism, and the Virtually Forgotten Prohibition of Voluntary Peonage." *Columbia Law Review* 112 (June 2012): 1607–39.

Stegmaier, Mark. "'An Imaginary Negro in an Impossible Place'? The Issue of New Mexico Statehood in the Secession Crisis, 1860–1861." *New Mexico Historical Review* 84 (Spring 2009): 263–90.

———. "A Law That Would Make Caligula Blush? New Mexico Territory's Unique Slave Code, 1859–1861." *New Mexico Historical Review* 87 (Spring 2012): 209–42.

———. "New Mexico's Delegate in the Secession Winter Congress, Part 1: Two Newspaper Accounts of Miguel Otero in 1861." *New Mexico Historical Review* 86 (Summer 2011): 385–92.

———. "New Mexico's Delegate in the Secession Winter Congress, Part 2: Miguel A. Otero Responds to Horace Greeley, and Greeley Takes Revenge." *New Mexico Historical Review* 86 (Fall 2011): 513–23.

Swadesh, Frances Leon. "The Social and Philosophical Context of Creativity in Hispanic New Mexico." *Rocky Mountain Social Science Journal* 9 (January 1972): 11–18.

Sweeney, Edwin R. "'I Had Lost All': Geronimo and the Carrasco Massacre of 1851." *Journal of Arizona History* 27 (Spring 1986): 35–52.

Taylor, William B., and Elliott West. "Patrón Leadership at the Crossroads: Southern Colorado in the Late Nineteenth Century." In *The Chicano*, edited by Norris Hundley Jr., 73–95. Santa Barbara, CA: Clio, 1975.

Theriault, Sean M., and Barry R. Weingast. "Agenda Manipulation, Strategic Voting, and Legislative Details in the Compromise of 1850." In *Party, Process, and Political Change in Congress: New Perspectives on the History of Congress*, edited by David W. Brady and Mathew D. McCubbins, 343–91. Stanford, CA: Stanford University Press, 2002.

Thomas, Alfred Barnaby, ed. and trans. "Governor Mendinueta's Proposals for the Defense of New Mexico, 1772–1778." *New Mexico Historical Review* 6 (January 1931): 21–39.

Tjarks, Alicia V. "Demographic, Ethnic and Occupational Structure of New Mexico, 1790." *Americas* 35 (July 1978): 45–88.

Tyler, S. Lyman, and H. Darrel Taylor. "The Report of Fray Alonso de Posada in Relation to Quivira and Teguayo." *New Mexico Historical Review* 33 (October 1958): 285–314.

Van Hoak, Stephen P. "And Who Shall Have the Children? The Indian Slave Trade in the Southern Great Basin, 1800–1865." *Nevada Historical Society Quarterly* 41 (1998): 3–25.

Vigil, Donaciano. "Arms, Indians, and the Mismanagement of New Mexico." Edited and translated by David J. Weber. *Southwestern Studies* 77 (1986): 1–50.

Worcester, Donald E., ed. and trans. "Notes and Documents: Advice on Governing New Mexico, 1794." *New Mexico Historical Review* 24 (July 1949): 236–54.

Newspapers and Periodicals

Albuquerque Journal (Albuquerque, NM)
"Suit Says Man Held in Peonage 33 Years," March 23, 1967.

"Peonage Claim to Be Probed by Justice Department," March 24, 1967.
"Workers in Peonage, Says Attorney," March 28, 1967.
"Rancher Answers Charge of Peonage," April 26, 1967.
Daily Albany Argus (Albany, NY)
"New Mexico—Slavery Recognized in Her Constitution," July 24, 1850.
"The New Mexican Delegate," July 26, 1850.
Deseret News Weekly (Salt Lake City, UT)
"Brigham Young's Address to the Utah Legislature," January 5, 1852.
El Sonorense (Ures, Sonora)
"Manuel Martinez Sr. to Commander of the State," April 23, 1850.
Harper's Weekly (New York City)
"Incidents of Travel on the Tehuantepec Route," January 15, 1859.
Memphis Daily Appeal (Memphis, TN)
"Miguel A. Otero to Senator G. E. Pugh," January 20, 1861.
Mesilla Times (Mesilla, NM)
"Greely's [*sic*] Article on New Mexico—Reply of Hon. M. A. Otero," March 2, 1861.
Montpelier Watchman and State Journal (Montpelier, VT)
"Interesting Letter from New Mexico," June 10, 1859.
National Era (Washington, DC)
Response to Richard Weightman, January 1, 1852.
"Scoundrelism in Our Territories: Kidnapping Under a Governor's License," February 26, 1852.
New-York Daily Tribune (New York City)
"Later from New Mexico," March 3, 1847.
"Peon Slavery on the Rio Grande—Letter from the Border," July 15, 1850.
"New-Mexico," December 31, 1860.
"Mr. Robinson's Proposition," January 5, 1861.
"A Few Questions About New Mexico," January 23, 1861.
"Shall We Give Up New Mexico?" February 25, 1861.
"The Slave Code of New Mexico," April 16, 1861.
"Governor of New-Mexico," July 15, 1861.
New York Herald (New York City)
"Important from New Mexico—Slavery and Peonage," July 18, 1850.
New York Times (New York City)
"The Disunion Troubles," December 27, 1860.
Santa Fe New Mexican (Santa Fe, NM)
Report on Navajo Indians, August 6, 1868.
"William T. Sherman to George W. Getty," September 26, 1868.
Santa Fe Weekly Gazette (Santa Fe, NM)
"New Mexico and Disunion," May 11, 1851.
Message on Slavery, July 20, 1852.

"Fatal Accident—A Soldier Shot Himself," June 17, 1854.

"The Killing of Jim," July 24, 1858.

"Death of Jim at Fort Defiance," August 21, 1858.

"Samuel Yost to James L. Collins, September 9, 1858," October 2, 1858.

New Mexico Slave Code, January 29, 1859.

"Peonage in New Mexico," February 2, 1867.

"The Supreme Court on Peonage," February 2, 1867.

Dissertations and Unpublished Papers

Córdova, Gilberto Benito. "The Genizaros." Unpublished conference paper presented at Taos, NM, 1999.

Rael-Galvéz, Estévan. "Identifying Captivity and Capturing Identity: Narratives of American Indian Slavery, Colorado and New Mexico, 1776–1934." PhD diss., University of Michigan, 2002.

Index

Abert, James W., 74, 89, 94, 96

Abiquiú, NM, 62, 74, 168, 231n90; genízaros at, 10, 171

Abolition/abolitionists, 15, 24, 30, 31, 33, 35, 40–42, 44, 46, 48, 53–55, 76, 87, 98, 117, 121, 127, 136, 139, 143, 145, 149, 155, 165, 166. *See also* American and Foreign Anti-Slavery Society; Free-soilers; Greeley, Horace; Mann, Horace; Need, William; Sumner, Charles

Abrego, Juan de, 59

Acculturation, 10–11, 58, 80–81

Acoma Pueblo, NM, 204n46

Adams, Charles Francis, 145

African slavery. *See* Chattel slavery

Alabama, peonage in, 179

Albuquerque, NM, 62, 113

Alcohol, 30

Alencaster, Joaquín Real, 72

American and Foreign Anti-Slavery Society, 53–54, 206n65. *See also* Abolition/abolitionists

American Insurance Company v. Canter (1828), 46

Analla, Juana (peon), 108

Angel, José Manuel (patrón), 88–89

Antislavery activism. *See* Abolition/abolitionists

Apache Indians, 4, 17, 62, 66, 170, 204n46; baptized, 5–6; as captives, 10–11, 75; Chiricahuas, 67, 69; Gilas, 67–68; Jicarillas, 150, 170; Mescaleros, 59, 67, 68, 69, 84; raiding, 7–8, 65

Arizona Territory, 29, 132

Arkansas River, 66

Armijo, Ambrosio, 106

Armijo, Manuel (patrón), 101

Armstrong, George W., 76, 81

Army of the West, 44, 88, 118–19

Arny, William F. M., 139, 146, 149–50, 155–56; background, 227n20

Arroyo Seco, NM, 62

Arvisu, Jesús (captive), 204n46

Assimilation, 1, 6, 11, 60, 66, 70, 81, 87, 150, 154, 168

Ayers, John, 97

Bacon's Rebellion, 3–4

Backus, Electus, 70

Baird, Spruce M., 54

Baptism: explained, 5; of Indians, 1, 12, 60, 74, 80–81, 156, 165–66, 184n21, 184n22; statistics, 5–7. *See also* Catholicism; Mormons

Barboncito (Navajo chief), 86

Bartlett, John Russell, 67–69, 91

Bautista de Anza, Juan, 10

Beall, Benjamin, 66

Belen, NM, 174

Bell, John, 34

Benedict, Kirby, 50–52, 57, 58, 61, 152, 224n101; background, 103, 105, 217n81; rules on peonage, 103–11, 149, 177

Bennett, James, 60

Bent, Charles, 65

Bent, María Guadalupe (captive), 65

Bent's Fort, CO, 66

Benton, Thomas Hart, 30, 31, 47, 56, 196n37, 199n102

Berrien, John M., 27, 46

Bingham, John A., 135, 137

Black slavery. *See* Chattel slavery

Blackwood, Mary Josephine, 127–28

Blaylock, Leonard, 173

Bonciargo, Felix (captive), 59

Bonneville, Benjamin, 74

Acknowledgments

In the process of researching and writing any scholarly work, one incurs many personal and professional debts, and my case is no different. In varying ways, the following individuals and institutions contributed to this book, and for their assistance I am most appreciative.

At Arizona State University, the advice and collaborative efforts of many people contributed to my research and writing of this book. I am grateful to Donald Critchlow, Donald Fixico, Matthew Garcia, Brian Gratton, Paul Hirt, Peter Iverson, Christopher Jones, Kyle Longley, Katherine Osburn, Calvin Schermerhorn, and Brooks Simpson for assisting me in various ways.

Informal conversations and professional collaboration with a number of scholars also helped to shape the content and structure of this book. I express my appreciation to Durwood Ball, James Brooks, Pete Daniel, Ross Frank, Charles Harris, Rick Hendricks, David Holtby, Paul Ortíz, Charles Rankin, Andrés Reséndez, Sherry Smith, Edwin Sweeney, and John P. Wilson. I extend a special word of gratitude to Brian DeLay, the coeditor of the University of Pennsylvania Press series in which this book is published, who carefully read drafts of the manuscript and provided invaluable feedback. I also thank Bob Lockhart at the press, who showed tremendous confidence in this project from the outset and helped by reading chapters and sharing thoughts and suggestions. Finally, Ed Westermann pored over the page proofs with a keen eye, and I sincerely appreciate his help in catching lingering mistakes.

Central to every work of scholarship are the archives that hold the source material from which we derive our interpretations of history. Repositories that I drew upon include the New Mexico State Records Center and Archives, the Center for Southwest Research at the University of New Mexico, and the Archives of the Archdiocese of Santa Fe, where Marina Ochoa and Bernadette Lucero provided access to documents. Richard Szary, Elizabeth Shulman, and Rebecca Williams at the University of North Carolina at Chapel Hill's Special Collections Library graciously scanned materials from the Abraham Rencher Papers for my use. I also thank the Charles Redd Center for Western Studies at Brigham Young University, which provided funding for a summer research trip to Santa Fe.

Several small portions of this work appeared in " 'A Charming Name for a Species of Slavery': Political Debates on Debt Peonage in the Southwest, 1840s–1860s," *Western Historical Quarterly* (Summer 2014). I thank David Rich Lewis, editor of the quarterly, for his careful readings of several drafts and for his patience during revisions. Five anonymous reviewers also provided feedback that contributed not only to the published article, but also to this larger book project.

I conclude by acknowledging my many friends and family members who have expressed enthusiasm for my academic endeavors and/or listened patiently to my ramblings about this book's topic. Most of all, I thank my parents, Dan and Jerine Kiser; my sister, Christine; and my wife, Nicole, for their unwavering support.

Lightning Source UK Ltd.
Milton Keynes UK
UKHW010935191021
392187UK00011B/218